HOW OTTAWA SPENDS

**The Politics of
Fragmentation**

1 9 9 1 - 9 2

GOVERNMENT OF ONTARIO
Ministry of Intergovernmental Affairs
Ottawa Office
45 O'Connor St. Suite 1410
Ottawa, Ontario K1P 1A4

HOW OTTAWA SPENDS

The Politics of Fragmentation

1991-92

edited by Frances Abele

Carleton University Press
Ottawa, Canada
1991

© Carleton University Press Inc. 1991

ISBN 0-88629-146-1 (paperback)

Printed and bound in Canada
Carleton Public Policy Series 6

Canadian Cataloguing in Publication Data

The National Library of Canada has catalogued this
publication as follows:

How Ottawa spends

1983-
1991-92 ed.: The politics of fragmentation.
Each vol. also has a distinctive title.
Prepared at the School of Public Administration,
    Carleton University.
Includes bibliographical references.
ISSN 0822-6482

1. Canada—Appropriations and expenditures—Periodicals.
I. Carleton University. School of Public Administration.

HJ7663.S6   354.710072'2   C84-030303-3

Distributed by: Oxford University Press Canada
                   70 Wynford Drive
                   Don Mills, Ontario
                   Canada M3C 1J9
                   (416) 441-2941

Cover design: Aerographics Ottawa

Acknowledgements

Carleton University Press gratefully acknowledges the
support extended to its publishing program by the Canada
Council and the Ontario Arts Council.

Contents

Preface

The purpose of the *How Ottawa Spends* series is to provide informed comment on public debate about federal government policies and practices. In this twelfth edition, particular attention is paid to issues of constitutional development, and to the increasing political and economic fragmentation of the country. Contributors from British Columbia, Alberta, the Northwest Territories, Ontario, Quebec and Nova Scotia have responded to the challenge. Their labours reveal much about the sources of our present dilemmas, and about how the governing Progressive Conservatives have responded to the very fundamental challenges of the year just past. In all of this analysis may be found, we hope, the basis for economic and political renewal.

How Ottawa Spends is produced by the School of Public Administration at Carleton University. It is a truly collaborative venture whose success depends upon the prompt contributions of many people. On behalf of all the authors, I would like to thank the government officials, staff of non-governmental agencies and academic colleagues who have been generous with their time and information. Marina Devine, Shirley Squires and Maxine Grier provided expert research assistance. I want to acknowledge particularly the major contribution of Ms. Grier, whose assignment carried the heaviest workload and who exceeded all reasonable expectations of intelligence and efficiency. Under the direction of Allan Maslove, she also produced the tables and charts that appear in the appendix to this book.

Production of an edited collection of peer-reviewed articles in less than one year is very close to an academic miracle. It is accomplished principally by Margaret Bezanson and Martha Clark of the School's administrative staff. They are skillful, inventive, firm, and kind—in appropriate measure. Carleton University Press staff, particularly Michael Gnarowski and Pauline Adams; our copy editor, Nancy Warren; and our French translators, Sinclair Robinson and Nandini Sarma, all provided invaluable professional service. Finally, I would like to thank my husband, George Kinloch, for unfailing support, remarkable patience and for raising inconvenient but most useful questions.

Frances Abele
Ottawa
April 1991

The opinions expressed by the contributors to this volume are the personal views of the authors of the individual chapters, and do not reflect the views of the editor or the School of Public Administration of Carleton University.

CHAPTER 1

THE POLITICS OF FRAGMENTATION

Frances Abele

Résumé: Une crise constitutionnelle profonde, la guerre et la récession ont dominé le programme politique fédéral au cours de cette dernière année. Le gouvernement progressiste-conservateur a l'employé pour relever ces défis fondamentaux les mêmes instruments que depuis 1984. Pour des raisons idéologiques et pragmatiques, et dans l'impossibilité d'utiliser leurs resources financières pour atteindre leurs buts, les conservateurs ont compté de plus en plus sur les symboles, la rhétorique, l'"image," et surtout diverses tractations. Le pénible échec de l'accord du lac Meech a démontré le danger inhérent à ce style de politique fédérale. Le budget de février 1991, qui a poursuivi la restriction des dépenses fédérales jusque dans la première récession depuis l'arrivée au pouvoir des conservateurs, n'a pas fait grand-chose pour réparer les dommages faits aux programmes sociaux ni pour remédier aux divisions grandissantes au sein du pays. Il n'en reste pas moins que la base d'un renouvellement constitutionnel et économique se trouve peut-être dans certaines initiatives gouvernementales "en marge" ainsi que dans le nouveau programme politique élaboré par des citoyens à travers le pays. Les autres chapitres de ce volume explorent ces possibilités de divers points de vue.

Abstract: A deep constitutional crisis, war and the recession drove the federal policy agenda during the last year. The Progressive Conservative government approached these fundamental challenges with the same tool kit they have been using since 1984. For ideological and pragmatic reasons, unable to wield federal spending power in meeting their goals, they increasingly relied on symbols, rhetoric, "image," and above all, deal-making. The acrimonious failure of the Meech Lake Accord demonstrated the danger of this style of federal leadership. The February 1991 Budget, which continued federal spending restraint into the first major recession since the Tories came to power, did little to repair earlier damage to social programs, or to remedy the widening divisions in the country. Yet perhaps a basis for constitutional and economic renewal may be found in some government initiatives "at the margin" and in the new agenda being set by people across the country. The other chapters in this volume explore these possibilities from a variety of perspectives.

War, recession and a deep constitutional crisis dominated the federal policy agenda during the last year.[1] The Progressive Conservatives approached these unusually fundamental challenges with the same tool kit they have been using since 1984. They relied upon symbolic gestures, rhetoric, and the Prime Minister's penchant for "deal-making." In the general atmosphere of long-term fiscal restraint, even expenditure decisions

2 / How Ottawa Spends

themselves tend to be signals or symbolic gestures, as often as they are actions intended to have a major effect on social and economic affairs. Arguably, both Canada's Gulf War effort and some expenditure control initiatives in the February 1991 Budget fall into this category, while the general strategy of fiscal restraint continues to be the single most effective Tory initiative. With the country at a serious constitutional impasse, in the midst of the first recession in a decade, it is more important than ever to assess realistically the wisdom of such a course.

The acrimonious national debate about the Meech Lake Accord, and the Accord's ultimate defeat in the summer of 1990 by Aboriginal leaders with the backing of large segments of Canadian society, may have been a mixed blessing for Canada and Quebec, but it was an unmitigated disaster for the Mulroney Tories. The protracted agonies of the unravelling Accord underlined Cabinet's inability to deliver on a central programmatic promise. Further, it displayed the weakness of the Mulroney style of leadership, and—much more serious in the long run—at once inflamed centrifugal forces and discouraged constitutional optimists across the country.

The Conservatives have been successful in reducing federal spending, though expenditure control has had much less impact on the deficit and the debt than they had projected, due to high interest rates. The February 1991 Budget follows the same pattern as the previous six Tory budgets, continuing the erosion of universality in basic social programs, of public service morale, and of the country's education and training infrastructure, all now under conditions of much higher unemployment and increasing poverty.[2] In addition, the direct assault on public sector collective bargaining rights announced in the Budget, coming as it has after years of uncertainty and declining working conditions, may propel the country into a period of major labour struggles.

Although this volume of *How Ottawa Spends* has no chapter on Canadian defence policy, both the Gulf War and the role of the armed forces in the confrontations at Kanesatake, Kahnawake, Chateauguay and Oka are considered briefly below.[3] After a summary of the main findings of the other chapters in this volume, there is a discussion of common themes emerging from these analyses. Then, in the next section, there is a brief discussion of the national and global, political and economic dimensions of the constitutional impasse and federal spending. This leads, in turn, to an assessment of the most recent federal budget, and finally to the conclusion that in the current circumstances the Tories' strategy of relying upon symbols, signals and prime ministerial persuasion in lieu of substantive initiatives is dangerous and divisive. Some basis for optimism about a reconsolidated federation is found, nevertheless.

Four chapters in this volume display the depth and dimensions of the current constitutional impasse. Deliberately, none focusses directly on federal spending, but rather upon **non-federal** (region-, province-, or nation-specific) political and economic dynamics. Canada is the sum of such independent and interrelated regional dynamics, all of which must be accounted for in any future constitutional resolution.

° David Hawkes and Marina Devine argue that the demise of the Meech Lake Accord at the hands of Manitoba legislator Elijah Harper, acting on behalf of a wide coalition of Canadian First Nations, opened a new phase in Native-state relations. Federal inaction at first ministers' conferences, in self-government and land claims negotiations, as well as program cutbacks and general foot-dragging is now confronted by a more solidaristic and powerful national Native movement. This will lead ultimately to new steps in Native policy; among these, Hawkes and Devine recommend particularly the establishment of an independent commission on land claims. They argue that the imperative of constitutional renewal to define Quebec's place in Canada will demand a constitutional resolution of Native-state relations as well.

° Alain Gagnon shows that none of the new constitutional proposals to accommodate Quebec in Canada represent an entirely novel approach to the old dilemmas of confederation. He argues, though, that with the failure of the Meech Lake Accord, a corner has been turned. The old-style federalist approaches of Liberals such as Trudeau and Chrétien (based on the linguistic and cultural dualism of "two founding nations") are dead. Quebec Liberals under Robert Bourassa are pursuing a careful, two-pronged strategy. On the one hand, they discuss fundamental changes to the structure of federalism (always involving a radical decentralization of jurisdiction to Quebec, as in the Allaire and Bélanger-Campeau reports) while, on the other hand and simultaneously, negotiating sub-constitutional special agreements (like the deal on immigration) that demonstrate the flexibility in the existing system. Yet there is no guarantee that this strategy will be successful, and as Gagnon concludes, "[i]n the end, the only available option for the rest of Canada may be to define its common values around the Charter of Rights and Freedoms...and let Quebec go its own way."

° The new politics of western Canada is characterized by the emergence of "Charter-induced identities" that challenge regional political identifications, and also by a rising environmentalism that may, in the long term, further reduce the political salience of "region." Roger Gibbins marks a sea change in the politics of western Canada, away from specific regional grievances towards national and "non-territorial" issues, such as environmental protection. In the long run, these changes will be positive for federal-provincial relations, though federal responsiveness may be limited in the short term by "the primordial electoral need to win Quebec," and a concomitant reluctance to extend the federal reach into any areas of provincial or concurrent jurisdiction.

° In Atlantic Canada, James Bickerton finds no parallel trajectory towards non-territorial politics, environment-alism, or Charter-rights-based communities. Bickerton shows that the priority for Atlantic Canada remains a continued federal commitment to policies of regional redistribution and development, for reasons of survival. Though the Atlantic provinces took different strategies and stances with respect to the Meech Lake Accord, they shared the reality that federal spending is central to Atlantic stability and welfare. "[I]n light of the emerging economic, fiscal and political realities of the 1990s—including free trade, deficit reduction and severe constitutional crisis," Bickerton foresees a period of insecurity and uncertainty for Atlantic Canada.

The diversity of constitutional requirements and perspec-tives identified in these reports on Aboriginal affairs, the Atlan-tic region, the West, and Quebec show how difficult forging a new national consensus will be. As the arrangements contained in the Meech Lake Accord itself suggest, fundamentally dif-ferent regional needs will have to be accommodated. Some further challenges, and also perhaps some clues to the shape of a new consensus, appear in the remaining chapters of this volume, which treat matters that all regions and collectivities have in common.

○ The Canada-United States Free Trade Agreement (FTA), and any subsequent agreement that includes Mexico, is bound to have an impact on Canada's economic capacity and needs. For one thing, the other shoe has yet to drop: the negotiations that produced the FTA did not yield a substantive agreement on the use of subsidies and trade remedies. Instead, the FTA contains an agreement to continue negotiations on these key matters. Bruce Doern and Brian Tomlin explain why an agreement has not yet been reached, arguing that neither Canada nor the US is likely to pursue an agreement before the 1992 elections, though the issues are ones that must be confronted in the 1990s. Doern and Tomlin find that the route for Canada is perilous and the choices difficult: contrary to the case in the FTA negotiations, in this second round Canada has no other issues on which to offer trade-offs. They predict that losses in policy capacity are likely to occur in industrial and regional policy, though protection of social programs from countervail action may be achieved.

○ Susan Phillips documents three trends in the relations between the federal government and interest groups. She finds that there is increased pressure for more meaningful consultation and a more client-centred public service, with a simultaneous reduction in resources. In the area of funding for public interest groups, there is a move away from operating grants, towards accountable project-specific funding. Furthermore, grants from Secretary of State over the last decade favour groups which support the symbolic order of Canadian identity (official language minority associations and multicultural groups) over those which promote the rights of other collectivities, notably women and Aboriginal peoples. Finally, Phillips explores the concept of "partnership" as it has been increasingly applied in state-citizen relationships by the Mulroney Tories, concluding that "[i]n this era of fragmented identities, public 'crankiness,' economic restraint and complex issues, there will be many innovative attempts to create less bureaucratic, more responsive government," all of which deserve public examination.

○ Daiva Stasiulis surveys Conservative government policies on race, racism and visible minorities since 1984. The Canadian Census, immigration policy, the federal employment equity program, multiculturalism, and the Royal Canadian Mounted Police are all examined in the context of the overall Tory economic and social agenda. Stasiulis finds a tendency towards superficial gestures and some contradictory policy directions, but also that Canadian Tories, unlike conservatives in the United States and Great Britain, have refused to pander to racist sentiment in the population, for example in such areas as immigration policy. Overall, though there has been a shortage of resources and administrative capacity, the Conservatives' multiculturalism policy has "legitimized a vision of Canada that reflects the reality of a multi-racial and multicultural country."

○ The 1988 Supreme Court decision that Canada's abortion law was unconstitutional presented the Conservative Cabinet with the need to forge a compromise among polarized and mobilized bodies of public opinion. The February 1991 Senate rejection of abortion legislation (Bill C-43) met with little resistance from Cabinet, which has now abandoned the issue at least until after the next election. Leslie Pal argues that the fortunes of Bill C-43 illustrate a "post-Meech syndrome," common to many public matters in contemporary Canada, turning on five "fragmenting forces:" the balance of national policy and regional variation, the role of public interest groups, the nature of rights, political leadership and the rule of law. These conditions, Pal concludes, require a degree of statesmanship that has so far been beyond the capacities of the current government.

○ Michael Prince explores the Tories' mixed record on retirement income policy. Despite seniors groups' victory in reversing federal policy on de-indexation of Old Age Security (OAS), the organized elderly generally have had little impact on the Conservative pension and social policy reform agenda, as the "clawback" of OAS benefits (effectively ending universality) demonstrates. Reviewing three possible scenarios for pension reform, in light of outstanding constitutional issues and the Conservatives' philosophy on federal-provincial transfers, Prince finds the most probable future course to be decentralization or devolution of old age pensions policy to the provinces.

Themes in Common: Identity, Equity, Survival

A number of important themes arise from the analyses just reviewed. First, while the failure of the Meech Lake Accord was widely interpreted in Quebec as the rest of Canada's rejection of Quebeckers' **minimum** requirements for survival as a "distinct society," it is clear that other constituencies—Aboriginal peoples, the West and the Atlantic region—reacted to the Accord from completely different perspectives, and on the basis of different needs.[4] A canvass of post-Meech political and constitutional agendas neither reveals nor predicts any magical convergence. Indeed, in western Canada, in Quebec, among Aboriginal Peoples, and in many other parts of the country, the Meech process seems to have made things much worse, at least in the short term. On the other hand, there are signs that the lessons of Meech might be applied in future negotiations. For example, despite the obvious interest of the Atlantic region in a continued strong federal spending power, most of the premiers from that region accepted what many expected to be the somewhat decentralizing effect of the Meech Lake Accord.[5] Without arguing the extent or desirability of decentralization, it is possible to see the Atlantic premiers' reactions, as detailed by Bickerton, as a sign that orderly negotiation in defence of enlightened self-interest may prevail—under the appropriate circumstances.

Second, the question of "appropriate circumstances" inevitably raises the question of leadership. Governing Canada in the current circumstances of political fragmentation and social fluidity would be difficult for any Cabinet; what is required, it appears, are very old-fashioned qualities of leadership: a positive vision of the country's future, a willingness to be criticized in the promotion of that vision, and a judicious openness to the considered views of the citizenry.[6]

Brian Mulroney has achieved the stature of the most unpopular prime minister in Canadian polling history. Both the style and the substance of his leadership have been under attack. What might in some quarters be seen as admirable personal loyalty to supporters has been read as "crony-ism," while a strong desire to charm has appeared as a fatal tendency to overstatement, insincerity, and boastfulness. Mulroney's style has held the Progressive Conservative caucus together (no mean feat), but it has alienated the rest of the population, including many party members. In politics, of course, personal unpopularity is always an ephemeral circumstance; beyond the personal, there is the fact that at least since the collapse of the Meech Lake Accord in June 1990, the Prime Minister and federal Cabinet have been in a largely crisis-driven and reactive mode, except for continued initiatives in deficit reduction. Even in fiscal matters, there have been no new initiatives, but rather simply a continuation of earlier strategies. As Gibbins and Gagnon note, in the absence of any substantive federal response to the collapse of the Meech Lake Accord,[7] regional forces have followed their own independent impetus, while Aboriginal-state relations, unattended, have gone from bad to worse. The nadir of political relations between Aboriginal peoples and the federal Cabinet was probably the long stand-off at Kanesatake and Oka, which began in the angry aftermath of the Meech Lake Accord when Mohawk land rights (a matter of federal responsibility) were challenged by a municipal government, backed by the Sûreté de Quebec and apparently by most of the provincial Cabinet.[8]

Federal neglect of the gathering confrontation at Kanesatake might be explained as an imprudent policy choice (the desire to avoid elbowing Quebec out of the way at a sensitive time in federal-provincial relations), but the lack of federal leadership is more general than this. For example, Pal attributes the failure of the Tories' abortion bill ultimately to its construction as "an enfeebled equilibrium of passionately opposed views" by a Cabinet lacking leadership and vision, while a similar condition was noted by Stasiulis in the Cabinet's unco-ordinated approach to employment equity. The major exceptions to the leadership vacuum appear to be in areas where a strong or determined minister has been able to impose her or his particular stamp (for example, Barbara McDougall on immigration policy, Michael Wilson on fiscal restraint, and some ministers of the outer circles of Cabinet who have clearly defined bailiwicks).

A third observation arises from a comparison of the constitutional aspirations of Aboriginal peoples and Quebec, as these are explored by Hawkes and Devine, and Gagnon. In each case, a "founding"[9] collectivity has identified certain minimum political rights as essential to survival and well-being. Both collectivities are constitutionally recognized. Yet one collectivity, Francophones in Quebec, has enormously greater security, a discrete and contiguous land base, language rights, and a wide range of special fiscal arrangements. As Hawkes and Devine very powerfully argue, there is no moral or logical case for denying these same arrangements to First Nations. The case against doing so is a practical one: members of the First Nations are not numerous, they live in communities scattered across the country, and they are not powerful. Hawkes and Devine suggest that the moral and political case for constitutional entrenchment of First Nations' collective rights is now "joined" with the case for Quebec. If it is true that a significant proportion of the electorate make this connection, and if Pal and Gibbins are correct in emphasizing the growing importance of Charter-induced political identities based on "rights," over time the practical strikes against the Aboriginal case may become less important.

The fourth implication of several chapters is that Canadian political identities are undergoing radical transformations that have yet to be reflected in the Constitution, nor, indeed, are they clearly understood and incorporated in our national self-image. Pal traces the influence of newly influential political constituencies on the abortion issue, while Stasiulis chronicles the struggles of Canadians of other than Aboriginal, British and French origins to register a presence in federal institutions and policy. Pal, Phillips and Stasiulis detect important patterns in the rather confused federal policy response to the pressure from these new (or newly organized and effective) communities. Phillips sees steady pressure for democratization of public service decision-making, and of the policy process, from a wide variety of citizens' groups. The federal response to date has relied upon the concept of "partnership" (implying not only shared decision-making but shared responsibility for funding, with both the provinces and the private sector)—but pressures from an organized citizenry may provoke other innovations towards less bureaucratic and more responsive government. Public Service 2000 and some longer standing experiments in decentralized decision-making are promising signs.[10] Stasiulis notes that despite a shortage of resources, the Progressive Conservatives have worked to avoid inflaming racist sentiment while supporting and legitimizing a vision of Canada as multiracial and multicultural. While this vision does not often find its way into the big-P politics of constitution-building, for example, it represents a promising initiative of the Tory Cabinet, "at the margin."

If the political power of Aboriginal peoples does not do it first, the reality that Canadians derive from virtually every culture on the globe must ultimately drain the positive political charge from the "two nations" view of the Constitution. The complexity of such matters is formidable: as the case for a constitutional accommodation of Quebec in Canada is more and more based upon collective "survival rights," rather than upon founding nation status, Aboriginal peoples' claim to "founding nation" or "first nation" status becomes more generally understood and accepted. At the same time, there is rising cross-pressure from "regionalist" forces, and from the rights-based social movements (feminism, anti-racism, gay rights) that transcend geography while, as Leslie Pal has observed, potentially "trumping" all other claims. It is no wonder that the Charter seems inimical to Quebec's constitutional position.

A fifth observation concerns the relationship between how Ottawa spends and possible outcomes in constitutional affairs. Federal spending is not only a matter for constitutional negotiation; it is also a conditioning and enabling factor in the negotiations themselves. As Gibbins and Bickerton separately establish, the importance of federal spending to the Atlantic region, and its relative insignificance in the West, probably accounts in large measure for the different attention spans and degrees of pliability of premiers in each region. The Atlantic premiers literally cannot afford to ignore federal initiatives to revise the Constitution, while western premiers (with the partial exceptions of Manitoba and Saskatchewan)[11] lack the direct fiscal incentive and always risk being associated with failure. As Gibbins' discussion of the Meech Lake adventures of western premiers suggests, these leaders still need a long spoon to sup with the federal devil. An even more direct impact of federal spending decisions upon the constitutional prospect is noted by Hawkes and Devine, who argue that restraint in federal spending on Aboriginal programs since 1987 influenced the strategic choices made by Aboriginal leaders in the Meech Lake debacle. The evidently low priority assigned Aboriginal needs by the Cabinet in the last Budget corroded already tarnished trust in federal good will. Prince's argument suggests that a similar degeneration may be building in other constituencies now feeling the brunt of restraint (such as the elderly and those who anticipate economic vulnerability when they are old).

Finally, it seems clear from all of the chapters in this volume that **whether** there will be a federal state for the forseeable future is not at issue. All proposals from Quebec and other parts of the country envision the continuation of Canada in some form—even though at the extreme, that form might be a much attenuated, residual superstructure. Doern and Tomlin document the adjustments to federal power already undertaken, and pending negotiated changes that may be more or less beneficial. Several other authors note the presence of fragmenting and decentralizing pressures shaped by ideology, political choices and the various and cumulative efforts of Canadians to cope with economic constraints. The outstanding questions concern what sort of federal state will be created in response to fundamental changes in the Canadian polity and the even more fundamental, and related, transformations in the international order. There are at this stage some interesting trends. A strong implication of many of the analyses in this volume is that the formal commitment to symmetrical federalism (which has for years been "symmetry if necessary but not necessarily symmetry" in any case) must be abandoned. Formal constitutional arrangements premised upon equal treatment for all provinces (symmetry), with many separate and different arrangements at the level of policy and administration (but not necessarily symmetry) have probably been pushed as far as they can go. In any case, the collectivities which must be accommodated in the federation are formed on incommensurate bases. Some are founded on the basis primarily of territory (most of the provinces), others are identified primarily by common language, culture and world view (Aboriginal peoples),[12] while only Quebec combines a distinct culture with a land base. These differences in principle are compounded by uneven development of the Canadian economy, creating widely divergent fiscal circumstances among regions.

How Canadians will move towards a discussion of these matters is also at issue. Clearly, some part of the revulsion against the Meech Lake Accord was a revulsion against executive federalism and secret negotiations. Recognition of this obviously informs the thinking behind the establishment of the determinedly participatory and extra-governmental Citizen's Forum on Canada's Future (the Spicer Commission). Gagnon, Hawkes and Devine, and Gibbins all document the exhaustion of elite accommodation as a strategy for national decision-making; perhaps for the reasons suggested by Stasiulis, Phillips and Pal, Canadians are now pressing for more direct political influence as a political right. Like citizens of the Soviet Union and eastern Europe, Canadians are demanding a more democratic form of government.[13]

The Constitutional Crisis in Context

The past year was one in which unusually fundamental domestic challenges confronted Cabinet even while international events impinged. As the Gulf War developed, a major recession brought new economic hardships to many Canadians, while ethnic and linguistic hostilities exceeded customary thresholds in the controversy surrounding the Meech Lake Accord and the confrontations involving Mohawks and their co-residents in Quebec. A particularly pointed illustration of this is the fate of the much-neglected Canadian Armed Forces, which saw its first non-peacekeeping international service in 40 years, and its first armed domestic intervention since 1970.

Maintenance of national security, of economic vitality, and of civic peace and a basic constitutional consensus are core requirements of good government. Though these are the age-old tasks of statecraft, in each era they must be accomplished in new circumstances. In the 1990s, citizens and policy-makers confront a world made new again. A new global political and economic order is emerging.

The characteristics of the new order are generally agreed upon.[14] It seems clear that the halcyon days of the industrialized west are over. Since the mid-seventies, in most places, it has no longer been taken for granted that expanding economies could finance an expanding welfare state, a problem that will become particularly acute as the population ages. What is often referred to as the "postwar compromise"—the political agreement among capital, labour and the state concerning the distribution of wealth and the regularization of conflict over distribution and other matters—began to break down in most capitalist countries in the 1970s. Through the 1980s, neo-conservative (or, more accurately, neo-liberal) economic philosophies replaced the Keynesian ideas that had given shape and substance to the postwar compromise, and virtually everywhere in the West, national governments were elected that held these views. Each, of course, had a flavour, pace and temper appropriate to the country in which it was formed.

Simultaneously with these developments, there has been globalization of capital and commodities markets, and the formation of new supranational economic (and, eventually, political) blocs. At the same time, non-militarized economic powers (Japan and West Germany) began gradually to challenge the United States' economic dominance. Finally, in 1989-90, a series of revolutions in the Soviet Union and eastern Europe brought about the end of the Cold War, the prospect of capitalism and perhaps democracy in the East, and an end to the deadly dualism of the post-World War II geopolitical systems. The United States is the world's military hegemon by elimination. While US President Bush's vision of the new world order is not shared by all, there is little doubt that a new order of some kind is taking shape.

Many observers noted that the Gulf War opened a new phase in international relations, the shape of which is not yet fully determined. How did Canada respond? The brief answer is: to US policy choices, with alacrity; to the military and diplomatic challenges of the Gulf War, with little effect. The hallmark domestic assignment of the Canadian Armed Forces is search and rescue; abroad, the accustomed role has been keeping the peace in other peoples' wars. Canada's first non-peacekeeping military action since the Korean War began and ended without Canadian casualties.[15] If this country's contribution to the war against Iraq was of little consequence to the Allied effort, it did correspondingly little to assist the governing party in overcoming the damage to their legitimacy wrought by the Meech Lake debacle and by sustained spending restraint.

To date, there is a paradoxical quality to the major changes that are under way. Both globalization and the formation of trading blocs tend to weaken national governments from "above" or "outside," while inside many nation-states, nationalism and renewed struggles for national self-determination of ethnic minorities proliferate. In none of these situations is it particularly clear whether nationalist sentiment will lead to the formation of new (and in most cases, much weaker) nation-states, or whether out of the various pressures on current state structures will come institutional innovation.

It thus is possible to see recent events in Canada as one relatively peaceful expression of a general global pattern.[16] In this light, renewal of the federation will require more than simply that the interests of all collectivities are satisfied to the greatest degree possible (though certainly this is part of what is required). In the first place, a global perspective suggests that the broad forces at work will not be so easily resolved within the old institutional framework; secondly, it is not at all clear what the future powers of the nation-state will be. Yet it is important not to lose sight of the fact that despite the large wheels turning beyond the power of any individual or government to change, there is still room for some choice and for preparation, to shape the institutional tools with which future generations will attempt to govern their affairs. In this light it is particularly important to attend to the *dénouement* of Canada-United States free trade negotiations, as well as to any future negotiations involving, for example, Mexico. As Doern and Tomlin document, it is through such negotiations that the policy capacities of the federal state are being defined.

The Budget

Federal budgets are necessarily perishable documents. They have a shelf life of one year at most, with the onset of decay usually much earlier, as unforeseen events and exogenous forces take hold. Nevertheless, particularly if attention is paid to explanations and predictions as well as to the numbers, budgets are arguably the central sources of information about a government's hopes, fears and purposes. The federal budget[17] released on February 26, 1991 thus provides an opportunity to assess the Cabinet's response to current political and economic challenges, particularly the constitutional crisis, the emerging new world order and the recession that began in the second quarter of 1990.

Finance Minister Wilson's seventh budget follows firmly the direction of restraint set by earlier budgets; in particular, despite the recession, there are no special counter-cyclical measures, while the "automatic" fiscal responses are either restrained, or in the case of unemployment insurance, offset by tax increases. The rationale for staying the course is much the same as in previous years.[18] The use of the federal spending power in traditional fashion, to create and support the institutions and infrastructure of Canadian unity, is not even considered; rather, there is the brisk injunction: "[o]ne of the best things we can do to strengthen the unity of our country is to strengthen our economic union and our fiscal position."[19] Strengthening the economic union is treated as indistinguishable from strengthening the federal fiscal position. As in previous years, deficit reduction through expenditure control governs the Budget. Except for a large (and presumably one-shot) allocation in support of the Gulf War effort, the Budget's contribution to finding a favourable place for Canada in the emerging world order entails expenditure restraint:

> Governments have a responsibility to create an environment favourable to the growth of competitive enterprise. In this budget we are acting to restore fiscal balance and attain price stability. This will strengthen our ability to compete in a tough economic world.[20]

The last federal budget (1990) introduced a two-year Expenditure Control Plan. The current budget extends this plan for three more years (beyond the next election to 1994-95), and adds a few more cutbacks for good measure. The main elements of the 1991 Expenditure Control Plan include:[21]

° Extension of the five per cent cap on the growth of Canada Assistance Plan payments to the "have" provinces of Ontario, British Columbia and Alberta, first announced for 1990-91 and 1991-92, now to cover an additional three years, to 1994-95.

° A freeze, to 1994-95, of total cash and tax transfers to all provinces under Established Programs Financing (EPF). The only source of increase will be increases in population. Because of the way in which EPF is calculated, this freeze has the effect of reducing the absolute amount of cash transfers, while the portion that comes from income tax will increase.

° A freeze on funding to selected other programs was continued, affecting *Public Utilities Income Tax Transfer Act* beneficiaries, Telefilm Canada and the Export Development Corporation.

° Extension of the three per cent cap on growth in science and technology programs and cash programs under Official Development Assistance for one more year.

° Another 15 per cent reduction in planned funds for new social housing was introduced, following a 15 per cent reduction in the year before.

° Grants and contributions to businesses, interest groups and individuals were reduced by $75 million in 1991-92 and by $125 million thereafter. (These reductions apply to discretionary grants only, not to entitlement programs such as Old Age Security and family allowance.)

A number of other spending cuts are presented under the rubric of "Reforming government management," but clearly what they "reform" is mainly the public service wage bill. There is, first, a three-fold attack on collective bargaining rights for public servants:[22] the Government has declared that it "is not prepared to contemplate wage increases beyond three per cent" per annum, while within this limit, departmental wage budgets will not be permitted to increase. In effect, this measure imposes a trade-off of salary increases for jobs; the Minister of Finance estimates that a one per cent increase in average wage settlements across the public service could lead to a loss of about 2,000 jobs. Furthermore, should increases of over three per cent be won by the unions at arbitration, arbitrators will be overruled, and the increases legislated back to three per cent.[23]

Salary increases for non-unionized "management exclusions," including deputy ministers and heads of Crown corporations, will be limited to the average of negotiated settlements; the ministerial pay of the Prime Minister and Cabinet have been frozen for one year; and the salaries of Members of Parliament and the Senate will not be allowed to increase at a greater rate than those of the unionized workforce. In addition, the Minister of Finance announced a decrease in the numbers of senior managers by 10 per cent over two years.

Not only will public servants' wages continue to fall behind those in the private sector and the provincial public service,[24] but they will have less money to spend in performing their jobs.

In this Budget, capital and non-wage operating budgets were also frozen at 1990-91 levels.

The Minister of Finance took the opportunity of the Budget and "difficult fiscal circumstances" to reverse a number of earlier spending decisions. Expenditure reductions in two key areas—environment and training—are worrisome, but perhaps were designed as once-and-for-all cuts to be remedied in the next, and almost certainly pre-election, budget. Already rather limited funds allocated to the implementation of the Green Plan were reduced, by spreading the Government's financial commitment over six instead of five years. Rather more ominous was the apparently arbitrary $100 million grab from the Canadian Jobs Strategy in 1991-92. In light of growing unemployment, the continued cutbacks to funding for education at all levels, accelerating business failures in the recession, and the repeated commitments made during the free trade debates that "structural adjustment" would be funded, this was a startling measure, indeed.

Several commitments of capital to develop cultural facilities were retracted. The federal commitment of $88 million to the Toronto Ballet Opera House was withdrawn, while $45 million in funding to the cultural research institute announced by Marcel Masse just two weeks before the Budget was "delayed," probably forever. Funding was also delayed for the construction of concert halls in Edmonton and Montreal.

Taxes were increased in two areas. Unemployment insurance rates were raised to $2.80 per $100 of insurable earnings for employees, and to $3.92 for employers—increases of 32 per cent and 27 per cent respectively. In line with revisions to the Unemployment Insurance Act in 1990, the UI account is meant to be self-financing. Apparently unanticipated increases in the unemployment rate would have resulted in a deficit. The Budget projects that the increase in unemployment insurance premiums will raise an additional $2.0 billion in 1991-92 and $2.4 billion in 1992-93.[25] Tobacco taxes were also raised, by three cents per cigarette and commensurately for other tobacco products. The increase in the tobacco excise tax was presented as a measure designed to discourage young smokers in particular, but it will almost certainly increase revenues as well.[26]

Some areas of government spending were not subject to further cuts, including federal income support programs (that is, pensions) for seniors, families and veterans, unemployment insurance transfers, the Equalization program, Canada Assistance Plan payments to all provinces except Alberta, British Columbia and Ontario, and Indian and Inuit programs. It is important to remember that the latter sustained cuts to crucial areas in the previous two fiscal years,[27] and that the Budget speech indicates federal interest in renegotiating (or at least thoroughly reconsidering) all aspects of fiscal federalism in the coming year.[28]

The annual Budget speech (and supporting information, including the Estimates) are instruments of fiscal control, key planning documents and a major opportunity for governments to communicate with the citizenry. In this latter sense, the whole budget is a signal, bearing a message made powerful by Cabinet's power to enforce implementation of all spending and regulatory decisions. This particular budget also contained an unusual number of essentially toothless or silly signs and symbols:

° The establishment of a Debt Servicing and Reduction Fund into which all Goods and Services Tax (GST) revenue will flow. The Fund is clearly an attempt to deflect some of the public grumbling about this very visible and unpopular tax, by offering assurance that at least the proceeds of the tax will be used for a worthy cause—debt reduction. Announcement of such a "fund," however, is purely a cosmetic gesture that can have no effect on the overall expenditure and revenue decisions outlined elsewhere in the Budget. Once the revenue is collected, there is no way to tell "GST dollars" from other tax income or from foregone expenditures. In any case, total GST revenues will amount to only about half of what the Government must pay annually to **service** the debt, and will certainly not justify the debt **reduction** part of the Fund's title.

° The imposition of "mandatory, legislated limits on annual program spending for the next five years."[29] Draft legislation for public discussion was scheduled for release in the spring of 1991, with final legislation promised "within the year." While allowing "flexibility" for a limited number of contingencies, the Finance Minister stated that the "law will bring a significant change to the way government manages its expenditures." This is a claim that is hard to credit. Who will be bound by the expenditure-capping law? The public service is already bound, firmly and legally, by parliamentary votes on expenditures and, off the budget cycle, by Cabinet decisions. Under the Canadian system of government, a government cannot pass laws that are binding on its future legislative capacity, or the legislative capacities of future governments.[30] The new legislated spending limits are constitutional nonsense; politically, this proposal amounts to a "cross-my-heart-and-hope-to-die" sort of assurance from the governing party itself. There is no legal or practical basis for accepting the assurance. It is hollow, and misrepresentative of parliamentary democracy.

° Finally, an essentially sanction-free but perhaps more meaningful signal was the joint announcement, on budget day, by the Minister of Finance and the Governor of the Bank of Canada of their mutual agreement on "intermediate inflation targets to serve as key steps on the way to price stability" (that is, to zero or near zero inflation). The inflation target was set at two per cent by 1995. A joint announcement by the Minister of Finance and the independent and non-partisan Governor of the Bank of Canada is an unusual event, underlining the commitment of the two public sector figures with the most power to effect change.

In an overall assessment of the 1991 Budget, two related questions may be asked. First, what does the Budget tell us, in general, about the Government's priorities? Second, what is the likely impact of the Budget on Canadian citizens?

Despite the onset of the recession, this is clearly a budget that continues to emphasize deficit and debt reduction. The document itself is reasonably blunt. While the recession will bring greater economic misery to the poor and to the growing ranks of the unemployed, the longer term well being of the economy precludes counter-cyclical spending:

In earlier times, periods of economic weakness have been occasions for Ministers of Finance to put some extra money in people's pockets, spend more on programs, and worry less about the government's fiscal situation. But in earlier times, we did not have to face persistently high deficits, high public debt and the economic damage that would result from ignoring these serious problems.[31]

Scant accommodation is made for the difficulties working people in Canada will face, though the difficulties were clearly anticipated. Access to unemployment insurance (UI) was reduced in earlier legislation (passed, finally and after much controversy, by the Senate in January 1990); in this budget, no measures were proposed to limit UI transfers, but premiums paid by both employers and employees were raised to cover the expected increase in claims as a result of the recession. The federal contribution to the Canada Assistance Plan (which provides for 50 per cent federal cost-sharing of transfers to non-working Canadians who are ineligible for other transfers, such as unemployment insurance) was restrained for only the three richest provinces, Alberta, British Columbia and Ontario, where it will certainly have some impact on either services or provincial expenditures.[32]

The impact of the continued freeze of the federal cash contribution to Established Programs Financing (which covers health care and education) is more difficult to assess. The National Council of Welfare calculates that the freezes thus far announced will lead to the total disappearance of the federal cash contribution under this scheme in some provinces by 1996-97, and everywhere by 2007-08.[33] The shift to a system financed entirely by tax points, which are much more directly under provincial control, results in a loss of federal leverage. The threat to withhold EPF cash payments has been used in the past to prohibit provinces from permitting physicians to extra-bill. Although the federal budget mentions that legislation to ensure national standards and universality will be introduced, it is not at all clear what sanctions are available to replace the cash transfer lever. It does appear that the shift from federal cash contributions to a tax-financed system will lead to a more decentralized, probably more diverse and possibly poorer health care system.

Since rejuvenation of the economy precludes spending to mitigate the impact of the recession on low-income Canadians, and depends upon restraint of federal expenditures, it is necessary to consider whether the restraint measures will be successful. The overall projected impact of the restraint measures announced in the February 1991 Budget is summarized in Table 1.1 Expenditure savings and revenue increases in 1991-92 are

expected to total $1,177 million, of which $50 million is identified as "Associated Public Debt Charge Savings" (savings
realized from foregone borrowing). The Budget predicts that the
total five-year savings will be $14,819 million (by 1995-96). In
light of the possible factors that might influence this latter
project (including a deepening recession, exogenously or at least
independently determined interest rates and a possible change
of government in 1992-93), the five-year project is best read as
a heuristic device, meant to signal determination and to suggest
that the tough measures in the current budget are worth it,
because success is in sight.

Table 1.1
Expenditure Restraint Measures
(millions of dollars)

	Savings 1991-92	Savings 1992-93	Five-Year Savings
Programs Constrained			
Canada Assistance Plan (non-equalization receiving provinces)	-	365	2,135
Official Development Assistance	-	262	1,610
Programs Frozen			
Established Programs Financing (per capita)	-	338	2,340
Public Utilities Income Tax Transfer Program	-	48	311
Canadian Film Development Corporation	-	7	28
Export Development Corporation	-	25	100
Programs Reduced			
Grants and Contributions	75*	125	575
CMHC Social Housing	32*	71	411
Canadian Jobs Strategy	100*	-	100
Green Plan Funding	125**	100	600
Management Measures			
Operating Budget Reductions	500*	500	2,500
Wage Strategy	185**	220	1,140
Increased Tax Compliance/Cost Recovery	50	53	1,009
Proceeds from Privatization	60	-	60
Associated Public Debt Charge Savings	50	200	1,900
Sub Totals			
Expenditure Savings	1,067	2,261	13,750
Initiatives Affecting Revenues	110	53	1,069
Total Fiscal Impact	1,177	2,314	14,819

Figures may not add to totals due to rounding.
*Not reflected in Main Estimates.
**Reflected in reduced reserve levels.

Source: Canada, *1991-92 Estimates*, Part I: The Government Expenditure
Plan (Ottawa: Supply and Services, 1991), p. 11.

Of course, even the projected savings for the next fiscal year must be viewed with some caution. Largely as a result of the recession and higher than anticipated interest rates, last year's federal expenditures overshot their target by 5.1 per cent (see Table 1.2). This year there may be somewhat more predictability, since the Minister of Finance achieved an agreement on inflation rate targets with the Governor of the Bank of Canada. Still, it appears that even under the best circumstances, there will be only an insignificant reduction in the nation's total debt. This is so for two reasons: first, the recession will result in some "automatically" increased expenditures and reduced revenues; and second, the portion of federal spending available for reduction (that is, the portion of discretionary spending) is relatively small.

Table 1.2
Total Expenditure Plan
(millions of dollars)

	Actual 1989-90	Forecast 1990-91	Planned 1991-92
Budgetary expenditures	142,703	151,250	159,000
Percentage change	7.5	6.0	5.1
Less: Public debt charges	38,820	42,950	43,200
Program Expenditures	103,883	108,300	115,800
Percentage change in program expenditures	4.4	4.3	6.9

Source: Canada, *1991-92 Estimates*, Part I: The Government Expenditure Plan, (Ottawa: Supply and Services, 1991), p. 11.

As Table 1.1 shows, expenditures have been reduced in part by direct action upon the statutory transfer programs that respond automatically to economic need—principally, unemployment insurance and social assistance. What is being restrained is the **anticipated increased spending** that is a result of the recession, and that is meant to cushion the effects of an economic downturn upon Canadian families and workers.

The remaining federal "savings" are achieved primarily by further reductions to the public service wage bill and to the operating and capital funding of the work of governing. The 1991 Budget backs the Government's decision to contain wage increases to three per cent and force a jobs-for-wages trade-off on public sector unions with the threat to legislate strikers back to work and/or render invalid arbitration awards. This is the toughest collective bargaining stance yet taken by the Tories, and the early response from public sector unions was militant. Whether or not there is ultimately a public service-wide strike, as was threatened by the leader of the largest public sector union, the Public Service Alliance, there is little doubt that the wage controls, together with the freeze on operating and capital expenditures by departments, will sap morale in an already demoralized public service. This in turn will surely affect public servants' capacity or willingness to respond to injunctions to improve responsiveness and service to the public.[34]

CONCLUSIONS

At least in the medium term, Canada must respond to a restructuring world economy within the framework of the Canada-United States Free Trade Agreement and in the wake of the United States' vigorous efforts to do the same, from a very different economic, military and geopolitical base. At least in the short term, this will occur under conditions of a recession. At the same time, in Canada as in many other federal countries, nationalist feeling is rising against existing governing institutions, even while other interests advancing other claims multiply pressures on state structure "from below." Simultaneous pressures "from above" (or from outside the nation-state) and for reform "from below" now shape a politics of fragmentation in many countries of the world, Canada included.

The Canadian politics of fragmentation involves conflicts over language, territory and citizens' rights. Though these are the old chestnuts of Canadian political life, and the staple of our odd national preoccupation with constitutional renegotiation,[35] the conflicts over the last two or three years have been unusually bitter and unusually barren. Not all aspects of social and economic life are susceptible to government influence, but at least some part of the responsibility for the current national distemper must lie with the Prime Minister's leadership and with the policy choices of Cabinet.

Federal initiatives and federal spending are the traditional glue in the Canadian federation. When asked to identify key elements of what is distinctive about Canada, most Canadians will quickly mention Medicare and the social welfare system, as well as a civic culture relatively free of interpersonal violence. Deeper than this, there is the reality that Canada is

largely the product of state initiatives—initially to protect
British North America from an expansionary United States, to
knit the disparate colonies together with compromise and accommodation, and then to create a national economy based upon
internal trade and western wheat. There has been much conflict over the terms of these arrangements, but they are at the
core of Canadian formation. The Progressive Conservatives'
decisions to privilege spending restraint over all other measures
to reduce the deficit, to carry restraint into the teeth of a
recession, and to limit the federal role in the economy through
the Free Trade Agreement and in other ways, are political
choices that move away from these traditional elements of the
Canadian polity.

Changing times require political leaders with a certain
vision, and a willingness to take positive initiatives towards
that vision. I have argued in this chapter that the Prime
Minister does not possess these leadership qualities, a circumstance that compounds the difficulties created by this
Cabinet's single-minded devotion to fiscal restraint. Thus,
through the relative prosperity of the 1980s and now in the
recession, the Tories provided no relief for the working poor and
the growing number of unemployed workers. There is no positive economic strategy, nor, apparently, any commitment to
easing the misery created by "structural adjustment" associated with their social and economic policy choices. Far from
conceiving of public spending as an aspect of federal power
capable of ameliorating hardship and easing the constitutional
impasse, the Progressive Conservatives remain preoccupied
with spending restraint (and with defending their right flank in
the next election).[36]

There have been some indications of a new direction for
Canada. Despite spending restraint and a relatively hostile
climate, the public service has begun to respond to demands for
less bureaucratization and more democracy. With the support
of some government agencies, and under the auspices of some
favourable government policies, Aboriginal peoples and new
constituencies of Canadians are in the process of organizing to
improve their influence and the terms of their lives. The
deliberations of all the commissions and inquiries, both federal
and provincial, may yet work through to a new vision of a
renewed federalism, and new expectations about popular participation in constitution-building and in political life in
general. The dominant factions of the Progressive Conserva-

tives in power appear to be at odds with these broad social movements.

Appendix 1.1
Average Percentage Wage Increases in Base Rates
for Collective Agreements Without Cost of Living Allowance (COLA) Clauses[1]

Annual Data Group	1975	1976	1977	1978	1979	1980	1981	1982	1983	1984	1985	1986	1987	1988	1989	Average 1975-89
Federal Administration	13.9	11.9	9.5	6.7	8.3	10.8	12.6	8.3	5.4	5.0	3.2	3.6	3.4	3.5	4.2	7.35
Provincial Administration	25.1	11.2	7.5	7.2	8.3	11.2	13.6	11.3	5.8	5.4	4.6	4.5	4.6	4.3	6.2	8.72
Local Administration	16.5	10.4	7.9	6.4	8.7	10.4	13.2	12.9	5.7	3.2	4.7	3.6	4.2	4.7	6.1	7.91
Health, Welfare and Education	21.8	10.8	6.9	6.5	8.1	11.1	13.7	11.1	5.6	3.1	3.4	3.6	4.0	3.8	5.9	7.96
Telephone, Electricity and Water	22.8	10.9	7.0	6.7	7.8	10.1	13.6	11.4	6.6	2.6	3.3	2.8	2.4	2.7	4.9	7.71
Total Public	19.7	11.1	7.8	6.7	8.3	10.9	13.3	9.9	5.6	3.9	3.9	3.8	4.0	4.0	5.3	7.88
Total Private	17.5	10.5	8.0	7.7	9.8	11.8	13.7	10.8	5.4	2.8	3.1	2.8	3.4	5.0	5.2	7.83

1   Bargaining units with fewer than 500 members are excluded.

Source: Data developed by Gene Swimmer from Labour Canada, *Major Collective Agreements.*

Notes

I am indebted to Katherine Graham, Allan Maslove, Susan Phillips, Daiva Stasiulis, and Gene Swimmer, for many improvements to this paper, and to Maxine Grier for superb research support.

1   The title, "The Politics of Fragmentation," is taken from Thomas O. Hueglin, "The Politics of Fragmentation in an Age of Scarcity: A Synthetic View and Critical Analysis of Welfare State Crisis," *Canadian Journal of Political Science* 20:2 (June 1987).

2   Even in the relatively buoyant economy of the 1980s, there was no ameliorization of poverty. Rather, income was redistributed upward, from middle- to upper- level earners. According to Statistics Canada figures released in March 1991, the 20 per cent of households with the lowest pre-tax incomes received just 5.5 per cent of national income, in 1989 as in 1981. With the recession, rising unemployment and restraint in federal spending, it is likely that the numbers of the poor will increase.

3   The last treatment of defence policy in *How Ottawa Spends* was Edgar J. Dosman, "The Department of National Defence: The Steady Drummer," in Katherine A. Graham, (ed.), *How Ottawa Spends 1988-89: The Conservatives Heading Into the Stretch,*" (Ottawa: Carleton University Press, 1988).

4   For a complete list of regional needs, it would be necessary to include similar chapters concerning the North and the industrialized parts of Ontario, at least. Criticism of the Accord came also from organizations representing feminists and ethno-cultural minorities. See Evelyn Kallen, "The Meech Lake Accord: Entrenching a Pecking Order of Minority Rights," *Canadian Public Policy,* v. 15, Supplement pp. 107-120.

5   For various perspectives, see Harvey Lithwick and Allan Maslove, "The Sum of the Parts: Free Trade and Meech Lake," in Katherine A. Graham (ed.), *How Ottawa Spends 1989-90: The Buck Stops Where?* (Ottawa: Carleton University Press, 1989); and all of the articles in

Canadian Public Policy, v. 15, Supplement, September 1988.

6   Susan Phillips suggested this line of reasoning.

7   Virtually the sole federal response, over nearly two years, has been to establish a number of investigatory and consultative committees and commissions. Appointment of such bodies to deliberate and to consult the public is a laudable if tardy initiative. As the next step after the overheated campaign for the Meech Lake Accord and the Accord's painful rejection, though, the various commissions are under considerable pressure. To demonstrate good faith, the Cabinet must in the end be able to show that the views expressed before these bodies have been understood and incorporated in any new proposals for constitutional change.

8   A good general account of events at Kanesatake and Oka will appear in Loreen Pindera and Geoffrey York, *The People of the Pines: The Warriors and the Legacy of Oka* (Canada: Little, Brown and Co., forthcoming 1991).

9   "Founding" must be understood in two senses for this description to be true. The First Nations, as the original inhabitants of what is now Canada, are obviously (and tautologically) the true founding nations. Europeans arrived, disrupted and displaced, but did not destroy them. On the basis of the sequence of migration, descendants of the French and the British migrants claimed founding nation status. From the long perspective of Aboriginal peoples, of course, the Chinese, Slavs and other ethnic groups arrived only slightly later than the first European migrants.

10   The design of the Canadian Aboriginal Economic Development Strategy reflects another such promising initiative. See Katherine Graham and Frances Abele, "Aboriginal People and Economic Development: Is It Business As Usual?" *Financial Times* [Toronto], September 16, 1989. [Frances Abele is now a member of the Eastern Board of the Canadian Aboriginal Economic Development Strategy, though Professor Graham is not.]

11   The two poorer western provinces have the fiscal incentive with the Atlantic region, somewhat counterbalanced by the potential for "regionalist" politics rooted in a political tradition of dissent and positive use of provincial states, and ultimately in the distinctive resource bases of these provinces.

12   This is tragically so, despite the overwhelming importance of land, and for many First Nations, land-based production. Reserves and traditional territories are scattered across Canada. For many Aboriginal peoples, an enhanced land base, and resolution of issues of contested jurisdiction are essential.

13   Of course, the comparison is accurate only up to a point, given the different starting points in Canada and the Soviet Union. Nevertheless, whatever else they may have brought, the eastern bloc revolutions of 1989-90 recalled international attention to issues of democracy (political and administrative) more powerfully than any events since the global popular risings of 1968. Other more extensive considerations of the need for renewed Canadian democracy appear in *Policy Options* 12:1 (January 1991); Roger Gibbins et al, (eds.), *Meech Lake and Canada: Perspectives from Western Canada* (Edmonton: Academic Printing and Publishing, 1988); and Institute of Intergovernmental Relations, Queen's University and Business Council on National Issues, *Canada's Constitutional Options*, Volume 1 and 2, Conference papers, January 16, 1991.

14   Hueglin, "The Politics of Fragmentation," cited earlier, draws on a wide variety of sources from different ideological perspectives to make similar points, emphasizing the fragmenting effects of these changes, and the widening class divisions being created. Other important and diverse Canadian sources include David Wolfe, "The Rise and Demise of the Keynesian Era in Canada: Economic Policy, 1930-1982," in M. Cross and G. Kealey (eds.), *Modern Canada, 1930-1980s;* Thomas J. Courchene, "Global Competitiveness and the Canadian Federation," prepared for the University of Toronto Conference, "Global Competition and Canadian Federalism," September 15, 1990; Jane Jenson, "'Different' but not

'exceptional': Canada's Permeable Fordism," *Canadian Review of Sociology and Anthropology*, v. 26, no. 1 (February 1989); Rianne Mahon, "Post-Fordism, Canada and the FTA: Some Issues for Labour," in Daniel Drache and Meric S. Gertler (eds.), *The New Era of Global Competition: State Policy and Market Power* (Montreal and Kingston: McGill-Queen's University Press, forthcoming 1991).

15   Estimates of the number of Iraqis who were killed range from 25,000 to 50,000 (United States) to 85,000 to 100,000 (Saudi Arabia). There were 79 Americans killed; no Canadians lost their lives; while figures for the other Allied forces were unavailable. The Department of National Defence estimates that the war effort has cost Canada $105 million per month since August. Seventy per cent of this has been identified as "incremental," that is, in excess of what would otherwise have been spent. The Canadian contribution to the environmental clean-up is at this stage difficult to estimate, as is the overall cost of the effort.

16   See Doern and Tomlin, "The Free Trade Sequel," in this volume, and for a positive exploration of this theme, see Robert Chodos, Eric Hamovitch and Rae Murphy, "Setting An Example: Could Canada Become a Pioneer in a Worldwide Redefinition of Nation and State?" *This Magazine* 24:7, excerpted from their forthcoming book, *The Unmaking of Canada* (Toronto: James Lorimer and Company, 1991).

17   I would like to acknowledge the particular assistance of my colleague, Allan Maslove, in developing this section. Also, it was he who drew my attention to the use of symbolic gestures in this budget.

18   See, for example, Michael J. Prince, "Restraining the State: How Ottawa Shrinks," in M.J. Prince (ed.), *How Ottawa Spends 1987-88: Restraining the State* (Toronto: Methuen, 1987); Katherine Graham, "Heading Into the Stretch: Pathology of a Government," in Katherine A. Graham (ed.), *How Ottawa Spends 1988-89: The Conservatives Heading into the Stretch* (Ottawa: Carleton University Press, 1988).

19 Canada, Department of Finance, *The Budget.* Tabled in the House of Commons, February 26, 1991, p. 5.

20 *The Budget,* p. 17.

21 *The Budget,* pp. 8-16.

22 *The Budget,* p. 9.

23 "Should it prove necessary...the government will not hesitate to use legislative means to avoid excessive wage settlements or third-party awards. Nor will the government hesitate to use legislation to prevent work stoppages that would hinder the delivery of services to Canadians." *The Budget,* p. 75.

24 *The Budget,* pp. 74-5; see Appendix 1.1.

25 *The Budget,* p. 93.

26 *The Budget,* pp. 15-6.

27 See Hawkes and Devine, "Meech Lake and Elijah Harper," chapter 2 in this volume.

28 *The Budget,* p. 19.

29 *The Budget,* p. 12.

30 Such a legislated spending cap makes more sense in the United States, since their system for expenditure management incorporates significant checks and balances, and significant negotiation and struggle between the legislative and executive branches. Canada's fusion of executive and legislative power in the Cabinet operates on just the opposite principle, with Parliamentary oversight and public debate providing the comparable "check." On the American budget process, and the American legal precedent for the Tories' legislated spending cap (the *Gramm-Rudman-Hollings Act*), see Aaron Wildavsky, *The New Politics of the Budgetary Process* (Scott, Foresman and Company, 1988).

31 *The Budget,* p. 5.

32   See Michael Prince, "From Meech Lake to Golden Pond,"
      in this volume; *The Canada Assistance Plan: No Time for
      Cuts* (Ottawa: National Council of Welfare, 1991); Allan
      Moscovitch, "Slowing the Steamroller: The Federal Con-
      servatives, the Social Sector and Child Benefits Reform,"
      in Katherine A. Graham (ed.), *How Ottawa Spends 1990-
      91: Tracking the Second Agenda* (Ottawa: Carleton
      University Press, 1990).

33   National Council of Welfare, "A Statement by the Nation-
      al Council of Welfare on the 1991 Federal Budget
      Speech," (Ottawa, February 28, 1991).

34   Federal public service salaries have in fact not kept up
      with salary increases in other sectors. (See Appendix 1.1)
      Also, see the discussion of Public Service 2000 in Phillips,
      "How Ottawa Blends," chapter 7 in this volume, and
      Canada, *Public Service 2000: The Renewal of the Public
      Service of Canada* (Ottawa: 1990); Canada, *Service to the
      Public Task Force Report*, Discussion paper (Ottawa,
      1990).

35   Donald Smiley once remarked that where other countries
      have developed a body of political philosophy, Canada has
      conducted such discussion in the language of fiscal
      federalism and constitutional division of powers.

36   See, for example, Miro Cernetig, "Reform Party rise wor-
      ries PCs," *Globe and Mail* [Toronto], March 25, 1991,
      p. 1.

CHAPTER 2

MEECH LAKE AND ELIJAH HARPER: NATIVE-STATE RELATIONS IN THE 1990s

David C. Hawkes and Marina Devine

Résumé: Ce chapitre retrace les événements cruciaux qui ont mené, en 1990, à la crise dans les relations entre les autochtones et l'État. On examine la crise constitutionnelle du lac Meech du point de vue des autochtones et on analyse les origines de la frustration de ceux-ci face à l'accord du lac Meech. On examine ensuite des méthodes alternatives de résolution de conflits, dont les conférences des premiers ministres sur les affaires constitutionnelles des autochtones (qui n'ont pas réussi); les dépenses fédérales sur les programmes; l'autonomie des communautés; les revendications globales et spécifiques; et les tribunaux. Toutes ces méthodes se sont avérées lentes et peu profitables.

L'inaction gouvernementale a accru le niveau de solidarité chez les divers peuples autochtones et a renforcé leur résolution face à l'injustice. Cela a été clairement démontré par les événements d'Oka. De nouvelles initiatives en matière de politique sur les autochtones s'imposent, telles qu'une commission indépendante sur les revendications territoriales. Le lien entre le rôle du Québec et celui des autochtones dans les questions constitutionnelles fait ressortir l'urgence qu'il y a à établir une nouvelle relation avec les peuples autochtones.

Abstract: This chapter outlines the crucial events that led to the summer 1990 crisis in Canadian Native-state relations. It examines the Meech Lake Constitutional crisis from an Aboriginal perspective and analyzes the roots of Native frustration with the Accord. Alternative methods of conflict resolution are then examined, including: the failed First Ministers' Conferences on Aboriginal Constitutional Matters; federal program spending; community self-government; comprehensive and specific claims; and the courts. All are marked by slowness of pace and limited success.

Government inaction has increased solidarity among diverse Aboriginal peoples and strengthened their resolve in the face of injustice, as events surrounding Oka brought home. New directions, such as an independent commission on land claims, are needed in Native policy. The joining of the Quebec and Aboriginal constitutional issues points to the urgency of establishing a new relationship with Aboriginal peoples.

... The end of the accord would invite economic calamity? We are already poor and unemployed, they said. The end of Meech Lake would kill constitutional change? We are already tired and frustrated by the

33

process, they said. The end of the accord would force
Quebec to leave Canada? Quebec has never been a
friend of ours anyway, they said.[1]

For many Canadians, Elijah Harper's successful stand against
the Meech Lake Accord was a shocking reversal of the expected
order. Through much of the past two centuries, the federal
government has dictated the outcome in its encounters with
Native peoples. In our view, although it would be unrealistic to
claim that Aboriginal peoples are now driving the Native-state
agenda, the demise of the Meech Lake Accord at Native hands
was not an aberration. It demonstrated both a depth of frustration and a degree of strength that have been building in the
Aboriginal movement for a long time.

In this chapter, we outline the events of the Meech Lake
constitutional crisis from the viewpoint of Native-state relations. We first examine the roots of Native frustration with the
Accord, stemming in part from the failure of a series of first
ministers' conferences (FMCs) to achieve agreement among
federal, provincial and territorial governments and Aboriginal
representatives to define and entrench an Aboriginal right of
self-government in the Canadian constitution. It is within the
context of this dispute that we review the recent restraint in
federal government expenditures on programs for Aboriginal
peoples. Other avenues of resolving Aboriginal-state disputes
are surveyed, including community self-government agreements and settlement of comprehensive and specific Aboriginal
claims. The courts appear to have been moving too slowly to
satisfy many Aboriginal peoples. The Aboriginal response has
included Aboriginal summit meetings, and attempts to get a
parallel accord and Companion Resolution on the political agenda. We conclude with suggestions for new initiatives to address
the fundamental disputes in Canadian Native-state relations.

ABORIGINAL PEOPLES AND CONSTITUTIONAL REFORM

On June 12, 1990, Manitoba Premier Gary Filmon asked his
legislature for unanimous consent to introduce a motion to
ratify the Meech Lake Accord. The clock was ticking towards
the June 23 deadline for ratification by Manitoba, New
Brunswick and Newfoundland. Elijah Harper, the sole
Aboriginal MLA in the Manitoba Legislature, refused to permit
Premier Filmon's motion to proceed without the usual notice.

This obscure and technical salvo, as we shall detail later, marked the beginning of the end of the Meech Lake Accord. However, it is important to realize that for Harper and other Native leaders, this was just one more battle in a war of words that began before the Trudeau government's attempts to patriate and amend the Constitution in the late 1970s.

The roots of Native frustration with the Meech Lake Accord are to be found in the failure of a series of constitutionally mandated first ministers' conferences on Aboriginal Constitutional Matte rs. The FMCs were, in turn, one consequence of the renewed interest in constitutional change that developed in response to the 1976 election of the *sovereigntist* Parti Québéois. What ensued was a "battle for the hearts and minds" of Quebeckers between the governments of Quebec and Canada. In 1978 the federal government introduced proposals for constitutional reform, *A Time for Action*, and its companion legislation Bill C-60.[2] Bill C-60 contained a proposed Charter of Rights and Freedoms as well as a provision which attempted to shield certain Aboriginal rights from the general application of the Charter. Nevertheless, the proposed Charter's emphasis on individual rights raised Aboriginal peoples' concern for the constitutional protection of their collective rights.

Although the Trudeau government set the stage for a national discussion of Aboriginal rights, it was the short-lived government of Progressive Conservative Prime Minister Joe Clark in 1979 that provided Aboriginal peoples with their first formal recognition as legitimate players on the constitutional stage, when Aboriginal constitutional matters were added as Item 13 on the First Ministers' Constitutional Conference agenda. At a meeting of the co-chairmen of the Continuing Committee of Ministers on the Constitution (CCMC), federal Minister of Federal-Provincial Relations Bill Jarvis, Saskatchewan Minister of Intergovernmental Affairs Roy Romanow and the "Native Presidents," Noel Starblanket of the National Indian Brotherhood (NIB), Harry Daniels of the Native Council of Canada (NCC), and Charlie Watt of the Inuit Committee on National Issues, a commitment was given to meet with Native leaders on constitutional matters that directly affected them.

With the May 1980 victory of federalist forces in the Quebec referendum on sovereignty association, the freshly re-elected Trudeau government set out to negotiate renewed federalism with the provinces. When an FMC on the Constitution held in

September 1980 failed to reach an agreement, the Prime Minister decided to seek patriation unilaterally. A month following the conference, the federal government's new proposal for constitutional reform was released. A proposed Section 25 provided for the non-derogation of Aboriginal and treaty rights with respect to the Charter of Rights and Freedoms. This would have the effect of shielding collective Aboriginal and treaty rights from the unintended application of individual Charter rights. In January 1981, following discussions with Aboriginal leaders, two other sections were added to entrench Aboriginal and treaty rights, and to provide for one further meeting of first ministers and Aboriginal leaders on constitutional matters.

Most provinces opposed the federal government's unilateral approach, and several launched court actions to stop it. They also lobbied for their case in London, in an attempt to persuade the British government not to accede to the request to patriate the constitution to Canada. The NIB and the NCC were already there to plead for the preservation of the special trust relationship between Indian people and the Crown (as represented by the Queen), which they thought was endangered by the federal proposals. Several Indian groups launched lawsuits in the British courts but were unsuccessful in blocking patriation.

The provincial court challenges had the desired effect.[3] In September 1981, the Supreme Court said that while unilateral federal action was legal in the strictest technical sense, it offended constitutional convention. By convention, a substantial measure of provincial consent was required on matters affecting federal-provincial relations before such a constitutional amendment could be forwarded to Westminster. The Court decision forced both the Prime Minister and the provincial premiers back to the bargaining table. An FMC on the Constitution was held in November 1981, in a last-ditch attempt to find agreement. On November 5, a constitutional accord was reached among the federal government and nine provinces, excluding Quebec. The government of Quebec would withhold its consent, the accord would remain partial, and the accommodation incomplete until the ill-fated Meech Lake Accord of 1987.

The 1981 constitutional accord was incomplete in other respects as well. Recognition of the rights of Aboriginal peoples, which was included in earlier draft amendments, had been

deliberately deleted at the last minute. Some provincial governments had become very concerned about the scope and meaning
of Aboriginal rights, due in part to the extensive lobbying efforts
of Aboriginal organizations in London.[4] Canadian women were
also concerned that the gender equality clause (Section 28),
guaranteeing rights and freedoms equally to male and female
persons, could be impaired by Section 33, the legislative over-
ride provision better known as the "notwithstanding" clause.
Only through the powerful combined lobby of Canadian women
and Aboriginal peoples, at both the national and international
levels, were these rights more fully protected in the new constitution at the time of patriation. The Aboriginal rights clause
was reinserted, albeit with the word "existing" placed before the
phrase "Aboriginal and treaty rights" in Section 35 (those rights
to be recognized and affirmed). The meaning of Section 35, never
clear, became even less so.

The *Constitution Act, 1982* was proclaimed on April 17,
1982. Three sections relate directly to Aboriginal peoples. Section 25 guarantees that the Canadian Charter of Rights and
Freedoms will not

> ...abrogate or derogate from any Aboriginal, treaty or
> other rights or freedoms that pertain to the Aboriginal
> peoples of Canada, including:
>
> (a) any rights or freedoms that have been recognized
> by the Royal Proclamation of October 7, 1763; and
>
> (b) any rights or freedoms that may be acquired by the
> Aboriginal peoples of Canada by way of land claims
> settlement.

Section 35 states that:

> (1) The existing Aboriginal and treaty rights of the
> Aboriginal peoples of Canada are hereby recognized
> and affirmed.
>
> (2) In this Act, "Aboriginal peoples of Canada" in-
> cludes the Indian, Inuit and Métis peoples of Canada.

Section 37 provided for the convening of a First Ministers'
Conference on Aboriginal Constitutional Matters by April 17,
1983, for discussions,

> ...including the identification and definition of the
> rights of those peoples to be included in the Constitu-
> tion of Canada...

and for the participation of Aboriginal peoples' representatives
and delegates from the two territorial governments in those
discussions.

That conference was held in March 1983, and an accord was
reached among the parties, resulting in the first amendments
to the newly patriated constitution. The accord covered five
topics: a process for negotiating the definition of Aboriginal and
treaty rights; an agenda for these discussions; and three different types of amendments.

Section 25 (b) was amended to protect existing and future
land claims settlements. To Section 35, two new subsections
were added: one included existing and future land claims agreements in the definition of "treaty rights;" another guaranteed
Aboriginal and treaty rights equally to male and female persons. A new Section 35.1 was added to provide for an FMC to
be convened, including the participation of representatives of
the Aboriginal peoples of Canada, before any amendment to the
Constitution which directly affects Aboriginal peoples, is made
(including subsection 91(24), the federal head of power over
"Indians and lands reserved for the Indians"). Native leaders
have claimed that such matters include Senate reform and
fisheries, given the Aboriginal interest in some form of guaranteed representation and the many disputes over Aboriginal
fishing rights. Section 37 was amended as well. Reference to
the "identification and definition" of the rights of the Aboriginal
peoples of Canada, contained in this section in 1982, was
deleted—the phrase "constitutional matters that directly affect"
Aboriginal peoples took its place. Perhaps of greater significance was the provision that mandated at least two more
First Ministers' Conferences on Aboriginal Constitutional Matters, in 1985 and 1987, with a further such conference agreed to
for 1984 by way of the political accord of March 1983.[5]

The three FMCs which followed focussed on the right of
Aboriginal self-government. This direction had been identified
in the accord and advocated in the 1983 Report of the House of
Commons Special Committee on Indian Self-Government,
known as the Penner Report.[6] Participants could not agree on
whether the right to Aboriginal self-government flowed from

inherent and unextinguished Aboriginal sovereignty, from existing treaty and Aboriginal rights or from federal and provincial governments. Other issues included financing self-government, especially the federal-provincial division of responsibility for that financing; land and resources; and a land base for the Métis. None of the conferences was successful in producing an accord, and the Section 37 constitutional negotiation process, which had begun with such bright hopes, ended. The next month, on April 30, 1987, the Meech Lake Accord was signed by the Prime Minister and all provincial premiers. First ministers could not accept an unclear concept of Aboriginal self-government after four years of exhaustive elaboration, but could endorse the equally vague notion of Quebec as a "distinct society" after only brief discussions. Louis Bruyére, former president of the Native Council of Canada, summed up reaction:

> Aboriginal peoples' view on the Accord can be summarized in four words: It abandons Aboriginal peoples. It does this by being silent about the uniqueness and distinctiveness of Aboriginal peoples.[7]

The immediate "success" of the Meech Lake Accord, and the ensuing constitutional resolution negotiated in the Langevin Block in Ottawa in early June, embittered Aboriginal peoples. The Accord obviously affected their interests, but the federal government had not consulted them. Meech Lake failed to recognize Aboriginal peoples' unique place in Canada, and it made northern provincehood more difficult. The Accord also proposed that the federal government would appoint Senators and Justices to the Supreme Court of Canada from nominees supplied exclusively by provincial governments, a suggestion which offended both Aboriginal peoples and residents of the Yukon and Northwest Territories.[8]

The negotiation process leading up to the Meech Lake Accord began during the Aboriginal constitutional process. During the annual Premiers' Conference in August 1986, premiers agreed with a request from Prime Minister Mulroney to give priority to the Quebec constitutional question. Negotiations on the Meech Lake Accord were quite different from those of the Section 37 process. Initially, Quebec Minister for Intergovernmental Affairs, Gil Rémillard, visited each provincial capital to make an assessment. He was followed by his federal counterpart, Senator Lowell Murray, who also undertook a series of private, bilateral meetings. It was only after many such meetings, when some chance of success was assured, that the federal government was willing to call first ministers together, as Mr. Rémillard phrased it, to negotiate Quebec's adherence to the *Constitution Act, 1982.* The first ministers' meeting was closed to the public and the media, with only the closest advisors allowed into the meeting room at Meech Lake. Any other process, it was argued, would not have allowed a deal to be struck. The characteristics of the negotiation process which purportedly led to its success—private and secret meetings, lack of public participation, closed to the public and the media, very few people involved—are the very characteristics which ultimately led to the undoing of the Meech Lake Accord.

The constitutional amending formula gave the federal parliament and each provincial legislature three years to pass the constitutional resolution. As time went on, it became increasingly obvious that, whatever Canadians thought about the substance of the Accord, they deplored the manner in which it was reached. What the federal and provincial governments failed to realize is that the Canadian Charter of Rights and Freedoms, and the revisions to the constitutional amending formula and procedure of 1982 (the "made-in-Canada" approach) had changed the nature of constitutional politics in Canada. Constitutional change is now a popular matter for all Canadians, and all wish to participate in the reform movement. The Meech Lake Accord represented yet another attempt by federal and provincial governments to promote constitutional change exclusively through executive federalism. Public consultation, to the extent it occurred at all, was held after the fact.[9] Even then, the Prime Minister and most premiers insisted that no changes could take place to the Accord as a result of these consultations, a move which further deepened the cynicism of Canadians.

The Aboriginal Response to Constitutional Inaction

In the meantime, however, the Section 37 process had served to aggregate Aboriginal interests at the national level. For the first time, Aboriginal peoples from across the country— Indian, Inuit and Métis—were working together at the national level. The "Aboriginal Summits," as they became known, brought together the national Aboriginal leaders to discuss the strategy of constitutional negotiations. By the end of the 1987

FMC on Aboriginal constitutional matters, a new Aboriginal solidarity had been established at the national level. This was remarkable, in view of the divisions among these peoples based not only on their different histories, but on their different entitlements under the law.

Just prior to the adjournment of the 1987 conference, the four national Aboriginal peoples' organizations tabled a draft constitutional amendment. The "Joint Aboriginal Proposal for Self-Government" would recognize and affirm the inherent right of self-government and land of all the Indian, Inuit and Métis peoples of Canada. Negotiations, which could be either bilateral (federal-Aboriginal) or trilateral (federal-provincial-Aboriginal) in nature, would be initiated at the request of Aboriginal peoples. Negotiations would include, but not be limited to: self-government, lands, resources, economic and fiscal arrangements, education, preservation and enhancement of language and culture, and equity of access (that is, availability to all Aboriginal peoples—Indian, Inuit and Métis). The rights defined in the agreements would be protected in the Constitution as are treaty rights.[10] The conference adjourned without addressing the Aboriginal constitutional proposal.

Although the process failed to produce a constitutional resolution regarding Aboriginal rights, the Aboriginal peoples emerged organized and united. The solidarity was more than symbolic. During the Meech Lake process, Aboriginal peoples prepared a "Companion Resolution" to the Meech Lake amendments, in yet another attempt to resolve, at least in part, Aboriginal constitutional issues. The concept emerged in 1987 from the Native Council of Canada but was supported by other national organizations as the fall-back to direct amendment of the Meech Lake Accord.[11]

The idea was to persuade governments to introduce into their respective legislatures, a constitutional amendment on Aboriginal rights and northern concerns that would take effect simultaneously with the Meech Lake resolution, without directly amending the latter (and therefore without requiring Quebec or other provinces to revisit the Meech Lake Accord). This would achieve the federal and provincial objectives of not altering the delicate balance achieved in the wording of the Meech Lake resolution, while at the same time addressing the needs of Aboriginal peoples and northerners.

A second initiative, to restart dialogue on a new package of substantive amendments addressing self-government, was also launched in 1987, this time by the NCC and the Inuit Tapirisat of Canada. In 1988, a revised package of principles was endorsed by all the national Aboriginal groups. In early 1989, the federal government sponsored a tour by three of the organizations to all provinces and territories, which yielded support from seven provinces (including Quebec) for a re-opening of at least informal dialogue on the basis of the proposal, while the Manitoba legislature passed a formal resolution calling for a FMC on Aboriginal constitutional matters by April 1990.

The struggle to address Aboriginal constitutional concerns, which were ignored in the Meech Lake Accord, also united factions within the status Indian community. In 1989, the Prairie Treaty Nations Alliance[12] buried their differences with the Assembly of First Nations (AFN), which was the NIB's successor as the organization representing Canada's status Indians. After November 1989, the failure of the Meech Lake Accord became a real probability, and the political context of Aboriginal efforts shifted from self-government proposals directly to the Companion Resolution.

Elijah Harper and Meech Lake

Aboriginal leaders had their own list of conditions, which, if met, might have rendered the Meech Lake Accord acceptable to them:

° recognition of Aboriginal peoples as a fundamental characteristic of Canada and as distinct societies in their own right;

° a constitutional process that deals with Aboriginal issues;

° guarantees that they will be involved in any first ministers' discussions that relate to or affect Aboriginal issues;

° a return to the original formula for creating new provinces, which required only the approval of Parliament (but no longer requiring the perfunctory approval of the Parliament of Great Britain).[13]

The AFN and most Native groups did not oppose the designation of Quebec as a distinct society, so long as Native peoples were recognized as having similar status.[14] The Aboriginal claim to "distinct society" status was not a mere "me too" reaction to the Meech Lake Accord. Aboriginal leaders regard the *Royal Proclamation of 1763* as a national founding document that establishes a partnership among three, not two, founding peoples: the English, the French and the Native people.[15] It is for that reason that they lobbied to have the *Proclamation* named in the *Constitution Act (1982)*. Until the end of the Meech process, however, Aboriginal demands were seen as add-ons, secondary issues lost in a crowd of higher political priorities, even by those premiers whose support for the Meech Lake Accord was tentative and conditional. The clauses on centre stage were "distinct society" status for Quebec, the federal spending power and the amending formula.

On March 21, 1990, Premier Frank McKenna of New Brunswick proposed a Companion Resolution that would, among other things, place Aboriginal issues on the agenda for the next round of constitutional talks, and drop the unanimity requirement for the creation of new provinces. McKenna's proposal was by no means as controversial as Manitoba's proposed "Canada clause," which was intended to replace the "distinct society" clause in the Meech Lake Accord, and which explicitly recognized the contribution of Aboriginal peoples to the fabric of Canada. Prime Minister Brian Mulroney agreed to bring the New Brunswick resolution before Parliament and refer it to a special committee for study.

The all-party committee, chaired by Quebec Conservative MP Jean Charest, began hearings on April 3. The Charest committee heard 160 witnesses and received 800 submissions including a forceful joint presentation by the AFN, the NCC and the Inuit. On May 18, the committee presented a unanimous report, which included recommendations to resolve Aboriginal concerns about the admission of new provinces and to place Aboriginal rights back on the constitutional agenda. More contentiously, the report included a proposal, similar in effect to Manitoba's "Canada clause," that Aboriginal and ethnic Canadians be recognized in the body of the Constitution. None of the recommendations technically involved re-opening the Accord.

The Charest report was still a possible framework for discussion when the first ministers met for supper at the Museum of Civilization in Ottawa on June 3. Manitoba Premier Gary Filmon suggested that it be the basis for a compromise. Then Prime Minister Mulroney proposed on June 4 that the Meech Lake constitutional amendment package be ratified without any changes by June 23, with further constitutional amendments to be passed later. Aboriginal rights were not first on the Prime Minister's agenda for future discussions. He wished to address such difficult issues as Manitoba's "Canada clause" and Senate reform later in the meeting. This meant that the Charest report, as such, could not be the basis of discussion.

Finally, on Saturday, June 9 at 10:30 p.m., after a week of protracted and secret discussions, the first ministers held a public signing ceremony for the document emanating from their negotiations. It included provisions for a Senate reform commission; for the provinces and the federal government to discuss as soon as possible amendments to ensure territorial representation on the Supreme Court, to strengthen women's rights and protect minority language rights; for Constitutional conferences on Aboriginal rights to take place every three years; for Parliamentary committee hearings on a "Canada clause" to begin in July; and for a review of the legal impact of the "distinct society" clause. The federal government expected that the Manitoba, Newfoundland and New Brunswick premiers would proceed to their legislatures and, however reluctantly, bring the Meech Lake Accord to a ratification vote by the June 23 deadline. New Brunswick did, in fact, ratify the Accord on June 15. But the Accord ran into trouble from an unexpected provincial source: Elijah Harper, the NDP Member of the Manitoba Legislative Assembly (MLA) for the riding of Rupertsland.

Premier Filmon's plan for passing the Accord, as agreed with opposition leaders Carstairs and Doer, called for the introduction of a motion of ratification in the Manitoba legislature, 10 days of public hearings, debate and a final vote, all in the less than two weeks left until June 23. On Tuesday, June 12, Filmon requested unanimous consent to introduce his motion without the usual two days' notice. With the encouragement of Manitoba Native leaders, Elijah Harper denied his consent. At first, this was thought to be merely a symbolic gesture.[16] But Harper again denied consent on June 13 and 14. This meant that the earliest the motion could be brought forward for debate was

Monday, June 18. On that day, the Prime Minister offered a six-point program for dealing with Aboriginal concerns:

1.   a Federal-Aboriginal process to set the agenda for the First Ministers' Conference on Aboriginal Matters; and the acceleration of the holding of the first Conference;

2.   a commitment by the Government of Canada to full constitutional recognition of the Aboriginal peoples as a fundamental characteristic of Canada;

3.   the participation of representatives of the Aboriginal peoples of Canada at any future first ministers' conference held to discuss the "recognition clause;"

4.   an invitation to participate in all first ministers' conferences where matters being discussed directly affect Aboriginal peoples;

5.   the joint definition of treaty rights;

6.   the establishment of a Royal Commission on Native Affairs.[17]

Native leaders refused to negotiate. Harper's stand was not a negotiating tactic; it was a real attempt to stop a process that Aboriginal peoples believed to be wrong and unacceptable.

The rules of the Manitoba legislature permitted Harper to delay the motion for six legislative working days. On Wednesday, June 20, Filmon was finally able to introduce his motion. By this time, Harper had become a national hero. The promised public hearings, with over 3,500 presenters signed up, had yet to be held. Debate on the motion went forward, but it was too late to save the Accord. At 12:30 p.m. in Winnipeg on Friday, June 22, the Manitoba legislature adjourned without bringing the Accord and companion agreement to a vote. Newfoundland premier Clyde Wells, whose legislature was also in the midst of debate, had been staying in close touch with Filmon and Carstairs, and spoke to Elijah Harper that day.[18] Later that afternoon, the Newfoundland House of Assembly also adjourned without a ratification vote. The Accord was dead. Having done so much, Native peoples once again found themselves invisible to the federal government—at least until July 11, when the Oka stand-off began.

For Aboriginal peoples in particular, the Meech Lake Accord represented a betrayal of self-government aspirations that had been nurtured, albeit sometimes reluctantly, by the federal government for nearly 20 years. Only a complete lack of faith in the federal government's sincerity can explain the absence of Aboriginal response to the Prime Minister's offers outlined in his letter of June 18, when it became clear that Aboriginal people had the unexpected power to break the Accord.

FEDERAL PROGRAM SPENDING FOR ABORIGINAL PEOPLES

Restraint in federal program spending for Aboriginal people may well have been a contributing factor in Aboriginal leaders' declining trust in government. An examination of federal expenditures on Aboriginal programs shows the government maintaining a direction that gave low priority to Aboriginal needs after 1987. The federal government pursued deficit-cutting objectives, perhaps without correctly evaluating the political consequences of its actions.

The Nielsen Task Force managed to uncover approximately 113 federal "programs" or federal activities for Aboriginal people in 1986. However, it appears that if a program particularly benefited Native people, it was included as a Native program, whether or not other persons also benefited.[19] If we include only those programs that serve Aboriginal people as Aboriginal people (and not, for example, as poor people or northerners), the number is reduced by nearly half.

There are a few minor programs for Native people scattered through various departments: programs for Native court workers and law students in Justice, the Canadian Employment and Immigration Commission (CEIC) Native internship program, Canada Mortgage and Housing's Rural and Native housing program and the Public Service Commission's northern careers and national indigenous development programs. Most of the more important programs are in Indian and Northern Affairs (INAC). As we shall note later, much of the actual administration of programs has now been devolved to Indian bands. The Indian and Inuit Affairs program of INAC, which accounts for the lion's share of federal expenditures on Native people, includes such activities as: negotiating self-government arrangements with individual bands; comprehensive claims negotiation and settlement administration; economic development; administration of lands, revenues and trusts; education, including funding for post-secondary education; social assistance and child welfare; capital facilities and community services, including housing and policing; and band management, as well as the usual internal component of program management and administration.

A number of grants and contributions within activities in the Northern Affairs program of INAC are specifically targeted for Native people "north of 60." These include: cultural grants, contributions to the two territorial governments for hospital and medical care of status Indians and Inuit, contributions to northern Native organizations for research and consultation related to northern development, and contributions to organizations and individuals for Inuit economic development.

The other main agencies offering specifically Native programming are Health and Welfare Canada, with Indian health services; Industry, Science and Technology, with the Canadian Aboriginal Economic Development Strategy (CAEDS) shared with INAC; and the Department of the Secretary of State. The contribution of the Secretary of State to overall spending on Native people is small, but the programs concerned have been extremely important to Native people themselves: funding for Aboriginal representative organizations, Native women's groups, Aboriginal Friendship Centres and for Native newspapers and radio and television production. In February 1990, cuts to the budget of the Secretary of State were announced, affecting over 100 Native political organizations and all the regional communications societies. The Minister received over 10,000 pieces of correspondence, nearly as many as were received protesting cuts to women's programs.[20] This funding was not reinstated in the 1991-92 Budget.

The adequacy of estimates of total federal expenditures on Aboriginal peoples has been controversial. When Native people and their supporters protested the $10 million cut in the 1990-91 Secretary of State budget, the Prime Minister and the Minister of Finance both pointed to an eight per cent increase in INAC, said to be the largest increase for any department that year, and said that the government was spending in excess of $4 billion on Aboriginal people. The AFN replied that the increase was $50 million short of what had been expected, and that it did not keep up with inflation and population growth.[21]

Total 1990-91 estimates for the specifically Native programs listed in this section did exceed $3 billion, with about $2.5 billion accounted for by INAC's Native programs. (This figure can thus be taken as a conservative, or low-side estimate.) These programs amounted to less than two per cent of the total federal budget, or about the same proportion as status Indians in the Canadian population. On balance, it appears that planned spending on Aboriginal people may not have kept pace with population growth and increases in the Consumer Price Index (CPI) over the past 10 years (see Table 2.1).[22] Given the continuing disadvantaged position of Aboriginal people in Canadian society, and viewed within the context of the failure of the constitutional process, expenditure restraint did little for the climate of Aboriginal-federal relations in the crucial years leading to the demise of the Meech Lake Accord. The federal government seems, to some extent, to have admitted this, in that Indian and Inuit programs were among those exempted from the federal expenditure control plan in 1991-92. The departmental spending plan for 1991-92 called for a 4.8 per cent increase over 1990-91 forecast expenditures.[23]

Table 2.1
Planned Federal Expenditures on Native People, 1981-90

Year	Planned Spending On Native People (millions) $	Growth (%)	CPI % Increase	Status Pop. Growth (%)
1990	3,150	9.20	5.0	5.30
1989	2,898	9.01	4.1	5.75
1988	2,612	9.12	4.4	6.34
1987	2,383	8.94	4.1	7.05
1986	2,130	9.33	4.0	7.08
1985	1,988	9.24	4.4	3.21
1984	1,836	8.80	5.8	2.91
1983	1,615	8.01	10.8	2.61
1982	1,293	8.72	12.5	2.52
1981	1,127	--	10.2	2.36

Sources: Federal *Estimates,* 1981-90; Statistics Canada, *The Consumer Price Index,* March 1990, and Hagey *et al., Demographic Trends,* INAC 1989.

OTHER AVENUES FOR RESOLVING DISPUTES WITH ABORIGINAL PEOPLES

Constitutional reform is only one of several avenues pursued over the past 20 years by the federal government and the Aboriginal peoples for resolving their disputes, particularly with regard to self-government. All are exasperatingly slow, partial and, most objectionable of all to Aboriginal peoples, controlled by federal conditions and federal funding. A summary review of the situation in each area drives home our point.

Devolution to Aboriginal Governments

One area in which Native people and the federal government seem to have found some common cause is in the transfer of responsibility for service delivery to Native people themselves. About 70 per cent of Indian and Inuit Affairs program expenditures are now administered by Indians.[24] During the period of INAC's five-year devolution plan, 1985-86 to 1990-91, the Indian and Inuit Affairs program staff complement was scheduled to be reduced from 4,256 to 2,913, as a result of devolution and efficiency measures.[25] The proportion of program expenditures administered by Indians almost doubled over the period 1981-1990. A new multi-year devolution plan was to be developed in 1990-91. Consonant with this movement toward devolution was the decentralization of administration to 33 district offices across the country.

However, administrative program transfers involve restrictions on the funding provided, and offer little flexibility for planning purposes. Alternative Funding Arrangements (AFAs), introduced in 1986, give eligible bands and tribal councils increased authority and flexibility in exercising local control and management of programs and services. These block funding agreements permit bands to design their own programs and transfer funds among activities, but bands must operate within the agreed funding ceiling over the multi-year term of the agreement. As of November 30, 1990, 77 AFAs had been signed, and annual funding amounted to $292.8 million.[26]

Many Native programs in other departments, such as the Secretary of State, consist of grants or contributions to bands, Native organizations or individuals. The largest exception is probably Health and Welfare's Indian health program. Partial devolution in this case occurred from Health and Welfare Canada to the Government of the NWT in 1988. Aboriginal organizations in the NWT supported the transfer because they believed that it would allow Native people to exercise more direct control over the health care system, through the mechanism of regional health committees.[27]

There are risks for both parties inherent in any devolution process. For the devolving agency, there may be additional costs due to diminished economies of scale.[28] In 1984, this was cited as one of the factors inhibiting further administrative transfers.[29] For the recipient Aboriginal government, the risks include accepting a transfer agreement with resources that may turn out to be partial or inadequate. Bands can avoid having INAC as a back-seat driver by negotiating AFAs, but they cannot then request additional funds during the life of the agreement.

Community Self-Government

In the fall of 1985, in the midst of the Section 37 constitutional negotiations, the federal government launched a program within INAC called Indian Self-Government Community Negotiations. It was thought that some practical experience using different approaches would build support for the constitutional initiative. The program enables Indian communities, if they so choose, to "escape" the *Indian Act* by replacing it with other federal legislation, which in turn delegates powers to the Indian band.

The Sechelt Indian Band of British Columbia's Sunshine Coast was the first to take advantage of such an approach, although negotiations between the Sechelt and the federal government had begun long before the federal program was announced. The *Sechelt Indian Band Self-Government Act,* and the accompanying provincial legislation, the *Sechelt Indian Government District Enabling Act,* set out the delegated powers potentially exercisable by the band, and recognize the band for all intents and purposes as a municipal government. Land is held in fee simple (and is thus alienable, can be borrowed against, and sold); fiscal arrangements between the Sechelt and the federal government are less conditional; and federal and provincial laws apply to the Sechelt only insofar as they are consistent with Sechelt by-laws.[30]

As of September 1990, five years after the policy was announced, 170 Indian bands were in the "developmental" phase of the program, 29 were involved in "framework" negotiations, and 30 were at the "substantive" negotiation phase.[31] However, no legislation has yet come forward which would bring these negotiations to fruition. This may change in 1991 with the impending ratification of the Council of Yukon Indians comprehensive claims agreement, which calls for band-by-band "opting in" to an umbrella Final Agreement and for the negotiation of a self-government agreement with each Yukon First Nation.

Parallel to these negotiations were ones held to address self-government for Aboriginal persons off-reserve. The federal government lead agency for this purpose was the Federal-Provincial Relations Office, not Indian and Northern Affairs. The process was to be initiated by provincial governments. Some discussions have been held with the governments of Manitoba, Saskatchewan and Prince Edward Island, but as yet nothing has advanced to even a framework stage.

Comprehensive and Specific Aboriginal Claims

In 1973, after the Calder case, the federal government embarked upon a policy of settling "comprehensive" Aboriginal claims. Comprehensive claims are those where the rights of the claimant Aboriginal group to traditional use and land occupancy have not been extinguished by treaty or superseded by law. While the principle of negotiated rather than litigated settlement was accepted, the federal policy of 1973 (reaffirmed in 1981) insisted on the extinguishment of Aboriginal rights in the claims area, and with the exception in 1981 of local governments, excluded self-government as an item for discussion. Both of these conditions acted as roadblocks to the settlement of claims. The Coolican Task Force on comprehensive claims policy led to significant policy changes in 1986, including a somewhat more open view of the extinguishment question. Nevertheless, no final comprehensive claims agreements have yet been ratified under the new policy. Extinguishment has proven to be of continuing concern to Aboriginal people in current negotiations.

Since 1973, three comprehensive claims have been settled, all of them while the lands concerned were under the threat of imminent resource development. These are the *James Bay and Northern Quebec Agreement (1975)*, the *Northeastern Quebec Agreement (1978)*, and the *Inuvialuit Final Agreement (1984)*. In April 1990, the James Bay Cree filed a lawsuit in the Quebec Superior Court to declare their claim agreement "unconstitutional, null and void," and to obtain a permanent injunction against any future hydro-electric development in their territory.[32] In essence, the Cree are suing for non-performance of contract.

While the federal government has abandoned its former policy of negotiating only six comprehensive claims at a time, negotiations in 1990-91 continued on the six previously accepted claims. The Attikamek-Montagnais signed a framework agreement in 1988; the NWT Dene and Métis are regrouping for negotiation of regional claims following the failure to ratify a final agreement in 1990; the Council of Yukon Indians' umbrella agreement is proceeding to ratification by March 31, 1991; the Nisg'a of British Columbia had a framework agreement in July 1989; the Inuit of the eastern Arctic signed an Agreement-In-Principle on April 30, 1990, which is expected to be ratified over an 18-month period; and negotiations began with the Labrador Inuit early in 1989. Nineteen other claims have been accepted on a waiting list, 17 of them in British Columbia; five have been rejected, including that of the Kanesatake Mohawks, and 11 are under review, as of July 1990.[32] This is obviously not a "fast track" to satisfactory settlements.

A complicating factor in the comprehensive claims process has been the necessity to involve provincial and territorial governments in the process, and their general unwillingness to be involved. The government of British Columbia, since it joined Confederation in 1871, has been especially adamant in refusing to recognize Aboriginal rights or to participate in treaty-making or land claims processes. The provincial government in 1990 reversed its traditional stand, sought ways to join the process and admitted the existence of "certain Aboriginal rights and interests."[34] It remains to be seen if this recognition will be adequate to open up the process with British Columbia's increasingly militant Native peoples.

The specific claims process has an even greater backlog. Specific claims are those resulting from grievances about government maladministration, unscrupulous land transactions or unfulfilled treaty promises. As of March 1990, 578 specific claims had been filed; 205 were classified as resolved; and 275 were under review or negotiation. Of the remainder, 55 were being reassessed by the claimants, 21 were suspended and 22 were under litigation. Of those classified as resolved, only 44 actually ended in settlements, while 44 were rejected (again including that of the Kanesatake Mohawks), 69 were referred to another administrative process and the file was closed on 48. One of the major problems with the policy on specific claims is that claimants must show they have occupied the land in question from "time immemorial;" this disqualifies colonial arrangements, such as that of the Kanesatake Mohawks.

While these claims are not as large as the comprehensive claims, specific claims settlements have resulted in $105.2 million in federal compensation, $37.4 million from various provincial governments, and the return of 143,055 acres of land to Indians.[35] It has been estimated that over 50 per cent of Canada may be under Aboriginal claim, including much of the northern territories, and 80 per cent of British Columbia and Quebec.[36]

The Courts

The courts provide an alternative method, albeit one which is exceedingly slow and very costly, of resolving disputes between Aboriginal peoples and the state. Recent decisions by the Supreme Court of Canada, especially since the constitutional amendments relating to Aboriginal peoples were proclaimed in 1982 and 1983, have begun to redefine the relationship between Aboriginal peoples and the Government of Canada.

The Supreme Court found in the *Guerin* case in 1984 that the Crown, in this case the federal government, is liable if it fails in the performance of its fiduciary duties (those of a guardian or trustee). The case involved the leasing of Indian reserve lands.[37] The import of the case, it is argued, is that Aboriginal title is a legal right that can be extinguished only with the consent of Aboriginal peoples, thus shifting the burden of proof to federal and provincial governments. They must show that Aboriginal land rights were lawfully extinguished in the past, or acknowledge their continuing existence.

In the *Simon* decision in 1986, the Supreme Court further ruled that treaty rights (in this case a right to hunt) set out in pre-Confederation treaties are protected under the *Constitution Act, 1982* (as amended).[38]

Some case law provides unforeseen guidance. In the decision of the Supreme Court on Bill 30, the Ontario government legislation proposing amendments to the Ontario *Education Act* (which, among other matters, would extend full public funding to Roman Catholic separate schools), the Court drew an analogy between Section 93 of the *Constitution Act, 1982*, that relating to separate schools at the time of Confederation, and Section 91 (24), the federal head of power relating to "Indians and lands reserved for the Indians."

> In this sense, section 93 is a provincial counterpart of section 91(24) (Indians and Indian land) which authorizes the Parliament of Canada to legislate for the benefit of the Indian population in a **preferential**, discriminatory, or distinctive fashion vis-à-vis others.[39]

Section 91(24) thus provides the federal government with the power to enact only preferential laws for the benefit of Aboriginal peoples, an interpretation quite at odds with the reality of the *Indian Act.*

The *Sparrow* decision of 1990 went several steps further. The case involved the Aboriginal right to fish in an area not covered by treaty, but which Aboriginal peoples historically occupied, and it was the first time that Section 35 (recognizing and affirming Aboriginal and treaty rights) was before the Court. The decision confirmed that the fiduciary or trust responsibility of the federal government with respect to Aboriginal peoples is part of Section 35 (1), that regulation of an Aboriginal right does not result in its extinguishment, and that there must be a clear and plain intention to extinguish the Aboriginal right in the particular legislation. The burden of proving extinguishment, as well as the burden of justifying legislation that has some negative effect on Aboriginal rights, rests with the Government.[40]

Many other cases are before the courts. One which could have the most far-reaching implications is that of the Gitksan-Wet'suwet'en of British Columbia, who have launched a court action against the province, declaring sovereignty over their traditional lands. (There is no treaty, and the lands have never been surrendered.)[41]

AFTER MEECH: THE NEED FOR NEW DIRECTIONS

Like so many federal government policies before it, the Meech Lake Accord mobilized Aboriginal peoples to take collective action, and provided them with an opportunity to build new solidarity. Following the failure of the Section 37 process, many Aboriginal leaders expressed a fear that their people would be excluded from future processes of constitutional reform. Over time, and without further involvement, it was thought that Aboriginal peoples would lose legitimacy as full participants at first ministers' conferences.[42] The Meech Lake Accord appeared as the realization of this fear. The solidarity among Aboriginal peoples that was required to make Oka a national issue was built upon the backs of the Meech Lake and Section 37 constitutional processes, together with the breakdown of alternative methods for resolving disputes between Aboriginal peoples and the Canadian state.

Renewed efforts at constitutional reform will hit an immediate reality—the joining of the Aboriginal and Quebec constitutional issues in the public mind. Both demand a constitutional status as distinct societies, both define themselves in national terms (e.g. Assembly of First Nations, Quebec National Assembly), both seek protection for their language and cultures, both are minorities with constitutional legal standing, and both, in a sense, are "founding peoples."

According to a fall 1990 Angus Reid poll, 85 per cent of Canadians approved of Elijah Harper's stand on the Meech Lake Accord. At that time, 50 per cent of Canadians thought that "Native issues" were the most important ones that our political leaders should address and most thought that the problems were caused by forces outside of the Native community. Federal policy was viewed in very negative terms and there was strong support for Aboriginal self-government for Native peoples. Based on his data, Mr. Reid has speculated that, among English-speaking Canadians, Aboriginal/non-Aboriginal relations had become tied to Quebec/non-Quebec relations.[43] The linkage of the issues is weaker in Quebec. Whatever constitutional reform process follows the report of the Citizens' Forum on Canada's Future (the Spicer Forum) it should involve Aboriginal peoples in the negotiation process, and consult Canadians on the proposed constitutional amendments.

There is a need to re-examine our federal structure, both in terms of Aboriginal-state relations and Quebec-Canada relations. If we are to live with asymmetrical federalism, there is no reason why it should not extend to Aboriginal peoples. This might take the form of a new head of power for Aboriginal self-government in the constitution (a "Section 93" approach), or recognition of Aboriginal governments as having powers similar to those of provincial governments. The idea of guaranteed representation in national institutions, such as the House of Commons and the Senate, should be reconsidered. Another possibility is that of an Aboriginal parliament, similar to the Saami Parliaments in Scandinavia, which represent the indigenous peoples, descendants of the traditional Saami reindeer herders of northern Europe. Although they control no territory, they provide a forum and a voice for Aboriginal peoples in decision making at the national and international levels. [44]

If this re-examination of Canadian federalism leads further, and some form of sovereignty association is to be negotiated between Quebec and "the rest of Canada," the legal status of Quebec's Aboriginal peoples will have to be resolved. Much of Nouveau-Quebec is inhabited exclusively by Cree and Inuit, and even to a modest degree, governed by them under existing land claims agreements. This territory was part of Rupert's Land and not part of Quebec at the time of Confederation. This raises a number of important issues for negotiation: do the Inuit and Cree have the same right to self-determination in Quebec, as Quebec has in Canada? Should they be represented directly in Quebec/rest-of-Canada negotiations? Who will assume the existing fiduciary trust obligation toward them? The answers to these questions, should they ever be addressed, may well determine the future self-governing status of Aboriginal peoples outside Quebec.

The structure of the relationship between Aboriginal peoples and the state is manifest in the machinery of government, especially at the federal level. Status Indians and Inuit relate to the federal government through the Department of Indian and Northern Affairs, a pre-Confederation, colonial and racist structural relationship built upon the *Indian Act,* and ill-suited to the 20th century. Non-status Indians and Métis peoples, despite the fact that they are defined as Aboriginal peoples in the Constitution, have no institutionalized relationship to the federal government. (Some provincial governments do have Indian, Métis or Aboriginal affairs agencies.)

This issue is one of some significance, and has not gone unnoticed. The Penner Report of 1983, for example, recommended that a Secretary of State for Aboriginal peoples be established in the federal government. The Report of the Canadian Human Rights Commission of November 1990 recommended an independent commission to resolve land claims, the abolition of the INAC and its replacement by a new federal-Aboriginal relations agency, and other measures which would prevent the federal government from straying from its trustee relationship to Aboriginal peoples. [45]

In our view, the federal government should give serious consideration to establishing an independent land claims negotiation commission which would report directly to Parliament. There appears to be a strong need for a process which will be perceived as more impartial. Policies on both comprehensive and specific claims should be reviewed, and efforts made to bring them into consonance with current legal thinking on Aboriginal rights. The expeditious settlement of both specific and comprehensive claims would do a great deal to improve Native conditions and federal-Aboriginal relations. Conflict of interest problems with INAC's funding program for Aboriginal court cases should be addressed as well. We endorse the establishment of an independently administered Aboriginal rights and title litigation fund, as recommended by the Canadian Bar Association. [43]

A willingness to recognize Aboriginal people as distinct, founding or fundamental peoples in Canada, the restoration of funding to Aboriginal political and communications organizations and a Royal Commission would round out this minimal list of measures required to restore some Aboriginal faith in the Canadian political system. If Aboriginal peoples do participate in a new constitutional reform process, the Royal Commission could be held after the shape of federal relations is known. The task of the Royal Commission would be to educate Canadians on Aboriginal issues, as well as to provide recommendations for action to resolve some of the many problems that will remain. [47] However, the federal response to the December 1990 proposals of the Canadian Human Rights Commission, which also called for an independent claims agency and a Royal Commission, was not encouraging.[48]

The federal government may soon have no choice in the matter. The imperative of constitutional renewal to define Quebec's place in Canada will inevitably demand a resolution of the self-government dispute with Native people. Elijah Harper's resistance to the Meech Lake Accord and the events at Oka, Quebec in the summer of 1990 were linked expressions of this necessity. Native people have considerable popular support, and they have become too angry and too strong to settle for less.

Notes

We would like to thank Michael Whittington, Susan Phillips, Frank Cassidy, Katherine Graham, Bob Groves and Bradford Morse for their helpful comments on an earlier version of this chapter. Daryl Reid provided helpful assistance on media reaction. We are also grateful to Frances Abele for editorial assistance and patience beyond the call of duty.

1   Andrew Cohen, *A Deal Undone: The Making and Breaking of the Meech Lake Accord* (Vancouver/Toronto: Douglas & McIntyre, 1990), p. 259.

2   For a fuller treatment of these constitutional negotiations see Roy Romanow, John Whyte and Howard Leeson, *Canada...Notwithstanding* (Toronto: Carswell/Methuen, 1984); Richard Sheppard and Michael Valpy, *The National Deal* (Toronto: Fleet Books, 1982), and Alain-G. Gagnon, chapter 3 in this volume.

3   *Reference re: The Amendment of the Constitution of Canada.*

4   Romanow, Whyte and Leeson, *Canada*, op. cit.,pp. 212-214.

5   Much of this descriptive history is abridged from David C. Hawkes, *Aboriginal Peoples and Constitutional Reform: What Have We Learned?* (Kingston: Institute of

Intergovernmental Relations, Queen's University, 1989), chapter 2.

6   Entitled *Indian Self-Government in Canada*, Ottawa, 1983.

7   Louis Bruyère, "Aboriginal Peoples and the Meech Lake Accord," in the *Canadian Human Rights Yearbook*, 1988, p. 51.

8   See Lorne Ingle, *Meech Lake Reconsidered* (Hull: Voyageur Publishing, 1989), especially chapters 10 and 13.

9   Five provincial governments held no public hearings whatsoever.

10 Assembly of First Nations, Native Council of Canada, Métis National Council, Inuit Committee on National Issues, "Joint Aboriginal Proposal for Self-Government," First Ministers' Conference on Aboriginal Constitutional Matters, Ottawa, March 27, 1987, CICS Document 800-23/030.

11 Much of this information comes from an interview with Bob Groves of the Native Council of Canada.

12 The Prairie Treaty Nations Alliance is an organization representing many First Nations in the prairie provinces, who view self-government as a treaty right, already protected by the Constitution.

13 Darcy Henton, "Why Canada's Native peoples want the Meech Accord changed," *Toronto Star*, June 20, 1990, p. A 23.

14 Henton, p. A23.

15 Peter Kulchyski, "Headwaters: A New History," *The Press Independent* [Yellowknife], November 9, 1990, p. 5.

16 Filmon accused Harper of abusing his position, and holding the rest of the country hostage until Native concerns about the Accord were dealt with. Roy K. Dahl, "Harper

rallies support in delaying Meech accord," *Native Press* [Yellowknife], June 22, 1990, p. 1.

17   Prime Minister Brian Mulroney, letter to Phil Fontaine, June 18, 1990, pp. 6-7.

18   Cohen, p. 265.

19   Thus, for example, of the 16 Canada Employment and Immigration Department programs listed, only one, the Native internship program, seems to have been specifically targeted for Native people. See *Improved Program Delivery: Indians and Natives*, A Study Team Report to the Task Force on Program Review, 1985 (the Nielsen Task Force).

20   Canada, Secretary of State, Correspondence Services, table: "Ministerial Correspondence on Budget Cuts," June 30, 1990.

21   J. Holman and R. Gougeon, "INAC's hike short of promised jump," *Native Press* [Yellowknife], March 9, 1990, p. 2.

22   We have used the figures from the *Estimates* as an indicator of planned government spending. This does not, however, include Supplementary Estimates, which in INAC's case, were sometimes considerable, at least before 1987. See Katherine Graham, "Indian Policy and the Tories: Cleaning Up After the Buffalo Jump," in *How Ottawa Spends, 1987-88*, p. 245. Similarly, the status Indian population growth rate has been shown because it is this group of Aboriginal peoples to whom most federal programs are directed.

23   Canada, *INAC Estimates, Part III, 1991-92*, pp. 1-5.

24   Canada, *INAC Estimates Part III 1990-91*, pp. 2-26 and 2-58.

25   Ibid., pp. 2-26.

26   Canada, *INAC Estimates Part III, 1991-92*, pp. 2-17.

27   Geoffrey Weller, "The Devolution of Health Care to Canada's North," in Gurston Dacks (ed.), *Devolution and Constitutional Development in the Canadian North* (Ottawa: Carleton University Press, 1990), p. 125.

28   See Canada, INAC "A forecast of expenditures associated with the policy of transfer" report, 1981.

29   Canada, 1985-86 INAC *Estimates Part III*, pp. 2-22.

30   See John P. Taylor and Gary Paget, "Federal/Provincial Responsibility and the Sechelt," in David C. Hawkes (ed.), *Aboriginal Peoples and Government Responsibility: Exploring Federal and Provincial Roles* (Ottawa: Carleton University Press, 1989).

31   Canada, *INAC Estimates Part III, 1991-92*, pp. 2-16.

32   Andre Picard, "Largest land claim settlement must be declared 'null and void,' Quebec Crees tell superior court," *Globe and Mail* [Toronto], April 4, 1990, p. A1.

33   Rudy Platiel, "Only 44 claims settled out of hundreds," *Globe and Mail* [Toronto], July 28, 1990, p. D2.

34   Deborah Wilson, "'Certain Native rights and interests' will be recognized, B.C. minister says," *Globe and Mail* [Toronto], July 26, 1990, p. A4.

35   Platiel, p. D2.

36   Barbara Frum, *The Journal*, CBC Television, December 21, 1990.

37   *Guerin v. The Queen*, [1984] 2 S.C.R. 335, (1984) 13 D.L.R. (4th) 321 (S.C.C.).

38   *Simon v. The Queen* [1986] 24 D.L.R. (4th) 390 (S.S.C.).

39   Justice Estey in Supreme Court decision on Bill 30, 1987, 40 D.L.R. (4th) 18 (S.C.C.), emphasis added.

40   *R. v. Sparrow* (1990), 46 B.C.L.R. (2nd) 1 (S.C.C.).

41   See for example Frank Cassidy and Norman Dale, *After Native Claims?* (Victoria: Institute for Research on Public Policy, 1988).

42   David C. Hawkes, *Aboriginal Peoples and Constitutional Reform: What Have We Learned?* (Kingston: Institute of Intergovernmental Relations, Queen's University, 1989), p. 50.

43   From remarks by Angus Reid to the "National Caucus on Aboriginal-Federal Relations" held in Ottawa on September 24-25, 1990.

44   See David C. Hawkes and Bradford W. Morse, "Alternative Methods for Aboriginal Participation in Processes of Constitutional Reform," in Ronald L. Watts (ed.), *Canada's Constitutional Options* (Toronto: University of Toronto Press, forthcoming 1991) for an elaboration of some of these approaches.

45   "A New Commitment," Statement of the Canadian Human Rights Commission on Federal Aboriginal Policy, Ottawa, November 21, 1990.

46   *Report of the Canadian Bar Association Committee on Aboriginal Rights in Canada: An Agenda for Action* (Ottawa: Canadian Bar Association, August 1988), Recommendation 7, p. 28.

47   Not all Aboriginal peoples have been so enamoured of a Royal Commission, noting that the Government could use it as an excuse to delay any action for several years.

48   Cooper Langford, "Abolish Indian Affairs, says commission," *The Press Independent* [Yellowknife], November 30, 1990, p. 1.

CHAPTER 3

EVERYTHING OLD IS NEW AGAIN: CANADA, QUEBEC AND CONSTITUTIONAL IMPASSE

Alain-G. Gagnon

Résumé: Ce chapitre analyse les forces politiques et historiques qui sous-tendent le cul-de-sac constitutionnel actuel. Au cours des trois dernières décennies, le Québec a acquis un statut particulier *de facto* mais non *de jure* que le reste du Canada a accepté puisque celui-ci répondait à certains besoins du Québec tout en maintenant une symétrie constitutionnelle. A la suite de l'enchâssement d'une charte des droits et des libertés, et au lendemain du fiasco du lac Meech, l'idée du Québec société distincte n'est plus acceptable au reste du Canada. Le Canada anglais (perçu *in toto*) n'est plus prêt à s'accommoder des besoins légitimes politiques du Québec et les arrangements politiques ad hoc ne répondent plus aux revendications du Québec. Tous ces facteurs, ainsi que le fait qu'un Québec indépendant pourra survivre économiquement, mettent en doute la survie du Canada en tant qu'entité politique.

Abstract: This chapter analyzes the political and historical forces that underlie the current constitutional impasse. During the last three decades, Quebec has developed *de facto* but not *de jure* special status which has been acceptable to the rest of Canada because it met some of Quebec's needs while maintaining constitutional symmetry. Following the entrenchment of a Charter of Rights and Freedoms and the Meech Lake debacle, the concept of distinct society for Quebec is no longer acceptable to the rest of Canada. English-speaking Canada (perceived *in toto*) is no longer willing to accommodate Quebec's legitimate needs and ad hoc political arrangements are not able to satisfy Quebec's demands. These factors, along with the knowledge that Quebec can survive economically on its own, cast doubt on the survival of Canada as a political entity.

Following the failure of the Meech Lake Accord, the government of Quebec no longer has a mandate to negotiate "integration" in the Canadian federation with honour and enthusiasm. The recent Commission on the Political and Constitutional Future of Quebec in Canada (the Bélanger-Campeau Commission) sought "a new definition of the relation between Quebec and Canada—and of Quebec's place within or at the side of Canada." This constitutes a unique moment in Canadian history. A province, through its governing party and with the full backing of the official opposition, decided to assess the appropriateness of its continued association with the rest of the country of which it was a founding member, renewing the 1981 unanimity that had condemned unilateral patriation of the BNA Act without Quebec consent.

During the last decade, Canada has experienced significant transformations, starting in 1981 with the patriation of the Constitution and the federal government's decision to append to it a Charter of Rights and Freedoms. Insertion of the Charter was a severe blow to parliamentary democracy and to executive federalism, as it gave added powers to the judiciary. The new sociological realities in Quebec and the rest of Canada constitute important changes that require attention: non-French and non-English communities are no longer insignificant minorities, and aspire to play an important role in modern-day Canada. The present constitutional debate is further complicated by the fact that in the 1988 federal elections, Quebec supported the Canada-US Free Trade Agreement more enthusiastically than the other provinces. This is said to have broken established solidarities between Quebec and the rest of Canada, and to have diminished the sympathies the Left in the rest of Canada[1] had for nationalist objectives in *la belle province*. In Quebec, the Free Trade Agreement was perceived as a desire to face new economic challenges and enter the global economy. In the course of the 1980s, the political dynamics of Quebec have changed fundamentally, with nationalist elements going through shades of popularity, undeniably growing support for sovereignty in the electorate and the formation at the federal level of a new political voice, the Bloc Québécois, in the spring of 1990.

This chapter will first discuss earlier negotiations between Quebec and the other constitutional partners, starting with the Quiet Revolution. Second, scenarios of things to come in a Quebec with or without Canada are assessed and weighed against economic and political objectives. Third, the potential for success of Quebec's pursuit of constitutional objectives is evaluated using domestic and external factors.

The Historic Legacy (1960-1990)

What have we learned from the last 30 years of our common existence? With the beginning of the Quiet Revolution, Quebec championed special arrangements in terms of programs, policies and constitutional modifications with the declared aim of increasing and, at a minimum, consolidating the province's power, resources and responsibilities. During this entire period, Quebec sought recognition of its special status, and ultimately at the end of the period under review, that that special status be entrenched through the Meech Lake Accord.

The Liberal Party's accession to power under Jean Lesage in June 1960 marked the beginning of the Quiet Revolution, and a sharp break with the previous Duplessis era. During the 1960s, there were more concerted efforts by Quebec and the other provinces to deal with the federal government as a bloc. At Lesage's invitation, the provincial premiers met annually in conferences intended to lessen the possibility for unilateral actions by the federal government in areas of provincial interest. Indeed, federal-provincial conferences took place more frequently, broadening the range of issues discussed and creating subcommittees and ministerial committees to deal with outstanding problems and administrative matters. Simultaneously, and respecting the Gérin-Lajoie doctrine of provincial autonomy,[2] Quebec began developing relationships with international organizations and other governments outside Canada. Quebec recognized that external affairs was a federal responsibility but asserted its right to act abroad in areas of provincial jurisdiction that brought about endless battles with Ottawa. Quebec was particularly successful between 1964 and 1966 in signing a series of agreements, covering youth, education and cultural affairs. Constitutional reforms were unavoidable as pressures mounted from Quebec and other parts of Canada for a "renewed federalism." The main stumbling block at the time was the lack of an amending formula in the British North America Act (1867).

During Lesage's tenure (1960-66), two proposals for constitutional reform regarding amending formulas were rejected, and there was a perceptible change in the Liberals' approach to the issue. In 1961, Lesage turned down the Davie Fulton (then Minister of Justice) amending formula because the federal government would not circumscribe the powers it had acquired in 1949, powers which allowed for unilateral amendment of the constitution in areas of exclusive federal jurisdiction. Moreover, Quebec would have had no voice in deciding reforms to national institutions such as the monarchy, the Senate and the Supreme Court. Similarly, in 1966, Lesage rejected the Fulton-Favreau formula, whereby constitutional amendments would have required the approval of the federal government and all other provincial governments for provisions respecting provincial

powers, use of the English and French languages, denomina-
tional rights in education, and representation in the House of
Commons. Other provisions respecting the monarchy, Senate
representation and the like could be amended by Ottawa with
the concurrence of two thirds of the provinces comprising more
than half the population.[3]

An amending formula based on unanimity was strongly
opposed in Quebec because it could threaten the possibility of
attaining agreements between Quebec and the federal government in such a culturally sensitive area as language policy, and
could discourage transfer of powers from the federal to the
provincial order. The central issue for Quebec was not the
amending formula, but rather the overhaul of the Constitution
and a new division of powers.[4] Faced with the prospect of a
provincial election, Lesage could not consent to proposals that
would run against strong provincialist and nationalist sentiments in the province. Lesage refused to consider patriation or
an amending formula unless this was combined with a clear
definition of Quebec's powers and responsibilities, and protection of the French language and Francophone culture. He thus
established the framework which would guide future Quebec
governments in discussion of constitutional reform.

Quebec's position on the Constitution underwent significant transformations. For instance, during the 1966 election, Lesage, afraid of being outflanked by Daniel Johnson,
adopted a more nationalist political platform by demanding a
special status for Quebec instead of advocating simple equality
among the provinces. Paul Gérin-Lajoie, then minister of education, remarked that:

> Up to the present, Quebec has asked nothing for itself
> which it would not be willing to recognize for the other
> provinces. But one may wonder whether this is the
> correct attitude to take...What objections would there
> be if Canada were to adopt a constitutional regime
> which would take into account the existence of the
> "two nations" or "societies" within one Canada?[5]

While Lesage was broadening the provincial position, he also
sought to influence the federal government. In the 1966 Quebec
budget, the government went so far as to suggest that the
province should participate directly in areas of exclusive federal
jurisdiction, by being associated in the development and execu-

tion of fiscal, monetary and trade policies. The federal government resisted such intervention.[6]

Although Quebec's relations with Ottawa on the matter of
the Constitution cannot be considered particularly collaborative, various other initiatives contributed to a more co-operative
federalism even as Quebec continued to press for greater
autonomy. The Lesage administration was resolute in pushing
for reform, ready to risk entangling relationships with Ottawa
if this could enhance Quebec's economic and political power and
status. In 1964 the Quebec government was granted control of
its own public pension plan. At that time, the federal government attempted unsuccessfully to convince other provinces to
follow Quebec's lead, so that the latter would not appear to have
gained special status. The establishment of the Quebec Pension
Plan gave the province greater fiscal autonomy, allowing for
new initiatives without continued federal involvement. The
Quebec Pension Plan constituted a major gain as it assisted
building the most important investment pool in the country,
the *Caisse de dépôt et placement*, the gem of Quebec financial
institutions.[7]

The push for constitutional reform and greater autonomy
that commenced under Lesage continued with the governments
of Daniel Johnson (1966-68) and Jean-Jacques Bertrand (1968-
70). Recognizing the success of the Liberals, the Union Nationale government continued to use an interventionist approach to
domestic policy and federal-provincial relations. Johnson's
theme for the 1966 election campaign—*Egalité ou
indépendance*—was in fact a stronger attempt to appeal to
nationalist forces than the Liberals were ready to make at that
time. Johnson went one step further than the previous government by making reference to the binational character of
Canada, and by putting forward a tentative proposal for special
status for Quebec.[8] Johnson, and subsequently Jean-Jacques
Bertrand, tended to concur with the *Report of the Royal Commission of Inquiry on Constitutional Problems* (the Tremblay
Commission) that the division of powers and revenues between
the provinces and the federal government should be based on
the Quebec interpretation of the *BNA Act.*[9] Under such a
proposal, the Union Nationale demanded limits on federal
government transfer payments to individuals through national
social programs, and complete federal withdrawal if these were
run on a shared-cost basis. The spending power of the federal
government was perceived as having a negative influence on

the maintenance of federalism since it did not respect a water-
tight division of powers between the two orders of government.
Johnson maintained, as does the Report of the Constitutional
Committee of the Quebec Liberal Party (Allaire Report) and
several briefs presented before the Bélanger-Campeau Commission 25 years later, that programs such as family allowance,
pensions, social assistance, health services, and labour force
training should be the sole responsibility of Quebec. Daniel
Johnson went on to stress that the uniqueness of Quebec war-
ranted bilateral arrangements between Quebec and Ottawa
that were not contingent upon the federal government's relations with other provinces. In short, this was an early call for
asymmetrical federalism as a means to respond to Quebec's
special needs, and was a major bone of contention during all of
Trudeau's reign in Ottawa, as the Prime Minister refused to
concede to Quebec what he was unwilling to give to the other
provinces.

Pursuing his demand for constitutional reform, and
benefiting from the momentum provided by the Royal Commission on Bilingualism and Biculturalism (the Laurendeau-Dun-
ton Commission), Johnson developed a binational solution to
Canada's constitutional problems. The way out of the already
looming constitutional crisis was based on a constitutional
interpretation that would define the country as a compact
between the French and English. Under Duplessis, the Union
Nationale had sought to protect the existing division of powers
from federal encroachment. The party, led by Johnson, asked
for additional powers to protect Francophones within, and to
some extent outside, Quebec. The modifications were seen to be
commensurate with Quebec's responsibilities as the primary
protector of the French-speaking community in Canada. The
government under Jean-Jacques Bertrand continued to argue
that the distinctiveness of Quebec deserved recognition in a new
Canadian constitution.

Quebec was not completely stonewalled during the second
half of the 1960s. For example, deals were made with Quebec
on tax revenues and an opting-out formula was implemented.
In addition, Quebec started to play an important role in *la
francophonie*, while an informal agreement with the federal
government allowed Quebec to expand the small immigration
bureau established during Lesage's mandate into a legitimate
government department.[10] This departure from standard practice opened the way for an asymmetrical federalism.[11] Under

the successive governments of Robert Bourassa (1970-76) and René Lévesque (1976-1985), Quebec and Ottawa reached more formal agreements broadening the province's responsibilities in these areas. Because the other provinces did not want to assume similar authority over international relations or immigration, Quebec thus gained the equivalent of special status in this policy field. Nonetheless, it should be stressed that neither Ottawa nor the other provinces have agreed to constitutional entrenchment of Quebec's rights in these domains, granting only the possibility of making reversible deals.

During the seventies, the Quebec government continued its search for greater autonomy by urging that it be given additional powers and the necessary revenues to exercise them with a view to preserving and promoting Quebec's distinct society and culture. It is in this context, that Robert Bourassa throughout his four mandates (1970-1976, and 1985-) has been pursuing the objectives of **profitable federalism** and **cultural sovereignty**. At first, Bourassa was not particularly concerned with the entrenchment of Quebec's national aspirations in the constitution, and looked instead for a revision of the federal system that would assign Quebec the requisite powers and resources needed for the "preservation and development of the bicultural character of the Canadian federation."[12]

At the Victoria Conference in 1971, it appeared that the constitutional debate would be successfully resolved, but at the last minute, when the time came to sign a formal document, Quebec declined. The reason given for this reversal was the imprecision of the text surrounding Article 94A, outlining responsibility for pensions and other social programs. For Quebec, 94A was a test of the extent to which its constitutional partners were willing to push for a significant new sharing of powers. Moreover, there was intense political pressure in Quebec regarding the proposed amending formula that would have given a veto to Quebec, Ontario, as well as one to the Western provinces collectively and one to the Eastern provinces. The package deal proposed by Ottawa failed to guarantee Quebec control of cultural and social policies. This resulted in a mobilization of nationalist forces in the province, and as opposition mounted in Quebec, forced Bourassa to decline the Victoria proposals.

Negotiations were reopened in 1975, with the federal government's suggestion that the issue of the division of powers be set aside in favour of simple patriation with an amending formula. This implied that any discussion of a new division of powers would be the subject of future multilateral and bilateral bargaining among Quebec, the other provinces and the federal government. Ottawa recognized that the protection and promotion of linguistic and cultural concerns were of primary interest to Quebec in modifying the federal structure of government. This was presented at the time as a recognition of Quebec's demand for "special status."[13] Quebec made public then that it accepted this approach providing that its linguistic and cultural concerns be entrenched in the Constitution.[14] It is evident that the federal government did not want to give ammunition to the Parti Québécois which was rapidly gaining popularity among the Quebec electorate.

In exchange for patriation, Bourassa asked that the following provisions be included in a new constitution: the right for Quebec to veto constitutional amendments; control of policies in the fields of education and culture in the province; the right to opt out of federal programs with compensation; a more important role in immigration, especially aspects dealing with selection and integration of immigrants into Quebec society; and limits on the federal government's declaratory and spending powers in areas of provincial jurisdiction.[15] Several of these ideas would continue in vogue in the Quebec Liberal Party, finding their way in Claude Ryan's 1980 Beige Paper, *A New Canadian Federation*, as Québécois were preparing to vote in a referendum reconsidering their future in Canada.

The 1975 federal initiative included a threat of unilateral patriation by Ottawa. Bourassa used this in the fall of 1976 to call an election. The PQ swept to power on November 15, 1976, with a program for sovereignty association. Under René Lévesque and, for a short time, Pierre-Marc Johnson, the PQ was committed to acquiring full political sovereignty for Quebec, with an economic association (later replaced by the notion of economic union) between Quebec and the rest of Canada. Following Lévesque's election in 1976, the federal government continued to press for patriation of the Constitution with an amending formula. In 1978, Ottawa introduced Bill C-60, *The Constitutional Amendment Bill*, containing terms very similar to the 1971 Victoria formula. The Quebec government showed no interest in this new initiative, as it was then elaborating its own political program, *Quebec-Canada: A New Deal* (1979). Another important federal initiative was the Task Force on

Canadian Unity, struck in 1977 to report in 1979. Known as the Pepin-Robarts Task Force, it recommended that Quebec be granted some form of special status, proposed a more decentralized federal system and introduced the notion of asymmetrical federalism as a "legitimate" political concept.[16] The main recommendations of the Task Force were largely ignored by Prime Minister Trudeau who pursued his own agenda.

In May 1979, Canada elected its first Conservative government since 1962. Prime Minister Joe Clark was better disposed than Trudeau toward a decentralized federalism, expressed in the conception of Canada as a "community of communities." At that time, Canada was in both a debilitating economic recession and a seemingly endless constitutional crisis. Despite the change in the federal position, the Quebec government remained committed to holding a referendum on sovereignty association. Then, unexpectedly, the cards were reshuffled. The Conservatives were forced to call an election, and the Trudeau Liberals returned to power in February 1980 with a renewed desire to crush the "separatists" and little interest in solutions to Quebec's claims. These claims were centred around the perennial notion that Quebec constitutes a distinct society in North America. Quebec, with its French-speaking majority, demanded sufficient powers to protect and preserve its character. This was felt to be especially important in policy sectors of communications, culture, immigration, international relations and language. During the 1980 referendum campaign, Trudeau challenged Quebec independentists, and sent his Quebec-based ministers to campaign for the "No" forces. Trudeau Liberals had promised that defeat of the referendum would not be interpreted as endorsement of the status quo, undertaking to elaborate policies that would respond to Quebec's special needs. Quebec's federal MPs, in an ultimate attempt to convince Québécois to vote against the PQ's proposal for independence, said they were putting their seats on the line. This was generally believed to mean that a genuine desire by the federalists to accommodate Quebec culturally and linguistically existed. When the Parti Québécois requested a mandate to negotiate sovereignty association, it was defeated (60 per cent "No", 40 per cent "Yes"). Contrary to promises made during the referendum, the federal government took this answer as an indication that Quebec wanted to remain in Confederation. The federalists proposed to continue constitutional discussions determined to be tougher than ever before since the so-called separatists were disorganized and demoralized. Trudeau challenged provincialism and decentralization as views of the past, and proposed a more centralist vision. The PQ was in disarray, the Quebec Liberal Party had fought a tough campaign against independence along with Ottawa, the Trudeau Liberals had a majority government, the state of the economy was abysmal, and a neo-liberal ideology was rampant.

Trudeau lost no time after the referendum and planned a constitutional conference for September 1980. Afraid of the possibility of a unilateral move by Ottawa if talks failed, Quebec was busy forging alliances with other provinces. The first ministers' conference failed due to a confrontation between two competing visions of Canada: centralization versus decentralization. The federal government kept the initiative by introducing on October 2, 1980 a "Proposed Resolution for Address to her Majesty the Queen Respecting the Constitution of Canada." Quebec and seven other provinces—the Gang of Eight—opposed the move, preparing reference cases in the Quebec, Manitoba and Newfoundland appeal courts that proved disappointing for the provincialist forces. Ultimately, the case reached the Supreme Court of Canada which ruled on September 21, 1981:

> That it would be legal for the Parliament to act without provincial consent, but that this would still be unconstitutional since it would breach an established convention of substantial provincial consent...The only way out was to return to the intergovernmental table. But now there was a critical difference: the convention, said the Court, did not mean unanimity; it required only "substantial consent." Two provinces was clearly not "substantial consent," but one province could no longer stop the process. The groundwork for a settlement without Quebec had been laid.[17]

Taking advantage of these circumstances, a constitutional conference was called by Trudeau for November 1981. With the support of the Quebec National Assembly and seven provincial premiers (Ontario and New Brunswick excepted), Premier Lévesque expressed opposition to the central government's plans to reform and patriate the Constitution unilaterally. Initially and strategically, Lévesque agreed to the principle of provincial equality. At the same time, he continued to oppose patriation in the absence of agreement on an amending formula and a new division of powers, demanded that Quebec be recognized as a culturally and linguistically distinct society, and asked for the responsibilities and resources which that implied. In return for Quebec's acceptance of the equality of provinces notion, the premiers confirmed the veto right of Quebec. It was believed by the Quebec delegation that this would have allowed the province to press for increased autonomy within a revised federal system, and would ultimately legitimize the Parti Québécois' pursuit of independence as defined under international law.[18]

Opposing any form of special status for Quebec, be it entrenched in the constitution or through international recognition, Trudeau shut Quebec out. On November 5, 1981, in the absence of Premier Lévesque, the other premiers agreed to patriation with a Charter of Rights and Freedoms. With agreement came their preferred amending formula,[19] and the right to opt out of the secondary provisions of the Charter, which were entrenched in the Constitution. The opting out (or "notwithstanding") clause ensured the Western premiers' support of the package deal. Quebec was isolated, with no other course of action but to make use of the notwithstanding clause, which it did systematically until the election of the Quebec Liberals in December 1985. The decision to patriate with an entrenched Charter of Rights and Freedoms proved to be a major assault on Quebec's vision of its own collective aspirations in an environment that was growing hostile to any protective measures. According to most Canadian federalists, time would heal everything. Ten years after patriation, the healing process is far from complete.

Before the election of Brian Mulroney's Conservative government in 1984, no new constitutional initatives to appease Quebec were undertaken by Ottawa. Following the election of a Conservative government, and the stated intention of Prime Minister Mulroney to reintegrate Quebec in the constitutional family with "honour and enthusiasm,"[20] Premier Lévesque spoke of *un beau risque*, and went on in May 1985 to present the new federal prime minister with a "Draft Agreement on the Constitution"[21] that embodied 22 claims made by Quebec since the beginning of the Quiet Revolution.[22] Differences between the Parti Québécois government, after the defeat of the referendum, and Robert Bourassa's Liberals following his re-election in 1985, were rather small. These were differences of degree, not of kind. It is to be noted here that between 1981 and 1985

Lévesque negotiated from a position of weakness, having lost the referendum. This changed when Bourassa, a *bona fide* federalist, became premier.

The Draft Agreement was used by the Quebec Liberals as a bottom line during subsequent negotiations.[23] Five conditions to be entrenched in the constitution included:

° the explicit recognition of Quebec as a distinct society;

° increased power to Quebec in immigration regarding recruitment, administration and integration;

° appointment of three Supreme Court Judges with expertise in Quebec civil law;

° containment of the federal spending power; and

° a full veto for Quebec in any new modifications to be considered to the Canadian constitution.

The Meech Lake proposals attempted to deal with most of these claims but failed, due at least in part, to a lack of openness to difference and a reform process (amending formula) that is insensitive to Quebec's distinct character.

For Ottawa, Meech Lake reflected a constant preoccupation with uniformity in Canadian federalism, except for the distinct society clause. By providing all the other provinces that which had been granted to Quebec, Ottawa intended to give what the other provinces demanded and remove any impression of giving Quebec a special status. In turn, the federal government obtained a major concession from Quebec, as it was willing to recognize for the first time the federal spending power in spheres of exclusive provincial jurisdictions. In the rest of Canada, there was a general understanding to the effect that the provinces had too much room to manoeuvre, as they were allowed to opt out of federal arrangements under certain conditions. In Quebec, the federal spending power was viewed as federal intrusion, but was still accepted by the Quebec government, to the great disenchantment of nationalists.

Several contingencies made it impossible for all premiers to agree on Meech Lake, despite these interlocking concessions.[24] Support for Meech was difficult to secure in Canada outside Quebec considering that several issues were said to be left unresolved. As the Meech Lake negotiations began (supposedly intended to bring Quebec back into the pan-Canadian family), other interests organized with the aim of defeating Quebec's vision of federalism. In the process, Quebec's claims became secondary to Natives, have-not provinces and universality of social programs. All of these reasons combined to deny Quebec recognition of its distinct character. It became an all-or-nothing issue: Meech Lake died. The events surrounding the failure of the Victoria Charter in 1971, when Quebec decided not to support proposed constitutional changes, and the failure to patriate the Canadian constitution with Quebec's consent in 1981, illustrates that difficulty with constitutional reform is a perennial feature of Canadian federalism. In part, this might well be because for most of the 1960s, 1970s and 1980s, Quebec pursued a strategy that consisted of being represented in Ottawa by one of the two major political parties. Through a strong presence within the federal governing party, Quebec was usually able to obtain some concessions at the administrative level, but failed to translate these to formal arrangements. The presence of the Bloc Québécois in Ottawa may well inject a new dimension to federal-provincial dynamics. Time and time again changes have been incremental and have failed to bring about a fundamental redefinition of the Canadian federation that could accommodate Quebec in the long haul.

In response to the failure of Meech Lake to confirm Quebec's distinct status, a democratization process that goes beyond anything we have experienced so far was launched, with the establishment of the Bélanger-Campeau commission that was formed by a broad coalition of interests.

Recycled Ideas and Scenarios

The push for autonomy by Quebec governments since the beginning of the Quiet Revolution has largely proceeded from two perspectives, the wish to remove the federal spending power in Quebec and the demand for increased autonomy for Quebec alone among the provinces. The greatest call for autonomy came from the Parti Québécois government which wanted to replace the federal system with sovereign, but economically associated states. If this cannot be achieved, the remaining option is full independence for Quebec. This scenario, once the most radical, is gaining popularity and currency in Quebec, and now constitutes a serious challenge to Canadian federalism.

Options being discussed are reminiscent of earlier debates, and tend to get more complicated and intermingled as the positions of various political actors are articulated. The deliberations of the current Keith Spicer Citizens' Forum, the Bélanger-Campeau Commission, and other commissions struck throughout the country to assess the crisis are attempting to influence the agenda surrounding the expected renegotiation of the Canadian federal union. The challenge for these commissions is major, if only due to the fact that English Canada has undergone substantial transformation during the last decades. Among the changes, one notes an increased significance given to entrenched rights and freedoms, a growing admission of a Native and multicultural heritage, a mounting recognition of the equality of provinces principle, ascending regionalism, and a growing disenchantment with executive federalism. In addition to these factors, there has been the impact of an increasing pull of the continental economy and its dangers for Canada's survival.

In response to the election of the Parti Québécois in 1976, several constitutional proposals were developed. We find ourselves again at a crossroads, and with few new alternative scenarios being proposed. Yet the seriousness of the crisis cannot be hidden and choices need to be made urgently. Possible scenarios include the status quo or renewed federalism of the Trudeau Liberals, the restructured federalism of the Pepin-Robarts Task Force, the sovereignty association of the Parti Québécois, the somewhat decentralized federalism of Claude Ryan's Liberals, and the ambiguous superstructure of Robert Bourassa.[25] A brief summary of these options is essential to clarify what is at stake, and what are Quebec's options.

The **renewed federalism** of the Trudeau Liberals, proposed under Bill C-60 in 1978, called for intrastate modifications that would strengthen provincial representation at the federal level, and be accompanied by a Charter of Rights and Freedoms (it was conceived as an "opt-in" arrangement for the provinces) and a constitutional amending formula. So far, both the amending formula and the Charter have been entrenched but with no fundamental changes in the division of powers or of provincial representation at the federal level. According to Bill C-60, these transformations would have involved replacing the

Senate with a House of the Federation, with half its proposed 118 members selected by provincial assemblies and the other half selected by the House of Commons. This would have been accompanied by entrenched representation of Quebec in the Supreme Court. In addition, the ability of the House of the Federation to veto changes to language legislation could be reduced to a 60 day suspensive veto, but could be overturned with the support of two thirds of the House of Commons.[26] In a reference decision, the Supreme Court of Canada ruled in 1979 that the Parliament of Canada was not empowered to modify itself in a manner that may affect the provinces. It was argued by the Court that despite the power of amendment in section 91(1), the House of the Federation, in substituting for the Senate, was affecting an institution that was of interest to the provinces. According to Verney, the Supreme Court based its decision on a 1965 federal White Paper that recognized a "provincial role in amendments to the BNA Act beyond those matters exclusively assigned to the provinces."[27]

It should be noted here that Jean Chrétien's intervention on December 17, 1990 before the Bélanger-Campeau Commission is reminiscent of the Trudeau years. Chrétien limited himself to raising the idea of a new sharing of powers between Ottawa and the provinces. Stressing that Quebec should not achieve a special status within the Canadian federation, he referred instead to special administrative arrangements that would leave the division of powers intact but allow Quebec to feel more at ease, therefore confirming his support for status quo federalism. In his brief, Chrétien argued for the need to protect against any challenge to the Charter of Rights and Freedoms special needs of the various communities. The renewed federalism options constituted an admission that if Canada was to respond to the Quebec challenge, a better representation within the federal order of government was required.

Unfortunately for the proponents of renewed federalism, this option was completely discredited in Quebec during the tenure of the Trudeau Liberals in Ottawa, as they failed to deliver on earlier promises. Many supporters of this option during the referendum campaign were made to believe that renewed federalism meant an official recognition of Quebec as a distinct society/people, and that new powers commensurate with this admission would be given to Quebec. One will remember that federalists of different persuasions had rallied around Pierre Elliott Trudeau to defeat Quebec's claim for a new agreement between Quebec and Ottawa. Instead of being granted special recognition, Quebec was weakened by the federal order. The federal government took the initiative by patriating the Constitution with a Charter of Rights and Freedoms against Quebec's will. This move was repudiated both by Quebec nationalists and federalists active at the provincial level, including federalists that in May 1980 were on Trudeau's side. These federalists felt betrayed. Trudeau's victory turned sour as opinion leaders who once fought for the federalist cause (such as Claude Ryan, Robert Bourassa and the business community at large), called for corrective measures to be implemented rapidly to keep Canada together. Two conceptions of Canada and two visions of liberalism were confronting one another. In the terms of Charles Taylor:

> Two conceptions of a liberal society meet head on. For one, this society is defined by individual rights and non-discrimination. Embracing as a common objective the furtherance of a particular culture or a way of life is seen as anti-liberal, (i) because it might justify over-riding rights (this is how some people see laws 101 and 178 in Quebec), and (ii) because, since some people belong to and some people don't to the culture in question, espousing such goals discriminates between citizens. For the other conception of liberalism, a liberal society always has some common goals, and interprets rights in their context. What makes a society liberal is its uncompromising stance on really fundamental rights (which on this reading are not at all at stake in laws 101 and 178), and its general openness and generosity in face of difference...Quebec can't live in a society which is defined rigidly by the first conception.[28]

Prime Minister Mulroney recently toyed with the notion of renewed federalism.[29] During the Bélanger-Campeau Commission hearings, this option has been equated with a looser federal association between Quebec and the rest of Canada. In any event, the chances of success of this option (and its many variants) appear remote, due to the fact that it proposes something which is much looser than anything that was proposed under Meech Lake.[30] Based on most reports and viewpoints heard from the rest of Canada so far, and even if this more recent version of renewed federalism were to make significant progress in Quebec, support for it seems faint at best. Available opinion polls suggest that status quo is the only viable option that *Canadiens hors Québec* are willing to consider.

Another expression of renewed federalism was the plan recommended by the 1979 Pepin-Robarts Task Force on Canadian Unity. It was based on three elements: the existence of different regions, the predominance of two cultures, and equality of two orders of government. The main thrust of the proposed changes was the institutionalization of **asymmetrical federalism** indicating that all provinces are not equal and the same. While avoiding a *de jure* special status for Quebec, Quebec's special relationship to the rest of Canada was said to be *de facto*, recognized in the arrangements that had been offered to all provinces but in which Quebec had been the only participant. The Quebec Pension Plan is the most potent example. This recognition of special status and asymmetry was extended to language, where it was admitted that each province had the right to determine provincial language policy.[31] Major institutional innovations included proposals for transforming the Senate, a partial introduction of proportional representation, an expanded Supreme Court, and changes to certain federal powers such as the abolition of the federal powers of reservation and disallowance. Concurrency was proposed for federal declaratory, spending and emergency powers. The Task Force also proposed replacement of the Senate by an 80-member Council of the Federation entirely composed of delegates nominated by the provinces. Moreover, seats based on proportional representation would be added to the House of Commons to redress the imbalances of the political parties. Expanding and dividing the Supreme Court into specialized "benches" (designed to address various deficiencies in the ability of the courts to rule in various jurisdictions) was also among the proposals. In an attempt to reconcile Western alienation and Quebec nationalism, this option attempted to address the issues of provincial autonomy, provincial control over language policy, an upper house response to provincial interests and recognition of Quebec's special status.

Short of a new Quebec-Canada union, asymmetrical federalism is probably the option that could gather most support in Quebec at the present time,[32] but this scenario appears to be totally unacceptable to Canadians outside Quebec. Both Mulroney and Chrétien insist that whatever Quebec gets, all other provinces should be able to obtain. The problem with Meech Lake, argued Mr. Mulroney, was that "it was perceived as an arrangement only for Quebec."[33] The debates surrounding the Meech Lake debacle[34] made clear that there was significant opposition to granting Quebec a special status in the Canadian federation. This idea has received support in only a few English Canadian intellectual circles.[35] Among the principal difficulties raised by asymmetrical federalism is the question of Quebec MPs, who would pronounce themselves on issues that concern residents outside of Quebec. Also, there is the impression that asymmetrical federalism undermines the principle of equality of provinces which appears to have gained genuine support among all significant constitutional participants with the exception of Quebec. In light of recent constitutional negotiations, an emerging minoritarianism tradition that is concerned with Aboriginals, multicultural communities, women's rights and other interests, displacing the notion of founding people as a fundamental pillar of Canadian society, and questioning parliamentary democracy has developed. The immediate consequence of this has been to undermine the leadership granted to elected representatives, and stress the new status accorded to groups via the Charter of Rights and Freedoms.[36]

The third option is the **sovereignty association** proposal of the Parti Québécois which, under this label, was somewhat discredited by the results of the 1980 referendum. In an attempt to rejuvenate this option, the PQ is calling for sovereignty with or without association so that Canada's refusal to enter negotiation with Quebec is no longer portrayed as *sine qua non* for Quebec independence. This option argues for the formation of "Two Communities" where nine provinces would reconstitute Canada and the tenth, that is Quebec, would exist as a separate state but part of the new Canadian economic union. The proposal includes a common market, with mobility of goods, services, capital and people in a monetary union. At a joint meeting of the Empire Club of Canada and the Canadian Club in Toronto, December 11, 1990, Jacques Parizeau confirmed that such a union between Quebec and the rest of Canada would entail "a free flow of goods and people, continuation of a customs union, maintenance of a common currency and common monetary policy and allocation of the federal government's debt." Parizeau stipulated that Quebec will be "responsible for its share of the public debt and entitled to the same share of [federal] assets."[37] The PQ has tried to revamp the old concept of sovereignty association, referring to the need to acquire full sovereignty before entering into association with economic partner(s) (as is the case in the European Community). Indeed, the Parti Québécois brief to the Bélanger-Campeau Commission argues that:

> The European Community truly serves as an example by the creation of the richest and most populous common market in the world, which permits the cohabitation of very different sovereign nations.[38]

The sovereignty association option is similar to what Daniel Latouche describes as a "supranational scenario." To quote Latouche, "Supranationalism is more radical than confederation, as it calls for the existence of two distinct countries, each with a separate international identity and enjoying full sovereignty on its respective territory."[39] From a Quebec point of view, the sovereignty association option has the advantage of dealing directly with the enduring issue of duality, whereas in the rest of the country it is perceived as ignoring a rapidly emerging minoritarian tradition and the equality of provinces principle especially claimed by provinces outside central Canada.

The fourth option, first developed by the Quebec Liberal Party under the influence of Claude Ryan, is a more **decentralized federalism.** Under these arrangements, more powers would be allocated to the provinces, two sovereign jurisdictions recognized and more direct provincial influence on federal activities accomplished through a provincially appointed intergovernmental body, called the Federal Council. Inspired by the German Bundesrat, this was an effort to meet Quebec's legitimate aspirations in the context of a Canadian federalism where the equality between the "two founding peoples" would be affirmed, and popular approval of change would take place in the context of an explicit agreement between the two historic communities comprising Canada.[40] Proposed changes involved the replacement of the Senate by a provincially appointed structure capable of curbing federal powers, proportional representation in the House of Commons and the abolition of the Monarchy. The proposed Federal Council would link the provinces, have its own source of funding and be free from federal manipulation and intrusion. Its roles would include the approval of federal appointments, ratification of treaties affecting provinces, a veto on federal emergency and spending powers, and an advisory role in matters of fiscal, monetary and transportation policy. In legislation regarding language and culture it would operate on a double majority principle. The Federal

Council would also be responsible for federal-provincial relations, thereby making federal-provincial conferences obsolete. A Canadian Charter of Rights and Freedoms was also proposed.

The chances for success of this option are limited since it is difficult to imagine provinces like Manitoba, New Brunswick, Newfoundland and Prince Edward Island accepting the decentralized option as a solution to the present crisis. There is a growing concern in the rest of Canada that decentralization endangers universality of social programs, especially in poorer provinces, which tend to oppose any challenges to maintaining national standards, or any diminution of the federal government's powers. In short, for these provinces, weakening the role of the federal government is not an option, as it could have a negative impact on their development. The decentralization option is gaining popularity among big business interests, and appears to be palatable to the federal government which is caught with a major financial burden. Nurtured by a neo-conservative political agenda, decentralization is definitely in the cards for the federal negotiators. Decentralization would also gain some support from Quebec's business community which finds the size of the current federal deficit, and its staggering debt, unacceptable.

The fifth scenario is Robert Bourassa's **superstructure**, building on his confusing idea of "two sovereign states associated in an economic union which would be responsible to a parliament elected by universal suffrage."[41] For some time, Robert Bourassa has been suggesting replacement of the Senate "with a permanent intergovernmental forum that has real powers in areas where the government operates concurrently." He also proposed institutionalizing federal-provincial conferences as means to achieve this objective.[42] At the outset, it should be pointed out that the possibility of having a commonly elected parliament is unacceptable to the supporters of sovereignty association, unless powers granted to that (joint) parliament are first delegated by an already sovereign Quebec.[43] In addition to creating a three-tier system of government, Bourassa's superstructure arguably would further complicate the division of powers by making governing less efficient, and by further challenging the principle of responsible government.

The Allaire report, entitled, *A Quebec Free to Choose*,[44] released January 28, 1991, proposed to diminish the federal government's scope and to transfer significant powers to the provinces. The federal government would be left with jurisdiction over defence, equalization payments, monetary policy and customs and debt management. Exclusive jurisdiction for the provinces is proposed in the fields of labour, natural resources, communications, health, agriculture, unemployment insurance, regional development, energy, environment, industry and commerce, language, research and development, public security and income security. Shared jurisdictions are demanded for Native affairs, taxation and revenue, immigration, financial institutions, fisheries, justice, foreign policy, post office, telecommunications and transport.

Bourassa's ambiguous concept of superstructure is presented in the Allaire report under the label of "a new structure." Inspired by the European community model, this new structure would allow for Quebec's special status to be recognized as well as accommodating the other provinces that wish to assume additional responsibilities. If they do not want such powers, the possibility to delegate them to Ottawa is open. Predictably, Quebec is demanding jurisdiction in all 22 domains identified as of provincial interest. Giving Quebec what it demands here would allow for asymmetrical federalism to take a significant hold in Canada. The Allaire report also proposes changing the amending formula, adding among other things, a Quebec veto. In addition, the report recommends the abolition of the Senate, the establishment of a community tribunal to oversee compliance with a new constitution to be drafted, and a regionally sensitive central bank. Finally, an argument is made for a Quebec Charter of Rights and Freedoms to be entrenched in a new Quebec constitution. This Charter would prevail, it is assumed, over the Canadian Charter in Quebec.

These options have become increasingly complicated of late as everyone is trying to discover the original idea that will resolve the present constitutional crisis. But as Jeffrey Simpson has put it, when assessing the Bélanger-Campeau Commission, the task is difficult, and the Commission is becoming "a forum for recycled ideas."[45] Nevertheless, Quebec requires the means for the maintenance of difference in order to feel comfortable in Canada.

The various mechanisms proposed in the five options outlined above, with the exception of sovereignty association, provide some promising avenues for representing provincial interests within federal institutions. Sovereignty association is, for a variety of reasons, difficult for the rest of Canada to accept. It is the aysmmetrical and restructured federalism options that could most strengthen provincial powers and allow for better control over their territories. Given the centrality of Quebec in the current crisis and its inadmissible eleventh hour exclusion from the previous round of negotiations in November 1981, any option that fails to establish both a credible augmentation in provincial powers, with the possible insertion of intrastate mechanisms for influencing federal policy, would fail to attract support.

Living Together: Domestic and External Factors

Since the failure of Meech Lake, the positions of political actors and of Canadians in general have hardened. Nothing points to an easy resolution of the current, and possibly fatal, constitutional crisis. It is difficult to see how Quebec's aspirations can be formally recognized, and very tough to imagine how the injustice of 1981 could ever be corrected. As Richard Simeon perceptively pointed out in his interpretation of the Meech Lake failure:

> Conspicuously missing...was a response to the Quebec agenda, which had always stressed the need for greater provincial autonomy. Indeed it could be argued that after 1982, Quebec had less rather than more authority: it had gained no new powers, had lost the veto over future constitutional change which most political actors assumed it always had and was now to be subject to a Charter which, in the public mind at least, was intrinsically hostile to collective rights and which opened the possibility of broad legal challenges to Quebec's attempts to shape its linguistic makeup through its language laws. Most telling, the *Act* had been passed over the objections not only of the Parti Québécois government, but also of Quebec federalists. The Supreme Court subsequently rejected Quebec's claim that the constitutional convention of "substantial provincial consent" should be read to include Quebec.[46]

To assess the viability of the preceding options, it is essential to consider domestic and external factors, including the Charter of Rights and Freedoms, economic and fiscal considerations and, not to be discounted, the capacity for constitutional engineering on the part of key political actors.

The Charter of Rights and Freedoms

To most students of Canadian federalism, the last 30 years demonstrate that Quebec has been able to exercise some autonomy as long as special arrangements were made on an ad hoc basis and, more importantly for the other provinces, that these were not constitutionally entrenched. Indeed, as the first part of this chapter shows, several initiatives were taken by the government of Quebec without fundamentally challenging the existence of the Canadian federal system. What changed the political dynamics, I believe, is the insertion in 1982 of a non-federal document into the Constitution Act of 1982, namely the Canadian Charter of Rights and Freedoms, and, to a lesser extent, the emerging view, as James Mallory recently put it,

> ...that a province is a province is a province. Whatever their strength, size or lack of same, provinces are the basic units of the system.[47]

This interpretation is substantiated by Charles Taylor who identified at least two irreducible collision courses endangering the country's survival. He refers to:

(1)   the conflict between the Charter of Rights and the recognition of Quebec as a distinct society, which raises the question of the procedural approach, implying that the Charter might well be differently interpreted in specific cases, and

(2)   the irreconcilable issue of equality between provinces in contrast to the special status demanded by Quebec.[48]

These two elements (the existence of a Charter of Rights and Freedoms that provides a definition of rights that are non-territorially based, conflicts with the "distinct society" view, and the equality of provinces principle clashes with Quebec's continued claim for special status) make it impossible to solve the present constitutional crisis within the present constitutional framework, and point in the direction of the sovereignty association option, or a variant, as the only realistic course of action for the Québécois. Following the failure of the Meech Lake Accord, such a prospect is not totally out of the question, as it would have the advantage of bringing the federation together again in a newly formed alliance between Quebec and the rest of Canada (or perhaps its successor-states formed by the regions of Ontario, the West, the Atlantic and eventually the North). Asymmetry or special status for Quebec during the Meech Lake debate proved to be a highly objectionable option to the rest of Canada. The Charter of Rights and Freedoms, perceived by most Canadians residing outside of Quebec as providing equal treatment without regard to territorial specificity, makes it difficult for French-speaking Québécois to accept its application. The decentralized model proposed by Claude Ryan offers some worthwhile elements of solution, but does not satisfy all of the other provinces, as it proposes both to empower provinces with additional responsibilities and to recognize the distinct character of Quebec. The have-not provinces object that this decentralization would leave the central government feeble and with little room to manoeuvre in its fight against inequality among regions and people.

The superstructure or new structure of Robert Bourassa constitutes a compromise (again) that risks disappointing everyone. On the one hand, Quebec nationalists would find highly objectionable any initiatives that create a new supreme body above the National Assembly. It is unlikely also that the rest of Canada would accept undermining the Charter of Rights and Freedoms by surrendering authority to this new body. For the rest of Canada, it appears that the only acceptable option is the status quo. One should not discount too rapidly the status quo outcome, if it means that Quebec would be granted special disposition at the administrative level as it has been able to achieve since the beginning of the Quiet Revolution.[49] However, the status quo scenario has been repeatedly denounced by all spokespersons at the Bélanger-Campeau Commission, including the Liberal Party of Canada, the Montreal Board of Trade, the Conseil du Patronat, and even the federalist Alliance Québec.

The tension between group and individual rights in an increasingly rights fixated society indicates that this will constitute a major stumbling block in any new federal arrangement.[50] In Canada, a "Charter culture" has developed and is having a significant impact on how Canadians in the rest of Canada view intergroup relations and the role of the state in citizens' affairs. The issue of rights is wrapped in the discourse of individual protection, and despite being applicable to groups, the Charter might well work against collective interests of those who predominate in a given region or province. In other words, the Charter of Rights and Freedoms has the potential to effectively undermine territorial diversity, especially in Quebec. However, a **re-negotiated federalism**, if it is still possible, must take into account the legitimating power of the "Charter" culture, but be willing to build institutions that are still capable of ensuring a greater degree of territorial autonomy than what is possible at the present time. The debate over the "distinct society" clause in the Meech Lake Accord and Quebec sign legislation (Bill 178) demonstrates the potential cleavage that such an issue is capable of generating. To avoid being trapped in a debate of individual versus collective rights,[51] one will have to take into account concurrently the question of territoriality so fundamental to Quebec's existence, and consider the collective goals pursued by both Quebec and the rest of Canada with a view to reaching a political compromise.

Economic Considerations

Economic considerations (for example, fiscal arrangements) will be an integral part of future negotiations about division of powers. All federalist options stress this element while the sovereignty association option presumes either the unwillingness or inability of the federal government to negotiate a suitable arrangement for Quebec within a federal context, raising instead the issue of deficit and assets sharing. Recognition of the advantages of economic association requires a level of negotiations unprecedented in contemporary Canadian history. If the experience of the European Community (EC) is any indication, substantial progress similar to the inter provincial arrangements already existing in Canada would be difficult. Each of the countries forming the EC still aggressively guards control over fiscal policies. Moreover, modelling a new Quebec-Canada relationship on the EC risks introducing a new array of interstate problems. If Quebec and the rest of Canada are to elaborate a new political arrangement, we should not copy the EC model. EC institutions are considered "creaky and undemocratic." Individual commissioners form the executive and are appointed by member states. The composition of the Council of Ministers varies according to the issue, with its discussions remaining *in camera.* Only the Parliament is directly elected, but it still serves primarily as a consultative body despite attempts to give it more clout.[52] In any event, if it comes to that in a new Quebec-Canada relationship, negotiations should not be restricted to a singular association with Canada, but should explore special bilateral arrangements at the economic level with other provinces such as Alberta or Ontario.[53] This economic strategy may develop within the federal context more easily than pursuing such arrangements after Quebec has unilaterally declared itself independent, particularly if separation is acrimonious. It is probably in this context that one should interpret Quebec's decision to ratify an interprovincial trade agreement that was signed immediately following the failure of Meech Lake.[54] The message was to stress Quebec's desire to consolidate the common Canadian market whatever the result of future negotiations.

Whatever the recommendations elaborated respectively by federalist and sovereignist forces, these will have to take into account the existence of a staggering federal debt. The accumulated deficit is such that collaboration between Quebec and the rest of Canada is compulsory if the two protagonists are to be taken seriously by international creditors. The federal government is burdened by an enormous deficit that deters it from any significant initiatives to respond to Quebec's challenge. This predicament must be taken seriously since the federal government has less financial leeway than it had in 1980 when it fought against Quebec's separation. In the end, economic considerations may well force Quebec and the rest of Canada to listen seriously to each other. Economic considerations are likely to play a significant role in the current crisis. But, as the economist Pierre Fortin remarked:

> In previous rounds of constitutional debate in Quebec, the drive for a greater measure of autonomy was constantly restrained by the general apprehension that any such occurrence would reduce the province's average standard of living. The main arguments were, first, that Quebec's economy was internally weak and highly dependent on external ownership, finance, manpower and technology; second, that any unilateral move by the province to appropriate greater constitutional powers would meet with swift trade retaliation from outside; and, third, that Quebec drew substantial net economic benefits from its participation in the federation. Today, all three arguments stand on their heads ....[55]

To substantiate his position, Fortin stresses that Quebec gradually narrowed the productivity gap with its traditional competitor, Ontario; that the province has introduced major financial innovations, starting with deregulation in the financial sector, encouraged collaboration between the private and public/parapublic sectors, and developed a more competitive tax system; that the business community involvement in the constitutional discussions has given credibility to Quebec's potential for independence; that trade retaliation in an international economy entering globalization would not be advisable, and would probably be challenged under the General Agreement on Tariffs and Trade (GATT), or the Free Trade Agreement with the United States; and, finally, that the federal deficit is so high that the Government's capability to resolve the crisis is seriously undermined.[56]

The business community in Quebec involved itself on the pro-Meech Lake side, providing an unexpected ally to forces asking for a new package deal with the rest of Canada. During the Bélanger-Campeau Commission hearings, the business community (through the Desjardins Movement, the Chamber of Commerce of the Province of Quebec and the Montreal Chamber of Commerce and, to a lesser extent, the Montreal Board of Trade) have asked for decentralization of several powers to the province. The business community seeks political stability to achieve bigger profits. If this means decentralization, so be it. Indeed, the status quo (meaning current federalism) is viewed as unacceptable by most economic actors.[57] In sharp contrast with the 1980 Quebec referendum, the current impasse will not be debated, or resolved around the economic issues. The federal government is viewed as moribund by most economic and political actors, and the place of Quebec in the new international economy is perceived as respectable. As Pierre Fortin argued:

> With increased globalization, economic boundaries transcend political boundaries as countries have to comply with international treaties. The correlation between income per capita and population size among industrial countries is almost exactly zero. The size of the Quebec economy is actually equal to or greater than that of Austria, Belgium, Denmark, Finland, New Zealand, Norway, and Switzerland, and not much smaller than that of Sweden.[58]

Constitutional Engineering and Politics

Politics being what it is, one should not completely exclude the possibility of a *rapprochement* between Quebec and the rest of Canada. On both sides, there will be attempts at developing face-saving measures to renew discussions between the main protagonists. Viewing the status quo and the normalization options (Meech Lake served with a different sauce) as an "unlikely scenario," Latouche recognizes the extent to which "inertia and the desire for *déja vu* solutions are strong forces in politics."[59] Pierre Fournier gave some additional weight to this possibility when he commented that the Bélanger-Campeau Commission may constitute nothing more than a trap for the sovereignists.[60]

For some time, Quebec nationalists have gone unchallenged, but it appears that federalist forces are regrouping for the final assault. To be credible, federalists will integrate in their counter-attacks two crucial aspects that arose time and again in the briefs presented to the Bélanger-Campeau Commission: the need for Quebec to operate within a more flexible system, and the economics-based definition of the new Quebec-Canada relationship, reminiscent of Bourassa's profitable federalism of the early 1970s. This, however, may be sneered at in the rest of Canada as being another play for more federal money by Quebec, and would probably bring about additional pressure on the federal government not to cave in to Quebec's demands. It is believed that concessions to Quebec would be acceptable to the rest of Canada only if these are perceived as bona fide cultural demands with little financial implication.

A series of interventions by Prime Minister Brian Mulroney and challenger Jean Chrétien call for a new division of powers between the federal and the provincial orders, with the combined objective of putting an end to overlapping jurisdictions and revising power-sharing arrangements with a view to transferring powers to the provinces as long as guarantees of national standards and universality are provided.[61] These propositions are reminiscent of promises made during the 1980 referendum debate in Quebec, and have accordingly been received with suspicion by sovereignists.[62]

Under the concept of **flexible federalism**, the federalist forces are elaborating a normalization scenario, as suggested by a series of recent initiatives put forward both on the Quebec and federal fronts with the possibility of identifying additional concurrent powers with potential provincial paramountcy.[63] For example, the deal reached between Quebec and Ottawa on the immigration issue indicates a political will to remove irritants between Quebec and Ottawa. It should resolve the issue of control of settlement and adaptation programs, and improve the likelihood immigrants will be better integrated into a French milieu.[64]

Following the immigration deal, Quebec has intensified pressures on the federal government to vacate fields of shared federal-provincial jurisdictions, and turn over responsibilities and powers related to, among others, the Canada Health Act, post-secondary education, unemployment insurance, and labour force training. Quebec's strategy appears to be operating at two levels: on the one hand, fundamental changes are proposed via the Allaire report and the Bélanger-Campeau Commission while, on the other hand, Ottawa and Quebec are trying to come up with deals that would demonstrate to Québécois the extent to which there is flexibility in the system.

One can speculate that a face-saving scenario is being written. Quebec will give the impression of making gains (gains that will also be made available to the other provinces so as not to challenge symmetry!), and the federal government will dump some of its responsibilities on the provincial order of government, due in part to lack of financial capacity. These changes will go some distance towards fulfilling Rémillard's demands that the federal government respect Quebec's jurisdiction under the Constitution Act (1867), implying that Ottawa should stop using its spending power to intrude in spheres of provincial responsibility.[65] Considering the financial strain under which the federal government is operating, it would not be surprising to hear the federal government agreeing to gradual withdrawal from social policies.[66] There are indications to the effect that the federal government had planned to continue gradually decreasing its contribution to health care systems to point zero in the second half of the 1990s.[67] The federal government could therefore vacate this policy sector as it pursues its fight toward deficit reduction, giving the impression that it is willing to initiate a major constitutional restructuring. This will not easily be done since Canadians have come to see programs, such as medicare as defining characteristics of what it is to be a "Canadian." The issues of national standards and universality will resurface again. However, arguing for the removal of provincial trade barriers as a first step to undertake reforms, Prime Minister Mulroney and Liberal leader Chrétien are already busy preparing the ground. In the meantime, Quebec has been careful to confirm its intention to sign a reciprocity deal, suggesting the elimination of trade barriers between provinces.[68]

In light of the continued disengagement of the state and its privatization agenda, the scenario is becoming clearer every day as Quebec displays its political strength to obtain control over jurisdictions that, to a large extent, the federal government will be well advised to vacate in favour of the provinces to diminish its deficit. These responsibilities are definitely less essential to Ottawa at a time when it attempts to modify its role in a globalizing international economy, and to decrease its financial commitments. One can also imagine a situation in which revenues raised with the Goods and Services Tax (GST) might allow the federal government to improve significantly its fiscal position by the time the next constitutional round comes up, in which case Ottawa could decide to assist provinces that will be asking for additional tax points to cope with their own financial burden.

CONCLUSION

The record indicates that since 1960 Quebec has been most successful in bilateral negotiations. Once concessions were obtained, these were then offered to all other provinces so that no asymmetrical federalism would ever develop in Canada. The convention against asymmetry has proven to be "problematic" during the Meech Lake discussions. Symmetrical federalism was often perceived by Meech opponents as the only valid doctrine from which to conduct federal-provincial negotiations in Canada. Whatever the end result of the current constitutional crisis, it surely cannot be resolved without an explicit recognition of Quebec's distinct presence and role in the Canadian federation. Given the new rules of the constitutional game in Canada (imposed by the Constitutional Act of 1981), special status cannot be achieved in the present context. However, bilateral deals through section 43 of the Constitution Act of 1981,[69] are possible. Backlash from other players is anticipated, though, making asymmetrical federalism untenable and demonstrating once again the extent to which the Constitution has become a strait-jacket for Quebec. Nevertheless, the only alternative left to Quebec and the rest of Canada is to work within the existing constitution.

The failure of Meech demonstrates the urgency of crafting political institutions that are sensitive to both individual rights and collective goals, at least if the intent is to propose enduring solutions. If Canada is to survive as a plural society, there is an immediate need to stop approaching federalism in reductivist ways. Instead of symmetry, consideration of a more generous kind of federalism is necessary, based on a vision that accepts asymmetry, as the Pepin-Robarts Task Force had already proposed in 1979. An acceptable solution for Quebec requires significant changes, allowing at a minimum for the recognition of asymmetrical federalism. With the Charter culture gradually taking hold in the rest of Canada, however, asymmetrical federalism will not be easily achieved.

The future of Canada depends on a variety of factors, among which are the imagination of its leaders, the will to accept Quebec's special place in Canada and, more importantly, the capacity of these leaders to find devices that subsume the application of the Charter of Rights and Freedoms under a territorial formula to account for Quebec's special and unique needs in the Canadian federation. This will be difficult to achieve due to:

° the rapid demise of first ministers' conferences (and executive federalism) which are perceived as too elitist;

° profound distrust of traditional forms of representation (for example, the major political parties) complicated by the emergence of regional blocs such as Reform Party and Bloc Québécois;

° the rapidly acquired faith in the Charter of Rights and Freedoms in English-speaking Canada, complicated by Quebec's cultural insecurity; and

° the equality of provinces precept that gained prominence with the growing popularity of province-building in the 1970s.

All of these factors coalesce in making a recognition of Quebec as a distinct society difficult. In fact, the combination of these elements make a solution to the present crisis improbable. First, Quebec will never agree to define itself as a *province comme les autres.* Second, Quebec cannot accept that the Charter of Rights undermines the supremacy of Quebec's National Assembly. Finally, Quebec, as the only province that has a Francophone majority, cannot accept having English-speaking Canadians decide the fate of the most important and viable French-speaking community in North America. The situation is further compounded by the fact that Quebec's conventional right of veto was denied by its Canadian partners when the time came to patriate the Constitution Act in 1981, and that so far no corrective measures have been implemented. It is ludicrous to imagine a country such as Canada that has not yet been able to obtain the consent of its second most populous province for its primary symbolic document, the Constitution Act of 1981. The legitimacy of the Constitution Act of 1981 is put in question due to the fact that Quebec is the only region of Canada where French has a majority status. An important caveat, however, is that the Charter of Rights and Freedoms weakens parliamentary supremacy, leaving the notwithstanding clause as the only instrument available to the Quebec government to protect its distinct character. In the process, the Canadian parliament becomes more responsive to special interests that are not territorially based (e.g. Natives, women, ethnic communities, and similar groups), and less responsible to its electors.

There remain several intangibles that could still have a crucial impact on the future of Canada. First, the capacity of political leaders to craft political institutions that tackle Quebec's distinct status, aimed at finding a territorial solution to the Canadian Charter of Rights and Freedoms. Second, elections are imminent in several parts of the country. The circulation of political leaders, both provincially and federally, should bring some fresh air into the process of constitutional negotiations. Finally, the recession may create a climate that encourages Canadians living outside of Quebec to be more receptive to a federalism that nourishes difference, instead of a federalism that stresses universal truths. Alternatively, the recession may discourage Quebec itself from taking the next logical step.

Failure to accept Quebec's distinct status, and its need for a constitutional veto, may have brought Canada to a point of no return, to be restructured around a new set of values rather than the ones that brought about its creation. In the end, the only available option for the rest of Canada may be to define its common values around the Charter of Rights and Freedoms, which has gained the adherence of English-speaking Canadians—including those in Quebec—and let Quebec go its own way. In this regard, there is growing support on the part of the rest of Canada to let Quebec do so.[70] If this is the conclusion reached, then Quebec and the rest of Canada should find ways to continue their economic association, as the Bélanger-Campeau Commission will probably recommend, and encourage economic solidarities that transcend political niceties. For instance, this could consist of bilateral arrangements between provinces and the federal government wishing to set up a supranational structure to regulate trade, monetary policy or fiscal policy. Creating economic solidarities has a potential to attenuate the current crisis. Whatever emerges from the Commission on the constitutional and political future of Quebec, it is certain that its co-presidents will approach the issue of Quebec in Canada as an economic challenge beneficial to all partners, and attempt to demonstrate the extent to which politics and economics constitute relatively autonomous spheres. In a sense, the Bélanger-Campeau Commission represents for Quebec the equivalent of the Macdonald Commission as it calls for globalization and "functional" federalism to become the new leitmotif.

Life without Quebec may be beneficial to a Canada that tries to find its own identity, and that has been hindered in that search by a definition of a Canada based on two founding nations. An independent Quebec could assert itself fully in the concert of nations, and aspire to face challenges that might never have occurred otherwise. Past guideposts may no longer serve any purpose as Quebec and the rest of Canada attempt to redefine themselves in relation to each other, and to the international political community.

Notes

For helpful comments, I am most grateful to Frances Abele, Daniel Drache, Scott Evans, Katherine Graham, François Rocher, Richard Simeon and Reginald Whitaker.

1   Philip Resnick (with a reply by Daniel Latouche), *Letters to a Québécois Friend* (Kingston: McGill-Queen's University Press, 1990).

2   This principle recognized, for instance, the provincial right to enter into negotiations with international organizations in matters exclusively assigned by the BNA Act of 1867 to the provinces. This is discussed fully by Claude Morin, *L'art de l'impossible: la diplomatie québécoise depuis 1960* (Montréal: Boréal, 1987).

3   Richard Simeon and Ian Robinson, *State, Society and the Development of Canadian Federalism* (Toronto: University of Toronto Press, 1990), p. 204.

4   Ironically, Quebec agreed to unanimity in 1980 as a last resort effort to block the federal government's patriation package.

5   Paul Gérin-Lajoie, Convocation Address at Carleton University, April 1965, quoted in Donald V. Smiley, *Constitutional Adaptation and Canadian Federalism Since 1945* (Ottawa: Information Canada, 1970), pp. 124, 158.

6   Donald V. Smiley, *The Canadian Political Community* (Toronto: Methuen, 1967), pp. 68-70; Claude Morin, *Quebec Versus Ottawa: The Struggle for Self-Government, 1960-1972* (Toronto: University of Toronto Press, 1972), chapter 8; and Richard Simeon, *Federal-Provincial Diplomacy: The Making of Recent Policy in Canada* (Toronto: University of Toronto Press, 1972).

7   For an interesting discussion on the *Caisse de dépôt et placement*, see Joseph Eliot Magnet, "La 'société distincte' et la spécificité économique du Québec: un modèle qui a fait ses preuves," *Le Devoir* [Montreal], July 4, 1990, p. 13. It is hard to imagine why such an initiative was not imitated by other provincial governments, though it could be suggested that the Alberta and Saskatchewan Heritage Funds are analogous. Of late, the Newfoundland business community is one of the rare financial groups to have shown excitement about such a prospect. The failure on the part of the provinces to imitate Quebec, it is suggested here, has cost provincial governments across the country, and their respective population, bil-

lions of dollars in wealth that could have been used more efficiently by the provinces. Pierre Fortin, "Quebec's Forced Choice," Remarks Prepared for the Conference on the Future of Quebec and Canada, Faculty of Law, McGill University, November 16-18, 1990. In the case of poorer provinces, it could be argued, however, that provincial control would have been a nightmare.

8   For a more detailed argument, see Alain-G. Gagnon, "Egalité ou indépendance: un tournant dans la pensée constitutionnelle du Québec," in Robert Comeau, Michel Lévesque and Yves Bélanger (eds.), *Daniel Johnson: Rêve d'égalité et projet d'indépendance* (Sillery: Presses de l'Université du Québec, 1991), pp. 173-181.

9   Following the Meech Lake failure, Gil Rémillard was quoted arguing "that the federal government must first respect Quebec's jurisdiction and powers recognized under the 1867 Constitution [following which] both sides can take into account the needs of modern Quebec and negotiate new power-sharing arrangements within a renewed Constitution." Rhéal Séguin, "Give Canada last chance, Grit adviser tells Quebec," *The Globe and Mail* [Toronto], December 13, 1990, p. A-5.

10 See Freda Hawkins, *Canada and Immigration: Public Policy and Public Concern* (Montreal: McGill-Queen's University Press, 1972), pp. 213-234.

11 For a convincing case, see Joseph Garcea, *The alignment of roles between the federal and provincial governments in the fields of immigration from 1970 to 1990,* PhD dissertation in progress, Carleton University.

12 Premier Robert Bourassa, Speech at the First Ministers' Constitutional Conference in Ottawa, September 14-15, 1970, quoted in Jean-Louis Roy, *Le Choix d'un pays: le débat Constitutional Québec-Ottawa, 1960-1976* (Ottawa: Leméac, 1978), p. 205.

13 Garth Stevenson, *Unfulfilled Union: Canadian Federalism and National Unity* (Toronto: Gage Publishing, 1982), p. 210.

14   See Prime Minister Pierre Elliott Trudeau, "1976 correspondence to all provincial premiers," in Peter Meekison (ed.), *Canadian Federalism: Myth or Reality* (Toronto: Methuen, 1977), 3rd edition, pp. 140-169.

15   For a fuller discussion, see John Saywell (ed.), *1976 Canadian Annual Review of Politics and Public Affairs* (Toronto: University of Toronto Press, 1977), pp. 43, 93-94.

16   Government of Canada, *The Task Force on Canadian Unity, A Future Together: Observations and Recommendations* (Ottawa: Ministry of Supply and Services, 1979); a useful account is given by Gérard Bergeron, "L'Etat du Québec sous le fédéralisme canadien," in Gérard Bergeron and Réjean Pelletier (eds.), *L'Etat du Québec en devenir* (Montréal: Boréal, 1980), pp. 331-350.

17   Simeon and Robinson, op. cit., p. 278.

18   Cf. Gil Rémillard, *Le fédéralisme canadien: Le rapatriement de la constitution* (Montréal: Québec Amérique, 1985), *pp. 115-17.*

19   The amending formula stipulates that constitutional changes can be made with the support of seven provinces totalling 50 per cent of the Canadian population, and indicates that the formula, along with a limited set of other changes, can be modified only with unanimity. This situation was forced onto Quebec which, against its consent, has to abide by rules that were set by others.

20   Brian Mulroney, "Notes pour une allocution de l'honorable Brian Mulroney," Sept-Iles, August 6, 1984, p. 4.

21   The Draft Agreement on the Constitution was largely inspired by a key document prepared by the Department of Intergovernmental Affairs, during the first mandate of the Parti Québécois. See, *Les positions constitutionnelles du Québec sur le partage des pouvoirs (1900-1976)* (Québec: Editeur officiel du Québec, 1978).

22   For a fuller account, see Alain-G. Gagnon and Mary Beth Montcalm, *Quebec: Beyond the Quiet Revolution* (Toronto: Nelson Canada, 1990), pp. 162-63.

23   Before coming to power in 1985, the Liberals had prepared a series of policy papers that pointed to areas where compromises needed to be reached. See, Quebec Liberal Party, *A New Canadian Constitution* (1980), *A New Political Leadership for Quebec* (1983), and *Mastering Our Future* (1985) that set the five conditions that would eventually constitute essential conditions for the Meech Lake Accord. These conditions were made public May 9, 1986, and are referred to as the Mont Gabriel proposals. For the Mont Gabriel speech, see Peter Leslie (ed.), *Canada: The State of the Federation, 1986* (Kingston: Institute of Intergovernmental Relations, 1987), pp. 97-105.

24   For two factual analyses, see Pierre Fournier, *Autopsie du Lac Meech: La souveraineté est-elle inévitable?* (Montréal: VLB éditeur, 1990); and Roch Denis (ed.), *Québec: Dix ans de crise constitutionnelle* (Montréal: VLB éditeur, 1990).

25   A July 9, 1990 poll, published in *The Globe and Mail*, indicates, and this was confirmed time and again in subsequent polling, that 81 per cent of Canadians (outside Quebec) want the status quo to prevail whereas 62 per cent of people polled in Quebec wish to have some form of separation, with 50 per cent saying that the province should move toward separation but retain a link to Canada, and 12 per cent stating that Quebec should be totally separated from the rest of Canada. A January 1991 poll shows that close to 70 per cent of Canadians outside Quebec say no to further concessions to Quebec, even if this means Quebec would separate.

26   Douglas Verney, *Three Civilizations, Two Cultures, One State: Canada's Political Traditions* (Durham, Duke University, 1986), p. 367.

27   Douglas Verney, Ibid., p. 367

28   Charles Taylor, "Collision Courses Québec-Canada." Keynote address given at the Conference on the Future

of Quebec and Canada, Faculty of Law, McGill University, November 16, 1990, pp. 2-3.

29   Discussed by Graham Fraser, "PM predicts no referendum in Quebec," *The Globe and Mail* [Toronto], December 31, 1990, p. A-3.

30   Charles Taylor suggested that it might be easier to negotiate successfully more important reforms than the ones proposed under Meech, as long as these are part of a significant constitutional restructuring of Canada. This view is, according to Taylor, also shared by constitutionalist Alan Cairns. See, Charles Taylor, "Lancer un ultimatum au Canada anglais," *Le Devoir* [Montreal], December 20, 1990, p. B-8.

31   In a recent paper, Robert Young argued that "It may be time to abandon a vision of the country that many English Canadians and Quebeckers never shared, and to jettison policies which have existed for twenty years but which are not working." Young goes on to propose "abandoning Trudeau's bilingual and bicultural policies" to avoid the risk of destroying the country, and recommended as Pepin-Robarts suggested in 1979, "A unilateral devolution of power over language, culture and communications" to the provinces. See, Robert A. Young, "Heading off the Constitutional Crisis," Mimeo, Toronto, November 1990.

32   During the Bélanger-Campeau Commission hearings, Léon Dion, a long-time defender of asymmetrical federalism, supported this option. This constitutional expert risks disappointment when he sees that his solution is not acceptable either to English Canadians or to the Prime Minister of Canada. Consistently with earlier statements, Léon Dion argued against the position defended by anti-Meech forces that the deal would have decentralized Canada too much, and then went on to propose, as an alternative, that only Quebec be granted special powers. See, Léon Dion, "Le chemin sera long," in *Le Devoir* [Montreal], December 13, 1990, p. B-8.

33   Mulroney quoted in Graham Fraser, "Mulroney facing constitutional puzzle," in *The Globe and Mail* [Toronto], December 28, 1990, p. A-4.

34   Daniel Latouche, "Quebec and Canada: Scenarios for the Future," in *Business in the Contemporary World,* Autumn 1990, vol. 3, no. 1, p. 58.

35   See, Daniel Drache, Mel Watkins, Frank Cunningham, Ashley McCall, Stephen Clarkson and Abraham Rotstein, "La solution: un Canada binational," *Le Devoir* [Montreal], May 24, 1990, p. 9.

36   Alan C. Cairns, "Constitutional Minoritarianism in Canada," in Ronald L. Watts and Douglas M. Brown (eds.), *Canada: The State of the Federation, 1990* (Kingston: Institute of Intergovernmental Relations, 1990), pp. 71-96.

37   Statements reported by Richard Mackie, "Parizeau gets tepid reception: Business apathy to speech on separation 'antediluvian'," in *The Globe and Mail* [Toronto], December 12, 1990, pp. 1-2.

38   Excerpt of the brief as translated by Jeffrey Simpson, "In discussing Quebec's future, everybody cites the European Community," *The Globe and Mail* [Toronto], December 21, 1990, p. A-16; also, see Parti Québécois, "La nécessaire souveraineté,"*Le Devoir* [Montreal], November 14, 1990, p. B-10. The influence of Jacques-Yvan Morin is noted, see, "La communauté économique Canada-Québec," *Le Devoir* [Montreal], December 14, 1990, p. B-8.

39   cf. Daniel Latouche, "Québec and Canada: Scenarios for the Future," in *Business in the Contemporary World,* Autumn 1990, vol. 3, no. 1, pp. 65-66.

40   See, Douglas Verney, op. cit., p. 374.

41   See, Rhéal Séguin, "The sober style of Robert Bourassa," *The Globe and Mail* [Toronto], October 6, 1990, pp. D-1-2.

42   See his brief to the Macdonald Commission, presented in February 1985 on behalf of the Quebec Liberal Party.

43   Jacques Parizeau made this point clear at the opening of the Bélanger-Campeau Commission. Jacques Parizeau, "La souveraineté, le premier geste à poser," *Le Devoir* [Montreal], November 7, 1990, p. B-12; for a similar point

of view, Jacques-Yvan Morin, "La communauté économique Canada-Québec," *Le Devoir* [Montreal], December 14, 1990, p. B-8.

44   Report of the Constitutional Committee of the Quebec Liberal Party (the Allaire Report), *A Quebec Free to Choose*, January 28, 1991.

45   Jeffrey Simpson, "Bélanger-Campeau Commission: A forum for recycled ideas," *The Globe and Mail* [Toronto], December 22, 1990, p. D-5.

46   Richard Simeon, "Why did the Meech Lake Accord Fail?" in Ronald L. Watts and Douglas M. Brown (eds.), *Canada: The State of the Federation, 1990* (Kingston: Institute of Intergovernmental Relations, 1990), pp. 17-18.

47   Comments made by James Mallory at a meeting of the Canadian Study of Parliament Group, Ottawa, November 9-10, 1990 on "The Future of Canadian Federalism."

48   Charles Taylor, "Collision Courses Québec-Canada," Keynote address given at the Conference on the Future of Quebec and Canada, Faculty of Law, McGill University, November 16, 1990.

49   For further details on the pursuit of a special status for Quebec, cf. Alain-G. Gagnon, "Quebec-Canada Relations: the engineering of constitutional arrangements," in Michael Burgess (ed.), *Canadian Federalism: Past, Present and Future* (London: Leicester University Press, 1990), pp. 95-119.

50   While the proponents of individual rights recognize the group character of many of the enumerated rights in the Charter, they frequently take issue when these groups of collective rights are tied to the question of territory.

51   Alan Cairns and Cynthia Williams provide a convincing argument concerning the impact the Charter has on both political culture and citizen-state relationships. If Cairns and Williams are correct in their assessment, the discourse of rights, either collective or individual, must be confronted in a **re-negotiated federalism** to be perceived as legitimate by the public. Alan Cairns and Cynthia

Williams, "Constitutionalism, Citizenship and Society in Canada: An Overview," in A. Cairns and C. Williams, (eds.), *Constitutionalism, Citizenship and Society in Canada* (Toronto: University of Toronto Press, 1985).

52   Michael Dolan, "The Single European Act—Its Origins and Implications," Paper presented for a Seminar on the European Community after 1992: Consequences for Africa, held in Lagos, Nigeria, June 13-15, 1990; and Michael Burgess, *Federalism and European Union: Political Ideas, Influences and Strategies in the European Community 1972-1987* (New York: Routledge, 1989).

53   This strategy was rapidly sketched out when Meech failed, see Pierre O'Neill, "Peterson et Bourassa jettent les bases d'un nouveau partenariat économique," *Le Devoir* [Montreal], June 27, 1990, pp. 1,8.

54   Michel Venne, "Québec dit oui au libre-échange entre les provinces," *Le Devoir* [Montreal], December 19, 1990, pp. A-1, A-4.

55   Pierre Fortin, "Quebec's Forced Choice," Remarks prepared for the Conference on the Future of Quebec and Canada, Faculty of Law, McGill University, November 16-18, 1990.

56   Pierre Fortin, op. cit; also his expert testimony before the Bélanger-Campeau Commission, "Le choix forcé du Québec,"*Le Devoir* [Montreal], December 14, 1990, p. B-8.

57   To name a few, the Royal Bank, Canadian Pacific, Bell Canada, the Conseil du Patronat, the Quebec wing of the Canadian Manufacturers' Association, the Forum de l'emploi. Some, such as the Desjardins Movement, do not hesitate to go as far as proposing full independence for Quebec. This reading emerged clearly out of the briefs presented at the Bélanger-Campeau Commission.

58   Pierre Fortin, op. cit.; also, an interview given by Thomas Courchene supports this interpretation, see Jean Blouin, "What does Canada Want?," *L'Actualité* March 1, 1990, pp. 12-13, 16.

59   Daniel Latouche, "Québec and Canada: Scenarios for the Future," *Business in the Contemporary World,* Autumn 1990, vol. 3, no. 1, p. 61.

60   Pierre Fournier, "Un guet-apens pour la souveraineté?" *La Presse* [Montreal], November 5, 1990, p. B-3; for some sobering thoughts on the sovereignty option, see his work *Autopsie du Lac Meech: la souveraineté est-elle inévitable?* (Montréal: VLB éditeur, 1990).

61   See, Marie Tyson, "Mulroney promet un nouveau partage des pouvoirs," *Le Devoir* [Montreal] December 17, 1990, pp. 1,4; Jean Chrétien, "Renforcer les régions," *Le Devoir* [Montreal], December 18, 1990, p. B-8.

62   See, Jean-Marc Léger, "L'auberge espagnole du fédéralisme renouvelé," *Le Devoir* [Montreal], January 4, 1991, p. 11.

63   This possibility was suggested by both David Milne and Peter Meekison at the January 16, 1991 Business Council on National Issues' special meeting held in Toronto on Constitutional Options for Canada.

64   Paul Cauchon, "Plus de pouvoirs au Québec en immigration: entente Québec-Canada sur le projet de Meech," *Le Devoir* [Montreal], December 22, 1990, pp. A-1, A-4; and Paul Cauchon, "Québec françaisera seul ses immigrants," *Le Devoir* [Montreal], December 28, 1990, pp. 1,4; and, Estanislas Oziewicz, "Quebec calls immigration pact model for future," *The Globe and Mail* [Toronto], February 6, 1991, p. A-4.

65   Rémillard made this point clear during the Bélanger-Campeau Commission hearings, reported in Rhéal Séguin, "Give Canada last chance, Grit adviser tells Quebec," *The Globe and Mail* [Toronto], December 13, 1990, p. A-5.

66   Graham Fraser, "PM suggests power shuffle with provinces," *The Globe and Mail* [Toronto], December 17, 1990, pp. A-1, A-2.

67   The leader of the Federal New Democratic Party, Audrey McLaughlin, was reported saying, "There have been successive cuts to health-care funding in this country. All of

the provinces and territories are aware of it. By 1997, Ontario and Quebec will be receiving no federal funding under the current formula; in the early 2000s, the rest of the provinces will follow with no federal funding," Graham Fraser, "Beatty rejects Quebec proposal," *The Globe and Mail* [Toronto], December 13, 1990, p. A-7.

68   Madelaine Drohan, "Quebec tries to change deal: wants to sign separate trade accords," *The Globe and Mail* [Toronto], December 20, 1990, pp. B-1, B-2.

69   Section 43 stipulates that "an amendment to the Constitution of Canada in relation to any provision that applies to one or more, but not all provinces" may be decided by Parliament and the relevant province(s) alone. This is available to all provinces, but gives some flexibility to the federal government to enter into some constitutional negotiations with Quebec.

70   This is suggested by a poll conducted by Decima Research Ltd. which reveals that 51 per cent of Canadians (with an analogous breakdown in both Quebec and the rest of Canada) believe that Canada should let Quebec go if it so desires. cf. *The Gazette* [Montreal], December 31, 1990, pp. 1-2.

CHAPTER 4

ANOTHER NEW WEST: ENVIRONMENTALISM AND THE NEW POLICY AGENDA

Roger Gibbins

Résumé: Ce chapitre traite des changements au programme politique de l'ouest du pays. Il examine en particulier la collision entre la vieille politique de langue et de territoire et la nouvelle politique de l'environnementalisme et des droits humains. Une analyse plus détaillée de l'environnementalisme suggère que le paysage politique de l'Ouest subit une transformation, et que la nature de cette transformation peut ouvrir la voie à de nouvelles initiatives politiques de la part du gouvernement fédéral.

Abstract: This chapter addresses changes to the political agenda in western Canada. More specifically, it examines the collision between the old politics of language and territory, and the new politics of environmentalism and human rights. The more detailed analysis of environmentalism suggests that the political landscape in western Canada is being transformed, and that the nature of the transformation may open up room for new policy initiatives by the federal government.

The early 1970s witnessed the emergence of what has been termed "the new West."[1] Resource-driven prosperity and aggressive, self-confident provincial governments moved the region to the centre of the Canadian political stage. The heartland of the new West was Alberta, where its lifeblood came from energy resources, its symbol of newfound wealth was the Alberta Heritage Savings and Trust Fund, and its constitutional point man in battles with the federal government was Alberta Premier Peter Lougheed. Then, in the early 1980s, the bloom came off the western Canadian rose. Energy prices fell, grain farmers faced higher costs and shrinking markets and western-based financial institutions collapsed like a house of cards. The movement of people and investment into the region from eastern Canada stopped, and then reversed itself as Ontario regained its economic prosperity and leadership. Far from permanently altering the distribution of economic and political power in Canada, the "new West" began to seem like a flash in the pan.

It can be argued, however, that the last few years have seen the tentative emergence of another "new West," although in this case the character of the region[2] is taking on a quite different cast. This second new West is not driven by economic prosperity, although conflict in the Middle East may temporarily fuel another oil boom in Alberta. In fact, the regional economic mood is hesitant and uncertain at best. Multitudinous problems continue to plague the grain industry as export markets for coal and forestry products soften, the national recession creeps west, and the anticipated largesse of the Free Trade Agreement remains more hope than substance. Nor is the emergent West marked by the profound **regional** alienation of the past. While western alienation is still very much in the air, and while the label of western alienation is still applied reflexively to political discontent within the region, such discontent now derives much of its motive force from national issues and national concerns. Indeed, it can be argued that the "new West" of the early 1990s is one in which national and non-territorial politics are coming to supplant the regional politics, and thus the regional alienation, of the past.

In even more expansive terms, it can be argued that the "new politics" is beginning to transform the face of western Canadian politics. What remains to be seen is whether this transformation will create a window of opportunity for new federal policy initiatives in the West. A preliminary look at the new politics of environmentalism suggests that this may indeed be the case.

The New Politics

Recent years have witnessed a growing scholarly interest in the emergence of a **new politics** or **new political agenda** (NPA).[3] Although the parameters of the NPA are somewhat loosely delineated, they are asserted to encompass at the very least environmentalism, feminism, Aboriginal claims, sustainable economic development, opposition to nuclear energy, an emphasis on human rights and, on an even more global basis, a concern with world peace. In the Canadian context, key components of the NPA are thought to capture changes in the political culture which find reflection in, and which have been energized by, the Charter of Rights and Freedoms. More broadly, the NPA is asserted to embrace the emergence of post-materialist patterns of ideological thought,[4] and to challenge older ideological patterns embodied in the left-right polarity.[5]

It would be a mistake, however, to assume that the NPA is uncontested, and that older patterns of ideological thought and political cleavage are on the ropes. Within the Canadian context, a resilient traditional political agenda (TPA) maintains a strong grip on political discourse and public policy. The TPA, or the old politics, stresses the primacy of territorial and linguistic identifications, and therefore federalism, in shaping political discourse and patterns of public policy. Thus the TPA embraces federal-provincial jurisdictional conflict, linguistic politics, an emphasis on economic growth and a concern with regional development. In the Canadian west, the TPA also embraces the territorial conflict associated with western alienation and Senate reform. The TPA has deep historical roots, and is firmly entrenched in the political institutions of the Canadian federal state.[6] Therefore, the task confronting the constituents of the NPA is indeed formidable: forging a new political agenda within the existing constitutional and institutional structures of the Canadian federal state will not be an easy task, nor one for which ultimate success should be presumed. As Krasner has so effectively argued, institutional inertia is a potent force.[7]

The question in the western Canadian context concerns the extent to which the TPA is being replaced, augmented or transformed by the NPA. To what extent, for example, does environmentalism (or feminism, or any other element of the NPA) crosscut or reinforce pre-existing patterns of regional conflict and institutional organization? In this respect, Cairns argues that the Charter of Rights will act as a solvent on the territorial, and eventually federal, organization of Canadian political life.[8] Following similar logic, it can be argued that environmentalism (and other elements of the NPA) has the same potential to transform the territorial (and perhaps even linguistic) segmentation of Canadian political life.[9] Just as the TPA stresses the primacy of territory, the NPA posits that other identities (e.g. gender) and other issues (e.g. environmentalism) are primary. In a general sense, then, the collision of the old and new political agendas represents a struggle over the centrality of territory, and hence federalism, to the ideological and institutional organization of Canadian political life. In the western Canadian context, the new political agenda, therefore, challenges the centrality and durability of western alienation as an organizing framework for political life.

In order to examine the regional interplay of the new and traditional political agendas, of the old and new politics, the stage must first be set by a brief look at the post-Meech political environment in the West. We can then take a closer look at how agenda conflict might shape the public policies and political perspectives of both the provincial and federal governments in the Canadian West.

Setting The Stage

The post-Meech environment in western Canada, as in Canada at large, is unsettled and confused. A good deal of uncertainty on the constitutional front is coupled with a sense of fatalism, and probably pessimism, concerning the future of the country. At the same time, there has been very little hand-wringing over the collapse of the Meech Lake Accord, very little sense that the country was brought to the brink, and that something must be done to accommodate the constitutional aspirations of Quebec. The constitutional mood in the region is probably less accommodating a year after Meech than it was before the collapse of the Accord; the inclination is to pull back, to argue that the Accord went too far. This sentiment, of course, puts public opinion, although not necessarily governmental opinion, in the west on a collision course with the proposals emerging from constitutional deliberations in Quebec. Nevertheless, if the danger, or threat, of independence has increased in Quebec, the increase has not generated any pronounced anxiety in the West. Bluntly put, western Canadians are torn between indifference, on the one hand, and a predisposition to play chicken with the nationalist movement in Quebec, on the other.

This unsettled constitutional environment contributes to a very fluid partisan environment. The federal Progressive Conservatives have all but collapsed across the region. As a consequence, an electoral vacuum has been created which Preston Manning and the Reform Party of Canada are filling. Recent opinion polls place the Reform party ahead of the Conservatives in all four western provinces, and well ahead of the Conservatives in that party's long-standing Alberta heartland.[10] In the battle over the western carcass of the Conservative party, the Reform party is the best positioned. The New Democrats are not well-placed ideologically to capture defecting Tories, and the Liberal "revival" in the West was stillborn with Jean Chrétien's leadership victory in Calgary in June, 1990. Thus, if mid-term opinion polls mean anything at all, the Reform Party is poised to capture as many as 40 or 50 seats. This possibility, quite apart from its realization, will shape the policy agenda in the West, and may even have a pre-election impact on "how Ottawa spends" as parties and governments respond to the fiscal conservatism and incipient tax revolt embedded in the Reform Party threat.

The federal Conservatives are not the only ones on the ropes; provincial governments west of Manitoba are also in disarray and under siege. At the time of writing, the provincial governments in Saskatchewan, Alberta and British Columbia were all trailing badly in the polls. (The Progressive Conservative government in Alberta was well behind the Reform Party even though the latter party had yet to enter provincial politics!) All three await an electoral verdict on Meech Lake. Thus the electoral atmosphere is not one which will encourage a thoughtful, reflective consideration of public policy issues, nor is it one that will encourage either federal-provincial co-operation or productive constitutional politics.

The Traditional Politics of Western Alienation

The 1984 landslide win by Brian Mulroney's Progressive Conservatives produced a clear but surprisingly short-lived hiatus in the traditional politics of western alienation. Discussion of constitutional and institutional reform was put on hold as western Canadians waited to see how Parliament would work now that the right party (the Progressive Conservatives, and not the Liberals) and the right leader (Brian Mulroney, and not Pierre Trudeau) held the reins of power.[11] Intergovernmental conflict was also put on hold as the western premiers met with a prime minister committed to national reconciliation, and as the federal government acted to remove important policy irritants including but not restricted to the National Energy Program. Ottawa provided substantial financial support for western agriculture and the Western Diversification Fund provided federal money for the long-standing yet elusive regional goal of economic diversification. On a broader level, the federal government produced the Free Trade Agreement, thus realizing one of the longest standing western Canadian policy objectives, and appeared able to produce constitutional peace through the Meech Lake Accord. It would seem, then, that the early Mulroney years were good years for western Canada.

Somewhere along the line, however, federal-provincial goodwill and regional contentment disappeared. The institutional experiment of 1984—would parliamentary institutions work under the best of conditions rather than under the worst of conditions?—has been judged a failure by large sections of the regional electorate. The federal government today is seen, fairly or not, as being no less preoccupied with Quebec, and no more sensitive to the West, than the Trudeau governments of the past. Initiatives like the Western Diversification Fund have left little, if any, mark on public perceptions of Ottawa. Thus, western alienation and federal-provincial conflict appear to be back with a vengeance, and the post-Meech environment finds the federal and western provincial governments once more at odds across a wide policy agenda. Both the fragile constitution consensus between Ottawa and the western provincial governments and electoral support for the Conservatives, have collapsed in the wake of the Meech Lake debacle, the GST and the plummeting popularity of the Prime Minister.

One of the policy fallouts from the Accord's collapse is a sustained effort by western premiers and their governments to downplay constitutional politics, to shift the national agenda's centre of gravity from the Constitution to the economy. In large part, this strategy reflects the fact that the three westernmost premiers have been badly burned by the Accord debate. Grant Devine and Don Getty, in particular, were enthusiastic participants in, and even cheerleaders for, a constitutional process which many western Canadians now believe to have been badly flawed at best, and pernicious at worst. The premiers' support for the Accord, and thus inextricably for the Prime Minister, was seriously at odds with public sentiment in the region. Hence the need to beat a hasty but hopefully dignified retreat from the constitutional field of battle.

Here it should also be noted that a continued high-profile discussion of constitutional issues would likely play into the electoral hands of the Reform Party and its vociferous quest for institutional reform, including, but by no means restricted to, Senate reform. The existing premiers have little to add to the constitutional debate; their positions have been well-established by their virtual silence during the Meech Lake process. Having failed to develop a western constitutional vision within the context of Meech, the premiers are not well-positioned to do so now; Mr. Getty may continue his quixotic search for Senate reform, but this issue has probably damaged him politically and again plays into the hands of the Reform Party.

Thus we should not expect bold constitutional proposals to emerge in the short run from western provincial governments. A more likely response is for the provincial governments to batten down the hatches in the hope that their electorates will forget the constitution, and in particular forget the Accord. The Lloydminster declaration by the western premiers in August 1990, a declaration which proposed fundamental changes to Canadian fiscal federation, can best be seen as covering fire laid down by the premiers as they tried to transform a constitutional rout into an orderly retreat. However, it also signals the constitutional strategy that western premiers are likely to pursue if forced back to the constitutional table, a strategy emphasizing fiscal issues. Certainly the call to shift taxing power to the provinces, and to make the federal government the recipient of provincial tax points, was not one that was met with any enthusiasm in Ottawa. If Ottawa's public reaction was mute, it was only because the federal government was mired in post-Meech and Oka doldrums at the time. Certainly the Lloydminster proposal flies directly in the face of the GST initiative. Whether it it will find common ground with Quebec remains to be seen.

The more general federal-provincial policy environment is likely to become increasingly conflictual and contentious as the western premiers struggle to distance themselves from a very unpopular federal government. The Meech process placed at least three of the western premiers in bed with the Prime Minister, and in a position which appeared to compromise western interests. Mr. Getty and Mr. Devine also share the misfortune of leading Progressive Conservative governments at a time when the federal Progressive Conservatives are so unpopular in the West that Pierre Trudeau is being revived as a regional folk hero. Thus it is an electoral imperative that the premiers establish some distance between themselves and the federal government, and particularly between themselves and the Prime Minister. This can be done by somewhat belated court challenges to the GST, by combat on the environmental front (discussed below), and by broad-gauge attacks on Ottawa's economic management, for which a first ministers' conference on the economy would provide an ideal setting. Fed-bashing has always been a popular sport in the West, but it is now also an electoral necessity.

All this may suggest that the traditional politics of western alienation are alive and well, and indeed in many respects they are. It can be argued, however, that the dynamics of western alienation have also changed in an important way, that they have become nationalized. The events and issues that are today driving western alienation, or at least what is seen and manifested as western alienation, are essentially the same events and issues that are driving political discontent elsewhere in the country outside Quebec.

Evidence for this transformation can be found in the character of the Meech Lake Accord debate in western Canada.[12] Although western Canadians did raise regionally specific concerns about such issues as Senate reform, the great bulk of the criticism and commentary was not regionally specific. Discussion turned around the impact of the Accord on the Charter, the North, women, and the strength of the national government. For the most part, the discussion could have been taking place almost anywhere in the country, excluding Quebec. Thus, while the Accord touched off a very heated debate in the West, it was not primarily a debate fuelled by regionalism. In this sense, the debate exposed an important face of the second "new West."

Now it may seem, of course, that the emergence of the Reform party provides clear and unequivocal evidence of vigorous regional discontent. Yet even here, the dynamics lying behind the growth of the Reform Party seem more national than regional. Reform protest about the GST and the deficit, about executive federalism and Meech Lake, and about the incumbent government and Prime Minister is by no means regional in character; it is to be found throughout the land. Even the party's emphasis on institutional reform, the holy grail of western Canadian politics, is finding a more receptive audience outside the region in the wake of the Meech debacle and the Senate debate on the GST. Thus, while the Reform Party is certainly the repository for traditional regional discontent, it also provides a protest vehicle through which Canadians in the West can vent their national concerns about national issues,[13] and through which a host of groups can potentially express their concern, if not outrage, at patterns of social change—liberalized abortion, increased immigration, feminism—threatening traditional social values. As a consequence, the party may turn out to have greater national appeal, that is to say appeal to the Ontario electorate and media, than its opponents suspect.

If there is an underlying theme to contemporary western Canadian politics, both protest and governmental, it is fiscal conservatism. Simply put, there is strong and growing support for deficit reduction, for constraints on government spending and for tax relief. In October 1990, the BC Minister of Finance called for spending cuts of five per cent across all ministries in the province. In Alberta, Premier Don Getty has been adamant that the surge in oil revenues generated by the Gulf crisis will be used to reduce the provincial debt, and will not result in any significant increase in provincial spending.[14] On the federal front, the Reform Party marches more to the drum of fiscal constraint than to the drum of regional discontent, although admittedly the two instruments find harmony in images of a spendthrift federal government dominated by a central Canadian political agenda.

Putting the latter images aside, there is little evidence that the fiscal conservatism of western Canadians is seriously out of line with sentiment elsewhere in Canada. For example, while the GST is very unpopular in the West, and particularly in once sales tax-free Alberta, it enjoys little support anywhere in the country. If western Canadians are teetering on the verge of a tax revolt, they are part of a much larger crowd. What gives fiscal conservatism a sharper political edge in the West is the Reform Party, for whom fiscal conservatism provides the central policy plank. At a time when the federal Conservatives are burdened with a perceived record of prolific spending and multitudinous tax increases, when the Liberals have not been able to replace their own profligate legacy with coherent policies adapted to new financial realities, and when the New Democrats are unwilling to bite the program bullet of spending cuts, the Reform Party has almost an open field as the champion of fiscal constraint. Had the GST been linked in the public's mind to effective deficit reduction or had the Conservatives been successful in selling the GST as a revenue-neutral component of more comprehensive tax reform, then the Reformers might have had a Conservative rival. However, given that the GST has instead been linked in the public eye with unconstrained federal spending, that it is seen to negate rather than reflect the need for expenditure control, the Reformers are unlikely to be challenged on this front.

A question to be asked is what impact, if any, fiscal conservatism in the West is likely to have on "how Ottawa spends." The most likely impact will not be on "how" Ottawa spends, but rather on "how much" Ottawa spends. If the West is able to exert any appreciable influence on the direction of national policy, and that is a big "if" indeed, then western predispositions should offer support for greater fiscal conservatism in Ottawa. Since the West is likely to be an electoral wasteland for the Conservatives in the next election, however, western predispositions are unlikely to account for much. National economic policy is more likely to be driven by the need to respond financially to Quebec's constitutional proposals, given that a constitutional response by English Canada will be difficult if not impossible for the federal government to orchestrate. It will also be driven by the need to respond to a recession that will have its greatest impact in central Canada; and by the need to firm up Conservative electoral support in Quebec in the run-up to the next federal election. Facing these realities, and with new revenue from the GST jingling in its pockets, the federal government is unlikely to respond to the fiscal conservatism of the West. A more probable response will be more comedy museums in Montreal and federal support for opera houses in Toronto, and more support for the Reform Party in the West.

Environmentalism and the New Politics

As noted above, the "new politics" is thought to encompass a wide variety of somewhat disparate elements, including environmentalism, feminism, opposition to nuclear energy, sustainable economic development and an emphasis on human rights. What these elements have in common, and what sets them apart from the traditional politics of western alienation, is their non-territorial and even transnational character. As Poguntke explains:

> ... new politics-related problems exist in all advanced societies to a substantial degree: the ecological crisis is a direct result of industrialization. Bureaucratization and the development of new technologies impinge on liberal freedoms and increase the possibility and likelihood of extensive state surveillance. The threat of nuclear annihilation is universally present, just as is the pressure to confront the problems of the Third World.[15]

Because the new politics is non-territorial, it has the potential to disrupt, and perhaps even transform or displace the territorial politics which underlie western alienation. To illustrate how the new politics might alter the dynamics of western Canadian politics, let us take a closer look at the possible impact of environmentalism, one of the key ingredients of the new politics.

No issue has climbed up the political agenda as quickly as environmentalism has done over the past few years. Accompanied by a barrage of media coverage, environmentalism has become **the** social and political issue of the 1990s,[16] one that challenges many of the economic shibboleths of western industrial states. Of particular importance for the present argument is the manner in which environmentalism challenges, or at least potentially challenges, the territorial organization of political life. To this point in time, admittedly, the challenge has been largely implicit in the logic of environmentalism. Few environmentalists in North America have explicitly challenged the values of federalism and national sovereignty, and thus the centrality of territorial politics, as the Greens have begun to do in Europe,[17] and most environmental radicalism has been directed towards targets contained within single political jurisdictions.[18] However, there are powerful reasons to expect an environmental challenge to territorial politics, and to expect it to be made with increasing force in the 1990s. At some point, the slogan "Think Globally and Act Locally" will give way to more broadly based political action.

Many environmental problems, and for that matter ecological perspectives on the world, show no regard for jurisdictional boundaries, for the "lines on maps" which give territorial definition to the federal and national organization of political life. Global warming, the threat to the ozone layer and to the rain forests of Brazil, acid rain and other forms of air pollution in Europe and North America, water pollution in the Great Lakes and European waterways, and the fall-out from Chernobyl are all examples of environmental effects which are unimpeded by jurisdictional boundaries. Yet while the effects may be unimpeded by jurisdictional boundaries, the existing territorial organization of political life, with national boundaries and provincial/state boundaries within federal states, limits our capacity to respond to environmental problems which have no respect for political boundaries. Note, for example, Carroll's argument that "transnational or transborder air pollution may be viewed as one of the greatest threats to the concept of national sovereignty and the notion of the nation-state yet to emerge."[19] Carroll goes on to argue that:

> The protection of the health and welfare of a nation's citizens, and therefore of their environment, is a fundamental *raison d'être* of government. To the extent that government cannot provide such protection, it loses its reason for existence. And this is precisely what is happening in the arena of international environmental relations.[20]

Thus individuals and groups who seek to address such environmental problems will increasingly chafe at the constraints imposed by both federalism and national sovereignty. When political boundaries appear to be an impediment to effective environmental action, the demand will grow to lower or even erase those boundaries;[21] international and even supranational solutions will be sought. Given that federal "lines on maps" are somewhat paler than those prescribed by national sovereignty, they may well be the first to feel the corrosive effects of environmentalism. Within this context, it will become more difficult to convince western Canadians, and indeed other Canadians, that the political claims of territory should be pre-eminent. To environmentalists, the only question is which level of government, federal or provincial, is prepared to impose the most rigorous standards; they are indifferent to the traditional importance ascribed by Canadian governments to jurisdictional niceties.

It should also be noted that, on many fronts, environmentalists confront a significant and troublesome "free-rider" problem, one that is entangled with the territorial organization of political life. With respect to continental and international politics, Canadian enthusiasm for a serious assault on carbon dioxide emissions and global warming is sapped by a number of realities: Canadian actions might not be matched by other countries, leaving Canada at risk in economic competition with non-participants; Canadian action by itself will not make a significant impact on global warming; and, if other countries do act, Canada can free-ride on their actions, enjoying the collective good (less global warming) while not contributing to the cost. What makes the problem a classic free-rider problem is the existence of national sovereignty. The solution is to be found in the reduction of national sovereignty through either international co-operation with teeth (coercion) or the creation of supranational political organizations. With respect to Canadian politics, the same logic calls for a strengthening of the national government and a reduction in territorial constraints on effective environmental action.

If this line of argument holds, if environmentalists are inherently indifferent to and even hostile to political lines on maps, then environmentalism should corrode the territorial organization of political life which underlies western alienation. Of course, for this impact to be felt, environmentalism must have some staying power on the political agenda. In this respect, I would agree with Rudig,[22] who maintains that the environmental movement has found a permanent home within western political systems. Its staying power is assured by the underlying reality of environmental problems; by the growing organizational power of environmental lobbies;[23] by the incorporation of environmentalism within state structures through the creation of provincial and national ministers and ministries of the environment; by institutional inertia once Green parties have been established;[24] and by the enthusiastic embrace and even promotion of environmentalism by the corporate sector. When McDonalds' restaurants take up the green crusade, as they have done, we can be confident that environmentalism is here for the long run.

It is important to stress, however, that although environmentalism may be here to stay, its specific impact on territorial politics is not predetermined. While the logic of environmentalism is intrinsically hostile to the territorial organization of political life, we must not underestimate the possibility that provincial governments will capture, at least temporarily, the green flag of environmental politics. Environmentalism has tremendous electoral appeal, and it is therefore in the interest of provincial governments to nail the environmental flag to their own masts. To the extent that they succeed, they will incorporate environmentalism (or other elements of the NPA) within the existing territorial and federal organization of the political world. Thus, just as environmentalists may attack the territorial organization of political life, provincial governments will seek to preserve that organization by drawing environmentalists into the existing federal structure.

Of course, the effort by provincial governments to capture the green flag will not be uncontested, and to this point has been notably unsuccessful as provincial governments have found themselves opposed to environmentalists across a wide range of conflicts. (Recent controversies concerning the development of

pulp mills in northern Alberta provide but one example.) Environmentalism can be expected to provide the central plank in
the federal Conservatives' 1992 campaign platform; with luck,
a campaign fought on the high ground of environmentalism will
distract voters' attention from the legacy of the GST, recession,
Meech Lake and other woes. Thus the hostility of environmentalists to political lines on maps potentially opens the door for
more assertive federal environmental initiatives. Ottawa has
the opportunity, and perhaps the obligation, to move across a
broad policy front, and may be able to do so despite jurisdictional
objections raised by provincial governments. To this point, the
federal government has managed to get its foot in the door
through both its Green Plan initiative and its success with
bilateral negotiations to reduce acid rain. What it now needs is
a period of calm on the national unity and fiscal fronts so that
these early gains can be consolidated in supportive public
opinion.

In pursuing this line of argument, we should not underestimate the creative capacity of political actors to recast elements
of the NPA into older ideological molds. Note, for example, the
September 3, 1990 attack by the *Alberta Report* on the federal
government's proposed environmental Green Plan:

> Cynics from government and industry in Alberta have
> already dubbed the Green Plan the "National Energy
> Program II." The punitive taxes and economic
> measures imposed by the Liberals of Pierre Trudeau
> in 1980 under the NEP drained an estimated $60
> billion out of the Alberta economy. "There is some fear
> that environmental assessment legislation would give
> the federal government opportunity to exercise some
> control over the resources of the province," noted a
> worried Alberta environment minister, Ralph Klein.

In Saskatchewan, the acrimonious legal fight between the
provincial and federal governments over the Rafferty-Alameda
dams provides a striking example of how an environmental
conflict can be transformed into a federal-provincial conflict,
and thus how the new politics can be recast as the old. In this
instance, the fact that the past and current federal ministers of
the environment, Lucien Bouchard and Robert de Cotret, were
from Quebec enabled participants to frame the dispute in the
classic terminology of western alienation. Hence we find one of
the strongest supporters of the dams, George Hill, arguing in

public that the federal Environment Department, and the environmental review panel established by the Department, showed an "overwhelming bias" against western Canada. Members of the panel, he argued, are:

> ...not only incompetent but are also insensitive to Saskatchewan or Western needs or feelings. Every one of the experts initially hired for the panel came from the great province of Ontario. Not one came from Saskatchewan or the West. Why should we put up with this insensitivity?[25]

It therefore remains to be seen if environmentalism will escape from or transform the traditional rhetoric of western alienation. In this respect, western Canadians can be expected to watch closely Ottawa's involvement in the second phase of the James Bay project. Any indication that Ottawa is less willing to wade into environmental conflict with Quebec than with western provinces will only enhance western alienation, and further curtail the transformative impact of environmentalism.

Some environmentalist policies may themselves stimulate important elements of the traditional political agenda, including regional conflict and the defence of federal lines of jurisdiction. For example, the imposition of a carbon tax in Canada would not only contribute to environmental goals but also be seen by Albertans as an unfair tax grab and as a federal assault on the resource underpinnings of the provincial economy. For just such reasons, a report by the House of Commons Committee on the Environment, released in mid-October, 1990, had to tread a wary path among regional aspirations. Its recommendation that Canada reduce its carbon dioxide emissions by 20 per cent by the year 2005 would have, if adopted, pronounced regional effects. At the present time, 66 per cent of Canada's primary energy comes from Alberta fossil fuels;[26] a shift, therefore, to other energy sources, such as substituting Quebec hydro power for Alberta oil and natural gas, is likely to induce regional conflict.

CONCLUSIONS

In the short run, the conventional politics and rituals of western alienation may inhibit the emergence of a clearly defined "new politics" in western Canada. Thus, for example, environmental politics may be folded into conventional patterns of federal-provincial conflict, although this outcome is far from inevitable. However, too tight a focus on the short term may obscure a fundamental transformation of the western Canadian political culture, a transformation that coincides with important features of national and international ideological change.

There is at least some evidence that new, Charter-induced identities are beginning to challenge territorial identities in the West, and that a new rights-based political agenda is diminishing the earlier centrality of territorial conflict. There is also evidence, albeit tenuous, and a more persuasive logical argument that environmentalism will strengthen the hold of non-territorial politics throughout the region. If we look ahead, then, to the turn of the century, we can see the sketchy outlines of a political agenda in which territorial and federal-provincial conflict play a substantially reduced role.

The outstanding political and constitutional problem is how to get to the turn of the century with the country still intact. In this respect, the contemporary political scene in western Canada provides less ground for optimism than do the broader patterns of ideological change that are transforming the Canadian political culture. If the Progressive Conservative government is to embrace the "new politics" with any positive electoral effect in western Canada, it must first get through the debris and dilemmas of the old politics. In this respect, any attempt to appeal to the western Canadian electorate with a campaign based on environmental activism will likely provoke hostility among Quebec voters grown increasingly wary of federal initiatives in areas of provincial or concurrent jurisdiction. Thus the primordial electoral need to win Quebec may once again pre-empt innovative federal initiatives in the West.

Notes

1   For a discussion, see Roger Gibbins, *Prairie Politics and Society: Regionalism in Decline* (Toronto: Butterworths, 1980) and John Richards and Larry Pratt, *Prairie Capitalism: Power and Influence in the New West* (Toronto: McClelland and Stewart, 1979).

2   At this point, a ritualistic caveat must be offered. The West is not, and never was, a homogeneous region, and therefore caution should be observed in applying the following analysis, in whole or in part, to particular segments of the region.

3   For example, see Wilhelm Buerklin, "The Greens, Ecology and the New Left," in H.G. Wallach and G. Romoses (eds.), *West German Politics in the Mid-Eighties* (New York: Praeger, 1985); Russell Dalton, *Citizen Politics in Western Democracies* (Chatham, N.J.: Chatham House, 1988); Scott Flanagan, "Changing Values in Advanced Industrial Societies: Inglehart's Silent Revolution from the Perspective of Japanese Findings," *Comparative Political Studies*, 14 (1982), pp. 209-221; P.R. Hay and M.G. Harvard, "Comparative Green Politics: Beyond the European Context?" *Political Studies*, 34 (1988), pp. 433-448; Markus Kreuzer, "New Politics: Just Post-Materialist? The Case of the Austrian and Swiss Greens," *West European Politics*, 13:1 (January, 1990), pp. 12-30; Warren Magnussen and Robert Walker, "De-Centring the State: Political Theory and Canadian Political Economy," *Studies in Political Economy*, 26 (Summer 1988); and Lester W. Milbrath, *Environmentalists: Vanguard for a New Society* (Albany, New York: State University of New York Press, 1984).

4   Ronald Inglehart, *The Silent Revolution* (Princeton, N.J.: Princeton University Press, 1977) and *Culture Shift in Advanced Industrial Society* (Princeton, NJ: Princeton University Press, 1990).

5   Neil Nevitte, Herman Bakvis and Roger Gibbins, "The Ideological Contours of 'New Politics' in Canada: Policy, Mobilization and Partisan Support," *Canadian Journal of Political Science*, xxii:3 (September 1989), pp. 475-504.

6   For a general discussion, see Alan C. Cairns, "The Governments and Societies of Canadian Federalism," *Canadian Journal of Political Science*, x:4 (December 1977), pp. 695-726; Roger Gibbins, *Regionalism: Territorial Politics in Canada and the United States* (Toronto: Butterworths, 1982); and Gibbins, "Federal Societies, Institutions, and Politics," in Herman Bakvis and William

Chandler (eds.), *Federalism and the Role of the State* (Toronto: University of Toronto Press, 1987).

7   Stephen D. Krasner, "Sovereignty: An Institutional Perspective," *Comparative Political Studies*, 21:1 (April 1988), pp. 66-94.

8   Alan C. Cairns, "Citizens (Outsiders) and Governments (Insiders) in Constitution-Making: The Case of Meech Lake," *Canadian Public Policy*, xiv (Supplement 1988).

9   Roger Gibbins, "Ideological Change as a Federal Solvent: Impact of the New Ideological Agenda on Continental Integration," paper presented to the Conference on "The Nation-State Versus Continental Integration: Canada and Western Europe Compared," Institute for Canadian Studies, University of Augsburg, December 11-14, 1990.

10   An Angus Reid poll in the early fall of 1990 gave the Reform party 36 per cent of the Alberta federal vote, compared to 31 per cent for the Liberals, 18 per cent for the Conservatives, and 16 per cent for the NDP. Other polls have not been as encouraging for the Conservatives.

11   The change was particularly pronounced in Alberta, which had failed to elect an MP to the government side of the House since 1979, or 1972 if we put aside the Joe Clark interregnum. Now Alberta had three powerful Cabinet ministers: Joe Clark, Harvie André and Don Mazankowski.

12   This conclusion is based on some 40 Alberta forums, panel discussions and phone-in programs on the Meech Lake Accord in which the author had the opportunity (or misfortune) to participate.

13   It is interesting to note that, in his speeches, Preston Manning draws a distinction between old and new politics, while placing the Reform Party firmly on the side of the new. The party's name should also be noted: The Reform Party of Canada.

14   The Getty government is concerned that any sustained increase in oil prices will generate irresistible consumer and central Canadian pressure for Ottawa's intervention.

Alberta's new-found, or once again found, wealth will be a less tempting target for other governments if it is directed to deficit reduction.

15   Thomas Poguntke, "New Politics and Party Systems: The Emergence of a New Type of Party?" *West European Politics*, 10:1 (January 1987), p. 77.

16   The overwhelmingly positive manner in which respondents reply to virtually any environmental question has caused a major headache for the polling industry. Even questions such as "would you sacrifice your first-born child to improve the quality of the environment?" tend to elicit a positive response. This breathless enthusiasm for environmentalism has elicited some scepticism among survey professionals.

17   Gregg O. Kvistad, "Between State and Society: Green Political Ideology in the Mid-1980s," *West European Politics*, 13:1 (January 1987), p. 212.

18   Christopher Manes, *Green Rage: Radical Environmentalism and the Unmaking of Civilization* (Boston: Little Brown and Company, 1990).

19   John E. Carroll, "Trans-Boundary Air Quality Relations," *Canadian-American Public Policy,* 2 (July 1990), p. 2.

20   Ibid., p. 3.

21   On a smaller scale, more radical environmentalists such as Manes (*Green Rage*, p. 25) also chafe at the political lines which establish parks, national forests and wilderness areas, but which, in so doing, fragment and isolate biotic communities.

22   Wolfgang Rudig, "Peace and Ecology Movements in Western Europe," *West European Politics*, 11:1 (January 1988), p. 37.

23   By early 1990, there were approximately 1,200 identified environmental groups in Canada (Farley Mowat, *Rescue The Earth! Conversations With Green Crusaders* (Toronto: McClelland and Stewart, 1990), p. 9).

24   Poguntke, "New Politics and Party Systems," p. 80.

25   John Dafoe, "Attack on Easterners is bunk," *The Globe and Mail* [Toronto] October 20, 1990, p. D1.

26   Ross Howard, "20% cut in carbon dioxide urged," *The Globe and Mail* [Toronto], October 8, 1990, pp. A1-A2.

CHAPTER 5

WAITING FOR THE FUTURE: ATLANTIC CANADA AFTER MEECH LAKE

James Bickerton

Résumé: Ce chapitre examine le rôle de la région de l'Atlantique dans la politique intérieure du pays, ainsi que le rôle du gouvernement fédéral dans cette région, en ce qui concerne trois domaines-clefs: la réforme constitutionnelle, la politique régionale et le développement économique. On soutient que l'engagement fédéral en matière de redistribution et développement régionaux représente la pierre angulaire de l'intégration fiscale et politique de la région dans la fédération canadienne. Si les gouvernements de cette région ont adopté diverses positions et stratégies constitutionnelles au cours des négociations du lac Meech, ils n'ont jamais cessé d'exprimer leur désir commun de voir continuer ces politiques fédérales. Le statu quo, et ainsi la place qui revient à la région de l'Atlantique, est loin d'être stable, vu les réalités naissantes des années 1990, dont le libre-échange, la réduction du déficit, et un état poussé de crise constitutionnelle. Malgré les initiatives de cette région favorisant une intégration et une réforme régionales, les dépenses fédérales resteront essentielles à la stabilité et au bien-être de cette région.

Abstract: This chapter examines Atlantic Canada's role in national politics, and the role of the federal government in the Atlantic region, in three key areas: constitutional reform, regional policy and economic development. It argues that federal commitment to policies of regional redistribution and development are the cornerstone of the fiscal and political integration of the region into the Canadian federation. Governments in the Atlantic region, while adopting differing constitutional positions and strategies throughout the Meech Lake round of negotiations, have consistently expressed a common concern for the continuance of such policies. However, in light of the emerging economic, fiscal and political realities of the 1990s—including free trade, deficit reduction and severe constitutional crisis—the status quo, and Atlantic Canada's place within it, seems far from secure. Maritime initiatives toward regional integration and reforms notwithstanding, how Ottawa spends in the region will remain central to the stability and welfare of Canada's Atlantic provinces.

In the aftermath of the failed Meech Lake Accord, the Atlantic region faces a period of political and economic uncertainty. The Free Trade Agreement has introduced new economic constraints and possibilities, fiscal arrangements in place since the 1960s are undergoing change, and continuation of the constitutional status quo seems highly dubious. The Atlantic provinces, however, are not particularly well-placed to shape their future.

While it is true that two Atlantic premiers were central to the Meech Lake debate and the events surrounding its demise, the region may now be able to exercise little or no influence on the course of events. Perhaps now more than ever, political and economic events seem beyond the control of governments in Atlantic Canada.

Since the re-election of the Conservatives in 1988, the direction of federal policy has been fairly clear and consistent. The passage and implementation of the Free Trade Agreement, with the restrictions it imposes on the use of non-tariff barriers and government subsidies, will limit and reorient the role of the federal government in regional development. Not only are the kind and direction of government supports for regional economies likely to be affected, but the sheer size of the federal role as well, especially in light of the current priority given to deficit reduction in Ottawa. The Atlantic provinces cannot expect to escape unscathed the federal retreat from economic intervention implied by these policies.

By the same token, the federal policy process (and Ottawa's spending plans) inevitably will be affected by the regional ramifications of past policies. Thus, in the case of Atlantic Canada, federal policies have created an entrenched interest in a strong central government able to redistribute national wealth; they have encouraged individual and governmental reliance on federal income and revenue supports; they have done little to strengthen and integrate the regional economy; and a key regional industry under federal control has been allowed to overdevelop its own forces of production, with regrettable long term human and social consequences.

This chapter will examine three key areas affecting Atlantic Canada—constitutional reform, federal regional policy and economic development—where change seems inevitable and imminent. Current circumstances have produced a growing political uneasiness in the region about the future; ultimately, however, this tension and insecurity may provide the necessary impetus for the construction of a truly regional polity and economy, and a policy agenda that will give Atlantic Canadians, at long last, greater influence over their own fate.

CONSTITUTIONAL REFORM

In 1981, the four Atlantic Provinces joined with all the other provinces except Quebec as signatories to a federal-provincial agreement that formed the basis for the *Constitution Act, 1982*, with its Charter of Rights, amending formula, and specific guarantees for women and Aboriginal people. Also entrenched in the new Constitution were the principle of equalization and the practice of equalization payments from the federal government to the poorer provinces. Although no specific formula or level of payments was indicated in the Constitution, the inclusion of this item in the supreme law of Canada was a clear victory for the poorer provinces, and especially for the Atlantic provinces. Over the two preceding decades, equalization had become the foundation of fiscal relations between provinces in the Atlantic region and—through the federal government—those in the rest of Canada. Placing it in the Constitution affirmed its sanctity and its centrality to intergovernmental and inter-regional relations.

Other than the fundamental item of equalization, there was little in the 1982 agreement that was specifically of concern to Atlantic Canada. Premier Hatfield of New Brunswick, a strong supporter of Trudeau's constitutional strategy during 1980-82, secured the constitutional entrenchment of bilingualism for his province. At the opposite extreme, Premier Peckford of Newfoundland was a leading exponent (along with Premiers Levesque and Lougheed) of a more decentralized federation reflecting a "compact" theory of Confederation.[1] For the most part, however, Atlantic premiers were wary of any erosion of federal capacity to redistribute wealth, or of the power of all governments to take measures to address regional disparities. In this connection, a concession was won on mobility rights. Limitations on the right of citizens to work in any part of the country would be granted insofar as such limitations involved a government program aimed at ameliorating economic disadvantages in provinces with high unemployment rates. Other substantive issues of concern to some or all Atlantic provinces, such as ownership of offshore resources or jurisdiction over the fishery, were absent from the final constitutional agreement.

In 1987, all four Atlantic premiers—Peckford, Buchanan, Hatfield, and Ghiz—endorsed the Meech Lake Accord, but then elections in New Brunswick and Newfoundland proved to be the undoing of this initial consensus. Soon after Richard Hatfield signed the Accord, and before the New Brunswick legislature could ratify it, he lost every seat in a 1987 provincial election. His successor as Premier, Liberal Frank McKenna, was a strong critic of the Accord and the process by which it was devised. In Newfoundland, Brian Peckford stepped down as Premier. In the ensuing election, the Liberals under Clyde Wells took power. Wells' sharp-edged criticism of the Accord became progressively more strident as his negative public pronouncements continued to draw little or no response from Ottawa. Unlike New Brunswick, however, the Newfoundland legislature already had ratified the Accord. So Wells would threaten to use, then finally to invoke the province's constitutional right to rescind its earlier ratification of the Accord and join New Brunswick and Manitoba as dissenting provinces.

Traditional regional concerns animated the Atlantic dissidents: they feared that allowing provinces to opt out of new national shared cost programs would discourage new federal initiatives; that equalization might be eroded; that the clause in the Accord designating Quebec a "distinct society" might undermine the equality of provinces and relegate provinces like Newfoundland to a constitutionally subordinate position; and that the federal role in promoting bilingualism would be limited or undermined.

Other concerns and criticisms, however, were less traditional in nature, and reflected new preoccupations with citizen rights and the role and performance of Canadian political institutions: Parliament, the federal system, the Supreme Court and the Charter of Rights. These criticisms—that rights in the Charter would be affected as the result of the distinct society clause; that behind-closed-door elite bargaining over constitutional matters was not a legitimate process of constitutional reform; that badly needed Senate reform would become impossible since the Accord demanded unanimity—were less Atlantic Canadian concerns *per se* than emblematic of a major shift in Anglophone Canadian political culture. The dissenting premiers on Meech Lake—McKenna, Wells, Filmon—were able to garner strong public support for their position not just in their own provinces but throughout the rest of Canada outside Quebec. This public reaction supports the argument of a number of observers of constitutional politics in Canada that the experience of constitution-making between 1980-82, and the subsequent widespread public acceptance of the Charter and its discourse of citizen rights, had fundamentally altered Canadians' attitude toward the Constitution and their place within it.[2]

The denouement of the Meech Lake round of constitutional negotiation is well known. Wells reluctantly agreed to place a slightly reworked Accord before the Newfoundland Legislature after an intense last-minute negotiation involving all first ministers—the Prime Minister's "roll of the dice." With a negative Newfoundland vote appearing ever more likely, however, federal authorities attempted to apply some last-minute pressure. In the confusion, a final vote on the Accord in the Newfoundland Legislature was deferred by an embittered Wells, even as Native legislator Elijah Harper was preventing, through procedural delay tactics, a similar last-minute ratification vote in the Manitoba Legislature. In New Brunswick, McKenna's 11th hour conversion ensured easy passage for the Accord through his Legislature. McKenna's was not a wholly popular decision with English-speaking New Brunswickers. As he noted in hindsight, "My position suffered by being associated with a process many Canadians found reprehensible."[3]

Following the death of the Meech Lake Accord, only McKenna among the Atlantic premiers continued to give a high priority to the constitutional stalemate. New Brunswick established a constitutional review committee to examine the province's role in Confederation. The committee is soliciting comment from New Brunswick residents and is to provide guidance to the provincial government on a broad range of provincial and national issues related to constitutional reform. No deadline was set for the committee, whose report eventually will be laid before a select committee of the provincial legislature. McKenna has also suggested that Quebec should not decide Canada's future alone, that the other provinces must remain active in "redefining our relationships and future," and that the federal government must play a leadership role in this process. McKenna himself has called for a new Rowell-Sirois Commission to examine Canada's fundamental fiscal arrangements. He also suggested a set of principles or guidelines for continuing constitutional review that reflect a sensitivity both to criticisms of the substance and process of Meech Lake, as well as the implications of accommodating Quebec's bottom-line demands: any new Constitution would have to be flexible enough to reflect shifts in Canadian society or values; personal freedoms, minority rights and linguistic equality must be constitutionally protected; Canadians should have an opportunity to express their views on proposed constitutional changes; and provinces need not be constitutionally identical.[4]

In the post-Meech period, Newfoundland's Premier Clyde Wells retains the support of the Newfoundland electorate and enjoys considerably enhanced status within the federal Liberal Party and throughout the rest of Canada more generally. Under these circumstances it is unlikely that Wells will alter fundamentally his principled stand on the main points of contention: the Charter's paramountcy, his opposition to constitutionally entrenched "special status" for Quebec or any other province, and the fundamental importance of a reformed Senate that would enhance regional influence. Thus, on hearing the news that Ottawa will cede wide-ranging powers over immigration to Quebec, Wells argued that other provinces should be offered the same deal; as well, he wished to determine whether the reported agreement respected the Charter of Rights.[5] Wells' own preference for constitutional reform, given the discredited Meech process, is a national public constitutional convention that would draft a new Constitution over a period of several years, and submit it for the approval of Canadians in a popular referendum.[6]

Nova Scotia and Prince Edward Island have been less active on the constitutional issue since the death of the Meech Lake Accord. While Nova Scotia has seldom been an innovator or taken a leadership role in constitutional matters, Premier John Buchanan's resignation as premier (and appointment to the Senate) in 1990 further distracted his already troubled Conservative government. The leadership contest which followed did not concern itself greatly with constitutional matters, revolving instead around the issues of honesty in government and political patronage. However, the new premier, Donald Cameron, quickly demonstrated that he had learned the lessons of Meech Lake when he promised to create a commission comprised of non-elected citizens to look at the future of Atlantic Canada in Confederation.[7] Prince Edward Island Premier Joe Ghiz, a strong supporter of Meech Lake and a vocal critic of the Newfoundland premier's principled (characterized by some as obstinate) opposition to the Accord, did not display any eagerness to revive or rejoin the constitutional debate in the wake of Meech Lake's demise, preferring to adopt a "wait and see" approach to developments in Quebec and elsewhere.

In some ways, the reaction of Atlantic Canadians to the Meech Lake Accord is similar to the region's reaction to the Mulroney government's other great first term initiative, the Free Trade Agreement with the United States. While three of four Atlantic premiers supported the Free Trade Agreement, all of them fretted about the fate of regional development and Ottawa's social programs, and made clear that their support for the federal government's initiative was premised on assurances that these programs would not be affected. The electorate in the region proved to be less sanguine. When the idea of free trade was first mooted, Atlantic Canadians were among its strongest supporters.[8] But after an intense debate during the 1988 federal election—which in Atlantic Canada largely focussed on the threat posed by the FTA to national social programs—the Conservatives managed to win only a minority of seats in three of the four provinces (they were shut out in the fourth) and only 10 in the whole region, compared to the 25 they won in 1984.

The debate over the Meech Lake Accord followed a similar trajectory. As with the Free Trade Agreement, the more debate there was about the Accord, and the possible changes or alterations to the federal role it might imply, the more it seemed to incite a defensive regional response. In the postwar era, political solidarities among Atlantic Canadians were created by federal policies and programs that became integral to the social and economic fabric of the region; political threats to the form and content of those specific programs, or in general to a continuing federal role in regional redistribution and stabilization, were bound to produce a largely unfavourable regional response. In the case of Meech Lake, however, opposition went beyond this regional reaction; it was part of a broader Canadian phenomenon, tied to changes in the political culture of all of Canada outside Quebec, changes induced by both the process and the substance of the 1982 Constitution. Atlantic Canadians for the most part shared the new norms, values and attitudes that lay behind the jaundiced view that the majority came to hold with regard to Meech Lake: no more backroom deals between political elites; in future an open and aboveboard constitutional review process; the rights and freedoms protected in the Charter must not be threatened or undermined.[9] While there was a regional component to Atlantic Canada's reaction to the Meech Lake Accord, then, it can best be understood within this wider context.

Regional Policy: Equalization and Social Programs

For some time it has been accepted as fact that the Atlantic region is too dependent on government spending. In some quarters this dependence on what has come to be characterized as "handouts" from Ottawa is seen to be excessive to the point where the outlook of the people of the region is being distorted; they are seen to be losing their individual initiative and their desire for self-improvement and self-reliance. The "psychology of dependence" in this way becomes the primary explanation for continuing dependence—the chief cause of the region's economic problems rather than a symptom.[10]

Beginning in the 1920s, Maritime provincial governments made the argument for some form of annual payment from Ottawa that would help them cover the cost of providing basic services to their residents. Without some such payment—one based on the difference between the actual cost of providing such basic services and the ability of provincial governments to raise the necessary revenues without resorting to prohibitive levels of taxation—the already noticeable disparity among provinces in the level and scope of public services would continue to grow. During the Depression years what had been a regional problem associated with the three Maritime provinces became a national problem. In 1940, the Royal Commission on Dominion-Provincial Relations (the Rowell-Sirois Commission) recognized that fundamental problems of vertical and horizontal equity lay at the base of federal-provincial fiscal relations.[11] They endorsed the principle involved in annual payments to the poorer provinces to enable them to provide an average level of services to their residents and recommended that the federal government make National Adjustment Grants to the provinces to achieve this objective. It was not until 1957, however, that this recommendation was given substance with the first equalization formula, and 1967 before all major sources of provincial revenue were included in this formula, ushering in the era of full equalization. By 1970 per capita provincial revenues, which had once diverged widely, were very close together.[12]

Equalization payments are today the cornerstone of the federal government's regional policy, and of enormous importance to the four Atlantic provinces. This is made clear not only by the size of these annual payments relative to provincial budgets in the Atlantic region (see Table 5.1) but, as noted above, by the entrenchment of equalization in the 1982 Constitution. Even so, in an era of government spending cuts, worries about potential threats to the level of payments to the poorer provinces (only the **principle** of equalization payments was constitutionally enshrined) led the New Brunswick premier to suggest a change to the ill-fated Meech Accord that would have mandated the Senate to review every five years the Government's performance in meeting its constitutional commitment to equalization.

While equalization payments are an essential component of the annual budgets of all four Atlantic provinces, they have greater importance for some than others. Moreover, it is not only the Atlantic provinces that are more or less permanent recipients of such payments. Manitoba and Quebec also benefit from equalization, though markedly less so on a per capita basis. It does appear that over the past decade, two of the Atlantic region's provinces—Newfoundland and Prince Edward Island— have **increased** their dependence on equalization, while the other two— Nova Scotia and New Brunswick—have **reduced** their dependence (see Table 5.1). This suggests that the 1980s were particularly hard on the "poorest of the poor," while those provinces within the region that traditionally have been better off have seen some improvement in the strength of their economies (and thus their revenue bases) relative to the national average.

Amongst other federal transfers, Unemployment Insurance payments continue to be of proportionately greater significance to residents of the Atlantic region than elsewhere in Canada. But again, not all provincial economies in Atlantic Canada demonstrate similar levels of dependence on this source of funds. Indeed, in 1988-89, Nova Scotia was roughly at the same level as Quebec and British Columbia, while Newfoundland's per capita rate of benefit payments was more than twice as high (see Table 5.2).

Table 5.1
General Purpose Transfers as a Proportion of
Total Provincial Expenditures
1989-90, 1979-80
(millions of dollars)

	PEI	NFLD	NB	NS	MAN	QUE
General Purpose Transfers	202	947	876	886	873	3650
Total Provincial Expenditure	665	3280	3719	4285	5986	39,556
GPT as % of Provincial Budget						
(1989-90)	30%	29%	24%	21%	15%	9%
(1979-80)	28%	24%	27%	25%	18%	10%

In 1989, 96 per cent of all General Purpose Transfers were
equalization payments.

Source: Canadian Tax Foundation, *Provincial and Municipal Finances*, 1989.

Table 5.2
Unemployment Insurance Benefit Payments
1988-89

	(millions of dollars)	Per Capita
Newfoundland	732.8	1289
Prince Edward Island	130.2	1008
Nova Scotia	510.5	578
New Brunswick	599.4	838
Quebec	3422.4	514
Ontario	2393.7	253
Manitoba	357.4	330
Saskatchewan	292.6	290
Alberta	879.4	292
British Columbia	1550.6	515
Northwest Territories	19.6	373
Yukon	20.6	811
Canada	10,912.0	419

Source: Council of Maritime Premiers, *Federal Expenditures as a Tool for Regional Development.*

Unemployment Insurance (UI) has been an important component of the federal government's regional policy since at least 1971, "when entrance requirements were relaxed, redistribution across income classes and regions was explicitly fostered, and various 'income security provisions'... were included, softening the strict insurance aspects of the system."[13] Changes were made in 1977 which introduced variable entrance requirements and benefits depending on the regional unemployment rate. The interregional redistribution effect was considerable. For example, as estimated by N.H. Lithwick, Newfoundland's regional benefit from UI (i.e. the extra amount received due to regionally variable eligibility requirements) in 1977-78 was $153 million, or 5.4 per cent of personal income. Other Atlantic provinces also benefited, though to a lesser extent (e.g. the benefits to Nova Scotia amounted to only 1.6 per cent of personal income, slightly higher than Quebec's regional benefit from UI). The total estimated amount conferred in 1977-78 in regional benefits from the Unemployment Insurance system was $900 million (over half of which went to Quebec), an amount 80 per cent larger than the Department of Regional Economic Expansion's entire budget for that year.[14]

The regional component of UI has made proposed changes to the system a regional issue. Thus, when the federal government's 1977 reforms initially proposed to strip away the regional component of UI (i.e., the regionally variable eligibility requirements), Atlantic region MPs of all party stripes joined forces to successfully scuttle the measure.[15] A similar fate befell the 1985-86 Commission of Inquiry on Unemployment Insurance (the Forget Commission). The Commission itself was badly split on its recommendations to the Government, with a minority dissenting report ferociously attacking the main report and Forget himself. The main report recommended sweeping changes to UI, including the elimination of regionally extended benefits and the variable entrance requirement, a change that would have saved the federal government $2.8 billion, but cost Atlantic Canada and Quebec dearly. Employment Minister Benoit Bouchard repudiated the final report in May 1987, and announced that there would be no fundamental reform to UI.[16] However, this proved to be only a temporary shelving of the issue.

The importance of programs like Unemployment Insurance to residents of Atlantic Canada can be gauged by the debate within the region over the free trade deal during the 1988 federal election and the regional outcome of that election. In fact, it did not take long after the 1988 election for regional concerns over the fate of social programs such as UI to be given some substance. Bill C-21, given Royal Assent in the fall of 1990, makes significant changes to the Unemployment Insurance system. The new legislation is designed to "save" nearly $1.3 billion in UI expenditures by tightening conditions of access. It will also cut the federal contribution, making the program exclusively self-financing, as it is in the US. Regional unemployment rates will still be a factor in determining conditions of access and duration of benefits, but entrance requirements and benefit periods have been raised for all areas but those with the highest unemployment levels (e.g. rural Newfoundland). This can be expected to result in a significant decline of the "regional component" of UI, with a narrowing of extended regional benefits to only the most desperate areas within Atlantic Canada and elsewhere.[17]

Immediate threats to equalization, presumably one of the "sacred cows" of Confederation, are less apparent. In the long run, however, as pressures increase for all Canadian provinces to emphasize the competitiveness of their economies over all other virtues, corresponding pressures will mount to decrease the burdens on the productivity of those economies, including and perhaps especially, the compensation they now indirectly pay to lagging regions. In the context of an increasingly permeable Canadian economy with stronger north-south trade links, interregional transfers make less sense from the perspective of contributing provinces such as Ontario. If the propensity of Atlantic Canadians to consume Ontario products and services declines as their consumption of American products and services grows, the economic logic of transfer payments within an integrated national economy is weakened. With a diminishing return to the Ontario economy relative to the burden imposed on that province by equalization payments, continuing political support for such payments will be less assured.

Another potential threat to equalization is tied to Canada's future constitutional order. What if the province of Quebec, a major receipient of equalization payments, leaves Confederation? On the one hand, while Quebec receives **on a per capita basis** much less in equalization than do any of the Atlantic provinces, it has always been the largest single recipient of equalization payments. Indeed, Quebec's annual grant is almost equivalent to the total amount transferred to the other five "permanent" beneficiaries of the program. In other words, the overall cost of equalization, in a Canada without Quebec, would be considerably reduced. On the other hand, Quebec independence would also mean the departure of a strong political ally for the other provincial beneficiaries of equalization (and presumably one of the key guarantors of the program's continuation). To say the least, in a Canada without Quebec, the political foundations of this central pillar of Canada's regional policy would be weakened.

ECONOMIC DEVELOPMENT

Regional Development Agencies

While fiscal transfers such as equalization or regionally extended unemployment insurance benefits help to ameliorate the effects of regional economic disparities, they do not deal directly with the underlying cause of those disparities: a less productive regional economy. Formal federal government recognition of this came in the early 1960s, with the establishment of the Agricultural and Rural Development Agency (ARDA) and the Atlantic Development Board (ADB). In 1969, these agencies were superseded by a more urban-focussed Department of Regional Economic Expansion (DREE). Originally, DREE was viewed as Atlantic Canada's agency in Ottawa. Its first minister, Jean Marchand, proclaimed that DREE would be remiss if it spent less than 80 per cent of its budget in Atlantic Canada.[18] It was also intended that DREE would undertake strategic economic planning for the Atlantic region as a whole, with at least two objectives: first, by removing the regional development emphasis and effort from rural development to urban growth poles within the region and secondly, by replacing direct federal-provincial negotiations with unilateral federal initiatives that would reflect a region-wide economic strategy.[19]

In the event, the designs of federal planners in DREE were more or less stillborn. The presumption that the federal government had, or was capable of producing a regional industrial strategy for Atlantic Canada, was mistaken.[20] Moreover, a key organizing concept for the Department's programs—the urban growth pole idea—was poorly developed and encountered political resistance from rural areas. Most tellingly, perhaps, was the obstacle posed by the need for provincial compliance and co-operation in the development field. There was both a program and a political price to pay for running roughshod over provincial sensibilities, and ultimately this more than anything may have determined a change in federal approach to regional development. For the balance of its departmental existence, DREE worked through formal federal-provincial agreements known as General Development Agreements that assumed that province was coterminous with region. While this bilateral approach was applauded by provincial governments, it sacrificed the incorporation of an overall regional perspective or strategy to the exigencies of intergovernmental negotiations.[21]

In the 1980s, as part of Trudeau's "new federalism" aimed at politically disentangling federal and provincial programs and spending, DREE was replaced by DRIE (Department of Regional Industrial Expansion) and the GDAs by ERDAs (Economic and Regional Development Agreements).[22] In the second half of the decade, under the Mulroney Conservatives and in a new era of "co-operative federalism," the hated DRIE (businesses and governments in the Atlantic region perceived it as biased toward industrial development in Central Canada) was in turn replaced. In a return to the days of the Atlantic Development Board, regional development responsibilities for Atlantic Canada were handed over to a separate agency, with a regional advisory board, reporting directly to a federal cabinet minister. The Atlantic Canada Opportunities Agency (ACOA) began operations in 1987, with a $1 billion budget over five years. In contrast to the infrastructure emphasis that characterized previous regional development spending, the new agency was mandated to focus on small scale projects and businesses and entrepreneurship development. It would also have responsibility for co-ordination of all federal economic programs in Atlantic Canada.[23]

ACOA was conceived and announced at a time when Atlantic Canada was only slowly overcoming the effects of the 1981-82 recession, while central Canada was enjoying an almost unprecedented stretch of economic growth and prosperity. Indeed, the "overheating" southern Ontario economy was keeping interest rates high, making economic matters even more difficult for the peripheral regions. The net result was growing regional disparities, and the re-politicization of these disparities, such that it became impossible for the federal government to avoid a new initiative in the regional development field. Yet only two years after ACOA legislation finally was given Royal Assent in December 1988, a new recession cast a pall on the Canadian economy as a whole, adding to the hardship in the Atlantic region caused by a disastrous decline in the groundfish sector of the Atlantic fishery. What kind of success can be hoped for under these conditions?

The inauguration of ACOA brought praise from regional businesses and politicians, although there were some concerns that the initial monies—$200 million a year for the four provinces—would not be sufficient to undertake the very large mandate for the region given the new Agency.[24] Then in May 1989, the federal government announced that this amount would have to be spread over seven years instead of five. Considerable claims were made for the Agency nonetheless. The minister responsible for ACOA, Elmer MacKay, made the rather dubious boast that $600 million, or almost two thirds of ACOA's total allotment, had been committed in 1988-89 alone. One third of all new investment in Atlantic Canada for that period, he said, was "ACOA-assisted."[25] This, of course, raises questions about how carefully or well those hundreds of millions were being spent. As has always been the case with regional development, the danger is that the Agency's political success counted for more than its program objectives, and for that reason, any number of high-profile projects would be supported, especially in the run-up to a federal election. This too-familiar pattern, of course, would not be the redirection of Ottawa's approach to regional development which was advocated by Donald Savoie and promised with ACOA's announcement. Nonetheless, it is plausible that just such an approach was a factor in a number of major business failures in 1990 involving substantial amounts of ACOA funds. In this connection, the government has launched a comprehensive review of ACOA's Cape Breton subsidiary, Enterprise Cape Breton. Announcement of the review followed quickly on the heels of an RCMP announcement of a criminal investigation into Technitread Tire Manufacturing Ltd., one of the failed businesses that just three days before the 1988 election campaign had received approval for $2 million in ACOA grants. Soon after, a second RCMP probe was announced into another ACOA client that went out of production in 1990 after receiving a total of $13 million in government aid.[26]

Besides the usual financial inducements to business, ACOA was also meant to be an advocate of the region's interests within the federal government and a co-ordinator of federal programs in the region. ACOA's designer, Donald Savoie, saw this as one of the Agency's most important and difficult tasks. Savoie also suggested that ACOA, due to its regionally sensitive structure and the clarity of its mandate, was in a better position to take up this challenge than any of its predecessor agencies.[27] But according to ACOA's second president, Peter Lesaux, over the first few years of ACOA's operation this advocacy role had not been performed very effectively.[28] This can hardly be considered surprising, given the federal bureaucracy's historic antipathy towards the whole concept of regional development.[29]

As well, ACOA does not appear to have even attempted to provide or develop a regional strategy or any sense of economic direction for the region beyond the vagaries of nurturing and rewarding indigenous entrepreneurship. This accords with the free market assumptions of much of the Conservatives' economic policy, the very same assumptions that had to be abandoned by Ottawa prior to the creation of ACOA when Mulroney admitted that the Atlantic region was not partaking in the central Canadian economic prosperity of the mid-1980s. This lack of a regional strategy makes policy drift and partisan political intervention more likely; it also hampers ACOA in its advocacy role, as the agency by and large is left without any strong sense of what it should be promoting in Ottawa, the "vision" that is in need of policy support. The Canadian experience has amply demonstrated that there is virtually no chance that one peripheral federal agency acting alone can ever eradicate, or even substantially reduce, the country's historic pattern of regional disparities. Without bringing the broader resources of the Ottawa bureaucracy to bear on the problem within the context of a more coherent regional approach, the future prospects for significant headway in addressing this problem seem slim.

Economic Development: Ottawa's Future Role

Regional development has always been affected by the actions of more than just one federal agency. A number of other federal policies and departments have had a traditional importance to the Atlantic region's economy as well. Under a regime of reducing government services in the name of deficit reduction, however, government spending decisions affecting Atlantic Canada tend to have negative implications for the regional economy. Major reductions in passenger rail service and rail subsidy cuts fall into this category. Other measures may be more indirect in their regional implications, but just as real: the privatization of Crown Corporations such as Air Canada which allows for a reduction in regional services; directives to Canada Post that it become profitable, leading to the closure of rural post offices; or budget cuts to the CBC, resulting in the elimination of all sub-regional production facilities. The point is that any reduction in the level or kind of service provided by public sector institutions in a region that remains inordinately dependent on public sector employment and spending, is bound to have a negative impact. Should such reductions and cutbacks continue, their cumulative effect will be profoundly negative.

Developments within the Atlantic fishery have not helped matters. A dramatic decline in groundfish stocks off the Atlantic coast has forced the Department of Fisheries and Oceans to drastically lower its fish allocations, a move which in turn has forced the closure of a number of fish processing facilities in the region.[30] Newfoundland and some areas of Nova Scotia have been particularly hard-hit by the crisis, the magnitude and nature of which appears to imply a long-term decline in the total fishing effort off the east coast. Indeed, the federal response to the crisis seems to be premised on just that. In the spring of 1990, it announced a $584 million, five-year adjustment program aimed at easing fishery workers out of the industry and retraining them for other jobs.[31] The Department of Fisheries and Oceans (DFO) has also begun assigning individual boat quotas, as a means of reducing in size, "a fishing fleet that is too big, too powerful and too competitive for fish stocks to bear." Individual quotas will be determined by the amount of fish caught by a fisherman in the best two of the past four years, setting in train a "cannibalization" process whereby a significant number of fishermen will be forced to trade their quotas and sell their boats, thereby rationalizing the fleet.[32]

For some time, provincial responses within Atlantic Canada to the fishery's problems have been at odds. Newfoundlanders and Nova Scotians are the two major participants in the Atlantic fishery, but adopt conflicting constitutional and management positions that are based on a long-standing competition between the provinces over access to and control over the resource. It was for this reason that Premier Brian Peckford of Newfoundland secured a provision in the Meech Lake Accord that would have made fisheries a perpetual item of discussion at federal-provincial constitutional meetings. The chief bone of contention between the two provinces is the issue of shared management of the fishery resource: Newfoundland wants a larger role and Nova Scotia wants to leave it with the federal government. The explanation for these opposing views is not difficult to discern: Newfoundland wants to sharply limit access to Newfoundland and Labrador fishing grounds by non-Newfoundland boats. A Newfoundland government White Paper on the fishery, a blueprint for the next decade, is due in the spring of 1991. The policy differences between the two main fishing provinces, however, are likely to remain for some time to come, given the apparently zero-sum nature of their conflict.[33]

If current trends within the Atlantic fishery continue—and all indications are they will—the transition to a smaller fishery seems inevitable. Currently, there are 250,000 Atlantic Canadians living in communities that have no other economic base but the fishery.[34] No doubt, given the fishery's problems, in coming years many of these people will continue to experience considerable economic and social stress. An ongoing restructuring and downsizing of the industry also suggests substantial direct and indirect costs to government, far beyond the amount already committed in the form of "transition costs." Federal-provincial and provincial-provincial relations in this field, thorny at the best of times, are unlikely to experience vast improvement in the near future. A strong, activist federal role, and innovative, flexible policy responses, will be needed.

A continuing role is also required in the field of transportation, a constant concern in geographically-fragmented Atlantic Canada. Highway construction and improvement have always been a central element of federal-provincial regional development agreements in Atlantic Canada, and this preoccupation seems destined to continue in the future. Indeed, with the total elimination of the Newfoundland railway and a substantial reduction in passenger rail service in the Maritimes, traffic on the region's highways, and especially truck traffic, is increasing. All four Atlantic provinces agree on the need for federal monies to help provinces upgrade and extend the regional transportation network.

In this connection, proposals for a fixed link crossing between Prince Edward Island and the mainland have been a prominent issue on PEI since 1988. Proponents laud the increased efficiency and lower costs in moving goods and people to and from the Island that such a link would afford; opponents warn of the dangers for the "Island way of life." Although the project is temporarily on hold due to an unfavourable environmental review of the potential effects on the lobster fishery in the area, both federal and provincial politicians have committed themselves to further investigation of the idea with a view to reviving it.[35]

As for the other provinces, both New Brunswick and Nova Scotia have made twinning of the Trans-Canada Highway through their provinces a major objective to be attained by the end of the decade. New Brunswick's McKenna has given highway twinning, described as a public safety issue as well as an economic development issue, a high priority. While negotiations with Ottawa are ongoing, New Brunswick will proceed with its plans to twin its highway with or without federal participation, despite the enormous costs involved. Spurred on by McKenna's example, Nova Scotia has made a similar commitment to its residents, though according it somewhat less urgency than does New Brunswick.[36] In Newfoundland, a federal-provincial agreement was reached in 1988 over the closure of the Newfoundland Railway. The Government of Newfoundland released the federal government from its constitutional commitment to maintain a rail link on the Island in return for a $500 million contribution toward the upgrading of Newfoundland highways.[37]

On other matters, however, Newfoundland stands somewhat apart from its east coast neighbours. In a province with the highest unemployment rates and lowest average incomes in Canada, there is a vision of a better economic future, at the centre of which is offshore oil. In September 1990, the $5.2 billion Hibernia oil project was finally approved, with involvement by Ottawa, Newfoundland and a consortium of four oil companies led by Mobil Oil of Canada. The project is expected to create 35,000 jobs during the five-year construction phase. The federal contribution is $2.7 billion in cash and loan guarantees. But the federal treasury should more than recover this in royalties and reduced equalization payments during the production phase. The provincial contribution to getting Hibernia started, under a statement of principles signed in 1988 (before Clyde Wells took power), is a raft of concessions that one Newfoundland economist estimates will slash the province's net income from royalties to a paltry $4 million annually. (This includes an almost dollar-for-dollar reduction in equalization payments once Newfoundland begins receiving royalties.) Premier Wells, while admitting that Newfoundland has made "one hell of a lot of concessions," hopes that Hibernia will merely be the first of a number of offshore oil developments, to be followed before the decade is out by Terra Nova, White Rose and other yet to be discovered fields. Presumably, it would not be necessary to favour the latter developments with the same deal given the Hibernia consortium, and other oil-related economic activities—such as petrochemicals—would become possible.[38]

While Newfoundland looks to Hibernia as an indicator of its future economic potential, Nova Scotia will be the first Canadian province to bring on-stream an offshore oil field. But the $565 million development of the Cohasset and Panuke oil fields off Sable Island, expected to start producing oil in 1992, is only one-tenth the magnitude of Hibernia in economic terms.[39] So Nova Scotia remains wedded to a more traditional energy strategy, one involving ever-larger quantities of Nova Scotia coal, despite the environmental costs associated with this option. Nova Scotia Power Corporation's $450 million Point Aconi plant currently under construction is the clearest case in point: the state-of-the-art coal-fired generating plant will consume 400,000 tons of coal per year using a high-technology process that will reduce acid rain-causing emissions by up to 90 per cent, but also produce up to 1.5 million tons of carbon dioxide emissions annually. The latter are thought to be a major contributor to global warming. Environmental opponents of the project also claim that the plant's enormous water requirements will have a deleterious effect on both nearby residents and the local ecosystem. A full-scale environmental assessment of Point Aconi, however, was never done. The federal government did not admit to the need for such an assessment and provincial legislation was altered to prevent the provincial Public Utilities Board from reviewing or halting the project.[40] It was this blatant political move by then Premier John Buchanan which gave impetus to those groups opposing the project. In contrast, a much larger coal-fired project in northern New Brunswick (the Belledune Generating Station) has produced little public outcry or controversy.[41]

At the same time, another proposed energy mega-project strongly backed by the Nova Scotia government was not supported by Ottawa. Like Point Aconi, the Scotia Synfuels synthetic fuel plant proposed for the Strait of Canso would have used 400,000 tons of Cape Breton coal per year. But unlike

Point Aconi, the Synfuels project required a major infusion of federal tax credit dollars (at least $200 million) to make it viable, an "achilles heel" which ultimately skewered the project.[42]

Maritime Economic Union

In 1988, the three Maritime premiers commissioned a study on the economic challenges facing the region. The study, by international business specialist and former federal policy advisor, Dr. Charles McMillan, was presented to the premiers in December 1989. McMillan's report, *Standing Up to the Future: The Maritimes in the 1990s*, made three key recommendations: removal of all interprovincial trade barriers in the region; establishment of a Maritime Savings Development Fund similar to Quebec's *Caisse de dépôt;* and a trade promotion strategy to increase the level of exports from the Maritime region by 50 per cent in five years. The aim and expectation, should this agenda be fully carried out by the three Maritime provinces, is that the region will be a "have" area of Canada by the year 2000. At the 78th session of the Council of Maritime Premiers (CMP) on October 10, 1990, the three premiers endorsed the thrust and principles of the McMillan Report and agreed to hold a forum of the three Maritime cabinets in Moncton during the first half of 1991 to discuss implementation of the Report. The Premiers noted that their governments, facing the prospect of continuing declines in federal transfers, out of necessity would have to increase their co-operative activity leading to rationalization of the three provincial economies.[43]

Even before the tabling of McMillan's report, Premier McKenna of New Brunswick had begun pushing the idea of Maritime Economic Union, a regional common market without any internal barriers to doing business. Hardly a radical idea, one might think, but given the extent to which Canadian provinces have sought to protect and preserve their own provincial market for their own provincial businesses, McKenna's proposal created a considerable stir. Beyond removing internal trade barriers, McKenna also suggested a closer integration of the strategic objectives of the three Maritime provinces on such issues as health care, energy, transportation, tourism and economic development.[44] His initiative was applauded by regional business associations and supported by governing and opposition parties in the three provinces. As for the general population, a survey by a regional polling agency in October 1990, registered nearly universal support amongst Maritimers for joint action by Maritime governments on social and economic issues, and between 60 and 70 per cent support for some type of political union of the three provinces.[45] Newfoundland, to date, has been left out of the discussions and timetable for implementing economic union, though its participation "at some point" has not been ruled out.[46]

Proposals for an economic or political union of the three Maritime provinces are, of course, nothing new. Maritime Union was the topic of a conference in 1864, before it was dropped in favour of a larger union: Confederation. In 1970-71, the Deutsch Commission, having been commissioned by the Maritime Premiers to look into Maritime Union, urged the Maritime provinces to move toward full political union as an important step in solving the economic and social ills of the region. The idea of political union, however, proceeded no further than the establishment of the Council of Maritime premiers. Of these two prior instances of Maritime union talk, perhaps 1864 is the more comparable context. Then, too, the established economic and political order was breaking up, as it appears to be doing in the 1990s, forcing the three Maritime provinces to reconsider their relationship with one another and with the rest of the world.[47] Whether a new confederation results from the current constitutional impasse or not, economic and fiscal pressures alone seem sufficient to force a closer integration of the Maritimes. As McKenna noted, "History teaches us that men behave wisely once they have exhausted all alternatives."[48]

CONCLUSION

The political and economic arrangements that have sustained Atlantic Canada in the postwar era—though admittedly as the least developed, least prosperous group of Canadian provinces—are now undergoing significant change. The causes of this change—the Free Trade Agreement, the continuing constitutional crisis and efforts to reduce the federal deficit—are beyond the control of regional politicians, who must now find ways and means to adapt to, and even exploit, the new realities of the 1990s.

The federal government has been the primary protagonist in these developments. Its manoeuverings and initiatives with regard to the Constitution have had the effect of dividing both the region's political leadership and its populace, generating debate about the implications of proposed constitutional changes for federal policies, political values and institutional arrangements important to the region. It can be expected that in future the constitutional positions taken by the Atlantic provinces will reflect the impact of this debate over constitutional first principles. In particular, it now seems more likely, in the aftermath of Meech Lake, that there will be stiffer opposition to further compromising, watering-down or eliminating the constitutional responsibilities and capacities of the federal government.

In the 1990s, some areas of federal spending and regulation in Atlantic Canada—the fishery, transportation and offshore oil development—can be expected to continue in ways that are congruent with the history of federal involvement in these areas. At the same time, free trade and federal deficit reduction efforts are combining to change other federal policies and to alter the pattern and scope of federal spending in key areas such as unemployment insurance and regional development. Federal expenditure on UI is being pared down as part of a larger design to enhance the efficiency of adjustment mechanisms within the labour market. With regard to regional development, a commitment was made by federal authorities to decentralize decision-making and to make ACOA the protector and promoter of Atlantic Canada's economic interests in Ottawa. ACOA was also mandated to alter the pattern of regional development spending in order to emphasize "entrepreneurship development" and support for smaller, regionally based enterprises. But ACOA's performance to date in fulfilling this mandate has not been convincing: it has not been an effective advocate for Atlantic Canada in Ottawa; large amounts of taxpayer dollars continue to be spent, with very mixed results, to entice capital into the region; narrow political considerations still appear to be a factor in the pattern and pace of regional development spending. Moreover, the regional development budget for Atlantic Canada has been reduced in terms of its annual allotment, and is now under direct threat from the provisions of the Canada-US Free Trade Agreement. At the very least, a further redirecting of federal spending in this area away from potentially countervailable subsidies seems inevitable.

While the region's economic future is expected, more or less, to be an extension of the past, economic and political developments in the 1990s have forced a rethinking of past patterns and alignments. In this connection, a strategic document advocating much closer regional integration and co-operation has been approved and a new initiative on Maritime economic union launched. The combined effect of the Free Trade Agreement, federal fiscal problems and the constitutional crisis is pressuring the three Maritime governments to move in a direction they have several times before contemplated. It reflects growing recognition of the need for a sense of economic direction, a strategic outlook that will enable the development of more coherent and co-ordinated economic policies for the region. In the current historical conjuncture, the benefits of union may finally be too compelling, and the costs of non-integration too severe, for Maritime governments not to engage in such a process. Contemplation of the "one region" concept may finally be replaced with concrete action leading toward its realization.

Notes

1   The compact theory of Confederation is one interpretation of the intentions of the Fathers of Confederation in framing the British North America Act. It states that Confederation is a compact between provinces, who together determine which powers and responsibilities they will grant to the federal government. The province is the primary community and the federal government their creature.

2   See for example, Alan Cairns, "Political Science, Ethnicity, and the Canadian Constitution," in David Shugarman and Reg Whitaker (eds.), *Federalism and Political Community: Essays in Honour of Donald Smiley* (Peterborough, Ont.: Broadview Press, 1990), pp. 113-140; Richard Simeon and Ian Robinson, *State, Society and the Development of Canadian Federalism* (Toronto: University of Toronto Press, 1990), chapters 11 and 12.

3   As quoted in Jeffrey Simpson, "Frank McKenna reflects on a climate of retrenchment and division," *The Globe and Mail* [Toronto], September 21, 1990.

4 Staff, "Quebec can't decide Canada's future—McKenna," *The Chronicle-Herald* [Halifax], September 14, 1990.

5 Canadian Press, "All provinces should be offered immigration deal—Wells," *The Chronicle-Herald* [Halifax], December 24, 1990.

6 Canadian Press, "Wells breaks silence on federalism debate," *The Chronicle-Herald* [Halifax], January 14, 1991.

7 Brian Underhill and Brian Ward, "Tories pick Cameron," *The Chronicle-Herald* [Halifax], February 11, 1991.

8 "Support slipping for freer trade," *Globe and Mail* [Toronto], December 23, 1985.

9 This argument has been made elsewhere by Alan Cairns in "Political Science, Ethnicity and the Canadian Constitution," in David Shugarman and Reg Whitaker (eds.), *Federalism and Political Community: Essays in Honour of Donald Smiley* (Peterborough, Ont.: Broadview Pres, 1989), pp. 113-140. See also chapter 4 by Roger Gibbins, elsewhere in this volume. For evidence regarding Anglophone opinion and attitudes on Meech Lake, see Kathy Brock, "A Mandate Fulfilled: Constitutional Reform and the Manitoba Task Force on Meech Lake," a project sponsored by the University of Manitoba Outreach Fund, December 1990; New Brunswick, Transcripts of the Meetings of the Select Committee on the 1987 Constitutional Accord.

10 For an example of this type of analysis, see Thomas Courchene, "A Market Perspective on Regional Disparities," *Canadian Public Policy*, VII:4 (Autumn, 1981), pp. 506-518.

11 The problem of vertical equity refers to the revenue-responsibility imbalance between Ottawa and the provinces that left Ottawa with unrestricted taxing powers and the provinces with responsibility for areas of rapidly growing government expenditure; the problem of horizontal equity refers to the much greater capacity of some provinces within the federation to raise revenues compared to other provinces.

12   R. Simeon and I. Robinson, *State, Society and the Development of Canadian Federalism* (Toronto: University of Toronto Press, 1990), p. 198.

13   Leslie Pal, *State, Class and Bureaucracy: Canadian Unemployment Insurance and Public Policy* (Montreal: McGill-Queen's University Press, 1988) p. 45.

14   N.H. Lithwick, "Regional Policy: The Embodiment of Contradictions," *How Ottawa Spends, 1982*, p. 141.

15   Cindy McKinley, "Regional Accommodation in Canada: The Atlantic Caucuses of the Liberal and Conservative Parties." Paper presented to Conference on Political Development in the Atlantic Provinces, Queen's University, Kingston, July, 1981.

16   Leslie Pal, op. cit., pp. 46-7.

17   Final Report of the Senate Committee on Bill C-21.

18   Canada. House of Commons, Standing Committee on Regional Development, *Minutes and Proceedings*, April 15, 1970, p. 62.

19   James Bickerton, *Nova Scotia, Ottawa and the Politics of Regional Development* (Toronto: University of Toronto Press, 1990), pp. 211-13.

20   In the words of then-DREE deputy minister, Tom Kent, "DREE cannot be expected to plan good regional development strategies unless there is a national industrial strategy of which regional programs are part and with which they can be co-ordinated. We do not have such a strategy." Paul Phillips, *Regional Disparities* (Toronto: Lorimer, 1982), p. 91.

21   Donald Savoie, "The General Development Agreement Approach and the Bureaucratization of Provincial Governments in Atlantic Canada," *Canadian Public Administration*, 24 (1981), pp. 116-131.

22   David Milne, *Tug of War: Ottawa and the Provinces Under Trudeau and Mulroney* (Toronto: Lorimer, 1986), pp. 131-2.

23 Sue Calhoun, "Agency will take yet one more kick at regional development," *Atlantic Business* (October, 1987) pp. 21-4 and Judy Myrden, "ACOA head rules out infrastructure," *The Chronicle-Herald* [Halifax], November 4, 1987.

24 Staff, "Regional assistance comes home," *The Chronicle-Herald* [Halifax], June 9, 1987.

25 Elmer MacKay, "MacKay singing ACOA praises," *The Chronicle Herald* [Halifax], October 6, 1989.

26 Deborah Jones, "Federal review planned for Cape Breton agency," *The Globe and Mail* [Toronto], October 6, 1990; Julie Zatzman, "RCMP probe C.B. firm," *The Chronicle-Herald* [Halifax], December 20, 1990.

27 Donald Savoie, "Atlantic Canada Opportunities Agency (ACOA): Something Old, Something New, Something Borrowed, Something Blue," in Katherine A. Graham (ed.), *How Ottawa Spends, 1989-90* (Ottawa, Carleton University Press, 1989), pp. 124-5.

28 Tom McCoag, "ACOA's Lesaux never shied away from a challenge," *The Chronicle-Herald* [Halifax], December 15, 1989.

29 See *The Politics of Regional Development*, chapters 4-8; "Atlantic Canada Opportunities," pp. 124-5.

30 While much media attention was given to Canso, a 300-year-old fishing community that refused to die and was eventually saved by a deal worked out between the federal and provincial governments and Seafreez Food Ltd.—who were given millions of dollars worth of fish and permitted to barter with a foreign country in return for saving 500 jobs in Canso—most of the plants closed by the downturn in the Atlantic fishery were not reopened. Rob Gorham, "The Seafreez shuffle," *The Chronicle-Herald* [Halifax], October 6, 1990.

31 Kevin Cox, "Solutions found scarcer than fish," *The Globe and Mail* [Toronto], September 17, 1990.

32   Kevin Cox, "Fishermen decry individual quotas," *The Globe and Mail* [Toronto], January 29, 1991.

33   Staff, "Casting a watchful eye," *The Chronicle-Herald* [Halifax], September 17, 1990.

34   A.P. Pross and S. McCorquodale, "The State, Interests and Policy-Making in the East Coast Fishery," in W.D. Coleman and S. Skogstad (eds.), *Policy Communities and Public Policy in Canada* (Mississauga, Ont.: Copp, Clark Pittman, 1990), p. 35.

35   Public Affairs International, *The PAI Report: Analysis of Developments in Public Policy* (October, 1990), p. 23.

36   Brian Underhill, "Region unites on highway twinning," *The Chronicle-Herald* [Halifax], July 16, 1988; Hattie Dyck, "Highway twinning plans expected by mid-summer," *The Chronicle-Herald* [Halifax], June 14, 1990.

37   Canada, Department of Regional Industrial Expansion, *Towards 2000: A Newfoundland and Labrador Transportation Initiative*, June 20, 1988.

38   Drew Fagan, "Wells cautious about Hibernia," *The Globe and Mail* [Toronto], September 17, 1990; Sylvie Caron, "Hibernia announcement due Friday," *The Chronicle-Herald* [Halifax], September 13, 1990.

39   Deborah Jones, "Nova Scotia offshore oil contracts awarded," *The Globe and Mail* [Toronto], October 10, 1990.

40   Alan Jeffers, "C.B.'s future black like coal," *The Chronicle-Herald* [Halifax], December 6, 1990.

41   Randy Jones, "Environmentalists quiet on NB's power plant front," *The Chronicle-Herald* [Halifax], January 15, 1991.

42   Malcolm Dunlop, "Synfuels not viable as planned," *The Chronicle-Herald* [Halifax], November 17, 1990

43   Council of Maritime Premiers, *Press Release*, 78th session, October 30, 1990.

44 Canadian Press, "McKenna pushes Maritime Coalition," *The Chronicle-Herald* [Halifax], September 12, 1990.

45 T. McKegney, "Maritime union support strong," *The Times-Transcript* [Moncton], October 16, 1990. This level of public support drops off when Atlantic union is the issue, with opposition strongest in Prince Edward Island. Loss of provincial identity was the main concern of those opposed, while those in favour expected more political clout for the region within Canada. "Atlantic Canadians split on political union," *The Chronicle-Herald* [Halifax], February 15, 1991.

46 Brian Underhill, "Summer talks on Maritime union likely," *The Chronicle-Herald* [Halifax], January 17, 1991.

47 In the mid-1860s, uncertainty clouded the future of the Maritime colonies; British trade preferences that had provided the region with a protected market for its products and services were disappearing; the 1846 Reciprocity Treaty that had provided access to the American market was not renewed by the United States in 1866; the end of the American Civil War in 1865 was followed by a military threat to British North America from Irish-Americans (the Fenians) hostile towards Britain; and the Government of Upper and Lower Canada was proposing a union of all the British North American colonies.

48 As quoted in Tom Kierans, "How To Save the Maritimes," *Report on Business Magazine* (December, 1990), p. 27.

CHAPTER 6

THE FREE TRADE SEQUEL: CANADA-UNITED STATES SUBSIDY NEGOTIATIONS

G. Bruce Doern and Brian W. Tomlin

Résumé: L'accord canado-américaine sur le libre-échange exige la négociation d'un nouveau régime de l'application des subventions et des remèdes commerciaux. Dans ce chapitre, on explore les raisons pour lesquelles un tel régime ne s'est pas réalisé au cours des négociations de 1987-88, et on examine les questions-clefs du débat ainsi que la dynamique complexe politico-économique impliquée dans la définition et l'évaluation des subventions.

Les auteurs en viennent à la conclusion d'après laquelle ni le Canada ni les États-Unis ne risquent de vouloir poursuivre des négociations sérieuses d'ici les élections de 1992 dans les deux pays. Ils en concluent également que le Canada a raison d'user de prudence puisque celui-ci est beaucoup plus vulnérable dans des négociations sur les subventions, où les concessions touchant d'autres questions ne sont guère possibles. Les choix à faire posent des problèmes au Canada, vu les différents effets qu'aura un accord sur les subventions sur différents champs de la politique. Le Canada risque de perdre de sa capacité d'agir en matière de politique industrielle et régionale, mais il pourra faire des gains si l'entente établit clairement que les programmes sociaux ne sont pas soumis à des mesures compensatoires. Que de telles négociations aient lieu ou non, on devra finir par faire face à ces questions relatives aux subventions au cours des années 1990.

Abstract: The Canada-United States Free Trade Agreement (FTA) requires the negotiation of a new regime to govern the use of subsidies and trade remedies. After exploring why such a regime failed to materialize in the 1986-87 FTA negotiations, this chapter examines key issues in the debate and the complex political-economic dynamics of defining and assessing subsidies.

The authors conclude that neither Canada nor the US is likely to be eager to pursue serious negotiations before the 1992 elections in both countries. In addition, Canada is right to be very cautious about such negotiations because it is far more vulnerable in a subsidy negotiation than it was in the FTA negotiations where it could secure tradeoffs on other issues. The choices are also difficult for Canada because an agreement on subsidies will have varying effects on different policy fields. Losses in policy capacity are likely to occur in industrial and regional policy but gains may accrue if such an agreement clearly establishes that social programs cannot be countervailed. Whether or not negotiations proceed, these subsidy issues will eventually have to be confronted in the 1990s.

After almost three years of political warfare over free trade, Meech Lake and the GST, Canadians are understandably worn out, and more than a little fed up with battle lines drawn over fundamental aspects of the political and economic life of the nation. While Canadians may not yet have the punched-out look of Rocky V, they are nonetheless weary of sequels. Yet one sequel that is in store for the early to mid-1990s has the potential to be nearly as divisive as the Free Trade Wars of the late 1980s. It centres around the undertaking in the Free Trade Agreement (FTA) by Canada and the United States to negotiate basic rules regarding the use of subsidies and antidumping and countervailing duties.

Efforts to establish such rules were at the core of the 1986-87 FTA negotiations, but the profound differences between the two countries could not be resolved in the time available. Instead, they agreed to continue to apply their existing trade remedy laws, but to substitute binational panel review for national court reviews of trade remedy actions. The binational panels are only a temporary solution to the impasse, however. Chapter 19 of the FTA established a bilateral Working Group to continue negotiations in search of a solution to the subsidies-trade remedies issue. The Working Group was given five years to complete this task, with the possibility of a two-year extension. If no agreement is reached at the end of seven years, then Chapter 19 stipulates that either party may terminate the entire FTA on six months notice.

This chapter examines some of the key issues and potential strategies involved in the continuing negotiations over subsidies. We want to determine why the subsidies issue almost became the black hole of the FTA, drawing the entire negotiation process into destruction. We also want to examine the essential politics and economics of defining and assessing subsidies for international trade purposes, as well as identifying the key subsidy issues in the conduct of Canadian industrial, social, regional and agricultural policy. Finally, we will explore the dynamics of the prospective negotiations, and ask whether Canada, in particular, will still be seriously interested in such a divisive negotiation in the politics of the 1990s. In addressing these questions, particular attention must be given to a series of events and concurrent pressures, some of which were not a direct part of the FTA negotiations of 1986-87, but which are clearly a part of the political and economic equation of the 1990s. These include the upcoming free trade negotiations between

Canada, Mexico and the United States, uncertainty over the outcome of the Uruguay Round of multilateral trade negotiations, and changes in the basic domestic politics of both Canada and the US since the free trade decision.

With regard to future bilateral negotiations, our argument is as follows. First, the conditions which produced an impasse in the original FTA negotiations are basically unchanged, and the prospect of substantial progress on the subsidy-countervail issue remains a long shot. Second, neither Canada nor the US is likely to be anxious to pursue negotiations in the short- to medium-term, because several political variables conspire against this. And Canada, in particular, is right to be cautious because it is far more vulnerable in a negotiation focussed exclusively on subsidies than it was in the FTA negotiations. Third, while liberal economic theorists strongly favour disciplining and even eliminating subsidies, the politics of this issue are less hospitable and vary greatly by policy field. Finally, while the subsidy issue must be confronted in the 1990s, Canada may wish to seriously consider whether the most prudent approach to the issue is through bilateral negotiations with the United States.

THE BLACK HOLE IN THE FTA

To understand the upcoming debate on subsidies, it is necessary to know the essence of what happened on this issue during the free trade negotiations of 1986-87.[1] Canada originally sought a free trade agreement partly out of a growing fear of US protectionism in the first half of the 1980s. The basis for this fear was the growing number of trade remedy actions initiated by US private interests against Canadian exporters, especially countervailing duties against alleged Canadian subsidy practices. These US actions were frequently seen in Canada as a harassment tactic which not only reduced access to the American market in an immediate sense, but also increased longer term uncertainty for investment in Canada.

Early in the negotiations, Simon Reisman, Canada's chief negotiator, proposed to the Americans that a regime be established to govern the use of trade remedy laws by defining new joint rules to discipline the practices that provoked the use of trade remedy actions by the US. A key element of the regime would be a subsidies code that would define exactly which subsidy practices were prohibited and which were permissible.

The Canadian proposal for a code was likened to a traffic light: acceptable practices would be given a green light, and no trade remedy actions would be possible against them (a non-actionable category); unacceptable practices would be given a red light; and a yellow, caution light would be given to any remaining, ambiguous practices, which would be reviewed by a binational panel to determine their final status.

While a Canadian proposal for a regime that would discipline its own practices may seem perverse at first glance, a subsidies code would allow Canada to side-step unilateral US definitions of what was subsidized and therefore countervailable. American recognition of a class of acceptable subsidy practices, against which they would not take trade remedy action, would achieve some measure of secure access for Canada to the US market. This would be especially the case because the Canadians intended to negotiate sufficient room to continue what they considered to be defensible subsidies, such as those used for regional development. Canada was rebuffed by chief US negotiator Peter Murphy, however. He argued that the problem, and solution, rested with Canada, since it was Canadian subsidy practices that required disciplining, not American. Murphy maintained that the US had already eliminated most federal subsidies, and as evidence he pointed to the absence of Canadian countervail actions against American producers. Obviously, American subsidies were not at issue. To solve its apparent problem, Murphy argued, all Canada had to do was discipline its own subsidy practices. No negotiated code was necessary.

Stonewalled, the Canadians continued to insist that a subsidies code was the key to any final deal. Late in the negotiations, US Commerce Department lawyers finally devised a counterproposal which was characterized by bright lines and safe harbours. The bright lines would provide a clear signal of the types of Canadian subsidies that were unacceptable, while safe harbour would be granted to a very small number of specific programs that would be exempt from trade remedies. Most important, the status of ambiguous practices would be determined through the usual countervail process, rather than by a binational panel. The US proposal also distinguished between subsidies with an export effect and those that were purely domestic, the former requiring disciplines, the latter not. The consequence of this last particular twist was not lost on the Canadians at the table. It meant that US subsidies directed to companies serving the huge American domestic market would be exempt, despite the fact that their effect was to displace imports. Under the American proposal, only Canadian subsidies would be targeted. In addition, the subsidy practices embodied in American defence spending were ruled off limits, on the grounds that trade policy could not be allowed to drive defence policy.

The US was not offering much with a proposal that was clearly designed more with an eye to winning Congressional approval than Canadian acceptance. But Canada was the *demandeur* on the issue, under intense pressure to get a deal. In addition, the Americans had been refusing for months to put any proposal at all forward on the subsidies-trade remedies issue. Now, they had finally relented with their offer of safe harbours. As a result, Reisman (who was unsympathetic to Canadian subsidy practices) and other senior officials in the Trade Negotiations Office (TNO), were determined give the US proposal a serious look. However, others in the TNO insisted that the US proposal was so one-sided that it was utterly unacceptable, and would provoke strong opposition in Canada. Provincial governments, especially in Atlantic Canada, had been given ironclad assurances by Ottawa that the integrity of regional development programs would not be placed at risk in the negotiations.² In the end, Reisman had to accept the fact that the American proposal offered no safe harbour for Canada.

This was the ultimate political paradox of the negotiations, and it almost transformed Canada's subsidy issue into a black hole in the FTA galaxy. A top Canadian priority was the establishment of a subsidies regime that would secure Canada's access to the American market by reducing the threat of countervail actions. But the more that subsidies were restrained through defined regimes and rules, the more likely it was that the majority domestic coalition favouring free trade would break apart. There would be widespread disbelief that a deal which imposed one-sided restraints on Canadian subsidy practices was a fair one, and it would be difficult to explain in the heat of an election in which the FTA was the central issue.

In the end, the FTA only became possible when the two countries decided to set aside the subsidies-trade remedies issue for future negotiations. At the time, the Chapter 19 provisions of the FTA represented the most the US would give, and the least that Canada would take, in a deal. The two countries agreed that each would continue to apply its existing trade remedy laws, but domestic decisions under these laws would be subject to procedural, although not substantive, review by a binational panel.[3] Panel findings would be binding and final. This proved to be enough to make a deal, but it did not resolve the issue.

THE POLITICAL ECONOMY OF DEFINING AND ASSESSING SUBSIDIES

The task of defining and assessing subsidies is not an easy one. We look at three different elements of the definition and assessment issue, first in the context of ideologies and academic disciplines, second as revealed in institutional practice under the General Agreement on Tariffs and Trade (GATT); and in the US, and finally in the light of selected empirical studies.

Subsidy Ideologies

The definition and assessment of subsidies is frequently heavily weighted by ideological views, because subsidies raise issues about the intent, degree and effects of state intervention in the economy. Practising politicians and political scientists writing about industrial policy have adopted a fairly benign view of subsidies, seeing them as an entirely predictable outcome of the special pleading that conventionally occurs in pluralist democratic politics.[4] Subsidies are simply the ways in which governments from time to time can help firms or industries or regions meet opportunities, overcome problems, or "buy time." This does not mean that politicians can subsidize every time someone asks, since pluralist politics also generate counterpressures against subsidization, including fiscal limits and opposition to specific subsidy proposals. Positive views of subsidies are also often based on considerations of national sovereignty. From this perspective, controls on subsidies may be viewed negatively simply because they reduce formal sovereign powers, or they eliminate a power which the state might need at some future date.

In contrast, economists and others who place their faith in economic development through free markets and free trade offer a more critical assessment of subsidies.[5] According to this view, subsidies are harmful to the Canadian, or any other, economy because they distort resource allocation and decisions on industrial location. By extension, this leads logically to the view that the availability of countervailing duties to the United States under its trade laws is actually of benefit to Canada, since this forces discipline on Canadian subsidy politics.[6] Canadian politicians are usefully restrained from catering to special interests seeking favours beneficial to them, but costly to the Canadian consumer. And by this logic, American consumers are actually penalized by US trade remedy laws, since they are prevented from buying low-cost imports subsidized by Canadian taxpayers.

This theoretical case against subsidies has been buttressed by numerous studies by economists in Canada and elsewhere.[7] These typically show how expensive each job saved is, how ill-defined the subsidy programs are, and how hidden the real costs are from the knowledge of the average taxpayer and consumer.

Subsidy Definitions

As Alan Oxley points out, the GATT is "remarkably permissive on the use of subsidies,"[8] despite its objectives of reinforcing and opening up markets. The GATT prohibits the use of export subsidies on manufactured goods, and countries are exhorted not to use subsidies if they harm trading partners. But subsidies can be used for non-manufactured products and can be paid to domestic firms in such a way as to displace imports. A subsidies code was negotiated during the GATT Tokyo Round, but it was only agreed to by a few countries, chief among them the United States.[9] The code does not speak of legal or illegal subsidies, but instead sets out a procedure indicating how a country should conduct subsidy and injury investigations, which may result in the right to impose a countervailing duty.

The US has gone further than any other country in entrenching the spirit of the GATT subsidy code in its trade remedy laws, and has added the proviso that producers, in addition to government, can initiate actions. The US Commerce Department initially defines a subsidy on the basis of whether a governmental program is generally available, or is targeted to "one company or industry, a limited group of companies or industries, or companies or industries located within a limited region or regions within a country."[10] Studies show that actual decisions can be quite arbitrary in applying this definition.[11] Some generally available programs have been ruled to be subsidies, and some targeted programs have been exonerated. These decisions are undoubtedly influenced by more general American views about what constitute appropriate functions for government. This was certainly the case in the second Softwood Lumber case, when provincial stumpage fees and related resource management practices were judged to be incompatible with US practices.[12] Furthermore, Canada's various regional programs have been determined to be countervailable subsidies.

Where does this leave the definitional debate? It would appear that, in principle, any government support—grants, tax breaks, concessionary loans or direct investment— could directly or indirectly assist an industry to penetrate export markets or to replace imports. Whether the support should, in fact, be considered a subsidy depends on how general or specific the intent and the effect of such policy instruments are, including their combined use. The first question that has to be posed in determining when a subsidy is present concerns whether the Government's support is intended to affect particular companies, an industrial sector, a region, all industries generally, or the population as a whole. Logic suggests that progression along this continuum, from company-specific to general support, should make actions less likely to be defined as a subsidy. This notion is important for our discussion below of industrial and social policy.

At the core of the definitional issue is the fact that the real concern of governments and firms is with subsidies that distort trade away from some natural state of comparative advantage. Distortion occurs when subsidies help increase exports or displace imports. But on this question, the asymmetry between the Canadian and US economies is vitally important. Canada is the more trade-dependent country, and most of Canada's trade is with the United States. The US, in contrast, is far less dependent on trade, and it trades extensively with Europe and Japan, as well as with Canada. It follows that any particular Canadian practice has a much greater chance of being alleged by the US to be trade distorting than does any specific US practice by Canada, simply because Canadian production affected by the practice is more likely to be exported, probably to the US.

Subsidy Practices

The debate over subsidies has led to a number of studies which attempt to compare subsidy practices and levels, both in the aggregate and by industrial sector. These studies are replete with methodological and measurement problems, and care must be taken to determine whether all policy instruments are included (taxation, spending, loans, regulation), whether all levels of government action are included (federal, provincial/state and local), whether activities such as defence are included or excluded, and of course what time periods are involved.

A study of federal subsidies by Bence and Smith showed that in 1984, explicit federal subsidies in the industrial and service sectors in Canada and the US averaged about 1.0 per cent of domestic shipments in Canada and 0.5 per cent in the US.[13] Out of 83 industries, only five in Canada and three in the US had subsidy rates greater than five per cent; in the range between one and five per cent, the US had 10 industries and Canada had six. The Bence and Smith study also pointed out that the Canadian figures had undoubtedly declined since 1984, primarily because of the elimination of large energy subsidies. Moreover, it stressed that if defence procurement were included in the US data, the average non-agricultural American subsidy rate would be about two per cent, larger than the Canadian rate, even after including Canada's defence procurement.[14] US studies also show that, overall, American subsidies tend to be lower than those of other industrialized countries.[15] However, most such studies exclude not only defence, but also regional location incentives provided by state and local governments.

Comparative studies provide a broader perspective on subsidy practices among industrialized countries, including the US and Canada. A recent study by Hufbauer confirms that the US is by far the least subsidizing of the G-7 countries, when subsidies are measured as a per cent of gross domestic product (GDP).[16] Another recent report by the Organization for Economic Co-operation and Development (OECD)[17] tries to put various studies on a comparable basis by converting the value of soft loans, equity participation and other (essentially non-regulatory) industrial policy measures into what they would be worth as a cash grant.[18] Expressed as a percentage of GDP, the OECD data show that since the early 1970s, the US rate has been at about 0.5 per cent, although it edged up to 0.7 in the 1985-88 period. Japan is the next lowest in the 1.2 to 1.4 per cent range. The European OECD countries had an average subsidy rate of 1.9 per cent in the early 1970s, but this grew to 2.7 per cent throughout the 1980s. Canada's rate was 1.1 per cent in the early 1970s, rose to 2.6 per cent in the early 1980s, but fell under the Conservative government to 2.2 per cent. Compared to the whole group of OECD countries, Canada's level of subsidizing was in about the middle of the pack.

While these data are instructive in an aggregate sense, and probably accurately indicate that Canada subsidizes more than the US at the federal level, they do not tell the whole story. In the US, federal assistance to business is less visible because it is provided through a complex tax code. In contrast, Canadian assistance is frequently provided through more visible grants to regions, or industries. In addition, state governments operate a diffuse system of direct assistance to industry, with all 50 states employing economic development offices to recruit investment.[19] Nor do the data indicate whether injury in particular industries is occurring. For example, even though Canada's regional programs have usually been determined by US decisions to be subsidies, most cases in dispute have also shown that the level of subsidization has been below 0.5 per cent, the minimum threshold (*de minimus* level) which must be surpassed under US trade law before a petition can proceed.[20] The actual levels in particular cases are of great importance because the inability of US firms to compete could be the result of a number of factors other than Canadian subsidization practices. These could include inferior products, inadequate technology, managerial incompetence, or inadequate financing, to cite only a few possibilities.

Other studies also point out practical problems of determining just what an "industry" is, and which parts of the industry or products within it, or adjacent to it, are benefiting from or being injured by an alleged subsidy. It has to be determined just how far up the production and value-added chain the subsidy-injury case should be taken. In the steel or lumber industries, for example, numerous primary and integrated mills are involved, leading to hundreds of later products that use lumber or steel.[21]

SUBSIDIES AND POLICY FIELDS

Problems associated with definition and measurement will loom large in the Chapter 19 negotiations to identify a new system of rules for subsidies and trade remedies. The negotiations will force a reconsideration of the role of subsidies in the Canadian economy, and will have direct consequences for Canada's capacity to make policy in various fields. In this section we look briefly at the implications of the negotiations for industrial, social, regional and agricultural policy. As we do, we want to keep in mind the continuum concept introduced earlier in our discussion of the definition of subsidies. According to this continuum, the more targeted and firm-specific governmental support is, the more likely that it will be viewed as a subsidy. And the more general support is, the less likely that it will be viewed as a subsidy. In terms of the traffic light system that was introduced in both the FTA and recent GATT negotiations, targeted programs would receive a red signal and generally available programs a green, while ambiguous cases would fall in the yellow zone.

Industrial Policy

Consider this continuum notion first in the area of Canadian industrial policy. Industrial policy consists of co-ordinated government actions targeted at key firms or sectors, and designed to enhance their international competitiveness in product development in the economic interests of Canada. In practice, this would mean the capacity of Canadian governments to assist firms such as Bombardier or Northern Telecom, or perhaps a consortium of firms. For our purposes, industrial policy does not refer to other so-called framework policies, such as general policies on research and development incentives, taxation, and education and training, that are pursued by governments to help business to compete in a general sense.[22]

It is clear that a subsidy regime that rules out such firm-specific actions will diminish Canada's capacity to make industrial policy. But many will question whether a diminished industrial policy capacity is a loss at all.[23] This was precisely the view of bodies like the Macdonald Royal Commission and the Economic Council of Canada, as well as numerous economists knowledgeable about Canada's past attempts at practising industrial policy. Conventional liberal economic approaches to this issue argue that governments should confine themselves to the establishment of good framework policies, that is, policies that are general and therefore less likely to be viewed as subsidies.

Assessments of past efforts to mount effective industrial policies have not been positive. Many studies have pointed to Canada's uneven success rate, arguing further that such policies have, in fact, seriously harmed, rather than helped,

Canadian economic performance by reducing Canada's capacity to adjust to international competitive forces.[24] Still others point to the absence of the political institutions and political consensus that are required to support a coherent industrial policy.[25] They also cite the absence of the necessary technical and organizational capacity within government to support the use of subsidies to promote international competitiveness.

Although much of this judgment of Canada's past efforts is accurate, it does not address the dilemma that Canada is going to face in the 1990s. While Canada, as a small trade-dependent country in an increasingly technological and global product market, undoubtedly needs free trade, it also requires a co-ordinated industrial policy to complement free trade. This is because the comparative advantage of nations is, to some extent, engineered. The economic rationale for firm-specific industrial policies, that is for subsidies, lies in the fact that some product development cycles are characterized by imperfect competition, or quasi-monopoly situations, and by increasing returns to scale.[26] This presents the case for governments to help Canadians achieve a share of some of these economic gains, or at least to prevent Canada from losing out altogether.

The Mulroney Conservative government does not currently see the need for such complementary industrial policies, however. Its official policy, centred in the Department of Industry, Science and Technology, has been to wean industry off grants and subsidies, in line with the economic arguments against subsidies set out above. It is, therefore, very likely that in any future negotiation the federal government will agree that firm-specific actions are subsidies and should be given a red light in any subsidy code. If this is the case, it will mean abandoning the possibility of a complementary industrial policy.

Social Policy

Social policy embraces the main elements of the modern social welfare state—health, education and welfare—but for our purposes it also includes areas such as unemployment insurance and training. Regional policy could also be included here, but for reasons set out below, we will treat it separately. During the 1987-88 free trade debate, opponents of the FTA argued that social programs should have been protected explicitly in the Agreement. Anti-free trade forces argued, quite misleadingly, that social programs were threatened by the FTA. They claimed the threat was both direct, coming from certain provisions in the Agreement, and indirect, arising from the pro-market ethos underlying the FTA, which would undermine Canadians' commitment to social values.[27]

The subsidy negotiations will resurrect the debate over these issues, but the lines may be drawn in a different way. Because social programs are generally available, the continuum concept suggests that they are unlikely to be viewed as subsidies, and therefore should not be subject to countervail. As former State Department official, Colleen Morton, stated recently,

> Although some industries in the United States would like to countervail broadly based Canadian [social] programs, it is highly unlikely that a positive final determination would be made under the current reading of the sector-specificity requirement in US cvd [countervailing duty] law.[28]

There has been speculation that income maintenance programs for the so-called "working pcor," either in their current form or in a future guaranteed annual income, may be viewed by the Americans to be a subsidy. They might take this position on the grounds that such programs benefit labour, frequently the largest cost component in many industrial sectors. However, many US social programs could be similarly attacked by Canada.

If, as seems likely, a negotiated subsidies code would give a green light to general social programs, then it may offer a new opportunity for social policy interests to rescue the notion of universality in Canadian social policy. For most of the 1980s, universal social programs have been under political attack by pro-market business interests making the case for more precisely targeted programs. But targeting may earn the programs a red light in any subsidies agreement, or, failing agreement, may render them more vulnerable to countervail action. Generally available social programs could, therefore, become an alternative policy instrument to enhance Canadian competitiveness, substituting for prohibited industrial policy programs. This result would not only bolster the principle of universality, but might also reduce opposition to a negotiated agreement on subsidies from social policy advocates, since it could further their own ends.

Regional Policy

If industrial and social policy represent opposite ends of the subsidy definition continuum, the former almost certain to receive a red signal and the latter green, then regional policy may fall in the yellow zone between them. The status of regional policy is ambiguous because, although regional support programs are aimed at enhancing regional development, Canada's heavy dependence on foreign trade increases the likelihood that the support will have an export effect. Past US trade remedy practice shows that the Americans will argue that regional programs constitute subsidies, and are therefore countervailable. The programs are made even more vulnerable by the fact that many benefit regionally concentrated industries. As a result, although regional programs may not be intended to be firm-specific, many end up being precisely this.

The regional policy issue has been divisive in Canada. Proponents of regional development programs take the view that policy should take "jobs to people" in the disadvantaged regions of the country. Opponents argue that a market-driven, adjustment policy is more appropriate, one that takes "people to jobs." There was strong provincial opposition to the inclusion of regional development programs in the effort to negotiate a subsidies regime for the FTA, and this is likely to persist for the Chapter 19 negotiations. In their FTA subsidies proposal, however, the Americans made it clear that regional development programs would be given no safe harbour, and this position is unlikely to change very much. If the US persists and regional interests prevail in Canada, then the impasse may force this issue into the yellow caution zone, where Canada's regional development programs would continue to be subject to countervail action.

Agricultural Policy

Canadian policy in the agricultural field reflects the same competitive subsidy binge that has marked the policies of the European Community (EC) and the US.[29] The Community's Common Agricultural Policy (CAP) to subsidize agricultural production was formulated in the early 1960s, when almost one quarter of the EC civilian work force was employed in agriculture. But this had declined to 7.5 per cent by the end of the 1980s, and was supported by a CAP that the rest of the world viewed with growing hostility. The CAP utilized some $44 billion of Community taxpayer money directly in subsidies, and it carried an additional cost of $54 billion in higher than market prices paid by EC consumers. Almost two per cent of the Community's GDP was devoted to assisting a small and declining part of its work force. Furthermore, as is common in most such programs, the bulk of the income support went not to needy farmers, who provided the official rationale for the program, but to wealthier farmers who had less need of the support. At the same time, the CAP seriously harmed the trade prospects of many agricultural Third World countries, as well as those of middle-sized agricultural traders like Canada, and they joined together in the so-called Cairns Group to oppose EC policies.

The attack on the CAP, however, was led by the United States, which made it a key issue in the Uruguay Round of multilateral trade negotiations (MTN) that began in 1986. The US, for some time generously endowed with its own support programs for agricultural producers, had greatly increased subsidies in the 1980s in order to retain its share of world agricultural trade. As both EC and US subsidies increased, other countries, including Canada, had little choice but to join the subsidy game. The Mulroney government's agricultural budget doubled between 1984 and 1988, mainly because of the mad rush to subsidize.[30] However, this is not a game that a smaller, debt-ridden country can afford to play for very long.

By the late 1980s, Canadian agricultural income support programs were being criticized on the same grounds as the Community's CAP: they produced higher prices for consumers, and support went disproportionately to larger or wealthier producers.[31] Furthermore, the programs distorted choices as to what to grow. Although Canada has attempted to achieve disciplines on agricultural subsidies through the GATT, it has been forced to deal with contrary pressures from contending domestic constituencies in the process. Some of the contours of the domestic battle over subsidies were revealed in the FTA negotiation process.[32] Here, the issue was whether agricultural marketing boards would be protected by Canada. It pitted farmers and producers against food manufacturers, who would soon face US competitors who could acquire their raw farm produce at lower market prices. The farmers won this original battle, but have since been under intense pressure from manufacturers to phase out marketing boards.

Canada and the US have agreed that problems related to agricultural subsidies, other than export subsidies, cannot be handled adequately in a bilateral forum, but must be addressed in multilateral negotiations. As a result, both countries have chosen to approach this issue through the current MTN, rather than through the bilateral subsidies negotiations.[33]Should the MTN fail to produce a satisfactory agreement, certain aspects of the agricultural subsidies issue could shift to the bilateral talks. However, an adequate solution requires a negotiated agreement between the EC and the US. Without this, the scope of any Canadian-American negotiation will be sharply limited, as will be its implications for agricultural policy.

NEGOTIATING IN THE 1990s: A FREE TRADE SEQUEL

In the original negotiations leading to the FTA, Canada was seeking some limits on the application of American countervailing duty (CVD) laws, which the US would consider only if Canada would agree to discipline its subsidy practices. Canada wanted to identify a non-actionable class of subsidy practices that would be exempt from countervail action, but the Americans rejected the Canadian proposal as offering far too broad an exemption to win acceptance in Congress. For its part, the US wanted to identify a prohibited class of subsidy practices that would apply to Canada, leaving the countervail system in place to target any programs not explicitly prohibited. The Canadians rejected this as insufficient and unbalanced.

Unable to resolve the stand-off, the two agreed to establish the bilateral working group to continue negotiations on the issue over a further five- to seven-year period, with the final deadline sometime in 1995.[34]However, the prospects for a negotiated agreement do not look much brighter now, almost four years after the original breakdown in talks in September 1987. The basic disagreement between the two countries over the nature of the issue remains. As well, there are good reasons for each to delay serious negotiations, and this will make a resolution of the very real differences between them more difficult.

Negotiation Dynamics

The 1987 impasse in the free trade negotiations resulted from a fundamental disagreement over the nature of the issue to be negotiated. For the US, the issue was, and remains, subsidies. The American countervail system is required to deal with Canadian subsidy practices; if subsidization is eliminated, then countervail will be unnecessary. For Canada, on the other hand, the issue was, and continues to be, American countervail actions. Although US subsidy practices are undoubtedly more widespread than the Americans would like to admit, and their import displacement effects are not trivial, they are not the major problem facing Canada. Instead, Canadian concerns centre on the growing tendency of the US to rely on countervailing duties to protect its domestic industries. Between 1980 and 1989, the US initiated or reviewed 16 CVD cases against Canada. As Colleen Morton states,

> ...as the trade deficit has climbed, both Congress and the Administration have become more willing to expand the application of cvd/ad [antidumping] procedures, to attack a wider array of foreign practices as 'subsidies' (especially upstream and natural resource subsidies) and to loosen the definitions of key concepts such as injury, specificity and causality.[35]

This basic disagreement over the nature of the problem at issue is reflected in the different labels assigned to the Article 1907 group by the two countries: the Working Group on Subsidies for the US, and the Subsidies-Trade Remedies Working Group for Canada.

Negotiating objectives for the US delegation to the Working Group were established in the FTA Implementation Act approved by Congress. The Act specifically requires the achievement of increased discipline over Canadian production and export subsidies. The Americans are most likely to focus their demands for Canadian disciplines on natural resource pricing and access policies and on regional development assistance programs, seeking Canadian agreement on the prohibition of subsidy practices in these areas. Canada's goal, on the other hand, will be the achievement of increased discipline over US trade remedy actions. As a key priority, Canada will probably seek American agreement to the identification of a class of non-actionable subsidy practices that will be explicitly exempted from countervail action.

Canada is also likely to pursue changes in the US countervail system in order to reduce its availability as an instrument to harass foreign competitors. For example, by getting the US to raise the *de minimus* level in US CVD cases beyond the current 0.5 per cent of production costs, Canada could eliminate countervail actions in cases where the cumulative effect of the subsidy on an American producer is minimal. Similarly, harassment would be reduced if the US would agree to adopt a more rigorous material injury test for CVD cases, one that is less biased in favour of the complainant in the determination of injury and requires the establishment of a direct causal link between the subsidy and the injury.

These divergent negotiating agendas will make agreement extremely difficult. The Americans are likely to press very hard on the subsidies issue, in an effort to target a wide range of Canadian subsidy programs for prohibition, while resisting Canadian efforts to place limits on the application of CVDs. For their part, the Canadians will want to push as far as possible on trade remedies, trying to get agreement on a class of non-actionable subsidies plus tighter rules governing CVD application. At the same time, Canada will want to preserve the integrity of certain sensitive programs, such as regional development assistance, and will resist US efforts to identify a broad class of prohibited subsidies.

Trade-offs across these two agendas will be difficult to engineer. In the face of the discord generated by the Meech Lake debacle, the Canadian federal government will not find it easy to agree to the prohibition of sensitive programs, such as regional development assistance, nor to undertake disciplines on provincial subsidy practices. The US, however, will be looking for major concessions. As one American analyst has put it:

> It would be a serious political mistake for the Canadian government to come to the negotiations demanding further limitations on the application of US cvd/ad laws without offering major concessions in return, in the form of substantially reduced subsidy programs.[36]

Incentives to Delay

Thus far, however, the problem of divergent negotiating agendas remains largely moot, since neither side has been anxious to move beyond preliminary discussions. Furthermore, it is unlikely that serious negotiations will occur in the medium term, at least until after the Canadian federal election that will probably occur late in 1992. This delay is in Canada's best interests. In fact, a maximum postponement is good for Canada for several reasons.

First, delay permits the FTA to become fully operational, and experience to be gained with the dispute settlement machinery created under Chapter 19. Second, it allows for a more considered discussion of the meaning of subsidies and who uses them. There is still a widespread American belief that other countries subsidize and the US does not. This fiction has been sustained in part by the virtual American monopoly in the subsidy definition business, and by the fact that few trade remedy actions have been launched against the US. In the early 1990s, however, it is increasingly apparent that Europe, Japan, the Pacific Rim countries and Canada are determined to break the American definitional monopoly. Discussion in the Uruguay Round has given these countries an opportunity to push the US further to test the definitional issue against a world standard. Buying time in this process is vital both for trade and other policy reasons, since the subsidies question goes to the core of defining what the proper role of the state is, or can be, under different democratic regimes. It is not a narrow trade matter.

A third reason for caution is that Canada is dangerously exposed in a negotiation that focusses exclusively on the subsidy issue. It will be a very different kind of negotiation than was the FTA itself, where the Americans might have had to pay on other issues for Canadian concessions on subsidies. In a subsidy negotiation, Canada's exposure is to both American demands and Canadian domestic political sensitivities. As a result, whereas the Canadians pushed the issue to the top of the agenda throughout 15 months of free trade negotiations, they might now be just as happy to have it go away. This is unlikely. While the US was willing to let the issue slide in the short term, at least as long as it was being addressed in the MTN, the Americans will be determined in the longer run to pursue subsidies negotiations.

Pressures in the US to obtain visible concessions from Canada are likely to increase. As was the case in the free trade negotiations, American negotiators will be more concerned with Congress than with Canada. And a Congress dominated by Democrats anxious to pursue a policy of "fair trade" as one of their main political weapons against President George Bush is unlikely to be very sympathetic to Canadian needs. Chapter 19 itself may also provide a lever for the Americans to use in pressing Canada for concessions. The panel review process approved by Congress as part of the Chapter 19 solution was intended to serve only until a new system of rules could be negotiated by the bilateral Working Group. It is not clear whether the review process itself will lapse in the event that the Working Group is unable to conclude a successful negotiation on the subsidies-trade remedies issue. For these reasons, the Americans may be expected to press hard for concessions on subsidies. But Canadian political conditions will make those concessions very difficult to grant.

In Canada, there will be much more tenacious vigilance on the part of the anti-free trade coalition that opposed the Mulroney free trade agreement. They will oppose in principle any demonstrable loss in formal federal powers, and they will be joined by anti-Meech Lake forces equally suspicious of federal giveaways. Provincial governments will also continue to be aggressive in their defence of subsidy programs, especially in Atlantic Canada, where regional development programs will be seen, correctly, as a major American target. In addition, the New Democratic government of Bob Rae in Ontario is likely to vigorously defend its powers to subsidize. All of this suggests that Canadian negotiators will be under intense scrutiny, and may have to set out for public discussion a far more open account of positions and strategies than was evident in the free trade negotiations. Because these conditions will make it difficult for Canada to respond to American pressures for concessions on the subsidies issue, the Canadians may prefer to delay negotiations until a more propitious political environment prevails.

Last, but hardly least among the factors suggesting continued delay is the upcoming Canada-Mexico-US trilateral free trade negotiation. In this case, however, the fate of the subsidy negotiations is far from certain. On the one hand, the separate negotiation on subsidies between Canada and the US might be simply postponed indefinitely by the larger issue of trilateral continental free trade.[37] If this is the case, then a decision would probably still have to be made on the fate of the temporary Chapter 19 panel review process. Even if the US is willing to let the process stand for Canada in the absence of a bilateral agreement under Chapter 19, its extension to include Mexico could be problematic.[38] On the other hand, the subsidies issue could be shifted from the bilateral negotiations to a trilateral forum, where Canada, the US and Mexico would attempt to define a system of rules to govern unfair trade practices between them. If the issue is transferred to the trilateral forum, then the Canadians will have to scramble to ready themselves for a negotiation on a tight schedule, in order to meet both US fast track legislative requirements and the Mexican Presidential electoral timetable.

CONCLUSIONS: THE POLITICAL ECONOMY OF SUBSIDIES

Although Canada originally pressed the subsidy issue on a reluctant United States in the FTA negotiations, the Americans have now become the principal advocates of a system of rules to discipline subsidy practices. There is more than a little irony in this. The threat of US protectionism, which dictated the priority Canada attached to the subsidies-trade remedies issue, was overblown from the outset. By early 1988, only four US countervailing duties were actually in place against Canada (excluding the softwood lumber export tax).[39] Even in the 1980-85 period, when Canadian governments were moving toward the decision to seek free trade, less than one per cent of Canada-US trade was affected by countervail actions. As John Whalley points out, this relatively small number of CVD actions on a small number of products is not terribly important in the scheme of overall economic activity.[40] Having opened the Pandora's box of subsidy disciplines, Canada may now wish things could revert to the *status quo ante*.

Canadians could get their wish, at least for the short term. On balance, it seems unlikely that bilateral subsidies-trade remedies negotiations can be concluded in the short term, especially since political forces in Canada weigh strongly against serious negotiations before midway through 1993. If they are undertaken bilaterally sooner than that, the prospects for success will not be bright. Even if the negotiations are postponed for a few years, however, Canadians will still need to face the issues raised by the subsidy debate sometime in the 1990s.

Whether in the process of bilateral or trilateral negotiations, or simply as a result of continuing GATT and FTA countervail cases, the role of subsidies in the Canadian political economy will continue to surface as an issue. The economic arguments for the most part suggest that it would be in Canada's interest to minimize subsidy activity. From this perspective, the best course would be to accede to US demands for greater disciplines on subsidies. But there are strong political, and even some economic, arguments in support of Canadian subsidy programs, and these will prevent easy compliance with US demands. The path to a new regime to govern subsidies and trade remedies will not be easily traversed, and whichever route is finally chosen, this free trade sequel is likely to receive mixed reviews from Canadians.

Notes

1   For a detailed account see G. Bruce Doern and Brian W. Tomlin, *Faith and Fear: The Free Trade Story* (Toronto: Stoddard, forthcoming 1991), chapters 7 and 8.

2   Ibid., chapter 6.

3   See Marc Gold and David Leyton-Brown, (eds.), *Trade-Offs on Free Trade* (Toronto: Carswell, 1988).

4   See Andre Blais, (ed.), *Industrial Policy* (Toronto: University of Toronto Press, 1986), chapter 1.

5   See Gary Hufbauer and Joanna Shelton Erb, *Subsidies in International Trade* (Washington, D.C.: Institute For International Economics, 1984) and Michael Trebilcock, M.A. Chandler and Robert Howse, *Trade and Transition: A Comparative Analysis of Adjustment Policies* (London: Routledge, 1990), chapter 3.

6   See John Whalley, "Now That the Deal is Over: Trade Policy Options in the 1990s," *Canadian Public Policy,* Volume XVI, No. 2 (June), 1990, pp. 121-136.

7   See Trebilcock, Chandler and Howse, op.cit., *passim.*

8   See Alan Oxley, *The Challenge of Free Trade* (London: Harvester Wheatsheaf, 1990), p. 243.

9   See Michael Finger and Julio Nogues, "International Control of Subsidies and Countervailing Duties," *The World Bank Economic Review* I:4 (1987), pp. 707-725 and Joseph Grieco, *Cooperation Among Nations: Europe, America and Non-Tariff Barriers To Trade* (Ithaca: Cornell University Press, 1990), chapters 3 and 4.

10   Quoted in Andrew Anderson and Alan Rugman, "Subsidies in the US Steel Industry: A Conceptual Approach to the Literature," *Working Paper Series*, No. 14, Ontario Centre For International Business, University of Toronto, April 1989, p. 29.

11   See Daniel Tarullo, "Beyond Normalcy in the Regulation of International Trade," *Harvard Law Review*, Vol. 100 (1987), pp. 547-626.

12   See Michael Percy and Christian Yoder, *The Softwood Lumber Dispute and Canada-US Trade in Natural Resources* (Halifax: Institute for Research on Public Policy, 1989).

13   See Jean-François Bence and Murray Smith "Subsidies and the Trade Laws: The Canada-US Dimension," *International Economic Issues* (April-May, 1989), pp. 1-36.

14   Ibid., p.ii.

15   See for example, John Mutti, *Taxes, Subsidies and Competitiveness Internationally* (Washington, D.C.: National Planning Association, 1982).

16   Gary Hufbauer, "A View of the Forest," in Bela Balassa (ed.), *Subsidies and Countervailing Measures* (Washington, D.C.: World Bank, 1989), Table 1, p. 22, cited in Colleen Morton, *Subsidies Negotiations and the Politics of Trade* (Washington, DC: National Planning Association, 1989), p. 6. The Group of Seven (G-7) includes the world's leading industrialized countries.

17   See Organization for Economic Co-operation and Development, "Industrial Subsidies in the OECD

Economies," *OECD Economic Studies,* No. 15, Paris, 1990.

18   The following data are taken from OECD, op.cit., Table 2.

19   During the FTA negotiations, the Canadian government compiled an extensive list of US federal subsidy practices, although most would displace imports rather than enhance exports and would therefore not be countervailable under the GATT or Canadian trade laws. See Ann Michel et al., *An Annotated Inventory of Federal Business Subsidy Programs in the United States* (Ottawa: Institute for Research on Public Policy, 1986), cited in Morton, op.cit., p. 10.

20   See Bence and Smith, op.cit., p. i.

21   See Anderson and Rugman, op.cit., pp. 1-4, and Percy and Yoder, op.cit.

22   For a review, see G. Bruce Doern, "The Department of Industry, Science and Technology: Is There Industrial Policy After Free Trade?" in Katherine A. Graham, (ed.), *How Ottawa Spends 1990-91* (Ottawa: Carleton University Press, 1990), pp. 49-72.

23   See Richard Lipsey and Wendy Dobson, (eds.), *Shaping Comparative Advantage* (Toronto: C.D. Howe Institute, 1987).

24   See Donald McFetridge, (ed.), *Canadian Industrial Policy in Action* (Toronto: University of Toronto Press, 1986), chapter 1.

25   See Michael Atkinson and William Coleman, *The State, Business, and Industrial Change in Canada* (Toronto: University of Toronto Press, 1989).

26   See Richard Harris, *Trade, Industrial Policy and International Trade* (Toronto: University of Toronto Press, 1985).

27   See Doern and Tomlin, *Faith and Fear: The Free Trade Story,* chapters 9 and 10, and Glen Drover, (ed.), *Free*

Trade and Social Policy (Ottawa: Canadian Council on Social Development, 1988).

28   Morton, op.cit., p. 11.

29   See "World Trade: Jousting for Advantage," *The Economist*, September 22, 1990, pp. 5-39.

30   Michael Prince, "Little Help on the Prairie: Canadian Farm Income Programs and the Western Grain Economy," in Katherine Graham (ed.), *How Ottawa Spends 1990-91* (Ottawa: Carleton University Press, 1990), p. 154.

31   L. Auer, *Canadian Prairie Farming, 1960-2000: An Economic Analysis* (Ottawa: Supply and Services Canada, 1989).

32   Doern and Tomlin, *Faith and Fear: The Free Trade Story*, chapter 5.

33   Morton, op.cit., p. 25. A significant number of American CVD actions against Canadian producers have targeted agricultural exports.

34   The Working Group established by Article 1907 of the FTA also has a mandate to deal with antidumping law, in addition to subsidies and countervail. We concentrate on the latter two in this section.

35   Morton, op.cit., p. 16.

36   Ibid., p. 26.

37   See Ronald Wonnacott, "Canada and the US-Mexico Free Trade Negotiations," *Commentary*, C.D. Howe Institute, No. 21, September 1990, and Richard Lipsey, "Canada at the US-Mexico Free Trade Dance: Wallflower or Partner?" *Commentary*, C.D. Howe Institute, No. 20, August 1990.

38   See Michael Hart, *A North American Free Trade Agreement* (Halifax: Institute for Research on Public Policy, 1990), p. 126.

39   Whalley, op.cit., p. 125.

40   Ibid., p. 125.

CHAPTER 7

HOW OTTAWA BLENDS: SHIFTING GOVERNMENT RELATIONSHIPS WITH INTEREST GROUPS

Susan D. Phillips

Résumé: Au cours du deuxième mandat du gouvernement Mulroney, trois tendances se sont dessinées dans les relations entre le gouvernement fédéral et les groupes d'intérêt. Premièrement, le public et les ministères gouvernementaux réclament une consultation plus positive ainsi qu'une fonction publique plus axée sur les clients. Deuxièmement, on révise la pratique qui consiste à accorder des subventions à des groupes d'intérêt. On essaie d'apporter plus de responsabilité à ce financement et on s'éloigne du financement global de l'opération des groupes en faveur du financement de projets spécifiques. Une analyse des subventions accordées par le Secrétariat d'État au cours des dix dernières années démontre une stabilité considérable dans le cas du financement de groupes tels que les associations de langue officielle minoritaire et les groupes multiculturels qui appuient l'ordre symbolique de l'identité canadienne mais en même temps une baisse importante dans le cas de groupes qui revendiquent des droits pour d'autres collectivités, les femmes et les autochtones notamment.

Finalement, le concept de collaboration entre "partenaires" est devenu très attirant. On examine quatre types de partenariat: 1) partenariats consultatifs, tels que la Table ronde sur l'économie et l'environnement; 2) partenariats accessoires, tels que la Semaine nationale pour l'intégration des personnes handicapées; 3) partenariats en matière de développement des communautés, tels que le projet Cités santé; 4) partenariats de collaboration, tels que la Commission canadienne de mise en valeur de la main-d'oeuvre.

Abstract: During the second term of the Mulroney government, three trends have emerged in relations between the federal government and client and stakeholder groups. First, there is a demand by both the public and government departments for more meaningful consultation and a more client-centred public service. Secondly, the practice of giving grants to interest groups has come under review. There are attempts to make this funding more accountable and there is a general move away from core or operational funding of groups in favour of grants for specific projects. Analysis of grants by Secretary of State over the past 10 years shows that funding is relatively secure for groups—official language minority associations and multicultural groups—which support the symbolic order of the **Canadian** identity, but has declined considerably for groups which promote rights of other collectivities, notably women and Aboriginal peoples.

Finally, the concept of "partnership" has become very attractive. Four types of partnerships are identified and examples of each briefly examined: 1) consultative partnerships, such as the Round Table on the Economy and the Environment; 2) contributory partnerships, using the example of National Access Awareness Week; 3) community development partnerships such as the Healthy Communities Project; and 4) collaborative partnerships, as illustrated by the Labour Force Development Board.

In the politics of the 1990s, interest groups are placing increasing pressure on Ottawa to blend their demands into the policy process. The traditional perspective on the relationship between government and interest groups has been to presume that organized groups lobby politicians and public servants to satisfy their special interests and that government responds to the group that is most vocal, most popular or most compatible with its own ideology.[1] There is no doubt that this type of pressure politics takes place on a daily basis in Ottawa by representatives of a plethora of interests. But the federal government is not merely a passive recipient of interest group demands. Rather, government departments shape the opportunities for certain groups—and not others—to participate in the policy-making process by creating mechanisms for public consultation. In addition, the federal government has a long-standing practice of providing funding to public interest groups so that they may organize their constituencies and represent their concerns.[2] During the second term of the Mulroney government, there have been three significant and, in some respects, contradictory developments in the ways in which the federal government deals with interest groups and the Canadian public.

First, the existing practice of public consultation increasingly is viewed as unworkable. Demands for more meaningful consultation and a more public-centred public service have been heard from many quarters including interest groups, public servants and the PS2000 Task Force on Service to the Public. Two of the most extensive—and most expensive—public participation exercises undertaken recently by the federal government have been the department of Environment's consultation surrounding the Green Plan and the Citizens' Forum on Canada's Future (the Spicer Commission). However, both illustrate fundamental flaws in the current practice of public participation in policy-making.

Second, faith has faded in the idea that government funding to public interest groups would create a level playing field among groups and promote citizenship in general. There is increasing selectivity in how Ottawa spends money on interest groups, resulting in cuts to some groups, and there are greater requirements for financial accountability. In particular, the federal government's role in core (sometimes called program, operational or sustaining) funding of interest groups gradually is being retracted in favour of project funding that is more easily controlled and more visibly accountable. However, many Aboriginal and women's organizations feel that successive funding cuts have been an attempt to muzzle them because they have been the most vitriolic critics of the Mulroney government.[3] Cuts in the 1990 Budget to these sectors resulted in innovative protests across the country consisting of "hot dog roasts" to commemorate the Minister of State, Gerry Weiner.[4] In spite of a general trend of more restrictive funding, support for associations promoting official language minorities (Francophones in English Canada and Anglophones in Quebec) and groups promoting multiculturalism has actually increased in recent years. In contrast to other social movements, their activities are integral to the campaign for national unity and the quest for a Canadian identity.

Finally, the greatest departure from old relationships is the concept of "partnership." In the proper sense, the term partnership necessarily involves a decentralization or sharing of power with non-government players—which may be either business, labour or citizen groups. However, the term, "partnership," has different interpretations in different departments. Indeed, partnerships may range from actual power-sharing arrangements, such as the Labour Force Development Board (LFDB) created in 1991 by Employment and Immigration, to vague notions in which the label partnership is used as nothing more than tinsel to adorn an existing arrangement. In spite of their popularity, partnerships should not be seen as direct substitutes for public consultation or funding of interest groups. Nor are they appropriate responses to all social policy issues. But, partnerships can be very effective under specific conditions for limited purposes.

The underlying impetus for these shifts in relationships with interest groups arises, in part, from significant changes in the structure of Canadian society. Specifically, in recent years Canadian society has witnessed:[5]

° increasing fragmentation and specialization of interests and identities that directs politics, not toward partisan ideology, but toward the concerns of language, region, gender, ethnicity, sexual orientation or other "minoritarianism."[6] Through social movements and interest groups, society has become increasingly organized to give voice to a multiplicity of collective identities, as well as to very specific interest group claims. As a consequence of the greater number of voices, political discourse on any given policy issue is much more complex than it was 10 or 20 years ago.

° embodiment of a rights-oriented political culture. Not only is this diversity of identities organized, but each feels it has a **right** to be heard in the policy process.[7] This notion of entitlement has been a direct result of the enhancement of both individual and collective rights in the Charter of Rights and Freedoms, the full force of which came into effect in 1985.

° growing uneasiness with elitism and increasing unwillingness to leave policy to our elected leaders.[8] The secretive and closed nature of the negotiations on the Meech Lake Constitutional Accord reinforced in Canadians a desire to make government decision-making processes more open and participatory for all citizens.

New ways of dealing with interest groups are also the result of global changes in the position of governments *vis-à-vis* markets and societies.[9] The factors that, in general, are requiring states to become less interventionist include:

° greater complexity of policy issues and a recognition by both government and interest groups that the state does not have a monopoly on expertise. In fields such as the environment or labour force policy, federal departments now argue that the issues have become so complicated that government alone no longer has the solutions, but needs to engage the active involvement of other private and public sector players.

° diminishing financial resources (due to the weight of the national debt) to pursue policy. In this era of economic restraint, the federal government is trying to find alternative solutions to policy problems than the old one of throwing money at them. Governments also are attempting to "lever" money from the private sector to spend on public policy.

° enhanced economic globalization has created a sense that governments, as well as business, must be more competitive. The interventionist state (one which tries to substitute itself or intrude into the private sector) has lost legitimacy, but governments, now more than ever, need to promote economic and social restructuring. They, therefore, must seek new forms of relationships with both society and the market.

This chapter examines the shifts in government-interest group relations and explores the implications of these changes. The first section considers the practice and pitfalls of public consultation, focussing on the Green Plan and the Spicer Commission. In the second section, we shall investigate the extent to which various departments, notably the Department of Secretary of State (SecState), finance public interest groups and we shall examine some issues concerning funding. An overview of the types of emerging partnerships is the focus of the third section. Examples of how they have been implemented are drawn from the departments of Environment, Secretary of State, Health and Welfare and Employment and Immigration.

Although seemingly distinct phenomena, the emerging developments in consultation, funding and partnerships must be considered as a package because the impacts of these changes are connected. To some degree, they are also contradictory. While there are public expectations of greater participation in the policy process, funding for interest groups that would permit disadvantaged constituencies to be represented is not increasing. Consultation and core funding of public interest groups emphasize the ability of groups to be advocates, critics and participants. However, the shift to project funding and partnerships stresses the role of interest groups as service-providers. In combination, these developments are a significant reorientation of the federal government toward organized interests in Canadian society. In general, they represent a move from encouraging interest group advocacy to improving client service.

PUBLIC CONSULTATION

The fundamental purpose of consultation with interest groups and the public at large is to democratize the policy-making process. Consultation is the process by which the views of all parties interested in a department's policies are integrated into its decision-making: " [it] is two-way communication, with the overall goal being better overall decision-making by the agency in question and the federal government in general."[10]

> Governments consult with groups and individuals in the private sector for many reasons: to collect information needed for policy making; to involve external groups in the policy development process so that they are comfortable with the outcome; to gauge the impact of public policy decisions on a particular group; ...to determine the level of support a proposed initiative might enjoy among the public...[and] to improve service consistently.[11]

One benefit of consultation is that it promotes participation as well as representation. While consultation encourages the **representation** of the range of interests or players that have a significant stake in a policy, it also promotes citizenship—empowerment of individuals and organizations—through the act of **participating** in making their views heard. Although in theory these are the functions of political parties, the complexity of policy and the dysfunctions of brokerage parties means that, in practice, parties do not adequately fulfill this role.[12] Therefore, consultation has become the responsibility of legislatures, through parliamentary committees, the public service and independent bodies, such as Royal Commissions.[13]

There are two broad categories of consultation, as defined by who is invited to participate. By far the oldest form of consultation in Canada, predating Confederation, is "elite accommodation."[14] This process involves accommodations among state elites and those with direct substantive interests in a policy. It usually is based on shared values and ongoing relationships and occurs as a result of informal and closed, sometimes secretive, meetings. However, in the past four or five years, opportunities to achieve consensus on important policy issues through elite accommodation have faded. This is partly a result of an increasingly fractured elite, but is also a by-product of the rise of a rights-oriented culture. Social groups which were formally granted the protection of equality under the Charter (and other groups not mentioned in the Charter) have come to feel that they are entitled to participation in all matters of government policy-making. In the minds of Canadians, the debacle of the Meech Lake Accord drove a final stake through the acceptability of a process of exclusionary accommodation among national elites—be they premiers or business leaders.

Although the legitimacy of elite accommodation may be undermined, the practice of closed one-on-one consultation has not died altogether. It merely has changed players. The colonization of Ottawa by fee-for-service lobbying firms over the past decade has produced an incredible professionalization of lobbying (the uninvited act of pressuring government for one's interests). This has enhanced inequities among types of interest groups because some (mainly corporations and economic associations) can afford the hefty fees of professional lobbyists, while others (public interest groups) cannot.[15] The professionalization of lobbying has also reinforced expectations on the part of many public servants that all interest groups should be able to act like professionals, armed with technical information, reasoned argument, something to bargain and the desire to avoid public criticism and confrontation at all costs. From the perspective of public servants, who naturally tend to be risk-averse, it is much easier to deal individually with polite, professional lobbyists experienced in the mores and norms of the public service than with "amateur," sometimes angry, representatives of citizen groups. In the present political climate of a lack of trust in government, the loss of legitimacy of elite accommodation has left a void and the success of the professional lobby industry, inadvertently, has put pressure on the public service to increase the spectrum of interests consulted.

The second type of consultation involves non-elites: representatives of public interest groups and unaffiliated individuals. However, non-elite consultation is not a new idea. In Canada the idea of **public** consultation by the public service has roots in the late 1960s with the involvement of the Citizenship Branch of the Department of Secretary of State in social development. It also was greatly stimulated by the creation of the Company of Young Canadians (CYC) in 1965. The CYC was to be a vehicle for actively involving middle class youth, and through them a means of accessing the poor, as an attempt at facilitating social change.[16] Trudeau's notion of "participatory democracy" as one of the conditions of a Just Society and, coincidentally, as a way of promoting national unity by building allegiance to the federal government, gave widespread visibility to the idea of public participation in policy-making. However, it was the experience of the Berger Commission of Inquiry into the Mackenzie Valley Pipeline in 1974 that established an important precedent that has forever changed how Canadians view public consultation. Not only did Berger break down the barriers of formality by encouraging people to speak out (in their own languages, their own time and their own communities), but he left the indelible imprint that all perspectives must be heard and that funding for disadvantaged or under-represented voices is a critical prerequisite to participation. More than that, Berger listened to, and acted upon, what people told him.[17] The rise of social movements and special interest groups during the 1970s and 1980s produced a growing number of consultations with government departments.[18] In part, this was due to a genuine interest in obtaining the range of public opinion and, in part, due to the desire to legitimate the process of decision-making because many of these groups were well prepared and willing to embarrass the Government if their concerns were ignored. The idea of extensive, open consultation was briefly resurrected as the way of governing in the first Mulroney term although, as in the Trudeau years, reality fell far short of the rhetoric.

The issues of who and how to consult are crucial because there are no formal institutionalized rules for this process. Consultation may be either **private** in which representatives of a few interest groups are invited to meet with public servants (such as representatives of the social policy or agricultural community) or **public** in which anyone who wishes can be heard. Royal Commissions, such as the current Commission on Reproductive Technology, and special Task Forces are often very useful vehicles for giving a full public airing to an issue. However, they tend to be time-consuming and costly. Often public servants need more flexible, informal and immediate means for tapping public and interest group views in the formulation of policy. Another way to think about consultation is based on the mix of interests solicited. Consultation may be limited to the **clients** of a policy or program (those who are its intended target and direct beneficiaries) or may include a diversity of **stakeholders** (those with a significant stake in the policy, but who are not direct beneficiaries). "Multistakeholder" forums which bring together representatives of different sets of interests (for example, environmental groups and industry) are becoming popular because they serve to sensitize the parties to each other's concerns, as well as providing information useful for policy-making.

In general, the fundamental dilemma of consultation is striking a balance between selectivity and openness: to consult with groups or individuals who can help inform policy through their advice and expertise, while being fair and equitable so that all interested parties have the opportunity to participate. This is not an easy balancing act and it is one which, to date, the public service has not done particularly well. Examination of two of the most visible public consultation exercises in recent years—the Department of Environment's consultation on the Green Plan in 1990 and the Citizens' Forum on Canada's Future in 1991—illustrate some of the basic flaws of consultation as it is practised by federal departments.

The consultation exercise surrounding the development of the Green Plan is an example of consultation which is open to the public and interest groups alike and which purposely attempts to create a multi-stakeholder mix in its meetings. In terms of numbers of people involved, the Green Plan consultations appear impressive. In the first eight-week phase, 6,000 Canadians attended 41 "information" sessions in cities and towns across the country and received information about the Department's general framework for discussion.[19] In the second phase which lasted four weeks, consultation sessions in 17 major cities were attended by 3,500 people, including representatives of interest groups, unaffiliated individuals and industry to discuss environment issues. The total cost of this consultation was approximately $6 million.

However, many environmental groups have harshly criticized the process. Some describe this exercise as a charade imposed upon a reluctant department by Cabinet and the public for purely political ends.[20] Perhaps the most serious criticism is that the consultation process built up expectations that the Green Plan would deal in specific and tough ways with environmental issues. Instead, the Plan contains only generalized objectives and unspecific resource allocations that have left interest groups disappointed.[21] Although Environment Minister de Cotret may be correct in his argument that it would have taken years to negotiate all the federal-provincial agreements necessary to provide the desired level of specificity, participants should have been apprised of this so that false expectations were not created. In addition, the fact that Cabinet insisted on keeping the plan top secret until its official unveiling on December 11, 1990 meant that during the consultations participants could not discuss actual policy alternatives in concrete terms. Therefore, neither industry, the public nor environmental groups, some of which are very sophisticated, could contribute as effectively as they might have if discussions had been framed in more specific ways related to actual policy options.[22] In the end, what might have been a very strong public support for the Green Plan backfired. Ultimately, it alienated the environmental constituency because the process appeared to be a legitimation exercise for political gain, designed to improve the Government's position in opinion polls.

One of the most talked about and expensive consultation exercises ever undertaken by Ottawa is the Citizens' Forum on Canada's Future chaired by Keith Spicer and 11 co-commissioners. The Commission was announced in November 1990 by Prime Minister Mulroney, undoubtedly as a counterweight to the Bélanger-Campeau Commission in Quebec which was soliciting the views of Quebec groups on the province's role in the federation and, in so doing, was leaning heavily toward a sovereignty solution. The Forum began to meet the public in January 1991 and Spicer has said that it is his goal to have at least one million Canadians participate in discussion groups over a three month period—a remarkable quantitative feat, if not a qualitative one.[23] The budget for the Forum appears to have been a blank cheque with an unanticipated cost of $27.4 million, making it the most expensive Royal Commission in Canadian history.[24] In contrast to most consultation exercises which stress representation of interests, the Citizens' Forum emphasizes participation. Its purpose is to encourage town hall-type meetings and grassroots discussion in church basements and around kitchen tables. The Forum, therefore, hears only individual Canadians, speaking as individuals, not as leaders of interest groups. Even Clyde Wells, who asked to address the Forum, was told by Spicer that he, too, could call the 1-800 telephone number for information and participate as a private citizen, but not as Premier of Newfoundland.[25]

The Forum got off to a rough start and its credibility remained constantly in question. Even before the public meetings began, journalists complained that the Forum office was excessively secretive and refused to give out information. At the kickoff in the Atlantic provinces, the supposedly "ordinary citizens" turned out to be hand-picked individuals invited to participate.[26] Simultaneous translation broke down and in Hull, Quebec many people were outraged because Anglophones and Francophones were separated into two different meetings.[27] Native peoples felt they were ignored entirely in participation and in the version of Canadian duality presented in discussion questions.[28] There appeared to be continual bickering and acrimony among the Commissioners themselves.

However, the problems of the Forum are more serious than a few mistakes at a rocky beginning. Its fundamental weakness is its lack of vision about what consultation should and realistically can accomplish as part of policy-making. If the flaw of the Green Plan consultation was that very sophisticated interest groups were dealing with simple, undefined or ambiguous questions, the problem of the Citizens' Forum is exactly the opposite. The 14 discussion questions which Canadians initially were asked to discuss—without any background facts, information or preparation—were exceedingly complex.[29] For instance, one question asked: "In an increasingly competitive global environment, what does Canada have to do to succeed in the 21st century?" Another asked: "We have a number of rights as Canadians. We have some of these rights as individuals. We have others because we may belong to religious, linguistic, Aboriginal or ethnic groups. How can we best balance our rights as individuals with our rights as group members?" Each is worthy of an entire graduate university course! It is hardly surprising that what the Forum heard was confusion and raw emotion, rather than informed discussion. Although it will be impossible to determine a final count of exactly how many people take part, estimates at the Forum's mid-point indicate perhaps 40,000 people sent in briefs or participated in discussion groups that filed reports—a far cry from the original goal. Spicer placed so much emphasis on numbers that this creates a severe problem of credibility for the Forum.[30] Because people enjoyed their participation and through it felt empowered, it is hard to imagine that the Forum's final outcome will be anything but incredible disappointment and widespread disillusionment, unless governments are prepared to implement at least some of its advice. The basic problem, which is inherent in many public consultation exercises, is how to reconcile divergent opinions into a single report that can be a useful input into policy-making, and how to get government to act on it.

The criticisms levied at the Green Plan and the Spicer Forum are not peculiar to them, but are typical of the problems of consultation as it is practised by many other departments. First, there is not a natural predisposition to consultation by public servants and, consequently, there is a significant gap between the expectations held by the public and those held by public servants. Evidence indicates that public servants and their stakeholders have very different perceptions about the effectiveness of consultation exercises. A study commissioned by the PS2000 Task Force on Service to the Public found that, in general, public servants held very positive views of their personal and their departments' performance in conducting consultation.[31] In stark contrast, citizens and interest groups feel that the public service is not committed to consultation and, in general, they do not believe that it is consulting properly. In fact, the dominant culture of the public service is seen to be "inward and secretive."[32]

> There is no consultative culture in the federal public service. Little premium is placed on consultative skills and few government departments have any established machinery through which ongoing consultation can proceed. Consultation tends to be an afterthought, rather than a first thought, and all too often, an exercise in window-dressing.[33]

In their defence, many public servants would say that citizen groups act merely as critics without anything constructive about concrete policy alternatives to contribute. But, from the groups' perspective, most struggle to forge expertise out of volunteer labour and a small support staff.[34]

If consultation is to provide useful information for the development of policy, there must be shared understanding about the limits of consultation. It should be seen as a kind of "contract" in which all players are aware of the extent to which their participation realistically can affect policy outcomes. They then could base their decision to participate and their expectations about outcomes on this knowledge. The right to participate is not the right to have one's position appear as public policy, but participants must be clearly informed of the real agenda and the limitations on a department to respond to their views. Groups should be aware that the Government cannot or is not willing to consider certain policy options.

Another problem arises from the fact that consultation seldom produces a consensus. Therefore, the information obtained often falls into a sink hole because minimal attention has been devoted to how the department will package, channel and present the diversity of views heard. A related problem is that frequently the process of consultation is not integrated with the process of policy-making. Many departments have a separate branch which conducts consultation so that senior policymakers may never actually be in contact with the public. In order to create a responsive culture within the public service, senior managers, at least from time to time, must be part of the face-to-face process as they are in private meetings with preferred stakeholders and professional lobbyists. Finally, consultation often fails because adequate time is not allocated. Consultation often is required at more than one stage in policy development. While it is important to attain interest group and public advice at an early stage before too many options have been foreclosed, it also is useful to get informed discussion on more concrete alternatives, thereby increasing the overall costs and length of time required to formulate policy.

Meaningful consultation is not something which can be legislated or imposed by central agency controls. Rather, it hinges upon a receptive organizational culture, an ethic of openness and interpersonal skills. It is certainly much easier for the public servant to deal with polite, discrete professionals who know their way around government, rather than with volunteers from the boards of citizen groups who often are deeply committed and emotional, sometimes angry, about their cause. However, if consultation is to serve a purpose of democratization, the process must be based on principles of fairness and equity of representation.

One of the strongest proponents within government of more open and meaningful consultation has been the PS2000 Task Force on Service to the Public. The Task Force recommendations include establishing principles of consultation, creating a position of Deputy Secretary of Consultation in the Privy Council Office, providing training for consultation, incorporating consultation in the accountability framework for deputy ministers and establishing a mechanism for monitoring consultation. However, the Task Force fuses consultation with service to clients.[35] In their interpretation, consultation is seen as a feedback loop from the clients of a "service transaction" (policy, regulation or program) to the "service provider" (government department). Of course, consultation and service to the public are not unrelated. But, the danger of collapsing consultation into service is that consultation then runs the risk of being limited to clients (direct beneficiaries) of a policy. However, consultation is not done merely to improve an existing service, but to question what types of services and benefits, at what costs, should be provided in the first place. This necessarily involves a broader range of interests, that is, it must include stakeholders as well as clients. Customer service involves a clientele relationship, but if such dependency were imposed on consultation, the relationship with stakeholders would be precariously close to co-option. In terms of changing the corporate culture of the public service, more open consultation with organized, vocal and critical interest groups is likely to be more threatening to public servants than is improved service to clients, who as individual recipients of benefits, often remain politically unorganized. On the other hand, while consultation can assist in setting a guiding direction and values, there is more to good delivery of services than consultation.

The success of consultation depends, in part, on the recognition that some interest groups naturally have greater resources, expertise and ability to organize and, thus have greater ease of access to government. As the PS2000 Task Force itself notes, a necessary principle and prerequisite for more open and meaningful consultation may be the provision of financial assistance or other support to some groups. In this way, consultation is directly linked to interest group funding.

TAKEN FOR GRANTED: INTEREST GROUP FUNDING

A distinctive feature of the Canadian political system is that the federal government provides funding to public interest groups, many of which engage in vociferous criticism of their own benefactor. Whereas interest groups in other countries must rely on their own members, charitable donations (promoted by the income tax system) or private foundations for revenues, financial support for public interest groups by the Canadian government has a long history dating from 1945. In the past four or five years, however, significant changes have occurred in funding of public interest groups by federal departments, and in particular, by the Department of Secretary of State, whose primary *raison d'être* is to promote citizenship and social development. First, criticism of government funding by ultra-conservative groups such as the National Citizens' Coalition or R.E.A.L. Women has fuelled a crisis of legitimacy because it has created the impression that criteria for awarding grants are arbitrary, decisions ad hoc and awards indefensible.[36] Second, reviews by the Auditor General and Public Accounts Committee of the House of Commons have reinforced existing trends to make groups more accountable for the funds they receive. Accountability is being intensified by making greater use of project-specific funding, rather than providing sustaining funding for the ongoing operation of groups, and by enhancing reporting requirements and government scrutiny in general.[37] Finally, significant cuts to groups in successive years, particularly to women's and Aboriginal groups, have thrown into question the government's commitment to the entire concept of state support. Commenting on cuts in 1990, "[o]ne veteran Tory MP, who wants to be unnamed, argues that government backbenchers have long wanted cuts to advocacy groups. 'Why give them the bullets to shoot us with?'"[38]

The rationale for government funding of public interest groups is embedded in the small-l liberal notion of the benefit of both a pluralistic society and a pluralist state. The presumption is that strong organizations of citizens have an intrinsic value and are essential for a healthy society.[39] Some constituencies of citizens naturally are more difficult to organize than others because they are geographically dispersed or politically unsophisticated and they may have great trouble obtaining sufficient financial support from their potential members because as individuals, they are economically disadvantaged. In addition, other sources of income, such as donations from corporations or private foundations, may be limited because the group's cause is not popular with them. Therefore, government funding to these disadvantaged constituencies adds an element of fairness in the representation of the spectrum of interests in Canadian society. It allows organizations of women, Natives, disabled, official language minorities and poor people to be heard among the voice of the economically powerful like the Pharmaceutical Manufacturers' Association or Macmillan Bloedel. In this way, government funding to normally underrepresented interest groups is linked to consultation. In order to ensure that all stakeholder interests are represented in the formulation of policy, the articulation of interests by the economically and politically disadvantaged must be assisted by the state.

In Canada, government funding also has had an important social development objective—one that would promote citizenship and self-help for marginal sectors of society:

> It was believed that disadvantaged people were isolated and depersonalized by mass society and that this could be overcome if they began to take some responsibility for their own future. The best way to do this would be through associations or coalitions which they themselves controlled and directed. Government's role would be to give individuals and communities which already shared Government's policy goals the resources needed to organize themselves, to develop a leadership and to allow individual participation and commitment to flourish. Once progress had been made in achieving goals, it was anticipated that Government could decrease or eliminate its direct support.[40]

As Pal notes, group funding has been criticized from both a conservative and a left perspective.[41] From a conservative viewpoint, interest groups should be competitive and, as in any market, those with a viable and popular interest will receive sufficient support from their own members. Government funding, in this view, simply makes groups dependent upon the state and estranged from their supporting constituencies.[42] In contrast, concerns from the left focus on the risks of cooptation and the taming effect of funding. From this perspective, government-dependent groups over time will become less willing to bite the hand that feeds them and thus become more conservative in their demands and tactics. Committed ideological activists exit and the groups lose their passion and vitality.[43] A second critique is that the state is not blind or neutral, but highly selective, in which groups it chooses to fund, offering grants to those which are relatively acquiescent in the first place and which generally support government policies. Ironically, the Women's Program has come under fire from both the right and the left because, on one hand, it refused to fund R.E.A.L. Women, but, on the other, it does not offer support to radical feminist or lesbian groups. Still other critics (and many group leaders) are skeptical of government funding on the basis that it is not good for the groups themselves: this concern is that it supposedly makes them flabby, vulnerable and easily manipulated.[44] Nevertheless, as long as one sees at least some merit in assisting public interest groups, a position to which the present government is still officially committed, the practical question becomes which ones to fund (as demand is inevitably greater than resources available) and how to do this in a manner that appears fair and defensible.

Although it represents only a fraction of a per cent of the overall federal budget, federal grants assist thousands of interest groups in a wide variety of policy fields. These funds are dispensed by a large number of departments including National Health and Welfare, Environment, Agriculture, Justice, Sports Canada, Consumer and Corporate Affairs and the Canadian International Development Agency (CIDA). By far the most visible funding department with the greatest expenditures and largest number of client groups is the Secretary of State and its new spinoff department, Multiculturalism and Citizenship.[45] These two departments have responsibility for funding the sectors of Canadian society that encompass the most important collective identities and social movements of the post war period.[46] In 1991-92 they will provide over $130 million in transfers to more than 3,000 organizations.[47] The five main programs of SecState and Multiculturalism and Citizenship which provide financial assistance to citizen groups are:

1) Official Language Communities which offers support to associations committed to promoting the social and cultural vitality of Francophone communities in English Canada and Anglophones in Quebec;

2) Native Citizens Program which provides grants to Aboriginal representative organizations, Friendship Centres, Native communications, languages, northern Native broadcasting and Aboriginal women;

3) Women's Program offering grants to national and regional women's groups which support equality;[48]

4) Disabled Persons Participation which as the newest granting program provides assistance to organizations of and for disabled persons; and

5) Multiculturalism which assists ethnic groups in activities that promote a multicultural society.

Are there discernible trends in the amount of money spent by federal departments or in the categories of interest groups receiving funding over the past 10 years? Although no systematic data exist across all departments, analysis of spending by a selection of four departments (excluding SecState at this point) reveals that, in general, the level of grants and contributions to advocacy-oriented interest groups has remained virtually static and, when the impact of inflation is considered, has diminished slightly. Moreover, as Appendix 7.1 illustrates, in absolute numbers these transfers are relatively small, ranging from approximately $6 million awarded by Health and Welfare to half a million by Environment Canada.[49]

The pattern of funding by Secretary of State, however, is quite different. As shown in Appendix 7.2, funding is in decline for two categories of interest groups—women and Aboriginal organizations—while, at the same time, it consistently has been rising for official language minority associations and multicultural groups.[50] These differences are not merely a reflection of the number of client organizations in each program. For instance, the $28.4 million which is allocated in 1991-92 to 337 Official Language Minority Groups is almost three times greater than the amount to be provided to women's groups and eight times as much as that to be given to organizations of disabled persons.[51] Yet there are 457 national and regional women's groups and 195 disabled persons groups assisted by their respective programs. (See Table 7.1.)

Table 7.1
Number of Groups Funded
by the Department of Secretary of State, 1990-91

	Official Language	Women	Disabled	Aboriginal	Multicultural
Ottawa	16	39	41	73	40
Newfoundland	7	17	13	1	4
Nova Scotia	10	15	4	2	4
N.B. & P.E.I.	41	32	9	2	7
Quebec	17	117	33	5	32
Ontario	101	76	33	17	30
Manitoba	32	20	10	11	15
Saskatchewan	60	26	14	21	8
Alberta & N.W.T.	32	50	15	17	19
B.C. & Yukon	21	67	23	10	16
TOTAL	337	457	195	160	175

Source: Secretary of State, 1991.

The dramatic cuts to womens' and Native organizations in the 1989 and 1990 budgets suggests that the political will to support these social movements, the organizations of which are expressly political rather than service-oriented, no longer is as strong as it was in the early 1980s. In contrast, support for official language groups unequivocally is yoked to the debate on national unity. It would appear to be political hypocrisy of the highest order if the federal government were to retreat from assistance to minority Francophone and Anglophone communities in these times of constitutional turmoil. Official language minority groups also give the federal government a useful vehicle for being involved, if indirectly, in social and cultural matters that are primarily under provincial jurisdiction. Support to advocacy groups undoubtedly is more palatable if those groups are advocating for policies primarily from other governments.[52] It appears that funding is relatively secure for groups which support the symbolic order of the **Canadian** identity, as bilingual and multicultural—but is unstable for groups that promote rights of other collectivities. The funding to interest groups by other departments is relatively invisible to the Canadian public and remains outside of the current crisis of legitimacy because these groups are not engaged in a discourse of rights. Rather, they are pursuing policies and providing services directly related to the mandates of their supporting department. The 1991 Budget announced that under the Expenditure Control Plan, there will be further cuts in grants and contributions, although specific targets were not identified. In 1991-92, $75 million will be cut from the $2.5 billion in discretionary transfers (which includes many other kinds of grants besides those to interest groups) and $125 million will be trimmed each year thereafter; a wide range of interest groups undoubtedly will be affected.

Not only level, but type of funding has become a matter of controversy. Financial assistance to interest groups may be provided as either a grant or as a contribution, the distinction being one of the degree of conditionality and accountability imposed on the group receiving the funds. Grants are defined by Treasury Board as unconditional transfer payments which are not subject to being accounted for or audited, but which are tested up-front on a number of eligibility requirements.[53] In contrast, contributions are "conditional transfer payments for a specified purpose which are subject to being accounted for and audited pursuant to a contribution agreement."[54] Most transfers to interest groups are made in the form of grants, whereas contributions normally are made to provincial or territorial governments, or to groups for large or capital projects, and often are provided on a shared-cost basis.[55]

The criteria which determine whether a grant or contribution will be given are set by Treasury Board. Three general factors are: 1) need for accountability; 2) level of comfort with the particular organization requesting funds; and 3) degree of control to which government wishes to subject the organization.[56] Although Treasury Board rules guide the general criteria and conditions of eligibility, each department establishes its own specific criteria that govern the compatibility of applications for funding with program objectives. For instance, the Women's Program of SecState sets specific criteria that apply to the eligible funding areas (they will fund programs that enhance economic equality, social justice and participation in decision-making, but will not fund activities that promote a view on abortion or sexual orientation), that relate to the capacity of organizations (such as a sound financial management system and member participation in organizational decision-making) and that establish the suitability of projects (for instance, length of project and objectives).[57]

Perhaps the issue which generates the greatest controversy is the distinction between grants which are given as project funding for limited purposes to carry out a predetermined project and those which are given as "core" funding aimed at paying a portion of the costs of the ongoing operation of organizations. A considerably greater degree of control can be exercised over project funding because the department has the opportunity to ensure that the activity complies with program objectives. In order to qualify for sustaining funding groups must have a proven ability to plan and implement programs and must submit a financial statement.[58] From the perspective of interest groups, most would prefer to obtain core funding because it is less intrusive and offers greater flexibility in its use. Many group leaders argue that in the absence of operating grants they create *de facto* sustaining funding through successive project applications which enable them to use a portion of project money to subsidize core operations. The organizational cost of this strategy is great because group executive and staff often become bogged down in filling out applications and activity reports or in undertaking projects that are not central to the primary mission of the group. Due to increased demands to participate in consultation, even many core funded groups are unable to sustain themselves on existing funding levels, and thus increasingly are being forced to supplement operating grants with project money.

For a number of reasons, there is a growing uneasiness within federal departments over the dispensing of core funding. First, there are no consistent and clearly articulated criteria used in the approval of sustaining grants.[59] A second concern is that core funding becomes an entitlement from which a department cannot easily extricate itself, particularly if there exist few other sources of funding for the groups. Finally, it is sometimes argued that core funding is not good for the groups because it reverses the direction of accountability from constituency to department, reduces volunteerism and makes citizen groups more professionalized, all of which isolate the leadership from its rank and file membership.

Given these perceived difficulties, many of the client groups believe that federal departments, especially SecState, are trying to retreat quietly from core funding for advocacy organizations.[60] When asked this question directly by a member of the Public Accounts Committee, however, a Secretary of State official was less than affirmative: "Core funding is a means by which the department can fund organizations whose objectives complement those of the department. I do not believe I can answer that question."[61]

The issue is an exceedingly difficult one for SecState and other departments because, while they may have a desire for greater discretion in funding by not being locked into ongoing commitments, they also have a symbiotic relationship with their recipient organizations. This produces a strong inertia against change. Because most of the core funded groups are highly dependent upon government revenues, withdrawal of sustaining grants would have to be done over many years in order not to decimate the groups.[62]

A related, but more visible development is the push to greater accountability for transfers to interest groups. In 1990, the Public Accounts Committee issued its sixth report on grants and contributions and the Auditor General independently reviewed the Native Citizens Directorate of SecState. Given the mission and orientation of both auditors, the similarities in their recommendations are not surprising.[63] Both the Public Accounts Committee and the Auditor General expressed concern that the criteria for funding are vague or poorly followed. Both recommended that grant applications be assessed against precise criteria and that reasons for decisions be documented. The Auditor General noted that in the absence of strict adherence to criteria, cuts to groups tend to be across the board without consideration of the relative merits or needs of the organizations.[64] Both reports also criticized the slow and cumbersome workings of the application approval process within SecState. The Auditor General lamented that "grants and contribution applications, regardless of size, must go through 10 review levels before approval. A process that took close to 21 weeks in 1989-90."[65]

On the issue of core funding, the concern was raised that the same groups tend to get funded year after year without adequate monitoring or accountability. The proposal was made that for core operating grants, accounting requirements be stiffened with both activity and financial reports being filed at two intervals during a grant. The Public Accounts Committee went so far as to suggest that every three years all granting departments be required to analyze and justify before Parliament the benefits of repeat funding in terms of competing government-wide demands for scarce resources: in effect, a kind of sunset clause that would put an end to automatic renewal of core funding.

It would be an extremely difficult task—and not one which will be attempted in this chapter—to evaluate in detail the impact of government funding on interest groups. Several general effects, however, are evident. First, the broad social movements which have been supported by SecState are relatively strong and healthy. In comparison to the US or the UK, for example, Canada still has a vital women's movement and the movement of disabled persons is becoming an important political force. It is likely that Canada's multicultural policy, in spite of all the criticism to which it has been subjected, would have been remote, artificial and unconnected to the grassroots if funding had not been available to community organizations for political advocacy or for "song and dance" celebrations of their ethnic heritage. In general, these social movements have been absorbed into "normal" politics rather than the confrontational, sometimes violent, conflicts that have characterized the politics of the new social movements in many European countries. A significant consequence for public policy has been that many identity-promoting groups, supported by federal departments, have come to look to government, and the federal government in particular, to protect or address their interests. On issues such as child care, violence against women or protection of heritage and minority languages, advocacy organizations have tended to turn first to Ottawa. In some measure, the expectation has been created that the funder of minority interests will also be their protector.

By creating highly organized social movements, the federal government has augmented, if indirectly, a political discourse focussed on collective rights. This does not imply that the programs of SecState created rights-seeking identities that would not have arisen without its support. Nor does it mean that cuts to funding would now reduce the emphasis on collective rights. As Pal argues, however, the financial assistance of the federal government promoted fragmentation among these movements:

> But the programs, by making it possible to organize and articulate demands, did amplify and legitimate a much richer diversity of identities and claims than would normally have been possible...The reality is a politics overdetermined by division and difference.[66]

This rights discourse also creates a strong resistance to change in the funding programs themselves because the client groups have assumed ownership of them. It has become extremely difficult to be more selective and to reduce grants, particularly core funding, because any organization not funded immediately cries that its rights, and by extension the group rights of the collectivity it represents, have been infringed. This rights-based ownership by the groups has reduced the Department's latitude for action and has created an internal crisis of management. In spite of client opposition, there is increasing political pressure on government departments to make funding more accountable and to be more selective in the grants made to interest groups engaged in policy advocacy. At the same time, however, the government itself is making increased demands on stakeholder groups for greater consultation. The two are inherently contradictory forces. One way in which the dilemma of achieving both greater accountability and more intense consultation is being resolved is through the move to strategic partnerships.

FROM CONSULTATION TO COLLABORATION: EMERGING PARTNERSHIPS

The term, "partnership" has become the buzzword of the 1990s. In his 1991 Budget Speech, Finance Minister Wilson spoke about building a new partnership for prosperity.[67] The Environmental Green Plan is replete with the language of partnership, positing the strengthening or forging of government partnerships with the provinces, Aboriginal peoples, industry, local communities, other nations, environmental interest groups and consumers. In its 1990 annual report, the Economic Council of Canada strongly recommended building a partnership among social-economic players to develop and deliver labour market programs.[68] Similarly, the Science Council asserts that success in science and technology policy in a globally competitive economy can no longer rely on solutions provided by centralized and insensitive national governments, but must involve both decentralization of decision-making to the community level and a partnership among levels of government, the business community, labour and educational/research institutions.[69] Even Premier Bob Rae, a social democrat, is stressing partnerships among government, industry and employees, as well as between Canada, the US and other economies.[70]

In spite of its ubiquitous popularity as a label, the meaning of partnership is sometimes chimerical. In its proper sense, partnership differs from consultation (an exchange of information) because it involves collaborative joint action in an effort to solve a problem. It requires an ongoing commitment, acceptance of shared contributions and recognition of mutual needs and benefits. A decentralization of power, responsibility and accountability from government to the partnership is supposed to occur.[71] Partnerships are one form of what Block calls, the "debureaucratization" of the state which he argues is essential in post-industrial economies.[72] In part, the push to these new power-sharing arrangements is a function of the failure of both consultation and group funding. While consultations seldom produce consensus, transferring money to stakeholders often merely enhances fragmentation and division because the interest groups simply become more expert in defending their positions.

The range of relationships that parade under the rubric of partnership extends from the "old wine, new bottles" variety to exciting fresh grapes and new vintners. In order not to render the concept meaningless through imprecise use, it is important to distinguish actual power-sharing relationships that, in fact, qualify as proper partnerships from those that are illusory new labels for old arrangements.[73] At least four types of partnerships can be identified.

Consultative "Partnerships": These refer to institutionalized stakeholder consultations of which the Round Table on the Economy and the Environment is a good example. In contrast to the one-shot consultation, Round Tables have the advantage that over time they can build trust, commitment and expertise among the members. In most cases, the members are carefully selected individuals who are typical of a particular stakeholder interest rather than representatives of a specific organization. Without strong government support in terms of mandate and personnel, however, Round Tables run the risk of impotence and isolation from both government and the public. Because no new powers are conferred on Round Table members, these bodies merely represent a new incantation for what we used to refer to as advisory councils and therefore should not be called partnerships at all.

Contributory Partnerships: These arrangements tend to be innovations of the Mulroney era and their primary purpose is to lever new resources or replace government with private sector money. Among the simplest form of these levering schemes is the Environmental Partners Fund under which Environment Canada will pay up to 50 per cent (to a maximum of $200,000 over three years) of local, small-scale projects if private or local authorities provide the remaining funds. More sophisticated versions are the two newest programs of SecState and Multiculturalism—the Disabled Persons Participation Program (created in 1985) and the Literacy program (begun in 1988)—both of them built on the strategy of partnership. For example, National Access Awareness Week (NAAW), supported by the Disabled Persons Participation Program, is an annual event which grew out of the momentum of positive publicity generated by Rick Hansen's "Man in Motion" tour. It is intended to promote public education of the physical and attitudinal barriers to disabled persons and recognize their accomplishments. Although supported by SecState, NAAW is built on the principle of corporate-group-government partnership. Two important features of NAAW are the contributions, both monetary and in-kind services, provided by corporate sponsors and the implementation of activities at the community level with no mandated requirement that activities follow a government-imposed plan.[74] Furthermore, SecState does not control the planning for NAAW events. Rather, the co-ordination of all aspects of planning is overseen by a national executive committee composed of provincial representatives, corporate sponsors and non-governmental organizations controlled by disabled persons; it is significant that SecState has no voting member on this committee. Although NAAW successfully has encouraged corporations to dedicate some of their marketing budgets to a social cause, the advantages of the model extend beyond contribution to communication. Greater understanding of the issues and application of the lessons to their own businesses has resulted from the direct interaction of corporate representatives with disabled persons in planning committees. Many corporate sponsors soon moved from simply printing posters to conducting audits of their own offices and retail stores to ensure accessibility. Similar models of contributory partnerships have appeared in other programs such as the National Drug Strategy sponsored by Health and Welfare and Environment Week run by the Department of Environment. Yet, it should be recognized that this type of partnership works best on very select issues that have a specific limited purpose for which the partners can agree on what needs to be done.

Community Development Partnerships: Cultivation of financial and human resources at the grassroots level so that local communities can develop and deliver government policy is the intent of this type of partnership. The emphasis is on replacing centralized, homogenous policy responses with community-sensitive, innovative ones. However, this is more than social "animation" because to be successful in policy delivery, at least some decision-making authority must be vested with local bodies. Examples of such decentralization are the Community Futures program created in 1985 as part of the Canada Jobs Strategy and the Canadian Healthy Communities Project funded by National Health and Welfare.

In communities of chronic unemployment or in those hit by plant closures, the Community Futures program funds committees composed of local government, non-governmental organizations, and private sector individuals to assess local economic problems, develop employment opportunities and act as a catalyst for sparking private sector and other governments to undertake new employment initiatives.[75]

The Healthy Communities Project, established in 1988, is jointly sponsored by the Canadian Institute of Planners, the Federation of Canadian Municipalities and Canadian Public Health Association, and is funded by Health and Welfare. Its purpose is to enhance health promotion by encouraging local communities to give greater emphasis to preventative interventions, such as improvements in environment, transportation and housing, rather than relying upon the curative health care system. Like the Community Futures program, there is a local steering committee that is the locus of issues, undertakes needs assessment and co-ordinates jointly-sponsored municipal projects. As the authority for implementation of most of the new projects and services already resides at the community level, no powers have had to be devolved. Instead the value of the program is derived from information-sharing and networking to develop new health promotion strategies. The focus on decentralized decision-making not only results from dysfunctional centralized policy, but it is a recognition that policies in themselves do not necessarily produce social change. Rather the **process** of policy formulation and implementation—an "empowerment" process—may be critical.

Collaborative Partnerships: This final category fits the true definition of partnership in that it involves power-sharing, active participation by partners and an attempt to develop broad policy consensus among major social partners. Historically or currently, there are few examples of truly collaborative partnerships in Canada. The proposed Labour Force Development Board (LFDB) which was constituted in January 1991 as part of the Labour Force Development Strategy, is a bold experiment that is intended to be a tripartite consensus-building institution.[76] The national Board is an independent agency reporting to Parliament that is composed of 22 members: eight each from national labour and business organizations, two representatives from the education community and four members from national organizations of the target groups of the Canada Jobs Strategy (one each from organizations representing women, visible minorities, Aboriginal peoples and the disabled). Government maintains only ex-officio status on the board. In contrast to the advisory Round Tables, the functions of the LFDB, while expected to evolve over time, are to make decisions, as well as offer recommendations, on counselling and strategic plans for training. It also will oversee monitoring of training programs. The LFDB is to be supported by a network of local boards that will take decisions and allocate funds regarding training initiatives at the local level. If members, who must be carefully selected, can put the old confrontational approaches aside and adopt new roles and modes of decision-making, and if the government is prepared to devolve sufficient power and provide enough time and resources for this to happen, the LFDB stands a chance of success—both in labour market policy and as a model of new partnership institutions.

An interesting question is whether these new collaborative partnerships constitute a significant change in the form of government. Specifically, are they a move to a corporatist system? Corporatism is popularly defined as:

> ...a system of interest representation in which the constituent units are organized into a limited number of singular, compulsory and non-competitive, hierarchically ordered and functionally differentiated categories, recognized or licensed (if not created) by the state and granted a deliberative representational monopoly within their respective categories in exchange for observing certain controls on their selection of leaders and articulation of demands and support.[77]

None of the creators and supporters of the Labour Force Development Board or other partnerships would claim these represent a form of corporatism. On the contrary, they argue, corporatism is alien to Canada for two reasons. The requisite supporting peak associations (business and labour) are too fragmented and historically confrontational to participate in sustained national corporatist structures and the third force of minority identities consider it their right to be represented alongside business and labour. In one important sense, however, collaborative partnerships have elements of what Jessop calls "ad hoc corporatism."[78] Although, as corporatism, they legitimize new forms of state intervention, these interventions also tend to be partial and tendential, rather than sector-wide and persistent. The institutional significance is that partnerships, like the LFDB, merge interest representation and policy intervention in the same organ such that the specific targets of intervention are directly and permanently represented.

It is very likely that Canada will see more collaborative partnerships, independent of which party is in power, due to evolving state-market-society relationships. An interventionist state no longer has legitimacy, the public service no longer believes it holds all the solutions or resources and the public is growing tired of unproductive conflict among social and economic interests. Several cautions about the viability of partnerships, from an institutional and a management perspective, must be exercised if these forms are to be successful.[79]

First, it should be recognized that, because a partnership depends on both a common interest and ongoing commitment, it is inherently fragile. Therefore, there must be careful selection of the issue around which a partnership is formed because it is vital that partners be able to find something upon which they can agree. In addition, there must be careful selection and balance among participants: the greater the scale of the issue, the more important it becomes to obtain involvement of the major social and economic players. Because only a very few representatives of an interest can participate in any given partnership, it is imperative that there be reporting and communication of the privileged partner with other organizations in the policy community so that the "in" players are not isolated from their outside constituencies. Second, flexibility to evolve as the relationship develops or goals change is also essential.[80] A partnership depends on trust among the partners which takes time to be nurtured. Results will not be immediate and mistakes may be made along the way. Third, a successful partnership relies on sufficient staff support and financial resources. The representatives of some interests (for example, representatives of the Aboriginal, disabled, women's and visible minority organizations on the LFDB) may need more assistance than others. Finally, it is essential to understand the limits as well as the potential of partnerships. They should not be a mere privatization of policy problems that departments themselves have been unable to solve or are unwilling to pay for, but must have a strong rationale and basis for collaboration. Not all issues are suitable for partnership and the existence of a partnership does not abrogate all government responsibility for the issue.

There are many sound financial, policy and institutional reasons for moving government into partnerships. This transition, however, is likely to have significant long-term effects on the system of political representation in Canada. The evolution of partnerships is a move away from support for interest advocacy and policy criticism to an emphasis on service delivery and implementation. While partnerships may provide secure funding and institutionalized access for participating interest groups, it is very difficult to be critical of government policy from within a partnership. The political advantages for the government are obvious, but the long-term effect on public policy may be to truncate or obscure the range of interest representation and public criticism.

CONCLUSION

The government can have an enormous impact on the ability of clients and stakeholders to influence the direction of public policy. Government departments can choose to, or not to have, have meaningful and fair public consultation that uses the information in decision-making. It can create comparative advantage in the ability to represent interests by funding some social movements or groups while ignoring others. It can select privileged partners to act as its proxy in developing policy and allow local communities to experiment with different initiatives, or it can stick to a centrally imposed "one size fits all" strategy. Public consultation, grants to interest groups and partnerships all have a role in government-society relations, but they serve different purposes. They are complements, not direct substitutes. In this era of fragmented identities, public "crankiness," economic restraint and complex issues, there will be many innovative attempts, some successful and some less so, to create less bureaucratic, more responsive government. Before the federal government slides into partnerships or slips out of core funding of interest groups, however, we need to encourage more public and scholarly debate about the potential, limitations and consequences of shifting government-interest group relations.

Appendix 7-1

Grants and Contributions to Interest Groups in Selected Departments

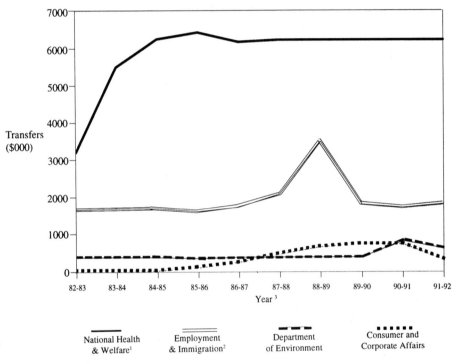

Note:
[1] National Health and Welfare includes transfers to voluntary national health and national social service organizations. These figures exclude assistance to amateur sport organizations which receive a much greater amount of money -- over $40 million in 1990-91.
[2] The transfers to voluntary organizations for literacy assistance are not included.
[3] The figures for 1982-83 through 1989-90 are actual expenditures; 1990-91 data are forecasts; 1991-92 figures are estimates.
Source: Part IIIs, *The Estimates*

Appendix 7-2

Grants and Contributions by the Department of Secretary of State

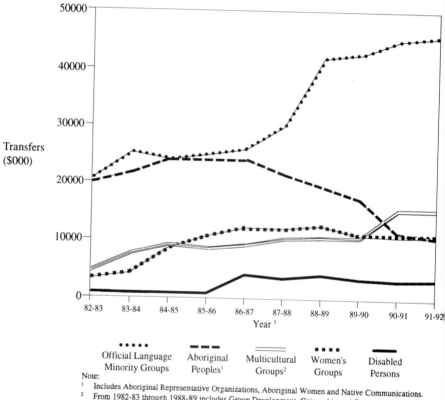

Transfers
($000)

Year [3]

•••••	– – –	══════	▪ ▪ ▪	▬▬▬
Official Language	Aboriginal	Multicultural	Women's	Disabled
Minority Groups	Peoples[1]	Groups[2]	Groups	Persons

Note:

[1]   Includes Aboriginal Representative Organizations, Aboriginal Women and Native Communications.

[2]   From 1982-83 through 1988-89 includes Group Development, Citizenship and Community Participation and Intercultural Communication; the figures reported through the Department of Multiculturalism and Citizenship are for the Community Support and Participation Program.

[3]   The figures for 1982-83 through 1989-90 are actual expenditures; 1990-91 data are forecasts; 1991-92 figures are estimates.

Source: Part IIIs, *The Estimates*

Notes

I wish to thank Frances Abele, Rianne Mahon, Leslie Pal, Marina Devine and Terry Milne for their very helpful comments on this chapter. I thank, too, the public servants and interest group leaders who generously gave me their time in interviews. The assistance of Terry Milne and Christine Bednarek in research is also greatly appreciated.

1   For excellent recent discussions of different perspectives on state theory, see: Bob Jessop, *State Theory: Putting the Capitalist State in its Place* (London: Polity Press, 1990); Rianne Mahon, "From Bringing to Putting: The State in Late Twentieth Century Social Theory," *Canadian Journal of Sociology,* forthcoming; Greg Albo and Jane Jenson, "A Contested Concept: The Relative Autonomy of the State," in W. Clement and G. Williams (eds.), *The New Canadian Political Economy* (Montreal: McGill-Queens, 1989); William D. Coleman and Grace Skogstad, "Policy Communities and Policy Networks: A Structural Approach," in William D. Coleman and Grace Skogstad (eds.), *Policy Communities and Public Policy in Canada* (Mississauga, Copp Clark Pitman, 1990.

2   A "public" interest group is defined as a group whose members act together to influence public policy in order to promote their common interest and whose objective is to benefit people beyond their own membership. In contrast to economic or business associations, their intentions are not centred upon providing direct economic benefit to their members. Membership is voluntary and relatively open such that anyone may join the group, thereby distinguishing them from unions or professional associations. Public interest groups are sometimes called "pressure" groups or "citizen" groups.

3   Deborah Dowling, "Muzzling Dissent," *Ottawa Citizen,* March 14, 1990, p. A4.

4   Two months after cuts were made in 1990, the government announced that it would restore $1.2 million in funding to 74 women's centres, but that another $400,000 slashed from the communications budgets for women and Native groups would not be reinstated. See, Ian Austen,

"Government restores some women's program funding," *Ottawa Citizen*, May 5, 1990, p. 3.

5   In addition to secondary sources, research for this chapter included interviews with 15 public servants from a variety of departments and seven interest group leaders. In interviews, there was consistent, spontaneous mention of the following societal and state factors.

6   Alan C. Cairns, "Constitutional Minoritarianism in Canada," in Ronald L. Watts and Douglas M. Brown (eds.), *Canada: The State of the Federation 1990* (Kingston: Institute of Intergovernmental Relations, 1990), pp. 71-96.

7   Cairns, "Constitutional Minoritarianism in Canada;" Seymour Martin Lipset, *Continental Divide* (London: Routledge, Chapman and Hall, 1990), pp. 104-5; Public Service 2000, *Service to the Public Task Force Report* (Ottawa: PS2000 Secretariat), p. 34.

8   Allan Gregg and Michael Posner, *The Big Picture: What Canadians Think about Almost Everything* (Toronto: MacFarlane Walter and Ross, 1990), chapter 3; Graham Fraser, "Meech Lake alone can't heal the rifts," *Globe and Mail* [Toronto], May 18, 1990, p. A7; Hugh Winsor, "Leaders get no respect," *Globe and Mail* [Toronto], October 29, 1990, p. A7. For an interesting perspective on the role of interest groups and the re-emerging importance of values, considered in the aftermath of the NDP victory in Ontario, see Jeffrey Simpson, "Looking for values in the political market," *Globe and Mail* [Toronto], September 19, 1990, p. A23.

9   For a discussion of the changing state in Canada see Jane Jenson, "'Different' but not 'Exceptional': Canada's Permeable Fordism," *Canadian Review of Sociology and Anthropology*, 26, 1989, pp. 69-94; Gilles Breton and Jane Jenson, "After Free Trade and Meech Lake: An Essay on the Challenges Facing Two Lefts," *Studies in Political Economy*, 34, Spring, 1991.

10   Federal Environmental Assessment Review Office, *Manual on Public Involvement in Environmental Assessment* (Ottawa: FEARO, 1988), pp. 1-2. For the present

discussion, we exclude consultation with other governments or other departments. Although the terms, public
"consultation," "involvement" and "participation" will
be used interchangeably here, there are subtle differences
in their history and practice. The term public participation (or public involvement) became popular in the late
1960s with the rise of social movements that stress community involvement in decision-making. It implies, at a
minimum, a two-way exchange of information and, at
best, shared decision-making. Consultation is a term
made popular in the 1980s which stresses information
exchange, but excludes joint decision-making as a possibility. In Canada, the broader term consultation seems
to have won favour—at least in the public service. The
distinction between consultation and lobbying is that consultation is invited, condoned and planned by government, whereas a lobby campaign (that may involve
letter-writing, press releases and demonstrations, as well
as meetings) often makes government the target, rather
than a willing participant.

11   Public Service 2000, *Service to the Public Task Force
     Report* (Ottawa: PS2000, October 12, 1990), p. 32.

12   Jenson, op. cit., pp. 87-88.

13   Consultation also includes the mandated formal hearing
     process such as that required as part of the Environmen-
     tal Assessment Review Process (EARP). There also have
     been attempts at various stages to establish national con-
     sultative bodies, especially between business and labour.
     On this see, John Crispo, *National Consultation:
     Problems and Prospects* (Montreal: C. D. Howe Institute,
     1984). While these formal or outside bodies have an im-
     portant role, a detailed examination of them is beyond the
     scope of this paper.

14   Robert Presthus, *Elite Accommodation in Canadian
     Politics* (Toronto: Macmillan, 1973), chapter 6.

15   Senator Pitfield argues that this professionalization is
     hurting the image of government and quality of the public
     service. See: Study of Parliament Group, *Interest Groups
     and Parliament* (Ottawa: Study of Parliament Group,
     1989), p. 10. For a discussion of types of clients of profes-

sional lobbying firms, see: *Lobby Digest* (Ottawa: Isis Research), November, 1982, p. 2. For a general discussion of lobbyists, see: John Sawatsky, *The Insiders: Government, Business and the Lobbyists* (Toronto: McClelland and Stewart, 1987) and Stevie Cameron, *Ottawa Inside Out* (Toronto: Key Porter Books, 1989), pp. 166-69.

16   Sandra Gwyn, "The Great Ottawa Grant Boom (And How it Grew)," *Saturday Night*, 87, October, 1972, pp. 22-23. Susan D. Phillips, Leslie A. Pal, David C. Hawkes and Daniel J. Savas, *Public Interest Groups in the Policy Process* (Unpublished Study prepared for the Department of Secretary of State, 1990), pp. 33-7.

17   Grahame Beakhust, "The Berger Inquiry," in Barry Sadler (ed.), *Involvement and Environment* vol. 2 (Edmonton: Environment Council of Alberta, 1979), pp. 312-320.

18   A parallel movement in the US for good government and public participation in policy-making had strong spillover effect for Canadian activities.

19   Government of Canada, *Canada's Green Plan* (Ottawa: Supply and Services, 1990), p. 7.

20   Personal communication. The representatives of these groups were not blindly critical of all activities of Environment Canada and, in fact, were quite positive about other consultations the department has conducted.

21   Ross Howard, "$3-billion Green Plan unveiled by Ottawa, but details scarce," *Globe and Mail* [Toronto], December 11, 1990 pp. A1, A6. The Plan was diluted further when it was announced in the 1991 Budget that its $3 billion budget would be spread over six years instead of five.

22   Environmental groups were also critical of the short time available, but argue that they could have dealt with the time element if they had had more details about potential alternatives that the government was actually considering.

23   Michael Valpy, "A noisy quest for a nation's values," *Globe and Mail* [Toronto], January 7, 1991, p. A1.

24 Joan Bryden, "PM defends beleaguered unity forum," *Ottawa Citizen*, March 6, 1991, p. A1. In comparison, the three-year Commission on Reproductive Technologies will cost $24.7 million, the MacDonald commission on Economic Unity cost $24 million and the Dubin inquiry into drug use in sports cost $4.48 million, See, *Ottawa Citizen*, March 1, 1991, p. A1. The Forum has 80 full-time employees in Ottawa plus another 40 regional field workers and 160 part-time "moderators" across the county whose job is to guide debate at the discussion groups. Mark Kennedy, "From out of chaos comes some order," *Ottawa Citizen*, February 16, 1991, p. B2.

25 Robert Mason Lee, "Forum is for grassroots, Spicer tells Wells," *Ottawa Citizen*, January 16, p. A3.

26 Michael Valpy, "Forum faces some criticism in first week," *Globe and Mail* [Toronto], January 11, p. A5.

27 George Kalogerakis, "Outrageous: Spicer Forum separates English, French," *Ottawa Citizen*, February 12, p. A1.

28 Joan Bryden and Elaine Flaherty, "Canadians speak up," *Ottawa Citizen*, January 9, 1991, p. A3.

29 These 14 questions have since been simplified to four more general, but broad discussion points.

30 Michael Valpy, "Citizens' Forum members vow to carry on with task," *The Globe and Mail* [Toronto], March 4, 1991, p. A1.

31 PS2000, *Service to the Public Task Force Report*, p. 39.

32 Ibid., p. 39.

33 This assessment was made by participants at a seminar sponsored by the Public Policy Forum; quoted in PS2000, *Service to the Public Task Force Report*, p. 40. However, the Economic Council offers equally harsh criticism: see, Economic Council of Canada, *Transitions for the 90s*, (Ottawa: Economic Council of Canada, 1990) p. 47.

34   Most public interest groups have a volunteer board of directors, a small staff (three or four people) and no paid researcher on staff. In contrast, economic associations usually have a larger, professional staff and can extract valuable services-in-kind (advice and research) from their member corporations. Although it is vital that public interest groups present their views when invited to do so, it often stretches their budgets to the limit. The internal difficulties that consultation may present for some organizations was noted in a program evaluation of the Women's Program of Secretary of State. Leaders of women's groups said: "Volunteers often have neither the time nor the resources to become expert on an issue, to discover who is who in Ottawa or in the province, to know what issues are on the agenda and how to present the strongest case. Staff also usually lack the flexibility of time to respond quickly and effectively." DPA Group Inc., *Evaluation of the Women's Program* (Ottawa: Program Evaluation Directorate, Secretary of State, 1985), p. 28.

      In contrast, some groups which have been identified as the lead organizations in their policy communities (such as **the** voice of the disabled community or **the** organization for poor people), are often consulted to death. In interviews, some public interest group representatives said that once they cultivated individuals with leadership skills and policy expertise, these individuals were often hired away by government.

35   Much of the service to the public rhetoric is borrowed from the management literature in the private sector and, in particular from Thomas J. Peters and Robert H. Waterman, Jr., *In Search of Excellence* (New York: Harper Collins, 1982).

36   The debate over the management and ideology of government funding was ignited in 1984 by R.E.A.L. Women's slam at the Women's Program of SecState which denied funding to them. Officials at the Women's Program refused because the group (which stresses ultra-conservative and family values) did not, in their view, support equality for women which is the primary objective of Program and is part of Canada's responsibility under United Nations conventions. With strong support from

Tory backbenchers, R.E.A.L. Women argued publicly that the Women's Program had a strong feminist bias that was not reflective of Canadian society. The group has been relatively quiet since it succeeded in obtaining funding of $21,000 in 1989. For a good discussion of this episode, see Leslie A. Pal, *Interests of State: Citizenship Policy and Language, Multicultural, and Women's Organizations in Canada* (forthcoming), ch. 7. See also "Women's Groups Hassle again over Handouts," *Ottawa Citizen*, January 15, 1990, p. A8. In 1989, the controversy expanded to other sectors when the National Citizens' Coalition (also an ultra-conservative group) issued *Tales from the Tax Trough* which complained of supposedly ludicrous grants by SecState, the Social Sciences and Humanities Research Council (SSHRC) and the Canada Council. For a comment on their position, see Roy Mac-Gregor, "Wingy citizens group a coalition of fools," *Ottawa Citizen*, November 22, 1989, p. A3. However, the concern about ad hoc decision-making also arose from inside the granting programs. See, Program Evaluation Directorate, Secretary of State, *A Framework for Cross-Sectoral Evaluation of Core Funding in the Secretary of State* (Ottawa: Secretary of State, 1986), pp. 12-13.

37   It is interesting to note that, in contrast, recent changes to funding provided to university and private scholars by the Social Sciences and Humanities Research Council (SSHRC) has moved in the opposite direction. Significant changes in the program in 1990 made SSHRC funding more flexible and placed greater emphasis on the ability of individuals, rather than the attractiveness of particular projects.

38   Deborah Dowling, "Muzzling Dissent," *Ottawa Citizen*, March 14, 1990, p. A4.

39   Program Evaluation Directorate, Secretary of State, *A Framework for Cross-Sectoral Evaluation of Core Funding in the Secretary of State*, p. 11.

40   Ibid., p. 9.

41   Pal, *Interests of State*, forthcoming, pp. xii-xvii.

42 The rationale for 1990 cuts to Aboriginal communication societies was offered by one public official: "Native media are businesses, not essential social/cultural services. They ought to be able to finance themselves just like the *Globe and Mail*," James MacDonald, Ontario Regional Director for the federal Department of Secretary of State, in Sean Fine, "Native media deride talks on budget cuts," *Globe and Mail* [Toronto], March 20, 1990, p. A10.

43 Anyone who has attended the annual lobby (sometimes jokingly called the "annual scream") held by the National Action Committee on the Status of Women (NAC) might question this. See "'Femocrats' advise feminists to improve lobbying tactics," *Ottawa Citizen*, November 3, 1990, p. D13; Robert Matas, "Change attitudes not laws, feminists told," *Globe and Mail* [Toronto], November 5, 1990, p. A3.

44 A. Paul Pross, *Group Politics and Public Policy* (Toronto: Oxford University Press, 1986), p. 198.

45 This new department, created out of SecState, was announced in 1988 as an institutional response to the government's strengthened commitment to multiculturalism under its New Multicultural Act of that year. The two departments still share certain common management functions and are joined at the regional level by sharing offices.

46 A discussion of the history of the development of SecState and Multiculturalism is a fascinating one, but is beyond the scope of this paper. It has been skilfully documented elsewhere by Leslie A. Pal, "Identity, Citizenship and Mobilization: The Nationalities Branch and World War II," *Canadian Public Administration*, 32, 3, 1989, pp. 407-426; Pal, *Interests of State*, (forthcoming).

47 These figures exclude transfers to the Race Relations Foundation, Citizenship Registration, Literacy, Heritage Cultures and Languages and Japanese Redress in the Department of Multiculturalism; they exclude Education Support, Native Social/Cultural Development and State Ceremonial transfers in the Department of Secretary of State.

48   Under its renewed terms in 1988, emphasis is now given
      to support for doubly disadvantaged groups such as im-
      migrant and visible minority women, disabled, rural and
      isolated women.

49   These figures are based on the Main Estimates and must
      be interpreted with caution because some grants are
      made under operating programs and are not readily iden-
      tifiable from the Estimates. There also is great
      variability in the types of groups supported, ranging from
      strictly advocacy to strictly social service.

50   The data shown in Appendix 7.2 are not adjusted for
      inflation. Also in 1989 and 1990, the amount allocated in
      the Spending Estimates for women's groups was less than
      what was actually (or forecasted to be) spent. This indi-
      cated that the Government's commitment to women's
      groups was even less than shown in the graph.

51   In Appendix 7.2, the amounts shown as transfers to Offi-
      cial Language Promotion are somewhat inflated because
      in 1988-89, the program of Official Language Minority
      Communities was amalgamated with Official Language
      Promotion. In order to compare the evolution of funding
      programs over 10 years, however, the amalgamated
      figures were used throughout the period. Of the $45.8
      million allocated to Official Language Promotion in 1991-
      92, $28.4 million will go directly to official language
      minority communities, but $500,000 is provided to com-
      munity radio stations, $12.4 million to intergovernmen-
      tal co-operation and $1 million to the administration of
      justice (although groups are also funded under these
      programs). In an attempt to maintain as much com-
      parability as possible, transfers to communications
      societies are included in the figures for funding to or-
      ganizations of Aboriginal peoples.

52   Leslie A. Pal, "Official Language Minorities and the
      State: Dual Dynamics in a Single Policy Network," in
      William D. Coleman and Grace Skogstad (eds.), *Policy
      Communities and Public Policy in Canada* (Mississauga,
      Copp Clark Pitman, 1990), pp. 170-90.

53   Treasury Board Guide on Financial Administration as
      reported in the Treasury Board Presentation, "Controls

over Grants and Contributions," made to the *Standing Committee on Public Accounts*, March 1990, issue 26.

54   *Standing Committee on Public Accounts*, March 1990, issue 26, p. 4.

55   Ibid., p. 14.

56   Of the 6,961 grants awarded by SecState and Multiculturalism in 1988-89, 87 per cent were for less than $25,000 and only 29 were in excess of $300,000. *Standing Committee on Public Accounts*, issue 32, p. 16.

57   Department of Secretary of State, *Grants and Contributions Manual* (Ottawa: Secretary of State, updated 1990), ch. 12.

58   The criteria for "program" (sustaining) funding varies across the programs of Secretary of State. The Department is in the process of drafting consistent criteria that will define eligibility for sustaining grants.

59   A cross-sectoral preliminary evaluation of core funding conducted by the Program Evaluation Branch of SecState was concerned with the inconsistency of criteria. See, Program Evaluation Directorate, Secretary of State, *A Framework for Cross-Sectoral Evaluation of Core Funding in the Secretary of State*, p. 3.

60   For instance, in 1989 NAC had the status of its operating grant changed to impose more stringent reporting requirements; in addition, its operating budget was cut by 50 per cent over three years. National Action Committee, "We're Worth More," (Bulletin published by NAC, 1990).

61   *Standing Committee on Public Accounts*, issue 32, p. 18.

62   The Voluntary Action Program of SecState has been helping groups learn new fundraising techniques that might reduce their dependency on government. However, government revenues are a large chunk of the budgets for most groups funded by SecState. See Sandra Burt, "Canadian Women's Groups in the 1980s: Organizational Development and Policy Influence," *Canadian Public Policy*, XVI, 1, 1990, pp. 20-22. Susan D. Phillips, Leslie

A. Pal, David C. Hawkes and Daniel J. Savas, *Public Interest Groups in the Policy Process*, pp. 91-92.

63 Earlier studies have also examined funding programs but were more divergent in their findings. For example, two separate studies of the Nielsen Task Force examined the Women's Program. While one study team (Citizenship, Labour and Immigration) generally supported the program and recommended maintaining the planned level of funding, a second study team (Culture and Communications) was wary that the Program was too focussed on upwardly mobile professional women and recommended that its objectives be reassessed and there be no funding increases.

64 Office of the Auditor General, *Annual Report* (Ottawa: Supply and Services, 1990), pp. 675-6. For instance, in 1989-90 funds to Aboriginal representative organizations were cut by 15 per cent, the same amount by which expenditure votes to SecState were reduced.

65 Auditor General, *Annual Report*, 1990, p. 677. Within SecState, the approval process is a highly regional one. First, an organization wishing to obtain funding submits an application to a regional office. The application is analysed by a local officer in terms of the criteria governing the program and he or she makes a recommendation to fund or not. This application then goes up the hierarchy to the local manager, a review committee and regional director; then on to the program director at headquarters, director general and, finally, to the Assistant Under Secretary of State. All applications in excess of $3,000 must be submitted to the Minister of State for final approval.

66 Leslie A. Pal, *Interests of State*, forthcoming, p. 452.

67 Department of Finance, *The Budget*, 1991, p. 18.

68 Economic Council, *Transitions for the '90s*, p. 53.

69 Science Council of Canada and the Canadian Advanced Technology Association, *Firing Up the Technology Engine* (Ottawa: Supply and Services, 1990), p. 6 and Canadian Advanced Technology Association, Science

Council of Canada and Canadian Chamber of Commerce, *Grassroots Initiatives, Global Success: Report of the 1989 National Technology Policy Roundtable* (Ottawa: Supply and Services, 1990).

70   Bob Rae, speech at a luncheon at the Plaza Hotel, New York City, October 30, 1990, pp. 6, 8.

71   Like the ideas about service to clients, the concept of partnership has been heavily influenced by private sector experiences and the management literature in which value-added partnerships and lateral linkages have come into vogue in recent years. See, for example: Sandra A. Waddock, "Building Successful Social Partnerships," *Sloan Management Review*, 17, Summer, 1988, pp. 17-23; Russell Johnston and Paul R. Lawrence, "Beyond Vertical Integration—The Rise of the Value-Adding Partnership," *Harvard Business Review*, July-August, 1988, pp. 94-101.

72   Debureaucratization includes internal changes to traditional hierarchical authority, such as decentralization from headquarters to local offices and greater reliance on teamwork, as well as power-sharing relationships with social partners. Fred Block, *Revising State Theory: Essays in Politics and Postindustrialism* (Philadelphia: Tempe University Press, 1987), pp. 29-33. The idea of post-industrial transition means that a number of current trends—cultural, technical and social—come into conflict with the patterns of social and economic organization that dominated the period of industrialism.

73   It should be recognized that there are also many partnerships **among** interest groups, but these are not the focus of the present work.

74   In 1990-91 the budget estimate for NAAW (including the Five Star Awards program) was $1.2 million. At the national level corporate sponsors supplied seven per cent and at the provincial or local level 22 per cent of the budget. However, their in-kind contributions (printing, mailing, providing meeting rooms) are also very significant.

75 As Prince and Rice note, decentralization had been tried at Employment and Immigration in the 1970s under the Liberal government, but had disappointing results because the department could not move away from a rigid, national approach to programming. They argue that the Community Futures program is a more promising attempt at decentralization. Michael J. Prince and Jim J. Rice, "The Canadian Jobs Strategy: Supply Side Social Policy," in Katherine A. Graham (ed.), *How Ottawa Spends 1989-90: The Buck Stops Where?* (Ottawa: Carleton University Press, 1989), pp. 258-63.

76 On the Labour Force Development Strategy, see: Rianne Mahon, "Adjusting to Win? The New Tory Training Initiative," in Katherine A. Graham (ed.), *How Ottawa Spends 1990-91* (Ottawa: Carleton University Press, 1990); on the LFDB, see: Canadian Labour Market and Productivity Centre, *A Framework for a National Training Board* (Ottawa: CLMPC, 1990).

77 Philippe C. Schmitter, "Still the Century of Corporatism?" *Review of Politics*, 36, 1, 1974, p. 13.

78 Bob Jessop, *State Theory: Putting the Capitalist State in its Place*, p. 191.

79 The management literature which has reported on value-added partnerships in the private sector for several years can offer some useful suggestions for practical implementation: Many of the ideas discussed here are borrowed from Sandra A. Waddock, "Building Successful Social Partnerships."

80 This includes structural and cultural change within the supporting department to make their mode of operations conducive and receptive to participation in a partnership. One of the debates in creating partnerships is how institutionalized versus ad hoc they should be. That is, should new permanent institutions, like the LFDB, be established or should emphasis be placed on working relationships, rather than structure? There is no easy answer to this, but either must permit flexibility.

CHAPTER 8

SYMBOLIC REPRESENTATION AND THE NUMBERS GAME: TORY POLICIES ON "RACE" AND VISIBLE MINORITIES

Daiva Stasiulis

Résumé: Ce chapitre examine la gamme de politiques fédérales en matière de race, racisme et minorités visibles. On examine la façon dont la diversité et la discrimination raciales ont été abordées par le recensement du Canada, la politique de l'immigration, le programme fédéral d'équité d'emploi et celui du multiculturalisme ainsi que par la GRC. A la différence d'autres gouvernements conservateurs en Grande-Bretagne et aux États-Unis, les conservateurs du gouvernement Mulroney ne se sont pas pliés aux sentiments racistes dans des domaines politiques clefs tels que l'immigration. Ils ont légitimé l'image d'un Canada multiculturel et multiracial, au moins sur le plan symbolique. Il n'en reste pas moins que les réformes antiracistes présentées depuis 1984 ont été peu systématiques et ont manqué d'inspiration. Il est difficile de réaliser des mesures plus positives et plus efficaces pour combattre l'inégalité raciale, vu le programme économique des conservateurs qui subordonne des soucis de justice sociale à une préoccupation avec le libre-échange, la compétitivité de l'entreprise privée et la réduction du déficit fédéral.

Abstract: This chapter examines the constellation of federal policies concerned with issues of race, racism and visible minorities. It analyses the approaches taken to racial diversity and racial discrimination within the Canadian Census, immigration policy, the federal employment equity program, multiculturalism and the RCMP. Unlike other conservative governments in Britain and the United States, the Mulroney Conservatives have not pandered to racist sentiment within key policy areas such as immigration. They have, at least symbolically, legitimized the image of a multicultural, multiracial Canada. The Conservative anti-racist reforms brought in since 1984 have, however, been piecemeal and uninspired. More meaningful and effective legislative measures against racial inequality are undermined by the Conservative economic agenda which subordinates social justice concerns to a preoccupation with free trade, the competitiveness of private business, and federal deficit reduction.

The history of Canada's immigration policies is replete with pressures to balance Canadian population and labour demands with efforts by the nation's official gatekeepers to limit the racial diversity of Canadian settlers. On the premise articulated by Prime Minister King in his classic 1947 statement that the people of Canada did not "wish as a result of mass immigration, to make a fundamental alteration in the character of the Canadian population," Canadian immigration policy included a variety of mechanisms—head taxes, "continuous passage" regulations and climate-based arguments—to maintain Canada as a "white man's country."[1] Indeed, King's statement guided the explicit denial of access to the country of racial minorities until regulations, passed in 1962 and 1967, eliminated racial considerations as criteria for entry. The fact that both Asians and Blacks nonetheless have been present in Canada prior to the "liberalization" of the immigration policy in the 1960s was mainly the result of their attractiveness to employers as cheap and expendable labour in arduous and hazardous jobs.

In 1991, the perceived legitimacy of immigrants still largely depends on their skin colour and country of origin. This is apparent in the various types of discrimination experienced by Canadians who are Asian, Black, or other racial minorities within the labour market, housing and all major institutions.[2] The majority of visible minorities are immigrants, although the proportion of immigrants varies by group and by region.[3] Yet racial minorities with roots in Canada extending back several generations, such as the Nova Scotian Black population, are also subjected to institutional and ideological forms of racism. The routine question asked of fourth and fifth generation Black Canadians—"Which island do you come from?"—reflects the profound sense in which skin colour continues to form part of a common-sense notion among whites of who is, and who is not, a legitimate Canadian.

Implicit racial distinctions are also evident in immigration policy discourse which continues to distinguish between "traditional" (white, European) and "non-traditional" (racial minority, Third World) immigrants and which continues to view the latter with apprehension.[4] In spite of Canada's policy on multiculturalism, assimilation, or rather the presumed ability to assimilate or to be "absorbed comfortably into Canadian society" is resuscitated as a guiding concern whenever there is a perception of an increase in the admission of Third World immigrants.[5] But the fact is that the shift from European to non-European sources of immigration has ensured that Canadian society has become increasingly racially and ethnically diverse, a trend that is not likely to alter in this century. Whereas 30 years ago, more than 80 per cent of Canada's immigrants came from Europe or were of European heritage, currently 70 per cent come from Asia, Africa, and

Latin America, with 43 per cent coming from Asia alone.[6] Racial diversity is most salient in Toronto, Vancouver, Calgary, Montreal and other urban centres that serve as magnets for immigration.[7] Thus, whereas "visible minorities" comprised an estimated 6.1 per cent of the Canadian population in 1986, 17.3 per cent of Torontonians and 16.9 per cent of Vancouverites were visible minorities.[8] In fact, in 1986, almost three quarters of the visible minority population in Canada were residing in five major cities—Toronto, Vancouver, Montreal, Calgary and Edmonton.[9]

Pressures to reflect this growing racial diversity within state policy have resulted in emergent forms of "race consciousness," at all three levels of the state. For instance, at the municipal level, a growing number of school boards, police forces and local governments have formulated policies that attempt to deal with racist incidents, racial discrimination and disadvantages, as well as accommodate a diversity of ethnocultural and religious traditions. At the same time, as indicated by the turmoil that accompanied the change in policy regarding headgear within the Royal Canadian Mounted Police (which now permits orthodox Sikhs to wear turbans), there is considerable resistance at both official and public levels to alter the racial and ethnic content of national symbols. Such resistance has been heightened by a growing fear of the balkanization of the country stimulated by the constitutional impasse connected with the ill-fated Meech Lake Accord.

This paper examines the policies of the Mulroney government since 1984 which are concerned with issues of race, racism, and visible minorities. More specifically, it surveys the approaches to visible minorities, racial diversity and racial discrimination taken by the Conservatives within the Canadian census, immigration policy, the federal employment equity program, multiculturalism and the RCMP. While each of these policy areas reflects individual policy and program responses by federal agencies to issues of racial diversity, racism and/or visible minority representation, a framework that considers the constellation of federal policies on race is more useful in evaluating the overall stance of the Mulroney Tories. The race relations policies of the Mulroney government reflect a commitment on the part of the Conservatives to retaining and building upon multicultural and anti-discrimination policies initiated under the Liberals. The chiefly symbolic and piecemeal character of the reforms are, however, in keeping with a neo-conservative economic agenda, such as a reluctance to infringe upon the operations of the "free" market, and a preoccupation with federal deficit reduction. It is beneficial to begin the discussion with a consideration of the use of such terms as "race" and "visible minority" within the federal state.

"RACE" AND "VISIBLE MINORITIES" IN THE CANADIAN CONTEXT AND CENSUS

Throughout much of Canadian history the concept of "race" was as likely to be applied to English, Irish, French, Ukrainian, and many other peoples, as to distinguish Blacks and Asians from Europeans.[10] The most enduring forms of discrimination and racist ideology were reserved, however, for members of the First Nations, Blacks and Asians, peoples whose skin colour was different from that of the "white settler colonists" and who were considered by the latter to be at the bottom of the ladder of racial and ethnic acceptability.[11] Given that variations existed in the racial heterogeneity of the population in various regions, the country as a whole did not have a consolidated policy on race.[12] The legislative base and severity of racism and the minority groups targeted by racial discrimination varied across regions and provinces. Thus, the civil and property rights of Asians were more consistently denied on the west coast, where the majority of Asians had settled, than in central and eastern Canada, where their numbers were negligible; the institutionalization of Black economic subordination was most profound in the Maritimes. Similarly, the legislation and policies developed after World War II to ameliorate racism and provide redress for victims of racial discrimination emerged unevenly across the country, with the federal state lagging behind provinces such as Ontario in the development of human rights legislation prohibiting discrimination on the grounds of race or colour.

Currently, several pieces of Canadian legislation, such as the Canadian Charter of Rights and Freedoms, the Canadian Multiculturalism Act, and policies in areas such as human rights and employment equity make reference to "race." However, as Juriansz notes,

> No guidance as to the meaning of "race" can be gleaned from jurisprudence developed in Canada under human rights legislation. Boards and tribunals which have dealt with complaints based on "race"

have simply assumed the ground to be established after seeing the complainant in the witness box.[13]

Nonetheless, there is a general unease expressed within much Canadian political discourse regarding the use of the concepts of "race," the "multiracial" character of Canada, and "racial minorities." Aversion to the term "race" is founded in postwar scientific conclusions regarding the absence of biological (phenotypical or genetic) divisions within humankind, and the fact that differences within groups popularly identified as races were as great or greater than the differences between racial groups. The argument to banish the use of the term "race" first received popular currency in postwar United Nations debates following the revelations of the murder of six million Jews in the name of "racial purity."[14] The argument that the idea of race lacks scientific credibility and is intellectually and politically indefensible was recently articulated by Gerry Weiner, Minister of State for Multiculturalism and Citizenship in his remarks to Parliament concerning the establishment of a Canadian Race Relations Foundation (Bill C-63):

> The idea of race is based on the long-held but discredited notion that cultural or physical differences are more than external, that they are biological, that a black person is inherently different than a white person, or an East Asian. Of course, there are profound consequences to accepting that there is more than one race in the human species. When we accept this notion we tend to reinforce claims of biological superiority or inferiority. We make discrimination intellectually feasible. We make it rational...Geneticists and anthropologists have discarded the concept of race because they have found it a useless construct for meaningful analysis of differences between groups, yet racist myth-making abounds.[15]

The entire history of racism in Canada and elsewhere demonstrates that "races" are socially and historically constructed, rather than founded in nature. The process of racial categorization is profoundly affected by economic relations of exploitation, political forms of oppression and exclusion, and "common-sense" forms of ideology. However, governments face a dilemma when they acknowledge and enact policies to deal with racism and discrimination based on race, yet simultaneously insist on the non-existence of race, on the supposition that to categorize people according to "race" is itself a form of racism. This dilemma is apparent in the federal government's Employment Equity program for "visible minorities" (to be discussed below) and also in the decision recently taken by Statistics Canada to **not** include a question on race in the 1991 Canadian census.

The term "visible minorities," which was recognized by Parliament in the 1986 Employment Equity Act, is an euphemism that seeks to avoid the words "race" and "colour."[16] The origins of the term are unknown.[17] Visible minorities are defined in the Employment Equity Regulations as "persons, other than aboriginal peoples, who are...non-Caucasian in race or non-white in colour." Thus, the definition refers to both race and colour, with some "intimation of synonymity in the descriptors,"[18] a synonymity that is problematic and that is not assumed by other government agencies that collect data on race.[19] As noted by Boxhill and Stanic of Statistics Canada, "the presumptions regarding a classification of the population into white/non-white are reasonable in the context of data collection and pose few problems of comprehension for respondents."[20] In contrast, the terms, "Caucasian" and "non-Caucasian" are not as well understood, nor as familiar as "white" and "non-white" in describing the Canadian population.[21] Interestingly, visible minorities had been earlier defined by the Abella Commission as "non-whites," rather than in terms of race, country of origin or some other criterion.[22]

While the Employment Equity Act identifies visible minorities on the basis of race and colour, recent Canadian censuses have not requested information on race, colour, or "being in a visible minority." In preparation for the 1991 Census, Statistics Canada had been testing differing versions of race/visible minority questions, using approaches such as surveys, focus groups and consultation with interested groups and individuals.[23] It was ultimately decided that there would be **no** question on race, colour or visible minorities within the 1991 census. The explanation provided from Statistics Canada for this decision was threefold. First, it was held that a question on race merely replicated information collected from responses to a combination of other questions. Thus,

> ...the test version on race and colour produced data comparable to estimates derived from the 1986 census questions on ethnic or cultural origin, place of birth

and language. Thus, in terms of providing data on visible minorities as defined for purposes of employment equity legislation, the direct question on race or colour would not appear to offer a significant advantage.[24]

Second, adding the race question to the ethnic or cultural identity question would increase costs and add to the burden on respondents, possibly resulting in reduced co-operation of respondents. And third, and perhaps most decisively, the race question could "be perceived as offensive by a significant number of Canadians," a view put forward by the Canadian Ethnocultural Council (a coalition of 39 national ethnocultural organizations) at Statistics Canada's public meetings.[25] It should be noted, however, that this argument concerning the "offensive" nature of a race question has been contested both between government agencies involved in the decision-making process concerning ethnic/race questions for the 1991 Census, and seemingly, within Statistics Canada itself. Thus, in a recent Statistics Canada report on visible minorities and the Census, Wally Boxhill counters the argument that a question on race was offensive to respondents in National Census tests, focus group discussions and consultations with special interest groups. Indeed, Boxhill plainly states that, "None of these activities generated strong empirical evidence to support the notion that respondents would be either offended by or encounter difficulty with a question on race."[26]

The decision to avoid mention of race or colour in the Census reflects an (arguably naive) Canadian predisposition to avoid the destructive phenomena associated with the term "race"—such as racism, racial inequality and racial violence—by avoiding use of the term, "race." Unfortunately, racism and racial inequality will not disappear, and racial violence will not become less likely simply by deleting the word, "race" from the federal bureaucracy's lexicon. Moreover, a dissonance exists when the Employment Equity legislation, the Multiculturalism Act, as well as longer-standing human rights legislation, are premised on the need to monitor, so as to better ameliorate, disadvantages based on race, and yet no consistency is provided for the definition and operationalization of "race." On balance, if the federal government continues to pursue employment equity for groups who are disadvantaged by virtue of their race or colour, then such programs are better served by inclusion of a census question on race or colour. Some of the consequences for decisions taken to avoid popular usage of "race" terms will be discussed below as they affect the race relations initiatives taken within Employment Equity and Multiculturalism and Citizenship.

IMMIGRATION POLICY UNDER THE TORIES

Immigration policy is a key plank of any national government's policy on race. If the racial composition of immigrants is treated as an issue, then it is likely that this will negatively affect the overall tone of a given government's policy on race relations. As discussed earlier, it has been less than 30 years since Canada's official gatekeepers stopped legally and explicitly judging potential migrants' worth on the basis of their cultural and physical similarity to the British. The official policy to maintain Canada as a white, if not British nation, most certainly legitimized discrimination and exclusion of racial minorities within Canada, even those of several generations standing here.

In evaluating the racial dimensions of the Conservative immigration policy since the Mulroney government took office in 1984, several observations are relevant. First, the Mulroney government has acted to significantly raise immigration levels from the previous Liberal administration. Indeed, in 1989, the total immigration intake (189,200) was more than double that of 1985 (84,302), the decade low.[27] A policy of "moderate and controlled" growth in immigration levels has been arrived at through large-scale commissioning of research and extensive consultation with provincial governments, the private sector and community organizations.[28]

In October 1990, Employment and Immigration Minister Barbara McDougall announced a five-year immigration plan that would continue this policy of moderate growth. The proposal would bring in 200,000 immigrants in 1990, 220,000 in 1991, and 250,000 during each of the years 1992-1995. As in the earlier Tory policy, the 1990 policy announcement singled out demographic considerations—i.e. a concern that the Canadian population will begin to decrease early in the next century because of below-replacement fertility rates—as a rationale for raising immigration levels.[29] It is notable that the Mulroney government has increased immigration levels, however modestly, in spite of evidence of public opinion polls that show Canadians are against increased immigration, and in spite of the economic downturn and rising levels of unemployment.[30]

The government has tried to allay the fears of the public concerning the economic impact of increased migration by stressing the potential long-term financial benefits. In support of a positive prognosis, the Immigration department cites data that suggest immigrants bring in up to $6 billion (in total) for capital investment, have a higher rate of self-employment and higher incomes than the Canadian-born, and receive less social assistance than other Canadians.[31] In addition, in order to assert greater control over the link between immigration and labour market changes, the Government has tightened the definition of "family class" immigrants by narrowing the types of people who are admitted as "family members" and using the notion of "real dependence" as the definitive criterion.[32]

The whole discussion of the projected levels of immigration in the federal five-year plan has noticeably downplayed issues of the racial and ethnic composition of immigrants.[33] The Immigration Minister's "Annual Report to Parliament" mentions the Middle East and Eastern Europe as regions from which large-scale pressure for migration are likely to be felt, but the report and the Minister's accompanying address to Parliament are otherwise devoid of mention of such issues as the increasing proportion of Third World, visible minority immigration.[34] Unlike the "Green Paper hearings," a series of lengthy public consultations that preceded the enactment of the 1976 Immigration Act, where the Liberal government itself focussed attention on the changing racial composition of migration to Canada, the immigration consultations conducted by the Mulroney government that preceded announcement of the five-year plan have not been similarly racialized. Where concerns regarding Canada's "absorptive capacity" in relation to new Canadians who are "culturally and visibly different," have been raised, this has occurred at the initiative of the mass media and research institutes rather than the Immigration Minister, Prime Minister, or members of the Conservative government.[35]

Some critics have suggested that the Mulroney government is shirking responsibility in not providing leadership in a debate about the impact on Canadian society of the new waves of visible minority immigrants. For instance, Islam argues that "such a debate is...in order because of the widespread belief that these immigrants are a burden on Canadian society."[36] Alternatively, the experience of past Canadian and other national governments which have made the racial composition of immigration a major reference point of their immigration policy discourse, has demonstrated that ensuing public debates have tended to encourage and legitimate hostility directed against racial minorities. With the exception of the seeming manipulation of the arrival of boatloads of Tamils and Sikhs to deal with the "refugee crisis" and bring in new (1989) refugee legislation, the federal government has avoided the mobilization of racist ideology in formulating immigration policy. In this important sense, the Conservative government of Brian Mulroney has distinguished itself from such neo-conservative governments as that of former British Prime Minister Margaret Thatcher, who had attempted to win favour with an insecure white British public through references to "swamping" of British culture by Black, New Commonwealth immigrants.[37]

Thus, the Conservative government should not be judged harshly for its silence on the racial composition of current and future immigration, given the almost certain nasty consequences such a public discussion is likely to have, especially for racial minorities. The major weakness of the Tories' five-year plan, which might be expected to fuel public anxiety over increased immigration and lead to greater levels of racial tension, is its failure to allocate adequate resources for settlement and administrative purposes. The Minister's announcement of the new levels of immigration was accompanied by a "federal integration strategy" which includes $200 million in extra funding for language training over four fiscal years.[38] Critics were quick to point out how inadequate the funds allocated for settlement were, suggesting that the federal government intends to place the burden of the increased costs of language and job training, and education of immigrant children, on the "already-stretched provinces and provincial education systems."[39]

Another concern with the new immigration plan raised by refugee aid groups was the absence of new initiatives to deal with the growing refugee backlog.[40] Inadequate resources to deal with the backlog might cause the number of people in "suspended animation" and with uncertain futures in Canada to grow. This in turn may incite racial antipathies given that a large segment of refugees are people of colour and of Third World origins.[41] Thus, in sum, the Tory immigration policy reflects an implicit de-politicization of race questions, combined with fiscal restraint and the shifting of costs of immigrant integration onto other levels of the state, the private sector, and most of all, onto the populations most vulnerable to racism and other forms of disadvantage. The groups most at risk include refugees and racial minority and non-English, non-French-speaking immigrant women. This approach is also reflected in the federal government's flagship program targeting racial discrimination in employment—namely, its federal employment equity program.

FEDERAL EMPLOYMENT EQUITY FOR VISIBLE MINORITIES: THE SIX PER CENT SOLUTION

The Employment Equity program is presented as one of the most extensive federal policy efforts to reduce institutional racism. Indeed, the Mulroney government claims that the Employment Equity Act is "[o]ne of the first of its kind both in Canada and internationally" and "represents a milestone in Canadian history."[42] The impetus for the development of the program was provided by recommendations for effective employment equity provisions in the reports of two royal commissions, and one standing parliamentary committee, all initiatives undertaken by the Trudeau Liberals.[43] Additional support for the development of the program was provided by the coming into force in April 1985 of Section 15(2) of the *Canadian Charter of Rights and Freedoms,* which rendered affirmative action programs legal.

The term "employment equity," was proposed by the Abella Commission to help defuse the negative emotional reactions evoked by the term, "affirmative action."[44] In 1986, after a decade and a half of voluntary affirmative action programs that showed no results, the federal government introduced employment equity for Crown corporations and federally regulated employers with 100 or more employees. The purpose of the Employment Equity legislation is to redress systemic discrimination against disadvantaged minorities—women, Aboriginal people, visible minorities and persons with disability, and to achieve workplace equality. The legislation requires federally-regulated employers to file an annual report with the Employment and Immigration Commission, reporting their work force profiles annually by sex, disability, visible minority and Aboriginal status.

The Employment Equity program has been under fire from visible minority and ethnic community organizations (among others) from its inception. Criticisms have centred on the legislation's lack of specific goals and timetables, systematic monitoring mechanisms or effective sanctions linked to **non-implementation** (as opposed to mere reporting) of employment equity measures.[45] The legislation requires employers under federal jurisdiction to prepare an annual employment equity plan with goals and timetables, but they are not required to submit this plan to the government. This is one feature which reveals the *de facto* non-mandatory character of the program.[46] Jain points out further flaws within the legislation:

> Much of the wording in the employment equity law is ill defined and somewhat loose in that positive policies and practices and reasonable accommodation do not lend themselves to precise interpretation. There is only a vague process of consultation between employers and designated group employee representatives to formulate the plan; meaningful consultation between the union or employee representatives is not possible if the employee representatives do not have a right to see the plan. What is more, there is no penalty for non-compliance with the action plan to prepare goals and timetables.[47]

The assumption of Employment Equity is that "public scrutiny" will provide the mechanism for enforcing the Act, an assumption that human rights activist Shelagh Day, calls "fanciful," and that places the burden of action on the victims of discrimination.[48] Under the Canadian Human Rights Act, the Human Rights Commission has the authority to initiate an investigation where there are reasonable grounds to believe that systemic discrimination exists. The Commission's approach, however, consistent with the soft-shoe tap dance of the Employment Equity program itself, has been to "avoid adversarial proceedings and to work with institutions to bring about the changes required by the Act."[49] The Commission's evaluation of the Employment Equity Act in its 1989 Annual Report called the progress made through the legislation:

> ...not very encouraging...[W]ithout an unequivocal commitment at the most senior levels of management it will not be accomplished at all...We certainly need a better law...not only to put to rest any doubts about

the obligations of those institutions covered by the Act, but also to give the Commission clearer authority to monitor compliance and ensure that there is genuine progress toward the objectives envisaged by Parliament.[50]

The major argument made in defense of the Employment Equity legislation is that it generates data that can be used to prove the existence and extent of systemic discrimination, and that can in turn persuade the federal government to eradicate such discrimination.[51] This argument is less than persuasive for visible minorities for several reasons.

First, there are real problems in the socio-political construction and operationalization of this category of disadvantaged group, some of which were raised earlier. Both in the 1981 and 1986 Census, the ethnic origin variable was the main variable used to define visible minorities. Data from other questions, such as place of birth, religion and mother tongue, were also used to "identify people who are likely to be visible minorities but did not indicate this information in their response."[52] Although such a combination of questions would appear to be a poor proxy for "non-white" and/or "non-Caucasian," this approach will be retained for collection of data on visible minorities in the 1991 Census, rather than a more direct question on "race" which might risk giving offense to respondents.[53] Thus, the success of employment equity—meant to remove discrimination based on race or skin colour—is hampered by the difficulties involved in obtaining meaningful statistics on the proportion of non-whites within the Canadian population.

A second problem with the program of employment equity for visible minorities is the assumption of homogeneous disadvantage for this designated group, which ignores the considerable socio-economic heterogeneity and social class differentiation both within each component group and within the category as a whole.[54] As Pendakur argues, the amalgamation of different groups may adversely affect the analysis of data concerning visible minorities in Canada. "For example, if one sub-group has a relatively high rate of achievement in occupation and income, it may obfuscate the fact that another subgroup is not faring as well. Thus, the impact of a program may not only be hidden, but also nullified by being improperly targeted."[55]

The need to confront the question of class in any long-term strategy to overcome racial and ethnic inequalities is particularly germane in Canada. Here, the history of importation of both cheap, unskilled, and professional, highly skilled immigrants from Third World countries has produced a bi-modal occupational and class structure among some, though not all, visible minority groups. The outcome of affirmative action programs, which tend to target upper and middle levels of management, is the promotion of minority candidates, who are in class terms relatively privileged, while there is inaction with respect to the many sources of class exploitation and racism among the least privileged strata within minority groups.[56] The current federal employment equity policy does nothing to redress the inequities in the labour market of those who are truly disadvantaged by virtue of their position in relations of class, race and gender—such as female minority domestic workers, chambermaids, building-cleaners, plastics workers, or those working in the needle trades and seasonal farm work. As important, the current employment equity policy diverts attention away from the costs of economic restructuring and policy harmonization processes involved in free trade with the United States, the brunt of which will be borne by older, non-English-speaking immigrant and refugee, and frequently, non-white women.[57] The appeal of employment equity to well-educated professionals, who have been excluded from the corporate boardroom or the upper levels of public service employment by virtue of their skin colour or visible cultural characteristics, is understandable. However, some minorities fear that they will bear a stigma through their participation within an affirmative action program of hiring or promotion. As described by Moodley,

> They will have to cope with the suspicion that they owe their position more to the colour of their skin than to their merit. Although affirmative action programs stress that they are no substitute for adequate qualifications, they are always perceived as overriding merit with ascriptive assets.[58]

The fact that the federal employment equity program is not effectively a policy which confronts and ameliorates structural barriers and institutional discrimination based on race is further observed in that its training component has been poorly developed.[59] For instance, the Canadian Jobs Strategy (CJS), the major job creation and training policy of the Conservative government, which was first introduced in 1985, sets explicit participation rates for the four designated groups within the federal Employment Equity program. However, the job creation and skills training within CJS is geared toward the lower end of the labour market in terms of income and skills, and thus fails to provide an appropriate link to the administrative, professional and technical, white collar occupations predominating within the Employment Equity program. Moreover, as Prince and Rice point out, "participants from visible minorities tend to be concentrated in [only] a few programs, Job Entry being the main one."[60]

The focus of the federal Employment Equity program on statistical representation of target groups in the federally regulated institutions suggests that equity for Aboriginal peoples, visible minorities, women and the disabled is achieved if those percentages match the percentages of the target groups in the Canadian labour force. For instance, the 1990 *Annual Report* for the Employment Equity program presents as a "positive change" an increase from 5.67 per cent to 6.68 per cent in visible minority representation in the labour force covered under the Act, a representation that is now slightly greater than in the Canadian labour force in 1986.[61] The sources for the increase in visible minority representation are far from clear, although the implication is that the increased percentage of visible minority employees is cause for celebration. Is the increase the result of a reduction in racial discrimination in hiring practices? Or is it largely the result of changes in the methods of counting visible minorities? Whatever factors underlying the percentage increase, such a reported statistical result may well relieve pressure on the federal government to deal with the unresolved problem of institutional racism. As argued by the Canadian Human Rights Commission:

> It is important...not to be mesmerized by definitional or statistical abstractions. We need to emphasize the qualitative and social goals of employment equity: positive structural and attitudinal achievements must underlie the numerical results.[62]

When Judge Rosalie Abella recommended that employment equity be implemented for visible minorities, she cautioned that:

> Focussing on visible minority groups through employment equity programs does not relieve society of the

responsibility to eradicate discrimination for all minority groups. It does not cancel the duty to provide for immigrants adequate language and skills training, bias-free mechanisms for determining the validity of foreign credentials, and experience, and vigilant regard for whether employers are unreasonably making Canadian experience a job requirement.[63]

Strategies to deal with the above-mentioned structures which exclude and adversely affect the employment status of particular groups within minority populations have not received much attention from the Conservative government, even though the effects of these structures are well documented.[64]

The Employment Equity program is scheduled to undergo a comprehensive review in 1991. This review is to involve consultation with affected groups, which will allow the latter to provide their criticisms of the program. It may also give minority groups the opportunity to re-appropriate the concept of "employment equity" and press for a reshaping of the program in a much broader and more comprehensive fashion to include issues such as official language and skills training, mechanisms for the more equitable recognition of foreign credentials and skills, and racism in the workplace.

RACE RELATIONS INITIATIVES IN MULTICULTURALISM AND CITIZENSHIP

The federal Multiculturalism bureaucracy has made race relations programs a major component of its activities since the early 1980s. In 1982, James Fleming, then Liberal Minister of Multiculturalism, made it a priority of his program to address the apparent upsurge in racial attacks, scapegoating and bigotry in Canada, and to take pre-emptive measures that would avoid the type of explosive race relations then dominating several British cities.[65] A Race Relations Directorate was created within the (then) Multiculturalism Directorate which sponsored several conferences targeting race relations, worked with the Treasury Board to prepare guidelines on the depiction of racial and ethnic minorities in government communications, and supported anti-racist and educational campaigns developed by organized labour, police forces and service agencies.

Under the Conservatives, multiculturalism has been given legislative status through the passage of the Canadian Multiculturalism Act in July 1988. As far as issues of race are concerned, the Act "recognizes the diversity of Canadians as regards race, national or ethnic origin, colour and religion as a fundamental characteristic of Canadian society." It recognizes and promotes the "understanding that multiculturalism reflects the cultural and racial diversity of Canadian society." And finally, it permits the Minister to "assist ethno-cultural minority communities to conduct activities with a view to overcoming any discriminatory barrier and, in particular, discrimination based on race or national or ethnic origin."

In September 1988, just before the federal election and following fast on the heels of the announcement of the new Multiculturalism Act, Prime Minister Mulroney announced an Agreement to provide redress to Canadians of Japanese ancestry for injustices suffered during and after the Second World War. As symbolic redress for the injustices, the Government offered a package that included $21,000 individual redress for victims of internment, $12 million to the Japanese community to undertake activities contributing to the well-being of the community and a further $12 million, on behalf of Japanese Canadians, for the creation of the Canadian Race Relations Foundation (to be discussed below). It is likely that other minorities—such as Canadians of Chinese and Ukrainian ancestry—who have historically suffered at the hands of Canadian authorities will also seek redress from a government that has shown itself willing to support such claims. Indeed, in September 1990, Prime Minister Mulroney extended an official apology to Italian-Canadians for their wartime injustices, a gesture that was entirely symbolic, however, and did not involve financial compensation.

The passage into law of the Multiculturalism Act was accompanied by an announcement by Gerry Weiner, the Minister responsible for Multiculturalism, of "Race Relations and Cross-Cultural Understanding" as one of four "new" directions to implement the "new" policy. The strategy for "national action on eliminating racial discrimination" was to include six areas of focus. These were: public education, institutional change, support for community advocacy, research and information, joint efforts to involve other levels of government, and direct action to change federal policies and practices.[66] In 1988-89, $3.07 million was allocated to Race Relations and Cross-Cultural Understanding. The amount spent in the following fiscal year (1989-90) was $6.42 million, and $7.27 million was forecast for 1990-91. An estimated $7.57 million is listed for the 1991-92 estimates.[67]

The major emphasis of the Race Relations program appears to have been in providing support for education and training within institutions in the areas of policing and justice, education, media and the arts, health and social services, and the workplace.[68] In many instances, such support has been limited to one-time workshops and conferences, but it has also been directed to programs to develop culturally sensitive services and training programs within particular institutions. Special attention has been given to institutions which have had protracted histories of racial exclusion and tensions with racial minorities, such as law enforcement. Such institutions have been encouraged to establish various administrative structures and recruitment programs to implement and monitor cross-cultural and race relations programs.[69]

With just over $7 million to allocate to the race relations program, Multiculturalism is limited in its resources, mandate and capacity to affect institutional change in the policies toward racial and ethnic minorities within other government departments and the private sector. Although with Bill C-18, which has attained third reading in Parliament, Multiculturalism and Citizenship is going to be upgraded to the status of a full department, this is unlikely to greatly enhance its capacity to effect major institutional change in combating racism, given the relatively scant size and low status of the proposed new department in the federal bureaucracy.[70] The extent to which real institutional change is occurring, and the efficacy of race relations and cross-cultural training is largely dependent upon the overall priorities of given institutions. It should be noted, however, that the majority of projects supported by Multiculturalism under the rubric of "institutional change" involve "cross-cultural" rather than "anti-racist" training.

Cross-cultural training tends to assume that lack of awareness of ethnocultural differences and the barriers that can occur in the absence of cultural sensitivity are at the root of inequities experienced by minorities. Anti-racist training focusses on the features of the institution which reflect the histories of racist exclusion and oppression of minorities, and attempts to eradicate those exclusionary mechanisms. Cross-cultural training may increase the efficiency and the productivity of workers within given institutions, a major priority of the Mulroney

government.[71] Such programs may, however, have little effect
on the experiences of racism of minority personnel or clientele,
insofar as they generally operate under the illusion of harmony
of interests, and equality of power and influence, between
generally white authorities and visible minority participants.
One outcome of cross-cultural training is that it may make the
participants "more sophisticated about their prejudices, to hide
them more effectively."[72] An evaluative study of an earlier
round of police sensitivity training workshops, developed
through liaison with the Canadian Association of Chiefs of
Police found that the workshops neither increased empathy nor
changed the attitudes held by police and minority civilians
regarding the other. The workshop achieved success only in
developing an understanding among participants of cultural
diversity.[73]

Multiculturalism has provided both sustaining and project
funds in support of community advocacy in anti-racist activities.
Fourteen organizations that have been provided Multiculturalism support in 1989 are listed in the Sector's "Overview of
Race Relations Initiatives," although this is apparently a
sample rather than comprehensive list of all funded race relations community-based projects. The Canadian Ethnocultural
Council (CEC) has recently been vociferous in its criticism of the
Race Relations Directorate because of its failure to support
particular community organization initiatives—specifically per-
taining to two of their own projectsdealing with media sen-
sitization and employment equity. According to Lewis Chan, the
President of the CEC, the Race Relations Directorate has been
"lacking a clear public strategy and has been subjected to
excessive political interference...The race relations policy and
program, we feel, responds less and less to the needs of the
communities, and more to the minister's office."[74] For their
part, Multiculturalism officials feared that the CEC's media
project would have created an adversarial relationship with
institutions that they felt were important to cultivate as
partners in efforts to eliminate racism. The Canadian Association of Broadcasters, for instance, had donated $10 million of
free air time during prime viewing hours for various public
education segments. In addition, an association of advertisers
is in the process of building awareness within its membership
of the importance of representative depiction. Multiculturalism
officials thus felt that to disturb these important relationships
through public criticism of the sort anticipated in the CEC

project, would be detrimental to the attainment of long-term goals.

The fear that partisan political interests will predominate and further weaken the support given by Multiculturalism to community advocacy in combatting racism was, however, also voiced in regard to another major initiative—the establishment of the Canadian Race Relations Foundation. The Race Relations Foundation was publicly announced as part of the September 1988 Japanese Canadian Redress Agreement, and will be funded with a $24 million endowment (providing the foundation, at current interest rates, with a $2.5 to $3 million operating budget). As conveyed in Bill C-63, the Act to establish the Foundation (which received Royal Assent on February 1, 1991), the organization's purpose is to undertake research and data collection in order to gain:

> ...further understanding of the nature of racism and racial discrimination and to assist business, labour, voluntary and other private organizations, as well as public institutions, governments, researchers and the general public in eliminating racism and racial discrimination.[75]

In the consultations with community groups and members of the Standing Committee on Multiculturalism over Bill C-63, particular concerns predominated. First, while a feasibility study on the Foundation discussed three options that the Foundation could take—primarily research, a more activist role with greater community representation and community empowerment, and a social council model—the proposed bill presents primarily a research model for the Foundation.[76] Several of the witnesses consequently criticized the passive and purely academic nature of the research foundation, and its lack of activist or grass-roots orientation or legislative authority in eradicating racism and racial discrimination.[77]

Second, community organizations expressed concern about the potential for partisan influence within the Foundation because of the power granted to Cabinet to appoint the Chief Executive Officer and members of the Board. Several witnesses recommended that appointments be made in a non-partisan fashion and that an arm's length relationship exist between the foundation and the Department of Multiculturalism and Citizenship.[78] This concern among organizations such as the

Canadian Ethnocultural Council was particularly acute given the Council's growing perception that the establishment of the Foundation was a means of supplanting grass-roots community groups. The impression that the Minister's office was acting unilaterally and without consultation with community groups was further enhanced by the unsuccessful efforts of the CEC and many other groups over two years to obtain a copy of the feasibility study on the Foundation.

A third recurring concern, voiced by representatives of community organizations outside the province of Ontario, was the issue of regional sensitivity. These witnesses objected to the planned location of the Foundation in Metropolitan Toronto, arguing that there already existed an abundance of resources to deal with race relations in Toronto and that, at the minimum, regional offices were required to take into account the different experiences of racism within different regions.[79]

Many questions remain, not only about the purposes and role of the Foundation, but also about the future relationship between the Race Relations Foundation and the new Department of Multiculturalism and Citizenship. One critical issue is if the Foundation is to take as its mandate race relations research and public education—currently two areas of focus of Multiculturalism in race relations that presumably are linked to the other areas of focus such as institutional change—then what would be left of the Race Relations program within Multiculturalism?

Ironically, the "new" direction in Race Relations and Cross-Cultural Understanding within Multiculturalism is in reality a continuation of several initiatives undertaken both by the previous Conservative Multiculturalism Minister, David Crombie, and former Liberal Minister, James Fleming. Much of the research, education and resource material financed through Multiculturalism reflects an effort of the Government to support the goal of anti-racism. But the Race Relations program within Multiculturalism does not follow any clear overall direction in confronting the many sources of institutional racism that have been identified by community groups and through research, although clearly its meagre resources and weak administrative capacity limit its interventions in initiating major costly institutional change. Unfortunately, the current approach is also lacking in creativity or fresh thinking. It is also problematic that Multiculturalism appears recently to have dampened its support for community advocacy on anti-racist issues, a necessary component for pushing a Conservative government, with quite different priorities, to seriously deal with racial inequities and discrimination. Indeed, those accomplishments within Multiculturalism that have been most publicized under the rubric of combating racism are easily read as efforts to draw favourable attention to the Minister's office, rather than well-considered programs providing long-term resources and commitment to protracted issues of systemic and ideological racism.[80]

MODERNIZATION OF THE RCMP: NATIONAL SYMBOLS, TURBANS AND BRAIDS

In March 1988, then Solicitor General James Kelleher announced that the RCMP wanted more Francophones, visible minorities and Natives to join its mostly white, male-dominated ranks. To meet what the Solicitor General called "the changing character and needs of the Canadian society," RCMP Commissioner Norman Inkster promised dress code changes to accommodate minorities such as male orthodox Sikhs, who are required to wear turbans and refrain from cutting their hair. Two years and two Solicitors General later, the decision to allow Sikhs to wear turbans was announced on March 15, 1990 in the House of Commons by Solicitor General, Pierre Cadieux.

In the two years that it took for the federal government to render a decision, the image of the Mounties had become a touchstone for racial and religious intolerance in Canada.[81] The announcement that headgear regulations in the 116-year-old force of 16,000 might be changed to accommodate the religious beliefs of Sikhs served as a catalyst for a storm of protest that was particularly strong in Alberta. By the end of 1989, more than 150,000 signatures had been collected on petitions which, in the words of one presenting MP,

> ...humbly pray and call upon Parliament to preserve the distinctive heritage and tradition of the RCMP by retaining the uniformity of the dress code with all the recognizable colour and trappings that have such great historical value to this country.[82]

Even more disturbing was the successful sale of pins and calendars which denigrated Sikhs, Chinese and Blacks. One pin which was reported to sell 30,000 copies around the country portrayed a white man, holding a Canadian flag and dwarfed by a Sikh in a turban, a Chinese man and a Black carrying a spear, bearing the words, "Who's the minority in Canada?"[83] The Canadian Ethnocultural Council considered a court challenge to stop the flow of the Taiwan-manufactured pins to Canada on the grounds that they constituted hate propaganda. Customs officials in Revenue Canada, however, decided that the pins did not fall within the guidelines which interpret hate propaganda within the Criminal Code.[84] Interestingly, in remarks which compared the wearing of the pins to the white hoods of the Ku Klux Klan, Prime Minister Mulroney indicated that he disagreed with Revenue Canada's judgment that the pins were not racist.[85]

While most of the petition-signing and entrepreneurial production and sales of anti-Sikh material occurred in Alberta, opposition to turbans for the RCMP emerged across the country. Many of those who opposed the dress code changes argued that the scarlet-jacketed RCMP in the flat-brimmed Mountie dress hat is one of Canada's best-loved symbols. Moreover, opponents argued that to allow Sikhs to diverge in the dress code of the force would be to give special privilege to one segment of the population—and risk undermining the liberal democratic, Judeo-Christian foundations of the country.[86]

Many Sikhs and others supportive of the change suspected that racism and fear among white Canadians of the changes wrought by non-European immigration were as much factors in the anti-turban campaign as love of Canadian heritage. This view was supported by the fact that, "since it was first formed in 1873, the RCMP has altered its official uniform several times, including a major change from a brimless pill box to a broad-brimmed scout charge."[87]

For the RCMP, the decision to modify dress regulations to accommodate religious beliefs is connected with the efforts of the force to recruit greater numbers of visible minorities, so that the national police force more clearly reflects the ethnocultural and racial composition of the country. In June 1989, in his comments to the Justice Committee, RCMP Norman Inkster pointed out the problems in policing created when minorities were not represented. An instance of this occurred in the RCMP investigation following the 1985 Air India crash where 307 passengers were killed, almost all of whom were members of the Canadian Sikh community. The force could call upon only two constables who spoke Punjabi to aid in its investigation.[88] Moreover, as demonstrated in one Canadian Human Rights case involving standard questioning of the citizenship by RCMP officers of those with "foreign ethnic backgrounds," the racially exclusionary nature of the Force had led to some routine racist operating procedures.[89] Interestingly, the exemption in wearing the stetson was legally justified in terms of religious freedoms consistent with both the Canadian Charter of Rights and Freedoms and the Canadian Human Rights Act which prohibit discrimination on the basis of religion, rather than tied to anti-discrimination arguments making reference to race.[90] Seven months later, religious freedom was again cited as the justification for permitting Native Canadians to wear braids in uniform.[91]

The long postponement of the government's decision on turbans in the RCMP, reflecting major splits within government ranks on the issue, has been widely criticized for contributing to the frenzied and racist character of the anti-turban campaign it seems to have inspired.[92] Nonetheless, the Mulroney government's decision to accept changes in the RCMP dress code to accommodate the changing ethnocultural, racial and religious character of Canada's population showed that it had travelled a fair distance since June 23, 1985. On hearing the news of the Air India crash on that day, the Prime Minister's response was to convey condolences to the Prime Minister of India, even though the vast majority of the 307 passengers killed were Canadians of Sikh origin.[93] Five years later, the Prime Minister supported a decision which acknowledged that people of Sikh origin were a part of Canada, and that major national symbols could be altered to reflect the current multicultural, multiracial diversity of Canadian society.

CONCLUSION

In evaluating the Conservative policies on issues of race and racism since the mid-1980s, it is important to keep in mind the larger political context in which these policies have been developed, and the limits imposed by the absences, contradictions and biases of the current political commitments to achieving racial equity in employment and other areas. Significant in this regard is the economic agenda of the Progressive Conservative government and its choice to vigorously pursue free trade with the United States. The philosophy underlying free trade— that unrestricted market forces are the most efficient allocators of economic resources—runs directly counter to public policies such as employment equity which interfere with the "natural workings of the market." Thus, it is not surprising that even supporters of employment equity acknowledge that the program involves little or no compulsion or intrusion into private decision-making.[94] As a strategy emphasizing upward mobility for visible minorities in some occupational and sectoral locations, employment equity by-passes those minority members trapped in low-wage, highly exploited industries and jobs. As a strategy to deal with racial discrimination in employment, its hypnotic fix on statistics draws attention away from the many sources of exclusion and subordination experienced by minorities where the federal government could play a leadership role. These include the inadequacies in official language and job training (which are particularly discriminatory in their impact on immigrant women), the over-burdened refugee determination system, the byzantine structure of overseas skills recognition, and the weak legislative protection for particular occupations within which new Canadians and visible minorities predominate—such as sewing machine operator, domestic worker and seasonal farm worker.

Within Conservative policies on race, there has unfortunately been a fair degree of muddling through (as in the Census and employment equity for visible minorities), preoccupation with superficial gestures in race relations programs, and in the RCMP turban issue, an absence of decisiveness at key junctures. In its favour, the Mulroney government has not, unlike other Conservative governments in Britain and the US, pandered to racist sentiment (for example, in immigration policy), which, given the uncertain economic times and anxiety over national unity provoked by the Meech Lake crisis, certainly exists in large measure. If the legislation that the government has brought forward to bolster multiculturalism has been lacking in terms of accompanying resources and administrative capacity, it has at least legitimized a vision of Canada that reflects the reality of a multiracial and multicultural country.

Notes

I am grateful for the constructive comments provided by Frances Abele, Yasmeen Abu-Laban and members of the Policy and Research division of the Multiculturalism Sector on earlier drafts of this work.

1   *Hansard*, May 1, 1947, Vol. 3, pp. 2644-2647. King was referring to immigration from Asia.

2   See Russell Juriansz, "Visible Minorities and Discrimination in Canada," Paper presented at the C.I.A.J. National Conference, Kananaskis Village, Alberta, October 11-14, 1989.

3   Of all those groups designated as "visible minorities" by Statistics Canada, only the Japanese are not dominated by immigrants. In 1986, in Canada as a whole, 42.8 per cent of Blacks were born in Canada; yet in Nova Scotia, 92.9 per cent of the Black population was Canadian-born. "The Visible Minority Population in Canada, 1986: Detailed Graphic Overview," (Policy and Research, Multiculturalism Sector, Multiculturalism & Citizenship, October 1990).

4   See, for example, Employment and Immigration Canada, "Immigration to Canada: Issues for Discussion," (Ottawa: Public Affairs and the Immigration Policy Branch, 1989), p. 8; Shirley Seward, "Immigration and Labour Adjustment," Paper presented to the House of Commons Standing Committee on Labour, Employment and Immigration, May 15, 1990.

5   Michael Valpy, "Ottawa should leave immigrant levels alone," *The Globe and Mail* [Toronto], October 22, 1990, p. A4.

6   "Immigration to Canada,", p. 8.

7   The majority (60 per cent) of immigrants to Canada in 1988 were destined for three centres: Toronto (35 per cent), Montreal (14 per cent) and Vancouver (11 per cent). Employment and Immigration Canada, "Immigration to Canada: A Statistical Overview," 1989, p. 18.

8   Employment and Immigration Canada, "1990 Annual Report Tables: Employment Equity Act, 1990, Table 1.2, p. 16.

9   Ravi Pendakur, "An Exploration of Race and State Policy," Department of Sociology and Anthropology, Carleton University, mimeo, 1990.

10   The racialization of differences between ethnic groups is reflected in the concept of Canada's "two founding races," referring to the British and French, a founding myth which is additionally flawed in its exclusion of the First Nations.

11   See Howard Palmer, "Reluctant Hosts: Anglo-Canadian Views of Multiculturalism in the Twentieth Century," in Canadian Consultative Council on Multiculturalism, (ed.), *Multiculturalism as State Policy: Conference Report* (Ottawa: Minister of Supply and Services, 1976).

12   See James Walker, "'Race' Policy in Canada: A Retrospective," in O.P. Dwivedi et al., (eds.), *Canada 2000: Race Relations and Public Policy* (Guelph: University of Guelph, 1989).

13   Juriansz, op. cit., p. 2.

14   See A. Montagu, *The Concept of Race* (New York: Free Press, 1964).

15   Gerry Weiner, *House of Commons Debates*, Vol.131, No.195, Tuesday, May 29, 1990, p. 11982.

16   Juriansz, op. cit., p. 1.

17   Boxhill and Stanic conjecture that the origins of the term may have been within the Abella Commission on Equality in Employment, which began its work in June 1983. See "Approaches to the Collection," p. 4. The term was also used in the Special Committee on Participation of Visible Minorities in Canadian Society, which received its mandate from Parliament in June 1983. The earliest reference I have found to this concept is an edited book published in 1980. See K. Victor Ujimoto and Gordon Hirabayashi, (eds.), *Visible Minorities and Multicul-*

turalism: Asians in Canada (Toronto: Butterworths, 1980).

18   Boxhill and Stanic, "Approaches to the Collection," p. 6.

19   For instance, the Statistics Canada's Centre for Justice Statistics includes persons who are South Asian (East Indian, Pakistani, Punjabi, Sri Lankan, Tamil, Bengali, Bangladeshi) under the category "Caucasian" along with persons who are European/"white." In contrast, the regulations accompanying the Employment Equity Act imply that South Asians are non-Caucasian by virtue of their inclusion under the category of "visible minorities." See Boxhill and Stanic, "Approaches to the Collection," pp. 12, 65-66.

20   "Approaches to the Collection," p. 6.

21   "Approaches to the Collection," p. 6.

22   See Judge Rosalie Silberman Abella, *Report of the Commission on Equality in Employment,* October 1984.

23   See Pamela White, "Testing 1991 Census Ethnic Ancestry, Ethnic Identity and Race Questions: Results of Two Surveys," Paper presented to the Canadian Population Society, Windsor, June 5, 1988.

24   Bruce Petrie, *Hansard,* Standing Committee on Multiculturalism and Citizenship, December 12, 1989, p. 1:40.

25   Ibid., p. 1:40. White also reports that, "From the 'public at large' focus group participants [organized by Statistics Canada] the view was expressed that the race question was racist and offensive. In particular, this group was concerned that visible minorities would consider the question to be objectionable because of its implied racist overtones." See White, "Testing 1991 Census," p. 14.

26   Wally Boxhill, "Making the Tough Choices in Using Census Data to Count Visible Minorities in Canada," Statistics Canada, December 1990, p. 18, emphasis added.

27   Employment and Immigration Canada, "Immigration to Canada: A statistical overview," (Ottawa: Public Affairs and the Immigration Policy Branch, 1989), p. 6.

28   Nasir Islam, "Canada's Immigration Policy: Compassion, Economic Necessity Or Lifeboat Ethics?" in Katherine A. Graham, (ed.), *How Ottawa Spends, 1989-90: The Buck Stops Where?* (Ottawa: Carleton University Press, 1989), pp. 222-4.

29   The Employment and Immigration Minister's "Annual Report to Parliament: Immigration Plan for 1991-1995," p. 5, cites the findings of the December 1989 report of Health and Welfare Canada's Demographic Review, "Charting Canada's Future" as evidence supporting the demographic argument for a modestly expansionary policy.

30   According to a *Globe and Mail*-CBC News poll taken October 15-20, 1990, 46 per cent of respondents favoured reduced immigration levels, 35 per cent favoured current levels, whereas only 16 per cent favoured increased levels. See Hugh Winsor, "46% want immigration levels reduced, poll finds," *Globe and Mail* [Toronto], October 29, 1990, p. A7.

31   See Hugh Winsor, "McDougall wins battle to increase immigration," *Globe and Mail* [Toronto], pp. A1, A2; Employment and Immigration Canada, "Immigration to Canada," p. 44.

32   As Nasir Islam points out, this restriction on the definition of "the family" within admissions policy is consistent with the Mulroney Government's earlier efforts to control the definition and size of the family class of entrants, which unlike the independent category of entrants is less subject to policy manipulations and short-term labour market changes. See Islam, "Canada's Immigration Policy," pp. 214-218.

33   In its background paper on "Immigration to Canada: Issues for Discussion," prior to the process of consultation, the Immigration department discusses the "socio-cultural dimensions of immigration." But it does so in a manner intended to reassure the public, distinguishing

between illegitimate racist responses to Third World migration and the legitimate desire of Canadians to "preserve national values." See "Immigration to Canada," pp. 8-9.

34   Employment and Immigration Canada, "Annual Report," p. 5; Barbara McDougall, "Notes for an Address on Tabling the Annual Report to Parliament on the Immigration Plan for 1991-1995."

35   Typical of the racialized discourse on immigration is this statement by journalist Michael Valpy: "Increasingly...Canada's immigrants are arriving from the Third World—from societies with structures and standards different from those in the industrialized world...We no longer are talking about a group of people who, in general, can be absorbed comfortably into Canadian society." "Ottawa should leave immigrant levels alone," *Globe and Mail* [Toronto], October 22, 1990, p. A4." See also Shirley B. Seward, "Immigration and Labour Adjustment," and Neil Swan, "Immigration: A Possible Study," Economic Council of Canada, November 15, 1988, p. 4.

36   "Canada's Immigration Policy, " p. 239.

37   See John Solomos, *Race and Racism in Contemporary Britain* (London: Macmillan, 1989,) pp. 59-63.

38   Overall, the federal integration strategy was to cost $525 million.   However, only $125 million is entirely new money, with the remaining funds obtained through increased visa costs and a reallocation of existing money in the department.   See Susan Delacourt, "Immigration gate opens wider," *Globe and Mail* [Toronto], October 26, 1990, p. A4.

39   Dan Heap, quoted in "Immigration gate opens wider," p. A4. Indeed, Immigration Minister Barbara McDougall responded to the criticisms made of the plan by Liberal and NDP MPs for its failure to help school boards cope with the influx of immigrant students by stating that "language training for school-aged children is a provincial responsibility," Joan Bryden, "Immigration plans stirs controversy," *(sic), Ottawa Citizen,* October 26, 1990, p. A3.

40   A $179 million program, announced by the federal
      government in December 1988, was supposed to clear up
      the backlog of 85,000 refugee claims within two years.
      But by the end of 1990, only 41 per cent of the claims had
      been resolved. In addition, by March 1991, approximate-
      ly 23,000 new claimants were waiting for a first hearing.
      Jacquie Miller, "New refugee system hitting same old
      logjams," *Ottawa Citizen*, March 5, 1991, p. A9. For an
      analysis of the overloaded and understaffed nature of the
      current refugee processing system, see Christie McLaren,
      "Jammed at the Door: Refugees in Canada," *Globe and
      Mail* [Toronto], Part One, February 23, 1991, pp. A1, A4;
      Part Two, February 25, 1991, pp. A1, A5; Part Three,
      February 26, 1991, p. A5; Part Four, February 27, 1991,
      p. A4; and Gwen Walmsley, "Living in Limbo, *Between
      the Lines*, Vol.1, No.6, p.5,

41   In 1988, Southeast Asia accounted for 25 per cent of
      refugees, and the Middle East and West Asia 16 per cent.
      However, the regional source for the greatest number of
      refugees was Eastern Europe which accounted for 35 per
      cent of the total number. "Immigration to Canada: A
      Statistical Overview," p. 50.

42   Employment and Immigration Canada, "1990 Annual
      Report: Employment Equity Act," p. 1.

43   Rosalie Silberman Abella, Commissioner, *Equality in
      Employment*; J. Patrick Boyer, Chair Sub-Committee on
      equality rights of the Standing Committee on Justice and
      Legal Affairs, *Equality for All* (Ottawa, House of Com-
      mons, October 1985); Bob Daudlin, Chair, *Equality Now!*
      Report of the Parliamentary Committee on Visible
      Minorities, (Ottawa, House of Commons, March 1984).

44   The negative connotations of "affirmative action" in-
      clude its association with "reverse discrimination," and
      practices of hiring and promotion based on target group
      membership, rather than merit. See Harish Jain, "Racial
      Minorities and Affirmative Action/Employment Equity
      Legislation in Canada," *Relations Industrielles*, Vol.44,
      No.3 (1989), p. 595.

45   Canadian Ethnocultural Council, "Employment Equity
      Review," 1988; Cross Cultural Communication Centre,

Employment Equity: How We Can Use It To Fight Workplace Racism, Toronto, 1988; Sheilagh Day, "Cries and Statistics: The Empty Heart of Federal Employment Equity," *Our Times*, (April 1990) 9(2): pp. 22-25.

46   Cross Cultural Communication Centre, pp. 5, 13.

47   Jain, "Racial Minorities," pp. 604-605.

48   "Cries and Statistics," p. 24.

49   Employment and Immigration Canada, "1990 Annual Report: Employment Equity Act," pp. 2-3; Canadian Human Rights Commission, "Annual Report 1989," p. 33.

50   Canadian Human Rights Commission, "Annual Report 1989," p. 31.

51   William F. Pentney, "Race Relations: The Legislative Base," in O.P. Dwivedi et al., *Canada 2000: Race Relations and Public Policy*, p. 60; Day, "Cries and Statistics," p. 24.

52   J. Coulter and A. Furrie, "Employment Equity Definitions of Visible Minorities, Aboriginal Peoples and Persons With Disabilities," Statistics Canada, Employment Equity Program, April 1989, p. 3. An example where place of birth would be useful in identifying members of a visible minority would be for "persons who checked French as their ethnic origin and Haiti as their place of birth who were assigned to the Black group." Coulter and Furrie, p. 3.

53   In discussions with a Statistics Canada official, it was pointed out that ethnic origin categories such as "Latin American" and "West Asian and Arab," two of the 11 groups counted as part of "visible minorities" were particularly problematic. Indeed, after lobbying from ethnic organizations representing Argentinean- and Chilean-Canadians, these groups were excluded from the visible minority category. The eleven visible minority groups are: Blacks, Indo-Pakistani, Chinese, Korean, Japanese, South East Asians, Filipino, other Pacific Islanders, West Asians and Arabs, Latin Americans, and "multiple visible minority." The "multiple visible minority" group

includes persons who fell into more than one of the visible minority categories by virtue of providing two or more visible minority origins. See Coulter and Furrie, "Employment Equity Definitions," pp. 6, 3-4; and Boxhill, "Making the Tough Choices."

54 See Daiva Stasiulis, "Rainbow Feminism: Perspectives on Minority Women in Canada," *Resources for Feminist Research*, 16(1): pp. 5-9; and Ravi Pendakur, "An Exploration of Race and State Policy," for analyses suggesting difficulties in treating the visible minority population as a homogeneous "disadvantaged minority."

55 Pendakur, "An Exploration," p. 17.

56 Kogila Moodley similarly argues that, "as in the cases of India and the United States, those who benefit most from affirmative action programs [in Canada] will be the least disadvantaged members of minority groups." Kogila Moodley, "The Predicament of Racial Affirmative Action," in Leo Driedger (ed.), *Ethnic Canada* (Toronto: Copp Clark Pitman Ltd.), p. 402; for a like-minded assessment of the American affirmative action program, see Richard P. Young, "History and the Politics of Race," *Socialist Review*, Vol.16, Nos.3 & 4, (May-Aug. 1986), pp. 67-75.

57 Marjorie Griffin Cohen, *Free Trade and the Future of Women's Work* (Toronto: Garamond Press), pp. 38, 46.

58 Moodley, "The Predicament of Racial Affirmative Action," p. 402. Similarly, within the focus groups tested by Statistics Canada, many visible minority participants expressed "that they wanted to obtain their employment on the basis of merit not quota. The desire to be treated fairly and equitably was at the centre of their concerns." White, "Testing 1991 Census," p. 14.

59 Pendakur, p. 21. An absence of a training component in any affirmative action program can have disastrous effects for target groups. Commenting on the poor results for Aboriginal peoples in the Employment Equity program, Narda Iulg, senior adviser on Aboriginal employment to the Native Council of Canada, said that the early years of Ottawa's 1983 affirmative action program ac-

tually did long-term damage to the viability of equality programs. "They grabbed anybody to put in a job. It was [taking] warm bodies off the street to keep dust off the chairs." Sean Fine, "Job equity eludes natives," *Globe and Mail* [Toronto], December 6, 1990.

60   Michael J. Prince and James J. Rice, "The Canadian Jobs Strategy: Supply Side Social Policy," in Katherine A. Graham (ed.), *How Ottawa Spends, 1989-90: The Buck Stops Where?* (Ottawa: Carleton University Press, 1989), p. 267. See Table 9.4, p. 278 for Participation Rate of Visible Minorities within the CJS.

61   "1990 Annual Report: Employment Equity Act," p. 5.

62   Canadian Human Rights Commission, *Annual Report 1989*, pp. 24-25.

63   Abella, *Equality in Employment*, p. 47.

64   For instance, immigrant women's groups have repeatedly lobbied against the networks of discriminatory regulations within Employment and Immigration which exclude many immigrant women from access to language and job training. While the federal government proposed a $15 million program for language training in the workplace for immigrant women, this proposal has not yet been implemented. See Seward, "Immigration and Labour Adjustment," p. 12. Similarly, in contrast to countries such as Australia, the Canadian government has provided very little leadership in dealing with the major problem (of which racism is a component) of recognizing overseas qualifications. See Daiva Stasiulis, "Multiculturalism and the Economic Agenda in Australia: Adult E.S.L., Overseas Skills Recognition and Anti-Racist Strategies," Prepared for Policy and Research, Multiculturalism Sector, Multiculturalism and Citizenship, June 1990.

65   See Daiva Stasiulis, "The Symbolic Mosaic Reaffirmed: Multiculturalism Policy," in Katherine A.Graham (ed.), *How Ottawa Spends, 1988-89: The Conservatives Heading Into the Stretch* (Ottawa: Carleton University Press, 1988), pp. 88-94.

66   Department of the Secretary of State, Multiculturalism and Citizenship, *Annual Report 1988-89,* p. 47.

67   Multiculturalism and Citizenship Canada, *1991-92 Estimates,* Part III, Expenditure Plan, p. 13. From 1989 onwards, 11 person-years were allocated within headquarters to the Race Relations and Cross-Cultural Understanding Program. Interview with Lizzy Fraikin, Director General, Programs Branch, Multiculturalism, January 5, 1991.

68   Multiculturalism and Citizenship Canada, *Working Together Towards Equality: An Overview of Race Relations Initiatives* (Minister of Supply and Services Canada, 1990).

69   For instance, beginning in October 1989, a National Action Plan on Police-Minority Relations was developed. It includes the establishment of a committee of federal/provincial/territorial deputy ministers responsible for policing, with representation from Multiculturalism and Citizenship. It also involves the creation of a national multicultural policing information centre and the development of a national framework for cross-cultural training of police officers. "Overview: justice for all," *Together,* Multiculturalism and Citizenship Canada, Vol. 2, No. 1, Winter 1990, p. 3.

70   One official within Multiculturalism pointed out that there were both advantages and disadvantages to the creation of a separate Department of Multiculturalism and Citizenship. On the positive side is the fact that the department that deals with race relations and multiculturalism will have its own financial credits and bureaucracy. On the negative side, the fact that the new department will be small (rather than part of a large department, the Secretary of State) will mean that its programs could become marginalized.

71   Indeed, the Multiculturalism program is justified by the federal government in terms of priorities established by the Free Trade Agreement: "If Canada is to respond successfully to the challenges of an increasingly competitive international economy and to the potential of the Canada-US Free Trade Agreement (FTA), equality of opportunity

and access to the economy are critical to ensure the fullest possible deployment of Canada's diverse human resource base." Multiculturalism and Citizenship Canada, *1990-91 Estimates*, p. 12.

72   "An interview with RCMP Commissioner, Norman Inkster," *Together*, Vol. 2, No. 1, (Winter 1990):15.

73   Charles S. Ungerleider, "Police Intercultural Education: Promoting Understanding and Empathy Between Police and Ethnic Communities," *Canadian Ethnic Studies*, Vol. 17, No. 1, 1985, pp. 51-66.

74   *House of Commons*, Minutes of Proceedings and Evidence of the Legislative Committee on Bill C-63, October 16, 1990, Vol. 5, pp. 7,6. To further support his view that community organizations had been by-passed within important decisions taken on Multiculturalism policy, Lewis Chan pointed out how two bills—"Bill C-18 on the department and...one on heritage languages have been...rushed through the committee stage, especially since they have been sitting months on the *Order Paper* and no serious amendments advanced by our council or other groups have been accepted." *House of Commons*, Bill C-63, p. 5:6.

75   "Bill C-63: An Act to establish the Canadian Race Relations Foundation," *The House of Commons*, First reading, February 1, 1990.

76   Margaret Mitchell, "House of Commons: Minutes of Proceedings and Evidence of the Legislative Committee on Bill C-63," Issue No. 5, p. 18.

77   For instance, Superintendent Julian Fantino of the Metro Toronto Police Task Force on Race Relations commented: "I do not see any power to seek documents, examine documents, power of subpoena to access things that normally would not be available to address these issues...I think the bill should have some...legislative power. It should compel certain compliance." "Minutes of Proceedings," October 17, 1990, Issue No. 6, p. 5.

78   "I would like to stress the importance of making an arm's length relationship between this foundation and the

Department of Multiculturalism and Citizenship. We must make sure the foundation is not something that will be subject to political patronage." Van Hori (National Association of Japanese Canadians, Canadian Ethnocultural Council), *House of Commons,* October 16, 1990, p. 9.; see also Alan Dutton, B.C. Organization to Fight Racism), *House of Commons,* October 18, 1990, p. 8.

79 See Alan Dutton, *House of Commons,* October 18, 1990, p. 8.

80 For instance, the Minister has developed "Awards for Excellence in Race Relations" which are given directly through the Minister's office, rather than through a more formal process. Also, a great deal of publicity has been given to short-term events such as a television public service announcement, a "Together We're Better" contest for teenagers and development of information kits as a central promotional vehicle—in commemorating March 21, International Day for the Elimination of Racial Discrimination. Given the small pool of resources provided to race relations within Multiculturalism, one must seriously question this allocation to one ceremonial anti-racist day.

81 "Symbol of tolerance," *Toronto Star,* editorial, March 8, 1990, p. A24.

82 Ian J. Kagedan, "As a symbol the Mountie is outdated," *Toronto Star,* February 6, 1990, p. A13.

83 "Calgarians' topical pins let buyers wear their opinions on their lapels," *Montreal Gazette,* February 27, 1990, p. B4.

84 "Pins not hate propaganda: Revenue Canada," *Saskatoon Star,* January 16, 1990, p. A11.

85 "Changing the uniform," *The Edmonton Journal,* March 12, 1990, p. A10. Given that many Tory MPs and some Cabinet Ministers opposed the move to alter the RCMP dress code, including Deputy Prime Minister Don Mazankowski, the Prime Minister's statement can be seen as reflecting personal rather than Conservative

Party sentiment. See "Mazankowski sets confusing example," *The Daily News* [Halifax], p. 18.

86   In late October 1989, delegates to the Reform Party's convention in Edmonton overwhelmingly supported a resolution that Sikhs be barred from wearing turbans in the RCMP. The Reform Party, whose base of support is widest in Alberta, has policies which are anti-immigration, anti-bilingual and anti-multicultural. "Ethnic groups accused of crying wolf," *Ottawa Citizen*, November 1, 1990, p. C16. One month after the federal government endorsed permitting Sikh RCMP officers to wear turbans, a Gallup poll found that this practice was favoured by only 22 per cent of Canadian adults. "Most oppose turban for RCMP," *The Gazette* [Montreal], May 7, 1990, p. A6. See also, Paul Jackson, *Calgary Sun*, February 25, 1990.

87   Bob Bragg, *Calgary Herald*, February 25, 1990.

88   "The RCMP needs turbaned Sikhs," *Edmonton Journal*, p. B4.

89   Juriansz, "Visible Minorities," p. 15.

90   Derek Lee, *House of Commons Debates*, March 15, 1990, p. 9308.

91   *RCMP News Release*, October 23, 1990. In the case of braids, the delay was accounted for in terms of the need of the RCMP to question "whether the braids are a religious symbol or merely an ethnic tradition which is not protected by human rights legislation." Geoffrey York, "RCMP permits braids," *Globe and Mail* [Toronto], October 25, 1990, p. A4.

92   "If former solicitor general Pierre Blais had quietly accepted the recommendation of RCMP Commissioner Norman Inkster last June, the few Sikhs in the force would be wearing turbans now with little public comment." "Changing the uniform," *The Edmonton Journal*, March 12, 1990, p. A10.

93   Clark Blaise and Bharati Mukherjee, *The Sorrow and the Terror: The Haunting Legacy of the Air India Tragedy* (Markham, Ont.: Penguin Books, 1988).

94   Dale Gibson, "Stereotypes, Statistics and Slippery Slopes: A Reply to Professors Flanagan & Knopff and Other Critics of Human Rights Legislation," in N. Nevitte and A. Kornberg, (eds.), *Minorities and the Canadian State,* pp. 125-138.

CHAPTER 9

HOW OTTAWA DITHERS: THE CONSERVATIVES AND ABORTION POLICY

Leslie A. Pal

Résumé: Depuis la déclaration par la Cour suprême de l'inconstitutionnalité de la loi canadienne sur l'avortement, les conservateurs fédéraux ont cherché avec beaucoup de difficulté un compromis pour combler le vide juridique. Leur tentative a échoué en 1988, mais ils ont failli y arriver avec la loi C-43, introduite vers la fin de 1989 mais défaite au Sénat en 1991. Une politique en matière d'avortement représente un défi de par la nature même de la question, les vues tranchées de chaque côté, et les divisions quant aux compétences en matière de droit criminel et de santé. Ce chapitre soutient, cependant, que la loi C-43 s'est noyée dans les eaux troubles du lac Meech. Le jeu politique de l'avortement n'est ni aberrant ni extrême, mais reflète plutôt le syndrome post-Meech impliquant la nécessité d'un équilibre entre une politique au niveau du pays et la variation régionale, le rôle des groupes d'intérêt public, la nature des droits humains, la qualité des chefs politiques et l'autorité de la loi. Si les manoeuvres derrière la loi C-43 ont failli réussir à produire une législation, elles font peu pour nous assurer que les conservateurs relèvent le défi d'un Canada divisé et découragé.

Abstract: Ever since the Supreme Court in 1988 declared Canada's abortion law unconstitutional, the federal Tories have struggled for a compromise to fill the legal vacuum. They failed in 1988, and very nearly succeeded with Bill C-43, introduced in late 1989 but defeated in the Senate in 1991. Designing an abortion policy is inherently challenging because of the sweeping nature of the issue, the firm views on each side, and jurisdictional divisions over criminal law and health. This chapter argues, however, that the fortunes of Bill C-43 reflect fundamental forces swirling in the wake of the failed Meech Lake Accord. The politics of abortion, far from being aberrant or extreme, is an exemplar of a "post-Meech syndrome" that wrestles with the balance of national policy and regional variation, the role of public interest groups, the nature of rights, political leadership, and the rule of law. While the manoeuvres behind Bill C-43 almost succeeded in producing legislation, they give little confidence that the Tories are equal to the challenge of a divided and despondent Canada.

Government is principally about two things: money and morals. Money—or rather lack of it—has dominated the Conservative agenda for seven years. The Meech Lake fiasco showed that the life and legitimacy of the Tory government depend as much if not more on contested visions of equality and ethics. But the Meech Lake Accord was only the first of Ottawa's confrontations with the politics of principle. As much as they twisted and squirmed, in 1990 the Tories finally had to face the question of abortion.

The abortion issue had simmered since January 1988, when the Supreme Court of Canada struck down the law that had regulated abortion in Canada since 1969. Pro-choicers rejoiced in the decision while pro-lifers attacked it. Promising an "immediate" response, the government tried to manoeuvre Parliament into accepting part of the responsibility for designing new legislation. This strategy failed and the government let the matter drop for a year, until the sensational Barbara Dodd and Chantal Daigle cases in summer 1989. The two women had decided to have abortions, but their former boyfriends tried to stop them with court injunctions. The government reluctantly launched another attempt at legislation, Bill C-43, that barely managed to get passed in the House, and then made its way to a Senate awash in the bile and vitriol of the GST. On January 31, 1991 the Senate defeated Bill C-43, and the government immediately announced that it would not attempt new legislation again, at least not before the next federal election. Bill C-43's defeat was humiliating, but ironically its passage would have been something less than a triumph for the Tories, since even Kim Campbell, the openly pro-choice Minister of Justice, admitted that it would have been challenged in the courts.

Abortion is often perceived as a distracting and somewhat anomalous area of contemporary public policy. It is central to sex and reproduction, topics that politicians treat squeamishly, if at all. It seems by its very nature to be unsolvable, with fierce and zealous exponents at both extremes. If contemporary politics is ultimately about compromise, then abortion must be our most intractable issue. Pro- and anti-abortion activists cannot bargain over lives or rights, they cannot make deals or trade-offs. To a government obsessed with the bottom line, with jobs and trade, with global competition and the budget, abortion policy is an unsavoury agenda item, something that wins no friends and makes many enemies.

While abortion is perhaps unusually complex and contentious, in fundamental ways the rest of the Canadian political system has caught up with it. Far from being anomalous, the politics of abortion is almost a template for contemporary Canadian public policy, particularly in an era dominated by what we may term the "post-Meech syndrome."[1] That syndrome consists of at least five characteristics that subject many of the federal government's policy initiatives—economic and other-wise—to forces similar to those that drive the abortion issue:

○ The Accord raised the question of the proper balance between national policy frameworks and permissible regional variation. This has been a leitmotif of Canadian federalism since Confederation, but the Accord's explicit acceptance of Quebec as a "distinct society" and its apparent constraints on Ottawa's spending power (coupled with other initiatives such as the Free Trade Agreement that seemed to reduce Ottawa's power) forced a much more pointed debate on the question.

○ The Accord's failure highlighted the new role of public interest groups, or citizens' coalitions against government policy. The Accord was damned as an issue of compromise and horsetrading that met no one's interests except those of an old-boys' club of power-grubbing politicians. Elijah Harper's *coup de grâce* on behalf of Aboriginal Canadians was only the most dramatic (and effective) example of opposition that swelled among women's organizations, ethnic groups, and linguistic minorities. These groups demanded that their rights be protected in Meech, and that they have more direct say in constitutional change.

○ As the first major attempt to amend the Constitution since patriation and the adoption of the Charter in 1982, the Accord threatened to rend the delicate and confused tapestry of "official" rights and freedoms. The 1982 Charter tries to affirm both individual and collective rights. The former apply to all Canadians, while the latter are focussed on particular categories of Canadians such as official language minorities, women, Aboriginals, and ethnics. What rights these groups enjoy is unclear, as is the hierarchy of rights among them. The Charter, while ambiguous, represented a sort of treaty among these groups and with the Canadian government. The Meech Lake Accord threatened to disturb the hierarchy (for example, in its final version affirming multicultural and Aboriginal but not women's rights), and potentially left **all** rights open to abuse in Quebec.

○ The death of the Meech Lake Accord was ultimately so farcical that it bred an unprecedented degree of public sourness and cynicism. While the politicians congratulated themselves for "nation-building" through the Accord, Canadians who watched the whole sordid process on television despaired of their country and its leaders.

° The Meech Lake Accord was the perfection of a peculiarly Canadian political practice that we might term "statutory exceptionalism." Whereas in most countries a law is a law is a law, and exceptions and exemptions are usually matters of administrative practice, the Canadian instinct is to embed or entrench exceptions directly into the letter of its laws and its constitution. The Canadian political community has from its inception been fragmented along linguistic and religious lines, and the fragmentation has only increased in recent times. Without national spirit or cementing traditions, sub-groups have jealously guarded their prerogatives to the point of insisting that any general laws or constitutional principle make explicit exception for them. The result is a political practice suffused by a duet of general principle and specific exception. The general principles often become exceedingly vague in order to accommodate those exceptions, further eroding any sense of overarching rule. The irritating ambiguity of the Accord's central terms (e.g. "distinct society") can be traced to this.

A post-Meech syndrome that reflects these fragmenting forces threatens to envelop Ottawa and the rest of the country for the foreseeable future. The failure of Meech means, for example, that constitutional discussions will continue to dominate the political agenda, and now those discussions will focus much more pointedly on the balance of national sovereignty and regional autonomy. Public interest groups, tempered in the fire of Meech, will be resilient and implacable opponents of any attack on fundamental rights as they perceive them. Public sourness and despair (at least outside of Quebec) can only increase as inept leaders bumble about trying to salvage a country from the ruins of the Accord. Their efforts will doubtless involve subterfuges of "statutory exceptionalism;" nothing else will now do for the nation's truculent mosaic.

The recent politics of abortion renders these themes, and echoes this syndrome, *pianissimo*. First, like the Meech Accord, abortion policy has been plagued by charges that **national** governments have abdicated their responsibility to regulate

termination of pregnancy. Because abortion is a medical procedure, provinces can control access to abortion through their
powers over health care. When Canada's previous abortion law
(section 251 of the Criminal Code)[2] was struck down by the
Supreme Court in 1988, provincial governments moved into the
legal vacuum and soon created a patchwork of jurisdictional
regimes governing abortion. Pro-choice critics have objected to
this, arguing that women must have equal access to abortion
across the country. Second, abortion policy is increasingly
driven by vocal and committed groups of citizens who will do
almost anything to achieve their goals. Since 1988, pro-life
groups have attracted the most attention for their dramatic
tactics (e.g. "Operation Rescue"), but pro-choice and feminist
groups have been equally active in the past and continue to hold
rallies and demonstrations in the present. Like Meech, abortion
has been the object of intense legal wrangles, but also like the
Accord it has become pre-eminently a "citizens' issue." Third,
just as the Meech Lake Accord was opposed for its potential
impact on collective rights, so abortion has become framed in
terms of the rights of women and of the fetus. Thirty years ago
the question of women's rights over reproduction was not
central to the debate over abortion, a debate incidentally that
was dominated by the legal and medical professions. Today, and
especially since the Charter, the question of abortion is assessed
primarily in terms of balancing rights: the right of women to
control their bodies and reproduction, and the right to life for
the fetus. Section 7 of the Charter (which states that everyone
has the "right to life, liberty and security of the person") has
been the basis of appeals **for** and **against** stricter abortion laws.

Fourth, the sad progress of abortion politics in Canada,
despite moments of enlightenment and good will, has contributed to and encouraged public disaffection and civil dis-
obedience on both sides of the issue. Henry Morgentaler, for
example, has successfully challenged federal and provincial
statutes by openly breaking the law, forcing the issue into court,
and winning jury acquittals. Pro-life activists see this as a
persistent pattern of criminal activity that deliberately ignores
the rule of law; at the same time, they themselves have adopted
more militant tactics, disobeying court injunctions in favour of
a "higher law." Finally, Canadian abortion law, both past and
present, is a prime example of "statutory exceptionalism." Section 251 and Bill C-43 had the same format: forbid abortion as
a crime, and then permit it under special circumstances. Under
section 251 those circumstances included a threat to life and

health and a certificate from a Therapeutic Abortion Committee, while Bill C-43 called for a physician's determination as to the medical necessity for the termination. As well, disputes have raged over the meaning of threats to "life" and "health" stemming from the pregnancy: pro-lifers claim that "health" is too broad and allows psychological and even eugenic grounds for abortion; pro-choicers have worried about narrow definitions that would exclude those grounds.

In its specifics, of course, abortion is substantially different from the Meech Lake Accord. The point is rather that, in terms of process and dynamics, the "post-Meech syndrome" will lead Canadian politics to reflect some of the generic features of abortion policy. The Tory government's record on abortion gives little confidence that it can manage the policy agenda in the aftermath of Meech.

CANADA'S ABORTION REGIME, 1969-88

Canada's abortion laws can be traced back to British common law tradition that made termination of pregnancy after "quickening" (the sensation of fetal movement sometime between the 13th and 16th week after conception) an offence. That tradition was codified in British legislation in 1803 and again in 1861, and Canada's first Criminal Code provisions against abortion simply copied the British statute.[3] With some minor changes, this legislation formed the foundation of Canada's abortion regime until 1969. Anyone who attempted to induce a miscarriage by chemical or mechanical means was liable to life imprisonment. It should be noted that as harsh as this was, it did not completely prevent abortions. There are no reliable data, but anecdotal evidence confirms that women self-induced, and that physicians would perform abortions either secretly or under the disguise of some other medical procedure. Back-street abortionists were available as well, though any woman who sought them out was usually risking her life.

Sexual mores had changed by the 1960s, not just in Canada but throughout the western world, and there was a general movement to liberalize abortion.[4] In sharp contrast to contemporary abortion politics, however, there was no mass movement and little visible public pressure for liberalization. An organized feminist movement which has been a key proponent of liberalized abortion, was only beginning to form in the mid-1960s. The pressure for liberalization came from the medical and legal professions, principally the Canadian Medical Association (CMA) and the Canadian Bar Association (CBA). The existing Criminal Code sections related to abortion were inconsistent, and doctors and lawyers wanted clarification. For example, while section 237 (as it was then numbered) of the Code explicitly forbade abortion and made it punishable by life imprisonment, section 209 (2) exempted it if performed to save the life of the mother. Another section of the Code protected physicians from liability in all surgical procedures (including abortion) as long as the procedure was done competently and out of necessity. Thus abortions were in fact sometimes performed openly in hospitals, though in most cases these hospitals had established Therapeutic Abortion Committees (TACs) to review and approve the procedure.

The CMA and CBA representations came at an opportune time since the federal government was in the midst of a review of legal provisions regarding the family and sexuality, particularly contraception. By October 1967 it turned its attention to abortion, and in December a parliamentary committee recommended a relaxed abortion law that would make it legal in cases where the pregnancy threatened the life or health of the mother. The Government (with Pierre Trudeau as Minister of Justice) accepted the recommendation and included almost identical wording in its omnibus bill to amend various sections of the Criminal Code. It took over a year for Parliament to pass the bill, but in June 1969 Canada had a new abortion law in the form of section 251 of the Criminal Code (Appendix 9.1).

Before discussing Section 251 in detail, it would be helpful to review some of the generic aspects of abortion regulation. First, abortion in Canada is an interjurisdictional matter. Abortion has always been a matter of criminal law, under federal jurisdiction. The **enforcement** of criminal law is left up to provincial authorities, however. Moreover, even though the primary regulatory instrument is a legal prohibition, abortion is also governed in some aspects by health policy, since termination of pregnancy is a medically delivered service. Whatever the federal law, provinces play a role in enforcement (and may on occasion, as Quebec did after 1976, refuse to enforce it), and in the way that they define hospitals, clinics, and medically insured services within their provincial health plans. Second, while abortion is regulated by governments, it is delivered by a self-governing profession. In order to practise medicine, physicians must be licensed by their respective provincial Colleges of Physicians and Surgeons. Hospitals are governed by their boards, which in some cases are elected members of the public, and as a matter of institutional practice can refuse to perform abortions. As members of a self-governing profession, and not simple employees of the state, physicians cannot be forced to provide a service. Personal preferences and informal professional standards can have an impact on the availability of the service.

The jurisdictional division coupled with the delivery of the service by members of a self-governing profession means that abortion policy and practice has the potential to be highly fragmented and regionally diverse, whatever the federal framework law might be. A third fact complicates this even further. The framework law may be quite vague, and so actually encourages fragmentation and diversity. Most of the world's abortion laws[5] stress **the detrimental effects** of the pregnancy as the primary basis for abortion. These effects may be defined broadly or narrowly. The broadest grounds would include anything the pregnant woman considered important, making the decision to terminate one that is completely up to her. Somewhat narrower grounds might include potentially detrimental effects on **health** and **well-being**. The most restrictive abortion regimes make termination of pregnancy illegal in all cases except those where there is a real threat to the mother's **life**.

In light of these general considerations it is clear that the pre-1969 Canadian abortion regime was highly restrictive. It simply made the attempt to perform an abortion a crime in all cases, whatever the reason. Section 251 of the revised Criminal Code continued to make abortion a crime, punishable by life imprisonment. However, subsection 4 then went on to say that abortion was legal as long as it met several conditions. These were: (1) it be performed by a qualified physician, (2) in an accredited hospital, and (3) approved or certified by a TAC whose majority opinion was that the continuation of the pregnancy "would or would be likely to endanger [the pregnant woman's] life or health." TACs had to consist of at least three members, all of whom had to be qualified physicians appointed by the hospital board. While the new legislation did liberalize access to abortion, it did so only modestly. The saving provision (life or health) was sufficiently broad that it could conceivably cover real physical threats to life as well as one's mental well-being. In practice, however, very few physicians at the time were prepared to allow expansive, largely social or psychological

grounds for abortion. The profession as a whole had its reserva-
tions about the procedure, and religious hospitals would rarely
if ever perform it.[6]

The widespread practice of TAC approval was now embedded in legislation, but without any guidelines as to how
expeditiously decisions would have to be made. The TACs
themselves were under the control of hospital boards, which
were either provincially appointed or elected. The very definition of an "accredited" hospital rested with the provincial Minister of Health, and always set such a high standard for
available personnel and equipment that "clinics," with more
modest resources, could not qualify. Years later, when the
abortion issue hinged on the legal establishment of free-stand-
ing abortion clinics, this provision of section 251 became central
to the debate.

The consequences of section 251 for Canada's abortion rate
may be seen in Table 9.1.

Table 9.1
Therapeutic Abortions in Canada, 1970-1986
Selected Years

Year	Therapeutic Abortions	Per 100 Live Births
1970	11,152	3.0
1973	43,201	12.6
1976	54,478	15.1
1978	62,290	17.4
1979	65,043	17.8
1980	65,751	17.7
1981	65,053	17.5
1982	66,254	17.8
1983	61,750	16.5
1984	62,247	16.5
1985	62,712	16.7
1986	63,462	17.0

Source: Statistics Canada, *Therapeutic Abortions, 1986,* Catalogue 82-211
(Ottawa: Minister of Supply and Services Canada, 1988), p. 1. The
second column on absolute number of abortions includes only those
performed on Canadian residents in hospitals, not in clinics. The
1986 Quebec figure for abortions performed in clinics was 3,498.

There was a surge in **legal** abortions immediately following the introduction of section 251. The number of abortions performed in hospitals peaked in the early 1980s and stabilized thereafter at a rate of roughly 17 abortions per 100 live births. Pro-life activists took these figures as a measure of how much section 251 had opened the gates to ease access to abortion. Those on the pro-choice side pointed instead to the administrative features of the abortion regime that inhibited access: the TAC approval process; agreement by a physician; provincial control over definitions of hospitals; and hospital board control. One independent estimate suggested, for example, that only 41 per cent of Canadian hospitals had the required obstetrical and gynecological resources to qualify to perform abortions. Of those, only 48 per cent chose to have TACs and actually do the procedure. Overall, by these data only 20 per cent of Canadian hospitals had TACs.[7] Not surprisingly, while the numbers of legal abortions increased in Canada, illegal ones continued to be performed, and women from smaller centres and smaller provinces often had to travel elsewhere to have an abortion.

As flawed as the legislation was, it was likely to persevere for several reasons. First, it threatened life imprisonment to anyone who broke the law, a strong disincentive for most physicians who might have disagreed with it. Second, the abortion law was drafted in such a way as to invite regional and even local variation, as preferences among hospitals, doctors, and women varied from place to place and time to time. While the pro-choice lobby could be expected to fight for further and more extensive liberalization, and while there may have been small battles over the law's implementation in different parts of the country, section 251 might very well have survived indefinitely had it not been for Henry Morgentaler's legal battles in the 1970s and 1980s.[8] Morgentaler was a family physician in Montreal, and had been an outspoken advocate of liberalized abortion before the parliamentary committees charged with reviewing the Criminal Code.[9] In 1968 he decided to fight the law. Aside from an implacable commitment to his cause, Morgentaler made another crucial contribution to the nature of abortion politics and policy in Canada. Prevailing abortion methods at the time called for a skilled surgeon and full anesthetic.[10] Morgentaler introduced the much simpler method of vacuum aspiration, first invented in China. The importance of vacuum aspiration cannot be underestimated, and it has changed the politics of abortion in Canada and elsewhere. Section 251 assumed that abortions had to be performed in hospitals; Morgentaler's technique could be safely and efficiently performed in a neighbourhood clinic.

Morgentaler established his first abortion clinic in Montreal in 1969. Quebec police raided the clinic in June the following year and charged him under section 251 of the Criminal Code with conspiracy to commit abortion and procuring abortion. His lawyer managed to postpone proceedings for two years, while Morgentaler was out on bail and continued to attack section 251. After the United States Supreme Court legalized first-trimester abortions in *Roe v. Wade* in 1973, Morgentaler publicly proclaimed that he had personally performed 5000 abortions and allowed a film of himself performing an abortion to be broadcast nationally. Morgentaler went to trial and was acquitted by a jury in November 1973. In 1975 and 1976 Morgentaler went before two more juries on additional charges, and was acquitted both times. In 1976 the newly elected Parti Quebecois government decided that the federal abortion law was unenforceable in Quebec and announced that there would be no further attempts to prosecute doctors performing abortions in the province. Morgentaler had won in Quebec, and roughly one third of Canadian women had relatively free access in clinics to abortions. Morgentaler remained happy with this situation until 1982, when he perceived that pro-life forces had gathered sufficient strength to impede even the limited access to abortion afforded through section 251. Working with pro-choice activists and women's health co-operatives, he established clinics in Winnipeg and Toronto. As in his early days in Quebec, he was immediately arrested and charged. The Toronto case eventually went all the way to the Supreme Court of Canada, but not before Morgentaler had won another jury acquittal at the Supreme Court of Ontario. *R. v. Morgentaler* was heard by the Supreme Court of Canada in October 1986, and a decision was released on 28 January 1988. By a margin of 5-2, the Supreme Court struck down section 251 of the Criminal Code as unconstitutional.

The unconstitutionality of section 251 was a relatively new twist on an old issue. In the 1970s some pro-choice activists had urged that the abortion law violated the Canadian Bill of Rights's equality provisions, but that Bill was merely another piece of legislation, not entrenched in the Constitution, and had been applied by the courts without enthusiasm. When Henry Morgentaler began his court challenges, he relied primarily on something called the "defence of necessity," a common law provision that abortion was permitted in order to save the life of the mother. (That "necessity" had never been proven in any of Morgentaler's trials, and so judges routinely told juries to disregard it, which they did not.) In 1982, on the eve of Morgentaler's Winnipeg and Toronto trials, Canada patriated its constitution with a new Charter of Rights and Freedoms. Section 7 of the Charter states:

> Everyone has the right to life, liberty and security of the person and the right not to be deprived thereof except in accordance with the principles of fundamental justice.

Morgentaler's lawyer appealed to the Supreme Court on 13 separate grounds, but the central argument pertained to the Charter's right to "security of the person."

The five judges who supported the appeal did so for different reasons. Chief Justice Brian Dickson argued, for himself and Justice Lamer, that the courts had a responsibility under the Charter to review the **substance** of legislation in cases where that legislation infringed on the security of the person. Commenting on section 251, he said:

> At the most basic physical and emotional level, every pregnant woman is told by the section that she cannot submit to a generally safe medical procedure that might be of clear benefit to her unless she meets criteria entirely unrelated to her own priorities and aspirations. Not only does the removal of decision-making power threaten women in a physical sense; the indecision of knowing whether an abortion will be granted inflicts emotional stress. Section 251 clearly interferes with a woman's bodily integrity in both a physical and emotional sense. Forcing a woman, by threat of criminal sanction, to carry a foetus to term unless she meets certain criteria unrelated to her own priorities and aspirations, is a profound interference with a woman's body and thus a violation of security of the person.[11]

Section 251 created delays and induced psychological stress and so thus violated section 7 of the Charter; thus its implementation was fundamentally unfair. While he recognized that state protection of fetal interests "may well be deserving of constitutional recognition" under section 1 of the Charter, Dickson concluded that the abortion law did this in an unfair and arbitrary fashion.

Justice Beetz, writing for himself and Justice Estey, also concluded that the abortion law was unconstitutional in terms of section 7 and that its violation of the security of the person was not saved by section 1 of the Charter.[12] He arrived at this conclusion by a different process of reasoning, however. Dickson had reasoned that the abortion law violated "security of the person," and that this violation did not accord with the principles of fundamental justice. Beetz reasoned that section 7 did not create a new right, but a right to "security of the person" in the sense of access to medical services to save one's life, and that the procedures under the abortion law prevented that. The procedural complexity of section 251, by unnecessarily delaying access to medical help, threatened pregnant women's health in arbitrary and unfair ways.

Justice Bertha Wilson, while also striking down the abortion law, reasoned that the law's procedures were irrelevant to the primary question of whether a woman could be forced to carry a fetus against her will. If she could not, even the best procedures in the world could not save the law. Wilson argued that section 7 of the Charter must be read as guaranteeing "life, liberty and security of the person," not just physical and emotional security as Dickson had presumed. Wilson concentrated on the importance of liberty and its connection to personal dignity. The decision to abort, in Wilson's view, was fundamental to personal autonomy, and to the reproductive rights that are a foundation for women's rights in general. The abortion law had clearly violated this right, and so contravened section 7 with respect to liberty. Finally, Wilson argued that section 251 had violated principles of fundamental justice, not in the sense of procedure, but in the sense of personal conscience and religious freedom. Section 1 of the Charter could not save the abortion law, because while the objective of protecting the fetus was valid, the law had taken inappropriate means to do it. Wilson suggested a permissive approach to abortion for the early stages of pregnancy and a restrictive approach in the later stages.

The dissenting opinion, drafted by Justice McIntyre for himself and Justice La Forest, argued that the Court could not invent rights. The Charter did not guarantee any "right to abortion," and to claim that it did required that it be read into section 7. The evidence for the law's procedural unfairness was questionable and sometimes weak, since thousands of abortions were performed each year in Toronto and there was no testimony from any woman who had ever been denied an abortion in Canada.

The Supreme Court's decision in *R v. Morgentaler* had a superficial clarity, and a singular result—the declaration that section 251 of the Criminal Code was unconstitutional. The actual texts of the decision were more complex and ambiguous. Only Justice Wilson had asserted a "right to abortion," though she agreed with the others in the majority that the state's role was to "balance" the rights of the fetus with those of the mother. While there might be a potential for new legislation, it would have somehow to be more "procedurally fair." When Henry Morgentaler started his legal battles in 1982, the Liberal government was in power in Ottawa. His legal victory dumped the entire issue into the lap of the Tory government under Brian Mulroney, a government that was close to the end of its first mandate. While abortion is perennially contentious, it had evolved well beyond the narrow circle of lawyers, doctors, and clerics who had dominated the debate in the 1960s. By 1988 the abortion issue was central to the Canadian women's movement, which by a vast majority favoured the pro-choice side. Morgentaler's sensational court cases in Montreal and then later in Toronto and Winnipeg had stimulated the establishment of various pro-life organizations with links to religious denominations. In Toronto, for example, the hierarchy of the Catholic Church urged Catholics to picket Morgentaler's clinic. Rallies throughout the country over the years had attracted larger and larger pro-choice and pro-life crowds, with thousands of participants. Abortion had turned into "movement" politics, linked with the judicial process through a strategy—on the pro-choice side—of deliberate law-breaking supported by legal arguments of unconstitutionality. If anything, the issue had become more explosive than it had been in the 1960s, when a Liberal government had cleverly slipped abortion amendments into an omnibus bill on the Criminal Code. The January 1988 court decision compelled a federal response.

SEARCHING FOR POLICY
COMPROMISE: BILL C-43

Abortion posed a challenge for the Mulroney Tories because it did not fit comfortably into the policy framework that had driven their agenda during the first mandate. The deficit, expenditure restraint, tax reform, encouragement of competitiveness, and the Free Trade Agreement were the engines that drove Tory policy, supplemented later by an agenda for "national reconciliation" through the Meech Lake Accord. Initiatives on the social policy front were either linked to the economic agenda (e.g. cuts to pension indexing, revisions to unemployment insurance) or criticized as anemic (e.g. equity employment legislation and child care). The most visible Tory initiatives on what might be termed the "moral" front had been in revisions to divorce law (enforcing support payment obligations), pornography (an attempt to restrict it), and more recently, refugee access (more stringent reviews of claims). It might have been expected, then, that the Tories would favour a moderate pro-life position on abortion and try to introduce legislation similar to but slightly stronger than the old section 251.

This was complicated by several factors. First, the Tory party is more heterogeneous on "moral/social policy" matters than it is on economic ones. For example, all Tory female MPs, including those in Cabinet, preferred policy options on the pro-choice end of the spectrum. Second, a substantial base of Tory support at the time was Quebec, a province in which virtually free access to abortion had been available since 1976. National opinion surveys consistently show that Quebeckers are more "liberal" on abortion than other Canadians, and introducing tough legislation threatened to erode Tory support in that province. Third, it was virtually certain that any new abortion law would be almost immediately challenged in the courts by one or conceivably even both sides of the issue. The 1988 decision, however, while it had upheld a role for the federal government, had implied that section 251 was unfair and too restrictive. Irrespective of the nature of an appeal, the Government had to design something that would withstand the court's scrutiny, a scrutiny informed by the 1988 decision. Finally, public discourse on abortion was dominated by the extremes (though neither extreme sees itself as extreme), and positions had hardened over the years to the extent that virtually no compromise could be imagined that would satisfy the majority of pro-choice **and** pro-life advocates. The Government would predictably be pilloried for almost anything it proposed. The Tory problem in the winter of 1988, then, was how to respond to pressures for new legislation without irrevocably antagonizing the courts, activists or citizens. The emerging strategy over that year and into the next with the introduction of Bill C-43 was "compromise." But "compromise," as it turned out, was a code for decentralization and diminution of federal responsibility, tactics that have been echoed in a wide range of Tory policies, from free trade to Meech Lake.

Within days of the Supreme Court decision, the Tories promised to "provide leadership and act quickly" to develop a new abortion policy.[13] The issue split the party caucus so severely, however, that in May the Prime Minister announced that there would be a free vote on abortion in the House. In the face of a divided caucus, the Government spent the spring and summer trying to identify the least controversial policy options. It had to show leadership, but also allow a free vote. Its solution, roundly criticized by opposition parties, was to offer a three-part resolution that set out different general approaches (pro-choice, moderate, pro-life) to new legislation. A free vote on this set of options would effectively have absolved the government itself from deciding on policy, particularly since the government proposed to allow no amendments to the resolution. Had the proposal been accepted, the Cabinet could have claimed that its legislation was not really **Government** policy, but the expressed will of Parliament. After protracted negotiations, the Government withdrew its original motion, submitted a revised version on July 26, 1988, and allowed MPs to make amendments. Rather than three options, the resolution offered a single set of principles for the drafting of future abortion legislation. MPs were to vote in favour of or against the resolution or amendments made to it.

The resolution said that any abortion legislation presented to Parliament should "prohibit the performance of an abortion" except:

> When, during the earlier stages of pregnancy: a qualified medical practitioner is of the opinion that the continuation of the pregnancy of a woman would, or would be likely to, threaten her physical or mental well-being; when the woman in consultation with a qualified medical practitioner decides to terminate

her pregnancy; and when the termination is performed by a qualified medical practitioner; and

When, during the subsequent stages of pregnancy: the
termination of the pregnancy satisfies further conditions, including a condition that after a certain point
in time, the termination would only be permitted
where, in the opinion of two qualified medical prac-
titioners, the continuation of the pregnancy would, or
would be likely to, endanger the woman's life or
seriously endanger her health.

MPs peppered the government with amendments to
restrict or expand these conditions. The core support for restrictions came from the Tory benches, while NDP members
favoured liberalization. The votes began on July 28, 1988, with
the peculiar result that **every** proposal was defeated. The
Government's main resolution was defeated 147 votes to 76. An
amendment which would have left the choice of abortion to the
woman in the early stages and demanded only one doctor's
opinion later was defeated 191 to 29. An amendment which
would have left the decision entirely up to a woman and her
doctor was defeated 198 to 20. An amendment which would
have restricted abortions to the first 12 weeks of pregnancy was
defeated 202 to 17. The most successful amendment—in that it
was defeated by the narrowest margin—would have prohibited
abortions except on the evidence of two doctors that the continuation of the pregnancy would endanger the woman's life.
None of the 29 female MPs supported this proposal.

The Government's resolution was demolished, and its
search for "guidance" had proved only how divided the legislature was on the issue. In September, the Government announced that it would not introduce new abortion legislation
until after the national election, widely expected to be held in
the fall. While Ottawa may have been trying to disengage itself
from abortion, the issue was actually developing greater
salience across the country. It surfaced, for example, in the
federal election campaign. At least 74 anti-abortion rights candidates were elected on November 21, 1988. Several nomina-
tion races were contested by pro-choice and pro-life candidates,
and pro-life activists targeted 30 ridings in which to mount
direct mail campaigns.[14]

Abortion gained more prominence as an issue in part because of the legal vacuum created by the Supreme Court's decision. Pro-choice advocates initially rejoiced at the 1988 decision, but the federal legislative void was rapidly filled by provincial regulations. Section 251 had been part of the Criminal Code, but abortion could also be regulated by provincial powers over health. One technique was withholding public payment for the procedure under provincial medicare schemes. Another was regulating where abortions could be performed (i.e. in accredited hospitals rather than clinics) and under what administrative conditions (e.g. committees of approval similar to TACs). The first to try to restrict access in this way was British Columbia. Within two days of the Supreme Court decision, the provincial government announced that it would pay only for abortions performed in accredited hospitals, approved by a TAC, and in cases where the life of the mother was threatened by the pregnancy. The British Columbia Civil Liberties Association then took the Government before the BC Supreme Court, which struck down the Government's action on technical grounds and strongly implied that other means to achieve the same ends would be impermissible. New Brunswick passed similar regulations, permitting only medically necessary abortions in accredited hospitals.

Within a year of Morgentaler, the combination of federal inaction and provincial initiative had resulted in less uniformity of access to abortion across the country. PEI performed no abortions at all, for example, and out-of-province abortions would only be reimbursed with the approval of a committee of five doctors. Ontario paid for the full cost of abortions performed in hospitals and clinics, while Manitoba paid for hospital but not clinic abortions. Saskatchewan, on the other hand, permitted abortions only in cases of "medical necessity."

Most of these provincial attempts to restrict access were successfully fought in the courts. But by this point the issue was once more on the streets, as pro-life activists began to use more militant tactics pioneered in the United States by such groups as Operation Rescue. For example, on January 21, 1989 about 150 protesters blockaded and shut down the Everywoman's Health Clinic in East Vancouver. Despite court injunctions against them, protesters continued the blockade, leading eventually to the arrest of 13 people (10 men and three women). They were all given short jail terms, joining almost 50 others who had refused to agree to stay away from the clinic. Eventually, a group of 104 protesters was found guilty of criminal offences for deliberately ignoring the injunction and obstructing access to the clinic. They were all given suspended sentences.

The federal government remained virtually silent throughout these events. Then came the "abortion summer" of 1989. It began with a decision by the United States Supreme Court in July upholding the constitutionality of some aspects of the state of Missouri's controversial abortion law, which banned public hospitals and public employees from performing abortions. The decision did not completely reverse the 1973 *Roe v. Wade* judgment, but it did open the way for more conservative states to restrict the right to abortion. Canadian pro-choice advocates were predictably shocked, but argued that despite provincial attempts to do much the same thing as Missouri had, Canadian women were better off than their American sisters because section 251—the federal law that had **controlled** access to abortion—was now null and void. The flaw in this argument was that it identified the "law" almost exclusively with the now moribund section 251. As provincial attempts to restrict abortion through health regulation had shown, there is potentially a broad range of legal constraints on abortion. This soon became clear in the Barbara Dodd and Chantal Daigle cases in July and August 1989. Both women had become pregnant in relationships that had subsequently soured, and both had decided to have abortions. Their former boyfriends very nearly succeeded in stopping them through court injunctions, something that while always possible had rarely been used in Canada.[16]

Gregory Murphy won his injunction against Barbara Dodd on July 4, 1989 from the Supreme Court of Ontario. Dodd was prohibited from aborting her 15-week-old fetus anywhere in Ontario. Murphy argued that the fetus's right to equality and life, liberty and security as guaranteed under the Charter would be violated if it were aborted.[17] He also claimed that Dodd, who was hearing impaired, had been pressured into the abortion by her parents. He promised to care for the fetus if it were born. Several days later, a Manitoba court facing the same arguments from a Winnipeg man who wanted to stop his former girlfriend's abortion decided that the woman had absolute control over her body.[18] The Dodd-Murphy case made instant headlines, and soon drew into its vortex a range of groups and actors. Women's and disabled persons' organizations complained that Dodd's rights had been flagrantly abused since the injunction had been granted in her absence and she had had difficulty finding a lawyer. It appeared that Dodd had been having sexual relations with another man as well as Murphy, and she did not know which was the father. Lurid details of Dodd's life with Murphy were revealed daily in the press: for example, that he had bullied her into working as an exotic dancer and demanded that she support him while he stayed home. These, along with other allegations, were argued before the Supreme Court of Ontario, which on July 11 set aside the injunction. Pro-choice advocates were obviously pleased, but even anti-abortion groups were encouraged by what they saw as a potential new legal technique to restrict access (the Court's denial of the injunction was on technical, procedural grounds, and so left open the possibility that injunctions might work if properly framed). Dodd immediately went to Henry Morgentaler's Toronto clinic and had her abortion. Astonishingly, within a few days Dodd (with Greg Murphy at her side) held a press conference and announced that she had been wrong to get an abortion, and that she had felt abandoned and manipulated by pro-choice groups. She later appeared at the Toronto headquarters of Campaign Life sporting a "Slavery Abortion" T-shirt.

While the Dodd-Murphy case was in its last stages, another attempt to accomplish the same thing was being undertaken by Jean-Guy Tremblay of Pointe-aux-Trembles, Quebec. Encouraged by Murphy's early success, on July 7 he filed for an injunction against Chantal Daigle, his former girlfriend. The two had lived together for almost a year, and after Daigle got pregnant, had planned to marry. The relationship collapsed in early July, and Daigle decided to abort her 20-week-old fetus. Tremblay's injunction was granted, with a hearing scheduled for July 17. Mr. Justice Jacques Viens of the Quebec Superior Court heard the opposing arguments. After the negative decision of the Ontario Supreme Court, almost everyone expected him to deny the injunction. In a surprise ruling, he upheld it, but not because of the Canadian Charter of Rights and Freedoms. Arguing that the Canadian Charter did not in fact give the fetus the right to life, Justice Viens instead cited the province's own Charter of Rights and Freedoms and some sections of its Civil Code. Articles 1 and 2 of the Quebec Charter refer to *être humain* (human being) while the remainder refers to *personne* (person), and Viens concluded from this that the fetus as a human being was guaranteed the right to life as well as the right to assistance. In English translation, the relevant sections were:

Article 1. Every human being has a right to life, and to personal security, inviolability and freedom.

Article 2. Every human being whose life is in peril has a right to assistance.[19]

Significantly, Viens acknowledged that Daigle too had certain rights, but in his opinion these were outweighed by those of the fetus. From the pro-life side, however, perhaps the most important aspect of the Viens decision was that the injunction was upheld not because it came from the father, but because it defended the fetus. Theoretically, since the injunction was contingent on the status of the fetus and not the parental status of the person seeking it, anyone might succeed with an attempt to stop any woman from attempting an abortion.

Chantal Daigle appealed the decision to the Quebec Court of Appeal, which delayed its ruling to consider the issues, but thereby made it impossible for her to get an abortion in Quebec, where they are not performed on women more than 20 weeks pregnant. If she were to get one at that point, it would have to be in the United States, where some clinics perform them as late as 26 weeks. The situation stimulated outraged commentary across the country, and particularly in Quebec. It was now clear that the absence of federal legislation was not an answer to the abortion question, and finally on July 20 the Prime Minister announced that an abortion bill would come before Parliament in the fall. A week later, the Quebec Court of Appeal in a 3-2 decision upheld the injunction. Even the majority on the Court, narrow as it was, was severely split in its reasoning. Two of them, for example, explicitly rejected Viens's reasoning, finding other grounds for the existence of fetal rights.[20]

Daigle then appealed to the Supreme Court, which granted her a hearing for August 8. but her advanced stage of pregnancy made every moment count. On August 1 a panel of five Supreme Court judges took 15 minutes to grant Daigle leave to appeal and state her arguments one week later. In a sense this was *Morgentaler* all over again, and the stakes were very high. The Supreme Court's composition had changed in the two years since its last major decision on abortion, and it was conceivable that the Quebec court's decision might be upheld. Several interest groups sought and received intervener status to make their own arguments in connection with the case: the Canadian Abortion Rights Action League, the Women's Legal Education

Action Fund, the Canadian Civil Liberties Association, the Campaign Life Coalition, Canadian Physicians for Life, *L'association des medicins du Québec pour le respect de la vie,* and REAL (Real, Equal, and Active for Life) Women of Canada. Along with the Attorney General of Quebec, the Attorney General of Canada sought to intervene on behalf of the federal government. Despite having virtually abdicated responsibility over abortion for the last year, Ottawa's interest was to ensure that abortion did not become a provincial jurisdiction.[21] Chantal Daigle finally lost patience with the judicial process. In the midst of hearing her appeal on August 8, the Supreme Court was suddenly informed that she had already had her abortion in Boston. The justices were momentarily confused, but then proceeded to render a unanimous decision quashing the injunction. The Court issued its reasons for decision later in November, and refuted each and every one of Tremblay's claims: the fetus had no status as a "legal person" that could be found in either the Canadian or Quebec Charters, or in common law. It also rejected "father's rights" to veto an abortion.[22] Despite its firmness, it is clear that the decision was primarily intended to forestall future injunctions of the type launched by Murphy and Tremblay; it did not say anything about the "right to life" or about section 7 of the Charter.

It was against this backdrop that the Tories finally introduced their new abortion legislation in fall 1989. After the legislative disaster of 1988, they were considerably more cautious. A caucus committee was established to review alternatives, and the Government's final legislative proposals were thoroughly vetted in the party. A free vote would be allowed, as in 1988, but this time the Cabinet (40 members) would support the Government's bill. With 295 seats in the House of Commons, the Bill needed 148 votes to pass. With some absences, Bill C-43 (Appendix 9.2) passed third reading in the Commons by only nine votes, 140 to 131.

It is important to understand what this legislation meant. Like section 251, Bill C-43 placed abortion once again in the Criminal Code. Unless performed under specific conditions, abortion was a crime. Bill C-43 proposed conditions that were similar to, but less stringent than, the old section 251. Abortions would be legal if done by or under the direction of a physician who believed that the pregnancy threatened the health or life of the mother. TACs were now no longer necessary under federal criminal law. In theory this did not amount to abortion on demand, since a woman who sought an abortion would still require medical approval, and the procedure would in principle have to be undertaken for medical reasons. The explanatory notes that accompanied the Bill, however, said that while eugenics, rape, incest, or socio-economic welfare were not specifically mentioned in the Bill, "these factors could be included in the determination of health if their effect was to threaten a woman's health."[23] In an important sense, then, the legislation was ambiguous on the central point that had bedeviled abortion policy since 1969: if criteria were to be used at all to justify abortion, precisely what were they? The provisions of Bill C-43 could in principle be interpreted quite broadly or quite narrowly. That is precisely what happened in Parliament and throughout the country.

Introduced to the House of Commons by Doug Lewis, Minister of Justice and Attorney General of Canada, on November 3, 1989, the Bill went to second reading on November 7, 1989. The Minister's second reading speech, while containing the usual self-congratulations that accompany a government's defence of its own legislation, was also careful to outline the rationale for several of the more contentious of the Bill's provisions. One such provision was the use of the criminal law to control abortion. Lewis argued that this was the only instrument available to the federal government to deal with abortion, since Ottawa has no jurisdiction over civil injunctions or health.[24] Denying that the Bill provided abortion on demand, Lewis admitted that "health" was defined broadly in the legislation to include "mental, physical and psychological health." It would be up to the medical practitioner to determine, in accordance with "generally accepted standards of the medical profession, whether there are health reasons to justify an abortion."[25]

> I would also say that doctors who, in the exercise of their medical judgment according to the standards of their profession, determine that a woman's health or life is threatened by a pregnancy, have no reason to fear potential criminal consequences of the legislation. We believe that this law is a reasonable solution which is sensitive to the differences of opinions among Canadians.[26]

As it turned out over the next year, this did indeed become one of the key worries of physicians across Canada, and many of them by late 1990 were openly stating that they would not perform abortions under the new legislation for fear of being prosecuted. In defending the Bill, the Minister argued that while it was not possible for the federal government to stay civil injunctions, the provincial attorneys-general could do so in the public interest. In any case, the Government's view was that such citizen-initiated prosecutions would be rare.

One of the most important considerations in the drafting of the Bill was whether it could meet the standards implied in the Supreme Court's decision in *Morgentaler*. That decision had struck down section 251 of the Criminal Code because it had unduly impeded women's access to abortion. In the Government's view, because Bill C-43 did not demand a TAC or an accredited hospital, it imposed only minimum requirements for abortion. The definition of "health" was broader, and so was also in the spirit of the Court's decision. Because the Bill did, however, stipulate some conditions (medical approval), it also protected the interests of the fetus, another concern voiced by the Supreme Court in *Morgentaler*. Later, before Committee, Lewis reiterated these points in a summary of how Bill C-43 differed from the old section 251.

> Under the old law there was a requirement for a therapeutic abortion committee; under the new bill it is one qualified medical practitioner. Under the old law there was no definition of "health;" under the new one we have defined "health." Under the old section 251 it required an accredited or approved hospital; under the new law there is no hospital requirement. That is left to the provinces to regulate. Under the old law the doctor who performed an abortion could not be on the abortion committee; under the new law the doctor who gives the opinion can be the same doctor who performs the abortion. Under the old law it was an expressed liability for women who intentionally seek an abortion; under the new law it is a liability for a woman only if she knowingly and intentionally seeks or has an abortion outside the exemption. Under the old law there was a requirement for a certificate from the doctor; under the new law there is no certificate.[27]

Ninety-seven MPs spoke during the second reading debate, elaborating the full range of pro-choice and pro-life positions, as well as more narrowly legalistic and political issues. Many of the latter were articulated at the outset of the debate by Robert Kaplan, the spokesperson for the Liberal Opposition. Kaplan argued that the Bill was not, as Lewis had claimed, a good balance between the rights of women and the fetus. On the first, the requirement of a medical determination of threat to health might pose an insurmountable impediment to some women in parts of the country because they might not be able to find physicians willing to provide that determination. Moreover, even if they found a physician willing to say that the pregnancy posed a threat to health, they might not be able to find a physician willing to do the abortion. On the second point, protection of the rights of the fetus, Kaplan noted that theoretically the legislation did not distinguish between early or late pregnancy. In terms of the legislation itself, abortions in Canada could legally be conducted well into the third trimester. The Bill's vague wording led Kaplan to conclude that it was an exercise in fraud. While having the veneer of restrictive legislation, it in fact invited Canadian women to "find the right doctor" who would then justify the procedure and perform it. On these grounds, Kaplan preferred, as did some other speakers, that the Government immediately refer the legislation to the Supreme Court for a ruling.[28] Finally, in a criticism that was to be echoed by both sides of the issue, Kaplan complained that the Bill in fact provided very little national leadership and virtually no national policy framework. All the important decisions related to accessibility—regulation of physicians, permission to perform abortions in clinics, the availability of medical services in remote areas—were under provincial control by virtue of their jurisdiction over health.

While Liberal MPs could vote according to conscience, and were therefore divided in support and criticism of the Bill, the NDP took a pro-choice position as a party. From this perspective, the Bill was fundamentally flawed for some of the reasons mentioned by Kaplan, but for others as well. The NDP found the criminalization of a decision as intensely personal as abortion to be particularly objectionable. The Government's unwillingness to use the Canada Health Act—passed to permit withdrawal of federal funds in cases of extra-billing and reductions in health care accessibility—to enforce accessibility was also criticized. Perhaps more fundamentally, the pro-choice position was that abortion was a right, and so the entire idea of regulating was objectionable. As Mary Clancy (Liberal) put it, "Women do not want their rights surreptitiously through the back door."[29] For pro-choicers, the Bill had a strong potential to actually reduce access: doctors fearing third party prosecutions would restrict abortion to narrow grounds, and moreover might even refuse, for personal reasons, to support a women's decision to abort. Dawn Black (NDP) attacked Lewis on this score:

> The Minister of Justice has been using the language of choice when discussing this bill. There is no choice for women involved in this bill. The minister is being hypocritical when he uses the language of choice in relation to this bill which makes abortion the doctor's decision based on health criteria, not the woman's choice based on her own personal criteria.[30]

These criticisms were echoed before the Legislative Committee on Bill C-43.[31]

A pro-choice position did not always lead to rejection of the Bill, however. This was particularly clear for Tory female Cabinet ministers, who as members of Cabinet were bound to support the Bill. Barbara McDougall, Kim Campbell (later to become Minister of Justice and responsible for the Bill), Mary Collins, Monique Landry, and Shirley Martin all indicated their pro-choice position, but argued that the Bill, with all its flaws, was better than no Bill at all. Interestingly, the only female MP to unambiguously take a pro-life position was Ethel Blondin (Liberal - Western Arctic), who based her position on her Dene culture: "I belong to a people who believe that life is sacred and always have under the harshest of circumstances."[32] Some of those on the pro-life side could also swallow their disagreement with the Bill on the grounds that it was the best that could be achieved. John Turner, leader of the Official Opposition, suggested this in his comments, as did the Prime Minister in the closing hours of the debate. Mulroney also reiterated a point that the government had emphasized when announcing the Bill: it would be this Bill or nothing. The Tories were not about to try again if Bill C-43 failed.

The pro-life reaction in the House and throughout the country focussed on the Bill's liberalizing aspects. Gone were TACs, and the legislation specifically exempted the use of "morning after" drugs like RU-486, currently used under strict control in France. From the pro-life perspective, the broader definition of health in the bill essentially meant abortion on demand. What was decried as undignified fraud by pro-choicers was seen as an enormous loophole that would allow any woman and her doctor to defend abortion at any time for virtually any reason. Moreover, since the legislation used the phrase "by or under the direction of a medical practitioner" it would allow non-physicians who qualify under medical standards legislation (e.g. nurses) to perform abortions under a physician's direction. Large scale, clinic-based abortion facilities would therefore be possible, run by only one doctor.

The government's threat that it was Bill C-43 or nothing, along with painful Tory memories of how badly its last legislative adventure on abortion had turned out, gave the party the incentive it needed to resist any amendments or changes in the Bill. The Legislative Committee on Bill C-43 took months to hear witnesses and study submissions, but then reported the Bill out without amendments. It came before the House for third reading on May 22, 1990, by which time Kim Campbell had assumed responsibility for it as Canada's first female Minister of Justice. Her defence of the legislation was the same as Lewis's, though as a committed pro-choice advocate, she insisted more strongly than he had that the Bill would not restrict access to abortion. Bill C-43 passed third reading by nine votes on May 29, 1990. From there it went to the Senate, which deferred consideration of the Bill as it struggled with the GST through the fall of 1990.

The GST dominated the Senate's time through December, and it only turned its attention to Bill C-43 in January. Like the Commons, the Senate was to have a free vote on the Bill, though the Government put pressure on its members to support the legislation. The arguments in debate and before the Senate Committee reviewing the Bill were precisely the same as those in the Commons six months earlier, and given the narrow passage in the lower chamber, the outcome was far from clear. In hindsight, three factors doomed Bill C-43 in the Senate. First, in the Commons, the Government had been able to count on at least 40 votes from the Cabinet (28 per cent of the total), but in the Senate it had no similar core. Second, the recent GST Senate debate had encouraged more legislative independence among Senators, and in any case, Bill C-43 was not central to the Government's mandate. Finally, opposition to the Bill among Canadian physicians had mounted dramatically over the fall, and moderately pro-choice Senators who might otherwise have been prepared to live with the legislation became worried about the "chill factor." Third reading was held on January 31, 1991, and the vote split evenly 43-43. Under Senate rules, a tie is considered a defeat, and Bill C-43 was dead. The Prime Minister and the Minister of Justice immediately announced there would be no attempt at new federal legislation on abortion.

Only 86 senators were present for the vote, and from the results it was clear that the Bill had been defeated by a curious alliance of pro- and anti-abortion forces. This had happened before in the Commons in 1988, as pro-lifers rejected legislation for being too permissive and pro-choicers rejected the same legislation for being too restrictive. On balance, pro-choice advocates were better served by Bill C-43's demise since federal legislation is not likely for several years, perhaps another decade. This shifts the battle to the provincial and local scene, where pressure will be applied to improve levels of funding and the numbers of clinics. Pro-life forces have a comparatively strong organizational presence at this level, but recent court cases on the use of injunctions and provincial attempts to restrict access through health legislation have constrained the available range of tactics.

Ironically, the effects of Bill C-43, had it passed, would not have been very different. Its use of the criminal law was deliberately feeble (though ultimately feared by some physicians), and left most of the important abortion issues up to the provinces. It is likely that had Bill C-43 become law, abortion regimes would still have varied across the provinces. They are certain to do so now.

CONCLUSION

In terms of what this chapter called the "post-Meech syndrome," the legislative agony over Bill C-43 was largely wasted. Even as parliamentarians sagely debated the issues, abortion refused to be bridled to the Tory agenda. For example, Henry Morgentaler, by opening clinics in Halifax, decided to challenge Nova Scotia legislation forbidding abortions in clinics. Later, he also opened clinics in St. John's and Edmonton. As a result of intense local opposition and subsequent trials, Morgentaler had ample opportunity to rehearse manoeuvres that he had perfected long ago in his Winnipeg and Toronto trials. The clinic in Edmonton was opened in part as a response to provincial physicians who declared that they would stop performing abortions once Bill

C-43 was passed. His activities underscored how **both** the pro-life and pro-choice sides had been wrong about the Bill. The early pro-choice criticism had been that the definition of health was so broad that virtually all abortions would be legal. They did not take account of the fear that most physicians had of being dragged into court by third parties for performing abortions. These fears were well-founded, since in medical terms there are few physcial risks to the mother's health associated with modern pregnancy. Doctors would thus likely have to justify abortions on psychological grounds, ones that they were not particularly competent to judge. The pro-choice side, on the other hand, had anticipated this but had not accounted for the possibilities that the legislation might open up for physicians like Morgentaler who were willing to operate clinics. A determined physician, prepared as Morgentaler was to apply a broad definition of health, could perform abortions with relatively few encumbrances. If taken to court, the physician would simply have to testify as to his belief or opinion that the pregnancy threatened health.

In one sense, then, Bill C-43 may be read as a brilliant tactical manoeuvre. It responded to the widespread demand after the Dodd and Daigle cases that Ottawa do something, by presenting legislation that seemed similar in form if not substance to the old section 251. It simultaneously re-criminalized abortion while making access to the procedure (in principle, at least) more liberal. It created a "national framework" without much substance: all the key issues would have to be resolved through provincial decisions on health care provision and access. To be fair, this had always been the case even under the previous legal regime, and was an artifact of provincial jurisdiction over health. Given the assumption that abortion should be controlled in some way, and that this control should apply uniformly across the country, only the federal government could legislate on abortion. But federal legislation would of necessity have to be something other than health regulation, which is provincial. The calls for federal use of the Canada Health Act to punish provinces that do not ensure full accessibility to abortion were plausible, but ran up against several objections. First, no province has forbidden abortions and so federal legislative measures to ensure "access" would have had to develop some measure of acceptable minimums in access. Second, by using the Canada Health Act in this way, the federal government would have linked its fiscal sanctions to a specific medical procedure, something that it does not do now. This might be seen as an encroachment on provincial jurisdiction, since if accepted there would be no limit on the specific things Ottawa could demand in provincial health administration. The third reason is perhaps the most important, and while it was never articulated, clearly was in the minds of ministers: by **stipulating** access to abortion through the Canada Health Act, the federal government would have appeared to be championing abortion. Much better to put the ball in the provincial court.

The Tory record on abortion should not be understood entirely as a matter of tactics, however. It echoes deeper chords in the contemporary Canadian polity, ones which have perhaps become dominant since the collapse of Meech. Ten years ago the ferocious dynamic of abortion was clearly unique in Canadian public policy. Other issues had their share of vitriol, of course, but abortion seemed to go well beyond them in terms of difficulty of compromise and entrenchment of position. Today, after the Mohawk confrontations at Kanesatake and Oka, and Kahnawake and Chateauguay, the fight over the GST, the painful debate over the Meech Lake Accord, and the demands from Quebec for political autonomy, the politics of abortion seem less strange—almost familiar.

Did the federal government have to take such an anemic leadership role on the issue? It might, for example, have coupled Bill C-43 to a broad and vigorous initiative to tackle some of the underlying social causes of abortion.[33] Germaine Greer, a prominent proponent of choice, once remarked that being **for** abortion was like being **for** amputation. No one defends abortion for its own sake, and the pro-choice side has never suggested that abortion should be or is taken lightly by women. Using its spending powers, Ottawa might have undertaken initiatives to encourage the provinces to fight poverty among women and help single mothers cope with pregnancy. The absence of such an initiative reflects less on the government's fiscal prudence than it does the troubled ambiguity that surrounds the role of the national government in Canada. The Tories began their mandates with a desire for national reconciliation, and so were prepared from the beginning to give provinces a greater role. The ultimate logic of this position resulted in the Meech Lake Accord, but was reflected in Bill C-43 as well.

Ironically, the same hubris affected Bill C-43 and the Meech process. Governments initially thought that they could control the issues themselves, both policy processes were tenaciously colonized by citizens' organizations and interest groups. On abortion, the federal government imagined that it was actually respecting provincial jurisdiction over health. In reality, all through the debate on Bill C-43 and after, the abortion issue has been on the streets and in the courts, pushed by partisans on both sides. They, like the groups that fought Meech Lake, see themselves as custodians of public will. In the wake of Bill C-43's defeat, pro-choice, feminist and women's health groups will fight a war of position, province by province, clinic by clinic. Recent legal opinions have tended to support their side (for example, by striking down provincial attempts to restrict access). The NDP government in Ontario is receptive to improved access and funding, and may thereby set a national example. Pro-life groups should not be discounted, however. While the Supreme Court appears to have definitively constrained the injunction weapon, there are other ways to legally harrass abortion clinics and physicians. Several legal questions—such as the status of the fetus in the later stages of pregnancy—arguably have not been resolved by the courts, and might provide openings for litigation. The absence of federal legislation may actually help the movement by encouraging a sense of crisis among opponents of abortion. Abortion politics, therefore, will continue to be fought in the streets and in the courts, showing that citizens simply refuse to accept the "final outcomes" of the legislative process.

The most important reason why groups and citizens no longer easily accept government control over the policy process is that they increasingly articulate their political demands in terms of rights. In this, abortion is an exemplar, albeit extreme, of the new age of Canadian politics. When a polity organizes a substantial part of its public policy debates in terms of rights, there are at least two consequences that tend to propel the process towards fragmentation. The first is that rights are not easily compromised. Rights are trumps over other claims, and almost by definition should not be sacrificed to expediency. In claiming women's right to abortion, for example, pro-choicers have quite logically demanded that abortion be publicly funded and widely available. Pro-life proponents, on the other hand, have posited a right to life that is equally absolute. One need support neither side to recognize that when claims are framed in this way, they are difficult to reconcile. It is precisely this type of political language that has increasingly structured

Canadian policy debates, from Meech to aboriginal claims to Quebec sovereignty.

The second consequence of a discourse dominated by rights claims is the difficulty of accepting hierarchies of rights. Rights should be equal, and demand equal respect and recognition. The abortion issue of course puts this conundrum pointedly, since the full recognition of either party—mother or fetus—will necessarily compromise the rights of the other. But the problem of balancing rights was clearly evident in the Meech Lake Accord, where key groups worried that the concession of a "distinct society" to Quebec would undermine their rights and status under the Charter.

The Tories are not, of course, responsible for these deeper undercurrents in either abortion politics or other areas. Nonetheless, the "post-Meech syndrome" is in part a Tory creation, and continued failures to deal with it will only encourage its corrosive effect on contemporary politics. The Bill C-43 experience casts doubt on Ottawa's capacity to deal with a policy agenda that threatens to be almost as divisive as abortion. In a pedestrian sense, Bill C-43 failed because the Tories bungled the legislative process. In a larger sense, Bill C-43 failed because it was designed merely to reflect the stalemates, ambiguities and tensions in the policy field. This was a strategy of compromise, but the issue demanded more than an enfeebled equilibrium of passionately opposed views. It demanded statesmanship. Tory fortunes and the country's future, in the face of a potentially explosive political agenda, demand it as well.

Appendix 9.1
Chapter C-34, Sect. 251

251.

(1) Everyone who, with intent to procure the miscarriage of a female person, whether or not she is pregnant, uses any means for the purpose of carrying out his intention is guilty of an indictable offence and is liable to imprisonment for life.

(2) Every female person who, being pregnant, with intent to procure her own miscarriage, uses any means for the purpose of carrying out her intention is guilty of an indictable offence and is liable to imprisonment for two years.

(3) In this section "means" includes

(a) the administration of a drug or other noxious thing;

(b) the use of an instrument; and

(c) manipulation of any kind.

(4) Subsections (1) and (2) do not apply to

(a) a qualified medical practitioner, other than a member of a therapeutic abortion committee for any hospital, who in good faith uses in an accredited or approved hospital any means for the purpose of carrying out his intention to procure the miscarriage of a female person, or

(b) a female person who, being pregnant, permits a qualified medical practitioner to use in an accredited or approved hospital any means for the purpose of carrying out her intention to procure her own miscarriage,

if, before the use of those means, the therapeutic abortion committee for that accredited or approved hospital, by a majority of the members of the committee and at a meeting of the committee at which the case of the female person has been reviewed,

(c) has by certificate in writing stated that in its opinion the continuation of the pregnancy of the female person would or would be likely to endanger her life or health, and

(d) has caused a copy of such certificate to be given to the qualified medical practitioner.

NOTE: Section 251 contained three other subsections not reproduced here. Subsection 5 gave the provincial Ministers of Health the power to demand copies of abortion certificates, while subsections 6 and 7 defined the terms in the other sections.

Appendix 9.2
Bill C-43
An Act Respecting Abortion

Her Majesty, by and with the advice and consent of the Senate and House of Commons of Canada, enacts as follows:

1.   Sections 287 and 288 of the *Criminal Code* are repealed and the following substituted therefor:

"287.   (1) Every person who induces an abortion on a female person is guilty of an indictable offence and liable to imprisonment for a term not exceeding two years, unless the abortion is induced by or under the direction of a medical practitioner who is of the opinion that, if the abortion were not induced, the health or life of the female person would be likely to be threatened.

(2) For the purposes of this section,

"health" includes, for greater certainty, physical, mental and psychological health;

"medical practitioner," in respect of an abortion induced in a province, means a person who is entitled to practise medicine under the laws of that province;

"opinion" means an opinion formed using generally accepted standards of the medical profession.

(3) For the purposes of this section and section 288, inducing an abortion does not include using a drug, device or other means on a female person that is likely to prevent implantation of a fertilized ovum.

288.   Every one who unlawfully supplies or procures a drug or other noxious thing or an instrument or thing, knowing that it is intended to be used or employed to induce an abortion on a female person, is guilty of an indictable offence and liable to imprisonment for a term not exceeding two years."

2.   This Act shall come into force on a day to be fixed by order of the Governor in Council.

Notes

1   On the Meech Lake Accord, see Michael D. Behiels (ed.), *The Meech Lake Primer: Conflicting Views of the 1987 Constitutional Accord* (Ottawa: University of Ottawa Press, 1989), and Roger Gibbins et al. (eds.), *Meech Lake and Canada: Perspectives from the West* (Edmonton: Academic Printing and Publishing, 1988.)

2   Under the Revised Statutes 1985 this section was renumbered as section 287, but for ease of reference this chapter will continue to refer to it as section 251.

3   The British statute was the Offences Against the Person Act, 1861. The relevant Canadian Criminal Code (1892) provisions were sections 271-74. The Canadian legislation was slightly different from the British in that it reduced the penalty for self-induced abortions and provided an explicit saving clause for anyone who was responsible for the death of a fetus in the course of trying to save a pregnant woman's life.

4   Daniel Callahan, *Abortion: Law, Choice and Morality* (London: Macmillan, 1970).

5   Mary Ann Glendon, *Abortion and Divorce in Western Law* (Cambridge, Mass.: Harvard University Press, 1987), and Canada, Law Reform Commission, *Crimes Against the Foetus*, Working Paper 58 (Ottawa: Law Reform Commission, 1988).

6   Committee on the Operation of the Abortion Law, *Report* (Ottawa: Minister of Supply and Services, 1977), pp. 30-31.

7   Ibid., pp. 27-28.

8   For details, see Eleanor Wright Pelrine, *Morgentaler: The Doctor Who Couldn't Turn Away* (Toronto: James Lorimer, 1983), and Anne Collins, *The Big Evasion: Abortion, The Issue That Won't Go Away* (Toronto: Lester and Orpen Dennys, 1985).

9   Canada, Parliament, House of Commons, Standing Committee on Health and Welfare, *Minutes of Proceedings and Evidence*, No. 3, October 19, 1967, p. 66.

10 Henry Morgentaler, *Abortion and Contraception* (Don Mills: General Publishing Co., 1982), chapter 4.

11 *R. v. Morgentaler* [1988] 1 S.C.R. 30.

12 Section 1 reads: "The Canadian Charter of Rights and Freedoms guarantees the rights and freedoms set out in it subject only to such reasonable limits prescribed by law as can be demonstrably justified in a free and democratic society."

13 *Globe and Mail* [Toronto], January 30, 1988, p. A1.

14 *Globe and Mail* [Toronto], November 23, 1988, p. A9.

15 For a discussion of attempts to regulate abortion through health legislation, see Sheilah L. Martin, *Women's Reproductive Health, the Charter of Rights and Freedoms, and the Canada Health Act* (Ottawa: Canadian Advisory Council on the Status of Women, 1989).

16 This tactic had been tried before without success as far back as 1984. The father got an initial injunction which was then overturned by the Ontario Supreme Court. It also failed in 1988 in Alberta. Private prosecutions had always been possible under Section 251.

17 The Supreme Court of Canada ruled on March 10, 1989 that the issues raised in Joe Borowski's challenge to Canada's abortion law—section 251—were moot since that section had been struck down in 1988. Borowski's challenge was based, as Henry Morgentaler's had been, on Section 7 of the Charter. Murphy's injunction in effect repeated Borowski's argument.

18 *Diamond v. Hirsch*, Man. Q. B., July 6, 1989.

19 *Daigle v. Tremblay*, (1989) S.C.R.

20 *Tremblay v. Daigle*, (1989) R.J.Q. 1735, 59 D.L.R. (4th), 609-642. The main dissent was written by the only woman on the Court, Justice Tourigny.

21 Doug Lewis, Minister of Justice, was quoted as saying that Ottawa was intervening only "to defend our right to legislate at the federal level." *Globe and Mail* [Toronto], August 6, 1989, pp. A1-A2.

22 *Tremblay v. Daigle*, (1989) S.C.R.

23 Canada, Minister of Justice and Attorney General of Canada, "New Abortion Legislation: Background Information," November 3, 1989, p. 6.

24 Canada, Parliament, House of Commons, *Debates,* November 7, 1989, p. 5640.

25 Ibid., p. 5641.

26 Ibid.

27 Canada, Parliament, House of Commons, Legislative Committee on Bill C-43, *Minutes and Proceedings of Evidence*, no. 1, December 5, 1989, p. 40.

28 Under the Supreme Court of Canada Act, the federal government has the power to refer a matter to the Court for a determination as to its constitutional validity.

29 Canada, Parliament, House of Commons, *Debates*, November 7, 1989, p. 5680.

30 Canada, Parliament, House of Commons, *Debates*, November 7, 1989, p. 5668.

31 See particularly the Brief by Canadian Abortion Rights Action League, Canada, Parliament, House of Commons, Legislative Committee on Bill C-43, *Minutes and Proceedings of Evidence*, Appendix C-43/3.

32 Canada, Parliament, House of Commons, *Debates*, November 7, 1989, p. 6160.

306 / How Ottawa Spends

33   Perrin Beatty, the federal Minister of National Health and Welfare, did promise several hundred thousand dollars for family planning and post-partum support programs, but these were clearly cosmetic.

CHAPTER 10

FROM MEECH LAKE TO GOLDEN POND: THE ELDERLY, PENSION REFORM AND FEDERALISM IN THE 1990s

Michael J. Prince

Résumé: Les conservateurs ont introduit plusieurs changements àla politique sur les prestations aux retraités depuis 1984, mais un certain nombre de questions restent non résolues. Malgré leur victoire sur la question de la déindexation de la pension de sécurité de la vieillesse, les groupes de l'âge d'or ont eu en général relativement peu d'influence sur le programme de réforme en matière de prestations et de politique sociale. Le "coup de griffe" met fin à l'universalité effective des prestations de la pension de sécurité de la vieillesse. On peut postuler trois scénarios concernant les relations fédérales-provinciales, et les relations Ottawa-Québec en particulier. Selon le scénario de la détente, les tensions intergouvernementales baissent, et Québec et d'autres gouvernements provinciaux évitent des changements majeurs à la politique des pensions avec la possibilité d'augmentations par l'un ou l'autre palier. Selon le deuxième scénario, celui de la décentralisation, le Québec peut réclamer des pouvoirs discrétionnaires pour varier le niveau des prestations et les critères d'admissibilité aux programmes fédéraux de prestations aux personnes âgées. Selon un troisième scénario, impliquant la dévolution, le Québec peut demander le transfert des dépenses fédérales en prestations aux personnes âgées et ainsi entrer dans le champ occupé actuellement par les programmes fédéraux de pension de sécurité de la vieillesse, de supplément de revenu garanti et d'allocation de conjoint. Vu que le Québec cherche une nouvelle relation avec le reste du Canada, une décentralisation ou une dévolution de la politique des pensions de vieillesse paraît très probable. A mesure que le drame constitutionnel se déroule, les pensions de vieillesse sont menacées par les retombées du lac Meech.

Abstract: The Tories have introduced several changes to retirement income policy since 1984, but a number of serious issues remain unresolved. Despite their victory on the OAS de-indexation issue seniors' groups have generally had little influence on the Conservatives' pension and social policy reform agenda, and the "clawback" of Old Age Security benefits effectively ends universality. Three scenarios are possible. Under a scenario of détente, intergovernmental tensions relax, and Quebec and other provincial governments avoid major changes to pension policy with the possibility of further incremental changes by either level of government. Under the second scenario of decentralization, Quebec may call for discretionary powers to vary the benefit and eligibility features in the federal elderly benefit programs. Third, under a devolution scenario, Quebec may call for the transfer of federal spending on elderly benefits to the province and move into the field now occupied by the federal OAS/GIS/SPA programs. With Quebec seeking some new relationship with the rest of Canada, decentralization or devolution of old age pensions policy appears most probable. As the constitutional drama unfolds, it seems that the troubled political waters of Meech Lake will spill into the Golden Pond of old age pensions.

Since 1984 the Progressive Conservatives have addressed, attacked, advanced and altered pension policies, at times in contradictory directions. This chapter has two objectives. The first is to describe and assess the policy changes made to the retirement income system by the Mulroney government. This also involves documenting federal spending trends on elderly benefit programs. The second objective, in keeping with the theme of this edition, is to speculate on how the demise of the Meech Lake Accord may influence intergovernmental relations and policy developments in the pensions field.

The Tories have introduced several changes to the Canadian retirement income system; some changes were progressive, others were not; some were substantial but most were marginal. After nearly seven years of pension reform, a number of serious issues remain unresolved. Unfinished business on elderly benefits and retirement income security represents a reform agenda for the federal and provincial governments in the 1990s. Federal spending on elderly benefit programs—that is, Old Age Security (OAS), Guaranteed Income Supplement (GIS), and Spouse's Allowance (SPA)—grew in absolute and relative terms over the 1984-90 period. We are not, however, witnessing a dramatic "greying" of the federal budget with rapidly rising expenditures for seniors. Relative to total federal program spending and to the Gross Domestic Product (GDP) of the Canadian economy, there has been a modest increase in federal elderly benefits spending.

Despite their victory on the OAS de-indexation issue, seniors' groups have generally had little influence on the Conservatives' pension and social policy reform agenda. Indeed, the elderly have not been immune from the federal tax increases and expenditure controls introduced since 1984. In 1990, for example, the additional net tax burden borne by the average elderly couple will be about $854 and for a single elderly person $244. Moreover, the "clawback" of Old Age Security benefits effectively ends the universality of this program, calling into question the future of the cornerstone program of the public pension system.

The chapter also explores possible pension policy futures in the post-Meech context. At least three scenarios can be postulated concerning federal-provincial and, in particular, Ottawa-Quebec relations. First, under a scenario of détente, intergovernmental tensions relax, and Quebec and other provincial governments leave pension policy alone, not addressing the division of powers, programs and expenditures in this field. This scenario would also include the possibility of further incremental changes to pension policy by either level of government. Under the second scenario of decentralization, Quebec may call for discretionary powers to vary the benefit and eligibility features in the federal elderly benefit programs. Moreover, the Canada Pension Plan (CPP) and the Quebec Pension Plan (QPP) might drift apart in terms of program design. Third, under a devolution scenario, Quebec may call for the transfer of federal spending on elderly benefits to the province and move into the field now occupied by the federal OAS/GIS/SPA programs. With Quebec seeking some new relationship with the rest of Canada, the détente scenario, in essence the status quo, seems least likely, and decentralization or devolution of old age pension policy appears more probable. As this constitutional drama unfolds, it seems that matters of social policy and income security will be involved. If so, then the troubled political waters of Meech Lake will spill into the Golden Pond of old age pensions.

THE MULRONEY GOVERNMENT AND PENSION REFORM

We first highlight what the Tories have said and promised with respect to pension reform by examining key statements and documents. Next we identify and describe what the Mulroney government has done in terms of policy initiatives in the retirement income system.[1]

Pension Promises and Principles

The Conservative government's pension reform agenda includes several promises and principles that have been articulated over the 1984-90 period. In August 1984, during the federal election campaign, Prime Minister Mulroney promised to improve income support for the elderly. Noting that 600,000 elderly persons live in poverty, he said:

There is no magic in the age 65. Sadness still intrudes. Hardships still exist. Poverty is not eliminated. It is a national disgrace that we have betrayed a generation of Canadians who have spent their lives building our country, raising families and contributing to the well-being, indeed the growth, of our regions, our provinces and our country. Basic pension reform will be a priority of a new Progressive Conservative government, because we are determined that growing old in Canada will not mean growing poor.[2]

During the campaign the Tories stated that their long-term goal in pension reform "is to maintain a mix of public- and private-sector pensions. Opportunity for individual planning for income security must co-exist with the CPP/QPP, if the long-term viability of the CPP is to be maintained."[3] The Tories' package of pension policy promises included six priority initiatives. These were: to extend the SPA to all widows and widowers in need aged 60 to 64; to restore full indexing of the OAS pension to the actual cost of living on a quarterly basis; to increase the GIS as soon as resources permit; to pursue negotiations with the provinces to include a homemakers' pension (worth at least $144 a month) in the CPP; to introduce a registered pension account to improve pension portability; and to encourage middle-income Canadians to invest in retirement savings plans by converting the existing deduction for contributions to a 40 percent tax credit. By 1991, only the first two of these priority items had been done.

In their first Throne Speech, pension reform was given prominence, suggesting it was a priority of the Mulroney Tories. The Throne Speech stated that the government "will enter discussions with the provinces aimed at a comprehensive overhaul of the Canadian pension system, including such matters as portability, vesting, survivors' benefits and pension coverage of women. An important element of this approach will be the consideration of measures designed to encourage Canadians to save for their retirement."[4] There was considerable similarity between these promises and those expressed in the last Liberal budget in February 1984. The pledge of consultation with the provinces was also planned by the Liberals in their "Action Plan for Pension Reform." The Tories' promise to consider measures to encourage Canadians to save for their retirement, implying there could be additional tax incentives for private savings and pension vehicles, was also foreshadowed in the Liberals' "Building Better Pensions for Canadians: Improved Tax Assistance for Retirement Saving."[5] In effect, the Tories inherited the occupational pensions policies from the Liberals. Proposals were already on the federal-provincial bargaining table under the Liberals. With the RRSPs, the first Tory proposals were nearly identical to previous Liberal proposals. Changes in the package came later as the enabling legislation was delayed numerous times over several years.

In November 1984, Finance Minister Michael Wilson presented a discussion paper entitled, *A New Direction for Canada: An Agenda for Economic Renewal,* which proposed, among other things, a sweeping and fundamental review of federal social policy. The *Agenda* paper argued that there was considerable scope for improving and redesigning social programs based on the twin tests of social and fiscal responsibility.

> **Social responsibility** dictates that wherever possible, and to a greater extent than is the case today, scarce resources should be diverted first to those in greatest need. **Fiscal responsibility** suggests that the best income security is a job, and that government expenditures must be allocated to provide immediate employment opportunities and better ensure sustained income growth.[6]

To begin this social policy review process, the *Agenda* paper raised for purposes of discussion and consultation some aspects of the elderly benefits system as well as other major social programs. The elderly benefits system was defined as including direct payments to persons in the form of the OAS, the GIS and the SPA, and two tax expenditures, the age exemption and the pension income deduction. After-tax expenditures (both direct and foregone tax revenue) for this system of elderly benefits was projected to be $11.8 billion in 1984-85. Excluded from this package were the tax deductions for contributions to registered pension plans, registered retirement savings plans, and the Canada Pension Plan as well as for interest and dividend income up to $1,000 on savings and investments. Also excluded were the retirement benefits component of the Unemployment Insurance program and tax exemptions available to families supporting their older members. Consequently, a comprehensive view of the total system was absent. In essence, the *Agenda* paper was focussing on a subset of the retirement income system in Canada.[7]

As a result of what the *Agenda* paper called the "rapid aging" of the Canadian population, costs for the elderly benefits were expected to grow significantly:

> It is therefore time to examine whether these federal transfer payments should continue in their present form or whether they need to be redesigned to increase fairness, assist those in greatest need, and reduce the burden on the federal government. If major changes were to be made, sufficient lead time would be required for current workers to plan for their own retirement needs. It will also take some time to make appropriate changes to public and private pension arrangements, and to related tax provisions, to encourage Canadians to prepare for their own retirement. Indeed, increased individual retirement savings will reduce the use of government revenues for financing old age assistance programs, and thus help to lower the tax burden on individuals and companies. It should be quite clear, however, that the government has no intention of reducing benefits for low- and middle-income individuals already retired or nearing retirement.[8]

In fact, in their Throne Speech the Tories had announced a reform to the SPA program. Previously, the SPA was paid only to spouses and widowed spouses of low-income old age pensioners who were between the ages of 60 and 64. The reform meant that all low-income widowed people between the ages of 60 and 64 would now be eligible for the SPA, whether their spouse had been receiving the OAS pension or not. This initiative was cited as evidence of the Mulroney government's desire to ensure that elderly Canadians enjoyed improved financial security, not less. The distribution of benefits by the elderly benefits system in 1984 is shown in Table 10.1. The table illustrates how benefits vary with income and raises questions about the design of federal elderly benefits, most particularly, "the fairness of providing assistance to high-income pensioners and the adequacy of benefits at low-income levels."[9]

Table 10.1
The Elderly Benefits System:
Net Annual Benefits for Single Individuals and
Two-Pensioner Couples at Selected Income Levels, 1984

Income*	OAS (after tax)	GIS	Tax Provisions	Total Benefits
		(dollars)		
Single				
0	3,219	3,419	0	6,638
4,000	2,809	1,525	410	4,744
8,000	2,361	0	925	3,286
15,000	2,272	0	1,022	3,294
30,000	2,009	0	1,308	3,317
50,000	1,767	0	1,569	3,336
Two-Pensioner Couple				
0	6,438	5,004	0	11,442
6,000	5,712	2,165	726	8,603
12,000	4,834	0	1,657	6,491
25,000	4,342	0	2,100	6,442
40,000	3,746	0	2,699	6,445
50,000	3,721	0	2,725	6,446
70,000	3,396	0	3,048	6,444

*   Income excludes OAS and GIS and is assumed to be earned by only one spouse, and residing in Ontario.

Source: Department of Finance, *A New Direction for Canada: An Agenda for Economic Renewal* (Ottawa: November 1984), p. 74.

The *Agenda* paper identified three possible options for changing elderly benefits. These were:

° reduce the amount of OAS available to high-income pensioners, by making benefits taxable at higher than normal rates or subject to some other tax recovery scheme;

° phase out the two tax provisions over several years;

° reduce the indexation of OAS while compensating pensioners in need (as was done in 1983 and 1984 under the Liberals' "6 and 5" inflation policy) or eliminate the indexation entirely.

All three options involved reducing benefits to higher-income pensioners, but none were aimed at directly increasing benefits to low-income seniors. None dealt with program enrichments or even reallocations between programs, say, from the tax provisions to the GIS or SPA. Instead, the sole focus was on program reductions, particularly the universal OAS program. The general impression was that there was a need to reduce the overall cost of the elderly benefits system while maintaining the "safety net" GIS and SPA programs. "In examining options for change to elderly benefits," the *Agenda* paper noted, "careful consideration should be given to the administrative implications of the various proposals as well as to their effects on Canadians' incentive to save for their retirement."[10] The paper did not, however, mention the political and symbolic implications of these proposals for reform.

Since much of politics is perception, the choice of words is extremely important. For many Canadians, the references in the paper to a "frank discussion" in order to "review" and "redesign" social programs so as to "divert" resources "to those in greatest need" were code words that more spending cuts in social programs were forthcoming and that no universal social program was a sacred trust, including the old age pension. It appeared that the Tories were seriously abridging, if not abandoning, their professed commitment to the principles of universality and social justice. The *Agenda* paper sparked six weeks of heated parliamentary debate. Subsequent remarks (some of them contradictory) by the Finance Minister, the Prime Minister, and the Minister of Health and Welfare led to greater concern and uncertainty about the Government's intentions for the universal OAS program.

Then in January 1985, Health and Welfare published a consultation paper on child and elderly benefits, describing the Government's approach to pension reform:

° The OAS pension is the foundation of the elderly benefits programs, and the concept of a universal base payment which is taxable and thus varies its after-tax benefits progressively is a sound one and should not be disturbed;

° A special surtax on OAS payments to recover more of the benefits paid to upper income pensioners would seriously disrupt our retirement income system and would unduly penalize those most affected by reason of retirement income resulting from private savings in earlier years;

° The age exemption and pension income deduction are the most regressive components of the existing elderly benefits system and are, therefore, those deserving most careful scrutiny;

° Changes in these programs which may result from this review should improve benefits for those in greatest need;

° Any net savings which may then remain, whether resulting from reductions in expenditure or additional revenues, should be applied to other priority concerns in the social affairs envelope. No such savings should be transferred to deficit reduction;

° No further expenditures additional to those already budgeted will be undertaken in 1985-86 on programs to provide social benefits, except where these can be funded by reallocating resources already committed for programs in the social field.[11]

The consultation paper attempted to reassure individual Canadians and organizations concerned with social policy that the focus of the elderly benefits program review was to have greater fairness in the distribution of benefits without disturbing the universality of the OAS pension. The consultation paper argued for a cautious and gradual approach to making changes in the elderly benefits system.[12]

While the consultation paper put forward options for change in child benefits for purposes of discussion, the Tories decided not to propose options for the reform of elderly benefits because, in their view, no change was required in the OAS or GIS. With respect to the tax provisions for the elderly, the Government believed that discussions with the provinces concerning comprehensive reform of the national pension system would provide the context in which to consider possible changes. This consultation paper released by Health and Welfare Canada, then, defended the concept of universality, emphasizing the progressivity of the OAS as well as of the selective GIS and SPA programs, while pointing to the regressive nature of the age exemption and pension income deduction. In effect, the consultation paper signalled that the options in the *Agenda* paper concerning cuts to the OAS program were not the Government's preferences, and that the elderly benefits system was "working well."

The May 1985 Budget proposal to partially de-index OAS benefits, however, contradicted the reassuring signal of the consultation paper. It certainly compromised the principle of help for those in greatest need because there was no GIS effect to the partial OAS de-indexing. This meant that low-income pensioners would also see their benefits decline in real value. Further, by appearing in the Budget section entitled "controlling the national debt," this measure compromised the principle that social policy savings would not be used to reduce the deficit.

A further statement on principles for social policy reform was made by Finance Minister Michael Wilson in his February 1986 Budget. In reforming social expenditures and related tax provisions, Wilson said that such reforms must respect several basic principles:

> They must maintain universal access. They must direct more resources to those most in need. They must improve the opportunities for individuals to become self-reliant. And they must reduce the after-tax value of benefits going to higher-income Canadians who do not need assistance.[13]

This statement is a mixture of ideas expressed in the *Agenda* paper and consultation paper. It is not only a reassurance that the "sacred trust" of universality is alive, but also a subtle reconstruction of the concept of universality that refers only to access and not benefit too. As well, the statement reaffirms the principles of social responsibility (that is, selectivity) and fiscal responsibility (that is, job creation and training), and revives the Finance Department's option of a surtax or clawback on benefits from programs such as the OAS.

During the 1988 federal election campaign, Prime Minister Mulroney promised to improve support for the elderly, no doubt to allay concerns over opposition claims that the Free Trade Agreement would threaten Canadian social programs. In a "special word to senior citizens," Mulroney stated in a speech on October 15, 1988, that "in the future Canada will be doing more, not less, for all of you."

Perhaps the most general and, in a sense, concrete state-ment of the Tories' approach to the retirement income system was in the December 1989 document, *Pension Reform: Improve-ments in Tax Assistance for Retirement Saving.*[14] Federal government policy on retirement income, it said, had two basic objectives: "to guarantee a basic level of income for all elderly Canadians; and to enable Canadians to avoid serious disruption of their living standards upon retirement."[15] A similar state-ment was contained in the Trudeau Liberals' 1982 Green Paper on pension reform.[16] With respect to the system of tax assis-tance for retirement saving, the Liberal and Tory documents also share the reform objective of providing Canadians with fairer and more flexible opportunities for tax assistance.

The Tory statement, however, has some distinctive fea-tures. One is the further reform objective of improving fiscal control over tax assistance costs by eliminating unintended tax-deferral opportunities by some high-income taxpayers. Another more important feature is that perhaps for the first time in a Government of Canada document an overall "target pension" is acknowledged and recommended by federal policy makers. In *Pension Reform*, the Department of Finance states:

> To maintain living standards, individuals need to replace income sources that cease at retirement, chief-ly earnings from employment or self-employment. Earnings do not need to be fully replaced, however, since work-related expenses, income taxes and savings requirements typically decline at retirement. A pen-sion of between 60 and 70 per cent of pre-retirement earnings is generally considered to be sufficient to avoid serious disruption of living standards.

> The adequacy of existing limits on benefits and con-tributions can thus be judged by whether they are high enough and flexible enough to permit individuals to attain a target pension of 60 to 70 per cent of pre-retire-ment earnings after a full career [30 to 35 years] of savings.[17]

The pension target adopted by the Tories is an income-re-placement ratio of pre-retirement earnings, based on a long career of regular savings. Perhaps we should not attach much importance to the target pension. It may be only a rationaliza-tion for bringing RRSP limits up to the limit in defined-benefit plans that have existed for many years (two per cent of earnings per year for 30 or 35 years = 60 or 70 per cent replacement). In any event, the target seeks to provide a measure of relative income security and stability for middle- and higher-income individuals. The federal government still has not authoritatively and explicitly stated what it regards as an acceptable level of income adequacy for elderly Canadians, regardless of their previous work histories. A minimum income floor is implied by the maximum OAS/GIS package, but this is widely held to be inadequate, especially for single women pensioners. For those Canadians with lower incomes, the income-replacement target offers a life of income insecurity and anxiety. Most working poor Canadians, for example, will be unlikely to attain a target level of 60 to 70 per cent of pre-retirement income. And even if they did, how adequate would 60 or 70 per cent of a subsistence wage be? Upon retirement, how many will have to resort to food banks and charities?

Canada's Retirement Income System

Canada's retirement income system comprises several policies and programs that directly affect the flow and level of incomes to the present elderly population and to those retiring in the future. The elderly benefits system discussed earlier is an important component of the larger retirement income system. In providing and regulating cash and tax benefits, and augmenting the incomes of older Canadians, the retirement income programs address states of dependencies and risks associated with aging and with the market economy.

The retirement income system contains a four-level structure of policies and programs. An overview of the Conservatives' retirement income policy record is shown in Appendix 10.1, which outlines the four levels of the system, lists the relevant federal programs and briefly identifies the major Tory pension reforms over the 1984-90 period.

Level one consists of direct transfer payments to older Canadians. These include the OAS, GIS and SPA programs, provincial income supplements as well as more specialized programs like veterans' pensions and retirement benefits in the Unemployment Insurance plan. Level two consists of the contributory public pension plans, the CPP and QPP. Level three concerns employer-sponsored or occupational pension plans. The federal role here is in registering all such plans for income tax purposes and in regulating those plans that lie within federal jurisdiction. Finally, level four deals with tax assistance for retirement savings and for the elderly. Ottawa plays the major governmental role in Canada in providing and governing tax assistance for saving in pension and retirement savings plans. Federal tax provisions apply to employer-sponsored registered pension plans (RPPs), deferred profit sharing plans (DPSPs), individual registered retirement savings plans (RRSPs), CPP contributions, pension income and old age (65 and over).

According to the Conservatives, the first two levels of the retirement income system relate to the objective of guaranteeing a **basic** level of income for all elderly Canadians, by providing transfer payments and a modicum of earnings replacement. These programs deal with Canadians as citizens and as employees. The third and fourth levels correspond to the objective of helping Canadians build **adequate** retirement incomes and thus maintain their living standards. Programs at these levels deal with Canadians as employees (or self-employed), taxpayers, investors and other private roles.

The Great De-indexation Fight

Arguably the best known pension initiative by the Tories, and clearly the most politically damaging, was the modified indexation of OAS payments proposed in the May 1985 Budget. As part of the Government's plan for controlling the national debt, the 1985 Budget announced that beginning in 1986 the indexation of OAS (as well as Family Allowance) payments would be modified, with benefits increasing yearly by the annual change in the consumer price index (CPI) in excess of three percentage points. This would provide for only partial protection against inflation and, therefore, old age pension benefits would no longer be fully compensated for increases in the cost of living. The selective GIS and SPA programs as well as veterans' benefits programs would continue to be fully indexed to any increases in the CPI.

The proposed partial de-indexation of OAS benefits engendered a swift, strong and widespread public outcry by seniors' groups, social policy groups, provincial governments and even business lobbies. The Great De-indexation Fight became the largest political protest by seniors in Canadian history.[18] By threatening and angering seniors, the de-indexation provision politicized many of them, expanding the membership of various seniors' and pensioners' groups, and prompting the creation of new groups and coalitions among groups. Barely four weeks after the Budget was delivered, Finance Minister Wilson withdrew the OAS de-indexation measure. To compensate for these lost expenditure reductions, estimated at $245 million for 1986-87, Wilson increased gasoline and corporate taxes.

Are seniors now a major force in the Canadian political system? Ann Finlayson claims that the message of the de-indexation retreat is that: "The rapidly growing army of older Canadians now has the numbers to make its wishes count. Age is becoming an ever more powerful political influence in Canada, even more powerful than such traditionally potent forces as race, class and sex."[19] In last year's edition of *How Ottawa Spends*, Allan Moscovitch suggested that the elderly were able to successfully press their case against the de-indexation of OAS, "because of their status in Canadian society as the most deserving of the poor and because of their political mobilization."[20]

In a thoughtful analysis of the de-indexation issue, Elizabeth and Gretta Riddell-Dixon note that the political mobilization and policy outcome in this case—a rapid, dramatic attack and reversal—are relatively rare in Canadian public policy. On the present state of provincial and national seniors' organizations, they conclude that, "the groups are too diversified to permit close co-operation except in crisis situations. This fact casts doubt on the idea that the pension controversy marked the beginning of a strong, unified seniors' movement in Canada."[21] In a similar vein, Mark Novak has identified three lessons about seniors' politics in Canada from the de-indexation case. "First, seniors can act as a group to change federal policy, but only if they speak with a single voice. Second, seniors can use opinion polls, the media and direct confrontation to pressure the Government. Third, seniors need to ally themselves with other power blocs in society—political parties, business and service groups."[22] We might also add that the Tories caved in because they were new to governing and were caught off guard.

To conclude, therefore, from the Great De-indexation Fight that "grey power" has emerged in Canada as a dominant political movement would be inaccurate. As we will show, seniors' groups have generally exerted far less influence on the Conservatives' social policy and tax reform agendas.

The Clawback on Pensions: Ending the Universality of OAS

"The central purpose of the social safety net," the 1989 Budget Speech argued, "is to assist those most in need, not to subsidize those with high incomes."[23] That Budget, therefore, proposed recovering old age security pensions (and family allowance benefits) from "higher-income Canadians" at a rate of 15 per cent of individual net income exceeding $50,000. The measure is being phased in over three years, with repayments calculated on the income tax return. Actual repayments in the 1989 taxation year were one third of the amount repayable; actual repayments in 1990 will be two thirds of the amount repayable; and the full amount will be repayable in 1991 and subsequent years. The amount of this special tax or clawback imposed on OAS benefits is deductible in computing a pensioner's income for the year. For 1990 and subsequent years the $50,000 threshold is partially indexed to inflation, that is, to the annual increase in the CPI in excess of three per cent. This is the same basis as most other indexed brackets and thresholds in the tax system. According to Budget papers, "The level of the threshold will be reviewed periodically and adjusted as appropriate."[24]

Table 10.2 shows how the clawback on OAS benefits operates for a single pensioner under the mature system effective in 1991. The surtax or clawback means that Canadian seniors repay 15 cents of their OAS pension for every dollar of net income above the threshold. Thus, seniors with net incomes of $50,000 or less will not pay the clawback; those with net incomes between $50,000 and $76,332 pay a graduated partial clawback, keeping some of their old age pension; and those seniors with net incomes above $76,332 pay the total clawback, forfeiting all of their OAS benefits.

Table 10.2
Impact of the Clawback on the Old Age Security
Benefits of a Single Pensioner, 1991

Seniors' Net Income	Gross OAS Benefits	Clawback
(Dollars)		
50,000 or less	3,950	0
51,000	3,950	150
55,000	3,950	750
60,000	3,950	1,500
65,000	3,950	2,250
70,000	3,950	3,000
76,332 or more	3,950	3,950

Source: Adapted from National Council of Welfare, *The 1989 Budget and Social Policy* (Ottawa: September 1989), Table B, p. 5. The figures are for 1989 but assume the clawback is fully in place.

Next, Table 10.3 illustrates how the introduction of the clawback alters the net benefit of the OAS realized by single pensioners at different income levels. OAS benefits are available to elderly Canadians independent of their income and for many years the benefits have been subject to personal income tax. As taxable benefits, OAS pensions "are of greatest value to low-income recipients and of progressively lower value as income rises and becomes subject to taxation at higher marginal rates."[25] Thus, operating in tandem with the income tax system, the universal OAS program has provided greater benefits to lower income seniors and smaller benefits to higher income seniors. This outcome, argue social policy groups across Canada, does not abrogate the universal nature of OAS, rather it affirms its universality. As the National Council of Welfare explains, universality means that all the recipients of a social program—made available regardless of their income—end up with some meaningful benefit.[26] Hence, prior to the clawback provision, seniors in the top tax bracket retained just over half of their OAS benefits after taxes.

Table 10.3 shows that pensioners with net incomes below $50,000 will experience no change in their net (that is, after-tax and clawback) OAS benefit. Those above the $50,000 threshold, however, keep smaller benefits, and a case can be made that pensioners with net incomes above $60,000 will no longer retain a meaningful benefit. Based on 1990 estimates, the Department of Finance projects that under the mature clawback system, 54,000 higher-income OAS recipients will repay all of their benefits and a further 74,000 will repay part of it. In total, benefits of about 4.4 per cent of all OAS recipients will be affected in the early 1990s.

Table 10.3
How the Clawback Alters the Net Benefit
of Old Age Security Benefits

Senior's Net Income[1]	Gross OAS Benefits	Pre-Clawback Net OAS Benefit[2]	After-Clawback Net OAS Benefit[3]
	(Dollars)		
10,000	3,950	3,950	3,950
20,000	3,950	2,909	2,909
30,000	3,950	2,358	2,358
40,000	3,950	2,358	2,358
50,000	3,950	2,174	2,174
55,000	3,950	2,174	1,762
60,000	3,950	2,174	1,349
65,000	3,950	2,174	936
70,000	3,950	2,174	523
75,000	3,950	2,174	110
76,332 or more	3,950	2,174	0

Notes: 1. Assumed to be a single pensioner 65 and over.

2. Refers to the benefits retained after federal and provincial income taxes payable on the OAS prior to the 1989 Budget.

3. Refers to the benefit retained after income taxes payable and the clawback repayment.

Source: Adapted from National Council of Welfare, *The 1989 Budget and Social Policy* (Ottawa: September 1989), Tables B and D, pp. 5 and 8. The figures are for 1989 but assume the mature clawback system is in place.

The Government contends that the clawback measure maintains the universal character of the OAS program because everyone eligible will continue to receive their benefits regardless of income. "Those who need assistance most will continue to retain all their benefits. Recipients with high incomes will retain less. This preserves the social safety net and helps provide a sound financial basis for social programs into the future."[28]

There are several problematic issues raised by this statement. First, it defines universality solely as an administrative process for program eligibility, completely ignoring the political, personal and sociological aspects of universality. These aspects include such ideas and experiences as nation building, citizenship, social recognition and inclusion. The Government's stated rationale for the clawback converts the role of the universal OAS into a residual program of assistance. As a policy tool, however, the clawback itself offers no direct enhancement of benefits to those seniors most in need. Second, with an initial 128,000 recipients receiving less or no OAS benefits than before, social policy groups are concerned that rather than preserving the social safety net, the clawback's impact will weaken general support for social programs. As the National Council of Welfare notes, "giving benefits with one hand and then taxing them all back with the other is a hypocritical policy that could engender middle-income voters' resentment at paying taxes for social programs to which they are not really entitled."[29] Third, because the clawback's $50,000 threshold is only partially indexed to the CPI, over a number of years inflation will pull the threshold down in real terms and more pensioners at increasingly more moderate income levels will end up with smaller OAS benefits. This likely scenario may not only further erode public support for the program, but also produce an uncertain basis for planning retirement income security.

Further criticisms and drawbacks of the clawback provision are summarized in Table 10.4. The clawbacks have been called "the most significant backward step in Canadian social policy in a generation, because they end the universal nature of the Old Age Security pension and family allowances."[30] The clawback ends the universal nature of the OAS because benefits are now subject to a special tax, no longer taxed at the same rate as other income; and because a growing number of seniors over time will not retain any after-tax benefits from the program. In essence, the OAS is now an income-tested selective program.

How did the Government succeed in implementing the clawback of pensions in 1989, a more radical policy change than the proposed partial de-indexation of OAS which was quickly withdrawn in 1985? Here we can only suggest in brief terms some pertinent factors: As the clawback affects far fewer seniors and is a more complicated measure to describe and debate, public opposition was not as widespread or strong—for example, there was no condemnation from provincial legislatures and business associations and no evident dissent within the Conservative caucus. Other items in the 1989 Budget such as the withdrawal of regular federal financing for the Unemployment Insurance program and further restraint in Ottawa's transfer payments to the provinces as well as the Goods and Services Tax debate overshadowed the clawback measure.

Table 10.4
Drawbacks of the Clawback on Old Age Security:
A Summary Overview

° Ends the universal nature of the OAS program as some seniors will not retain any after-tax benefits.

° Complicates the income tax return and introduces a confiscatory tax structure of 100 per cent.

° Clawback threshold of $50,000 is only partially indexed to cost of living, so each year more pensioners will lose all or part of their OAS benefits.

° Inconsistent with generous increases in RRSP contributions limits.

° Announced without any public debate or consultation with seniors' groups.

° The expected savings (about $300 million in 1991) are not earmarked to help low-income seniors as previously promised.

° A possible disincentive to private savings, it penalizes those who have invested, sacrificed and saved for retirement.

° Three-year phase-in too short as a transitional period for treating those nearing retirement differently from those younger.

° Unfair tax treatment of upper-income pensioners compared to upper-income persons under age 65.

° Destabilizes the retirement income system since the OAS, the basis of the system, is formally considered in the design of many private schemes.

° Creates a new tax haven, since it applies only to those who file Canadian tax returns. Canadian seniors living in the United States pay tax on the OAS only in the United States, where just half of the OAS income is taxable.

° Applies to some pensioners with incomes below $50,000 because the threshold is based on a definition of net income which includes a 25 per cent "gross up" of dividend income.

° Breaks a "social contract" between the federal government and the public, especially those seniors who paid the special OAS Tax, in place over the 1952-72 period.

Thus, the clawback issue received far less media coverage than the Great De-indexation Fight. Lastly, the federal opposition parties, seniors groups and other social policy organizations opposed to the clawback on universal programs faced a more experienced and determined Finance Minister and Conservative government, revived by their 1988 election victory.

Reforming the Canada Pension Plan

Amendments to the CPP were announced by the Mulroney government in 1985, enacted the next year and were effective as of January 1, 1987. The main reforms of the plan deal with financing, the retirement age, survivor benefits, splitting of pension credits, and disability benefits.[31] Specifically, they involve:

° Increasing the contribution rate for employees and employers by 0.2 per cent each year over the 1987-92 period. Increases of 0.15 per cent are scheduled for the succeeding 20 years to 2011, and can be amended by federal-provincial review. The combined contribution rate is projected to reach 7.6 per cent of pensionable earnings from the previously fixed rate of 3.6 per cent.

° Allowing more flexible retirement age, by enabling benefit claims as early as age 60 or as late as age 70. Benefits that begin between age 60 and 65 will be reduced by 0.5 per cent for each month before a person's 65th year, and benefits claimed after age 65 will be increased by 0.5 per cent per month.

° Ensuring that survivors over age 65 receive 60 per cent of a deceased spouse's retirement benefit even if the survivor is entitled to a retirement benefit.

° Guaranteeing that survivor benefits will no longer cease if the survivor remarries.

° Providing that pension credits (entitlements to future benefits) earned during marriage (legal or common-law) be split between spouses upon divorce or separation. This provision can, however, be overridden by provincial family laws.

° Improving orphans' benefits for dependent children of deceased CPP members.

° Increasing the flat-rate disability benefits from $93 to $233 (in 1986 dollars) and the earnings-related portion to the same levels as the Quebec Pension Plan.

With these changes the CPP is on a sounder financial basis and some benefits have been improved. Several of the program changes brought the CPP closer in line with the QPP. In 1988, under phase one of tax reform, the tax deduction for contributions to the CPP and QPP was converted to a tax credit.

Still, some shortcomings of the CPP remain. The principal weakness, many groups argue, is that the maximum pension payable is too low—a maximum of 25 per cent of earnings up to the average industrial wage. This low income-replacement rate was a deliberate limitation built into the plan when it began in 1966. The result, however, is that even with a full CPP pension and the OAS, a retired person living in a large city needs a sizeable GIS to get over the poverty line. Moreover, while more women are now claiming CPP retirement benefits than 10 or 15 years ago, many are retiring with relatively meagre pensions, commonly less than 40 per cent of the maximum benefit.[32] A second shortcoming is that the contribution system is a regressive payroll tax. The percentage of earnings paid in contributions declines once earnings exceed the pensionable limit. Hence, everyone making more than $30,500 in 1991 pays the same maximum contribution. A third issue concerns whether and how to provide direct coverage by the CPP for full-time homemakers. As an item on the national policy agenda, homemakers pensions seem effectively dead.

Reforming Occupational Pension Plans

For the third level of Canada's retirement income system shown in Appendix 10.1, the main federal law on occupational pension plans, the Pension Benefit Standards Act (PBSA) was amended in 1985 and took effect in 1987. The PBSA applies to federally regulated industries such as the banking sector, interprovincial transportation, radio and television broadcasting, telecommunications and federal Crown corporations. It covers about one million Canadian workers within federal jurisdiction (including Yukon and Northwest Territories), while provincial laws cover over 3 1/2 million workers.

In 1989, modest changes were made to eight other pieces of federal pension legislation by the Statute Law (Superannuation) Amendment Act.[33] This law removed the provisions that suspended surviving spouses' pensions upon remarriage and student allowances of surviving children upon marriage, and resumed payment of benefits that had been suspended or terminated. The law also ended the reduction of benefits to surviving spouses who are 20 or more years younger than the deceased pension plan contributor in plans that had this provision. The Government made these changes so that survivors of federal public service employees have the same protection found in most other pension plans. The total value of additional benefits resulting from this law was estimated to be $39 million for about 6,700 surviving spouses.

Inherited largely from Liberal efforts on occupational pensions, the Conservatives' results in reforming the PBSA were as follows:

° to ensure a higher degree of uniformity in pension plan standards across Canada;

° to increase vesting so that workers can acquire pension rights more quickly;

° to increase portability so that pensions are transferable when workers change jobs;

° to expand accessibility to plans so more workers will have the opportunity to join;

° to give workers more choice in determining their age of retirement;

° to improve pensions for women;

° to encourage inflation protection of pension benefits;

° to increase the disclosure of information about pension plans to members; and

° to encourage employee participation on pension management committees.[34]

These outcomes came from the pension reform debate of the previous several years, including a federal-provincial process of discussions in the early 1980s. In fact, many of the provisions in the PBSA passed by Ottawa in 1985 are similar to those in the Pension Benefit Act passed by Manitoba in 1983. A fair degree of uniformity in standards has since resulted with newly enacted, proposed or amended pension laws in British Columbia, Alberta, Ontario, Quebec, New Brunswick, Nova Scotia and Prince Edward Island. In general, the minimum legal entitlements to pension plans and retirement income have been raised and become more common across Canada over the 1985-90 period.

With respect to vesting, the PBSA provides that employees have a right to receive the benefits from their own pension contributions and those made by their employers after two years as a plan member. A person who ends employment prior to becoming fully vested loses rights to all or some of any employer-provided pension. This new rule applies to benefits accruing after 1986. For pre-1987 accrued benefits the old rule of age 45 and 10 years of service or membership applies. The PBSA improves portability by enabling workers who change jobs to transfer vested pension benefits to a new employer's plan or to place the benefits in a locked-in individual RRSP or to purchase a life annuity. Eligibility for occupational pension plans is eased and expanded somewhat by the PBSA. Full-time employees can join existing plans after two years and part-time workers can now join if they earn 35 per cent or more of the Year's Maximum Pensionable Earnings (YMPE) under the CPP for two consecutive years. The YMPE is a measure of the average wage determined by Health and Welfare Canada, and for 1991 it is $30,500. Unfortunately for many adult part-time workers, these earnings rules mean that private pension plans will remain inaccessible. The PBSA also requires that if membership to a plan is compulsory, exclusion for religious beliefs must be permitted.

On giving workers more choice in deciding their retirement age, the PBSA provides some standards on early retirement rights and on the treatment of employment after the "normal" retirement date. Election of early retirement must be allowed within 10 years of pensionable age, that is, the earliest age when a member may retire without consent and receive an unreduced pension. While a plan member is in continued employment after pensionable age, the pension is postponed and accruals continue on the same formula basis.

For women, PBSA reforms that seek to improve their pension opportunities and benefits relate to the improved vesting noted above as well as to prohibiting sex discrimination in calculating employee contributions and benefits, the splitting of pension credits upon marriage (legal or common-law) breakdown in accordance with provincial laws and various changes to survivor benefits. Plans regulated by the PBSA are required to provide pre-retirement survivor benefits of 100 per cent of the value of post-1986 accrued pension payable to the surviving spouse in the form of an annuity or RRSP. For a plan member who dies after retirement, plans must provide a pension of at least 60 per cent of the full pension. Furthermore, survivor benefits continue if the surviving spouse remarries. Survivor pensions provided under PBSA, however, can be waived with the consent of both spouses, so that they are not really mandatory.

On protecting the value of occupational pension benefits against inflation, the Mulroney Conservatives have adopted a voluntary rather than mandatory approach. In contrast, the Trudeau Liberals had announced in their last budget in February 1984, their intention to adjust pensions and deferred pensions annually by 60 per cent of the change in the CPI, to a maximum annual adjustment of eight per cent.[35] This change was not enacted before the September 1984 federal election. Ontario and Nova Scotia support, in principle, mandatory inflation protection of defined benefits in their pension laws but neither province to date has implemented such a policy. The federal PBSA does contain a modest incentive for indexation that is linked to the rules on the minimum contribution by employers to plans. For 1987 and later benefits, employers are required to contribute 50 per cent of the value of vested pension benefits. This 50 per cent cost rule can be waived if the plan provides for annual indexing of deferred pensions at 75 per cent of the CPI less one per cent.

Pension plan administration and disclosure of information are other key areas regulated by the PBSA. For plans having at least 50 members, the establishment of, and representation by members on, a special committee is required upon the request of a majority of members. Such committees serve in an advisory capacity to the plan administrator. The PBSA also provides for periodic benefit statements and requires employers to make available pension plan documents and actuarial and financial information filed after 1986.

The Office of the Superintendent of Financial Institutions is responsible for overseeing the administration of the PBSA. The Office carries out periodic on-site examinations of pension plans registered under the PBSA. In response to a recommendation by the Office of the Auditor General, the Superintendent's Office has, in recent years, been increasing the number of examinations conducted. From just a few inspections focussed on the larger plans, the Office now examines a wider cross-section of the federally regulated pension plans. By 1990, the Office was examining about 60 plans annually. These examinations have found that some plans are not in full compliance with the standards set out in the PBSA. Pension plan violations by employers relate to the vesting of benefits, sex discrimination, disclosure of information to plan members and the timing of remittances of employee contributions to the pension fund. Where such violations occur, the Superintendent considers the situation to be serious, warranting future examinations.[36]

The 1985 amendments to the PBSA have established some new rights to occupational pension plans within federal jurisdiction. These new rights, as we have shown, deal with such items as early retirement, access to pension plan survivor benefits and the eligibility of certain regular part-time workers. Some problems and unmet needs, however, remain. One critique of the Tories' record on private pension plans notes that:

> ...the federal government failed to prohibit employers from withdrawing surplus funds from their pension plans, to require worker/employer co-management of pension plans and to provide for automatic credit splitting upon marriage breakdown. The Conservatives also did nothing to rectify the fatal flaw of most employer-sponsored pension plans—their lack of full indexation of pension credits and benefits.[37]

Another recent study concludes:

> All in all, occupational pension plans play a limited role in providing retirement income for Canadians. Coverage continues to be concentrated in the public sector and in large industries in the private sector. Most women, most low-wage workers and most employees in the private sector continue to be left out. It remains to be seen whether this will change as a

result of the latest round of changes in federal and provincial pension laws.[38]

The Conservatives (and Liberals before them) subscribe to what could be called an optimistic model of private pension coverage development. According to this model, private plan membership can and will expand over the long run, aided by a supportive regulatory framework and tax system. In principle, then, the labour market is capable of providing adequate pension coverage of workers. Three criticisms can be made about this model. First, the inadequacies of coverage by occupational pension plans in the Canadian economy have not improved over recent years. In 1978, 47.9 per cent of all employed paid workers were covered, versus only 44.9 per cent in 1988. More than half of employed workers in Canada's labour force remain excluded. Second, the economic adjustments expected in the 1990s associated with free trade, corporate failures, mergers and other developments will likely be difficult times for workers and for firms establishing, maintaining and expanding private plans. Third, the supportive tax policies for encouraging the development of occupational pension plans are regressive in their impact. Under tax reform, the Tories did not convert the tax deduction for contributions to occupational pension plans to a tax credit.

Tax Reform as Pension Reform

Level four of the Canadian retirement income system, shown in Appendix 10.1, is significant in terms of the number of changes that have been made in recent years by the Tories as part of their tax reform process.

A main element of tax reform in 1988 was the conversion of tax exemptions and deductions to tax credits. The federal government emphasized that this produced particular benefits for elderly Canadians. By replacing exemptions and deduction with tax credits the Government estimated that this would completely eliminate federal income tax for 850,000 Canadians, 250,000 of whom are senior citizens. Moreover, the new credits would mean that about 90 per cent of Canadians aged 65 and over would pay less federal tax in 1988. Converting tax exemptions and deductions to tax credits also supported the Government's goals for reforming social policy noted earlier in this chapter, namely, to target assistance more effectively to those with lower incomes, and to reduce the after-tax value of transfer payments to those with higher incomes.

To be sure, the conversion of exemptions and deductions to tax credits makes the personal income tax system more progressive. Exemptions reduce the amount of income that is subject to tax, making their value greater for those with higher incomes because higher income people have higher tax rates. Tax credits, on the other hand, reduce tax payable and are worth the same regardless of income. For example, before the 1988 tax reforms, there was an age exemption of $2,670 (in 1987) for Canadians 65 and over. For a senior citizen with a $15,000 income, this was worth about $705 in lower federal and provincial taxes while for a senior with a $100,000 income, the same exemption was worth $1,410. As part of the tax reform package, the age exemption was converted to a non-refundable tax credit worth $850 (in 1988 with federal and provincial taxes included) to all seniors.

In addition to the age exemption, several other existing deductions for seniors in the retirement system were converted to tax credits. These are listed in Table 10.5.

In the tax reform arena, as with the OAS clawback issue, seniors groups were far less effective as policy advocates than during the Great De-indexation Fight. As one seniors' activist notes:

> The 1985 campaign against partial de-indexing of OAS is often depicted as the start of real "grey power" in Canada. Perhaps the fact that it was a campaign to stop the government from taking away a benefit rather than to seek a new one contributed in part to the extensive media coverage. However, partial de-indexation of income tax exemptions, both personal and age, was legislated in 1985. In the 1987 conversion to credits it was perpetuated. Seniors groups, along with many other organizations, protested strongly, but to no avail.[39]

In appearances before the House of Commons Standing Committee on Finance and Economic Affairs, dealing with the White Paper on Tax Reform, seniors groups (along with other social groups) called for certain policy measures. These included: the full indexation of tax credits to the CPI, the retention or conversion of the investment income deduction to a tax credit, higher refundable sales tax credits, and the conversion of the RRSP deduction to a credit or, failing that, not raising the contribution limits so sharply.

Table 10.5
Tax Reform as Pension Reform:
Changes to the Personal Income Tax System,
1988 and 1990

Provision	Pre-reform	Post-reform
Age (65 and over)	Standard exemption of $2,670 in 1987.	Tax Credit of $850 in 1988. Unused credit transferable to spouse.
Pension Income	Eligible pension income deductible up to $1,000. Unused deduction transferable to spouse.	17 per cent tax credit of eligible pension income, maximum $170. Unused credit transferable to spouse.
CPP\QPP Contributions (employee share)	Fully deductible.	Credit at 17 per cent of contributions for all employees and self-employed.
Investment Income	Interest and dividend income up to $1,000 deductible.	Abolished as of 1988.
Dividend Tax Credit	Combined federal-provincial credit of 33 1/3 per cent of dividends from Canadian firms.	Credit reduced to 25 per cent.
RRSPs, RPPs, DPSPs	Deduction limit on annual contributions is 20 per cent of earned income up to $7,500 for taxpayers not belonging to an RPP or DPSP or $3,500 less employee RPP contributions for other taxpayers.	Deductions maintained and limit on contributions converted to 18 per cent of earned income to $15,500 by 1995.

Note: Since the 1989 taxation year, the age tax credit has been partially indexed to inflation—the annual increase in the CPI in excess of three per cent. It is the only credit in this table that is partially indexed. Other tax reforms of interest to seniors include the Disability Credit, Medical Expenses Credit, Goods and Services Tax Credit, Married Credit, and the Basic Personal Credit.

Overall, the Standing Committee's final report contained relatively little discussion on elderly benefits and seniors, much less than on child benefits. The report largely accepted and defended the White Paper's proposals that concerned seniors and the retirement income system. The Committee argued that while full indexation of the tax system may be desirable, "seniors are less affected than some other groups of taxpayers, because the benefits most of them receive outside the tax system (OAS and CPP) are fully indexed." On the removal of the $1,000 investment income deduction, the committee contended that placed in the context of other personal income tax reform proposals, the elimination of the investment income deduction was "not a serious loss to the elderly." The combined effect of the new age credit, the pension income credit, and the basic personal tax credit is that lower income seniors—who represent about 70 per cent of senior tax filers—will pay less tax because of these reforms and a number will see their income taxes reduced to zero. The committee, therefore, accepted the White Paper's claim that personal income tax would be reduced for almost 90 per cent of elderly Canadians.

Seniors groups like One Voice: The Canadian Seniors Network and the National Pensioners and Senior Citizens Federation argued that the plans to raise the limits on contributions to RRSPs in stages to $15,500 a year was unfair, meant a significant loss of revenue to Ottawa, and contradicted the main tax reform thrust of converting exemptions and deductions to credits. The Conservative majority on the Standing Committee, however, did not see the proposal as unfair nor really as a seniors' benefit, but rather as a benefit for young and middle-aged workers to save enough money to live on in retirement. Upon the advice of Finance Department officials, the Committee concluded that there were "practical obstacles" to a tax credit for private retirement savings plans. The Committee's rationale is worth quoting:

> A tax credit at the 12 per cent federal rate would reduce tax assistance for employee contributions to RPPs and for RRSP contributions out of incomes in the middle and upper brackets. This would discriminate against contributory plans and RRSPs, and create a tax incentive to shift to greater employer contribution. High-income contributors approaching retirement would prefer to drop out of their plans instead of saving federal taxes at 17 per cent on contributions towards

benefits a few years later that would be taxed at 26 or 29 per cent. In other words a tax credit for contributions could not be introduced without re-examining how benefits should be taxed.[40]

Interestingly, a 1983 all-party Parliamentary Task Force on Pension Reform recommended that a tax credit for contributions could and should be introduced. And, as noted earlier, one of the Tories' pension policy promises made in 1984 involved converting the existing deduction for contributions to RRSPs to a 40 per cent tax credit. It is ironic that the government was upset about OAS benefits going to rich seniors at about the same time it was increasing the RRSP contribution limit for rich working people—a much larger net benefit than the OAS.

One of the Mulroney government's own stated tests with which to assess the tax reforms is the impact on the elderly. Do the tax reforms give senior citizens more peace of mind and security? The Government, of course, believes so: as a result of personal income tax reform, 1.2 million or 90 per cent of households with at least one individual aged 65 or over saw their taxes cut. Contrary to Government claims, however, tax reform did not yield a substantial benefit for senior citizens. The average reduction in federal and provincial personal income tax in 1988 for the elderly is estimated to be $290.[41] Indeed, the change in tax represents on average less than one per cent of income for elderly households. One seniors group, *Forum des citoyens agés de Montréal,* claimed that the 1988 tax reforms did not include any real reforms for the elderly. Rather, the *Forum* argued that the tax reforms threatened the peace of mind and security of seniors because "the value of these credits [will] be lower in the medium term since the reform does not provide for their full indexation."[42] For example, the age tax credit will decline by about 14 per cent in real value from 1988 to 1991. As the Federal Task Force on Retirement Income Policy put it: "The greater the conditionality and uncertainty associated with the real incomes of the elderly, the more likely it is that the elderly will be made to feel uncomfortable."[43]

The 1988 tax reforms were a case of the Tories appearing to be generous after being tax greedy and transfer grumpy. In fact, the appearance was deceptive. Many pensioners are worse off. A comprehensive analysis of the distributional impact of federal tax and transfer changes introduced over the 1984-1990 period found that an average Canadian family in 1990 will bear an additional tax burden, net of transfers, of $1,000 more than they would face under an extension of the 1984 system.[44] Of the 2.4 million taxpayers in elderly families, 1.7 million (72 per cent) will pay more taxes net of transfers in 1990 than they would pay if the pre-1984 system were still in place, and 554,000 (24 per cent) will pay less. The study reported that:

° An average elderly family that consists of one adult will have an income of $17,198 in 1990 and will pay $244 more in taxes, net of transfers, and an average elderly family that consists of two or more will have an income of $40,355 and will pay $854 more.

° Elderly families with incomes at $50,000 or more lose significantly more as a result of the tax changes than do other childless couples at the same income levels because of the clawback of the OAS pension.

° At low incomes between $10,000 to $15,000, 51 per cent of single elderly and 39 per cent of elderly couples are paying more in federal taxes in 1990 than in 1984.

° Across all income groups, 61 per cent of single elderly and 85 per cent of elderly couples are net losers with declines in consumable income.[45]

A Closer Look at Federal Spending on Elderly Benefits

Federal spending trends on the elderly benefits programs of OAS, GIS and SPA are given in Table 10.6. The data in this table span 1975 to 1990, covering the modern structure of the federal elderly benefits system. The SPA program was introduced in 1975 to join the previously established OAS (1952) and GIS (1966). Also in 1975 the OAS Fund was abolished and benefits have since been paid from the Consolidated Revenue Fund. The table shows the steady increases in spending for all three programs over the period. To show real trends, the figures have been converted to constant 1990 dollars. Over the Mulroney years shown here, 1984-85 to 1990-91, spending grew in both absolute and real terms. In fact, among the major federal statutory programs, the OAS was the only one that increased in real terms, 18.6 per cent over five years.

Table 10.6

Federal Elderly Benefits Expenditures, 1975-1990

Fiscal Year	current dollars				constant 1990 dollars			
	OAS	GIS	SPA	TOTAL	OAS	GIS	SPA	TOTAL
	(millions of dollars)							
1990-91[1]	12,878,000	4,105,000	519,000	17,502,000	12,878,000	4,105,000	519,000	17,502,000
89-90[2]	11,850,000	3,902,000	477,000	16,229,000	12,407,772	4,085,665	499,452	16,992,886
88-89[3]	10,963,365	3,765,839	473,220	15,202,424	12,053,374	4,140,249	520,269	16,713,691
87-88	10,247,941	3,618,244	482,561	14,348,746	11,723,363	4,139,172	552,037	16,414,570
86-87	9,520,047	3,451,376	473,239	13,444,662	11,367,756	4,121,240	565,088	16,054,084
85-86	8,857,668	3,319,428	347,752	12,524,848	11,009,204	4,125,720	432,221	15,567,145
84-85	8,215,898	2,952,921	248,782	11,417,601	10,620,677	3,817,236	321,600	14,759,513
83-84	7,648,959	2,524,450	232,914	10,406,323	10,318,067	3,405,358	314,189	14,037,614
82-83	7,005,302	2,416,263	221,468	9,643,033	9,995,643	3,447,689	316,006	13,759,337
81-82	6,140,552	2,241,914	202,844	8,585,310	9,708,028	3,544,399	320,690	13,573,117
80-81	5,322,086	1,918,066	177,653	7,417,805	9,464,633	3,411,029	315,933	13,191,594
79-80	4,679,030	1,494,585	145,983	6,319,598	9,166,550	2,927,998	285,991	12,380,538
78-79	4,130,613	1,234,161	126,302	5,491,076	8,836,773	2,640,286	270,203	11,747,261
77-78	3,668,559	1,077,621	114,999	4,861,179	8,541,799	2,509,111	267,761	11,318,671
76-77	3,318,919	1,017,128	100,626	4,436,673	8,341,989	2,556,516	252,920	11,151,425
75-76	2,975,000	939,009	34,936	3,948,945	8,039,976	2,537,684	94,415	10,672,074
Percentage change								
75-90	332.9	337.2	1385.6	343.2	60.2	61.8	449.7	64.0
84-90	56.7	39.0	108.6	53.3	21.3	7.5	61.4	18.6

Source: Public Accounts of Canada, Volume II, except as otherwise noted.

1. Forecast 1990-91 Estimates Part III, Department of National Health and Welfare, p. 3-22
2. Estimate 1990-91 Estimates Part III, Department of National Health and Welfare, p. 3-22
3. The total of the three amounts for 1988-89 represent the actual expenditures, while the figure for each program is an estimate of the breakdown.

The other programs—Established Program Financing, Canada Assistance Plan, Family Allowance, and Unemployment Insurance—either declined or remained flat.[46]

The upward trend in federal spending on the elderly benefits programs over the 1984-90 period is due to several factors: (1) in June 1984 and again in December 1984, as a result of a Liberal government decision, the GIS basic benefit was increased by $25 a month; (2) in May/June 1985, the Conservative government retreated from its proposed partial de-indexation of the OAS benefits; (3) in September 1985 the SPA program was extended to 46,000 people previously excluded; (4) given the aging of the population, the number of recipients of the three programs grew from 2.7 million in 1985 to 3.2 million in 1990;[47] and (5) the decision in the February 1990 Budget to exempt elderly benefits programs (among other programs) from the Expenditure Control Plan which capped annual increases in program spending at three per cent. The most significant determinants in the recent growth of federal spending for the elderly have been, in order of importance, price inflation and program indexation, client population growth and policy actions. All three elderly benefits programs remain fully indexed to the cost of living.

The spending trends in this area are influenced not only by what the Mulroney government has done—such as introducing the clawback of OAS benefits—but also by what it has not done. Spending on elderly benefits has been restrained by a number of Tory non-decisions, choices to do nothing new on certain issues and to confine actual reform to relatively inexpensive changes. The Tories have engaged in pension non-decision-making by not raising the basic OAS benefit or GIS benefit and in not extending the SPA to include low-income couples or single individuals aged 60 to 64. During the Mulroney years these policy options have been kept off the governmental agenda.

Although Ottawa's spending on elderly benefits has grown in recent years, we are not witnessing a "greying" of the federal budget with rapidly rising expenditures for seniors. Contrary to the implication of the *Agenda* paper, the "financial burden" of elderly benefits on Ottawa is not onerous. Table 10.7 puts elderly benefits expenditures in the wider contexts of the federal budget and Canadian economy.

Table 10.7
Elderly Benefits Expenditures in Context:
Selected Years

Year	As a % of Federal Program Expenditures	As a % of GDP
1990-91	16.1	2.6[1]
1989-90	15.7	2.5
1988-89	15.2	2.5
1987-88	14.9	2.6
1986-87	14.9	2.7
1985-86	14.6	2.6
1984-85	14.7	2.6
1983-84	14.7	2.6
1982-83	15.7	2.6
1981-82	16.3	2.4
1980-81	14.4	2.4
1975-76	13.5	2.3

Note: Elderly benefits refer to OAS, GIS and SPA payments reported in Table 10.6.

Source: Data from *Economic Review* and *Public Accounts of Canada*, various years.

1   Estimate for 1990.

When viewed in relation to total program spending and the GDP, there has not been a dramatic or rapid increase. In terms of federal program expenditures, spending on elderly benefits has fluctuated around 15 per cent in the 1980s, and in terms of the GDP the spending has remained fairly constant at about 2.6 per cent. True, the program spending targeted on older Canadians is growing, but that spending is not outstripping growth in the economy and the extent of "greying" of the federal budget has been gradual. In 1962-63, for example, federal expenditures on income support for seniors represented 13.6 per cent of federal program spending and 1.7 per cent of GDP.

The "greying" of how Ottawa spends has been a gradual and manageable process for over 30 years, and it will likely continue to be so for the next 30 years. The Canadian population is aging, but not rapidly. A recent study by the International Monetary Fund projects that Canada's share of GDP allocated to public pensions will be 3.1 per cent in 2000, growing to 4.3 per cent in 2025.[48] These ratios of pension expenditures to GDP were the lowest of the seven major industrial countries examined, reflecting Canada's lower average pension benefits and a relatively lower share of the elderly in the population.

The 1991 Budget, Pension Reform and Elderly Benefits

The February 1991 Budget contains several items related to pension reform and benefits for the elderly. Indeed, as a client group, the elderly are among the few "winners" in this budget of expenditure restraint.

To expand the range of equity investments in Canadian corporations that pension funds can choose from, the Budget proposes easing certain PBSA rules on portfolio investment performance. The Budget also proposes to increase the relative level of investment in equity markets by Canadian pension funds. The Government suggests that a tax credit and a levy be applied to holdings of Canadian common equity and other investments respectively. The credit would increase the return to the eligible equity investments held by pension funds while the levy would reduce the return to other investments like bonds and real estate. The Government's intention is to shift more of the $190 billion in Canadian pension fund holdings into the stock market. Recognizing that the proposal represents a major change, the Government intends issuing a technical discussion paper which will provide the basis for consultation with the financial sector.[52]

Initial reaction to this proposal by the pension fund and capital market communities has been critical.[53] They question the Government's proposed use of tax penalties to directly influence pension fund investment decisions on asset mix. They say that the problem is not a bias in the tax system in favour of debt instruments but rather the lack of available high-quality liquid stocks. They also express concern that the proposal opens the door to a tax on pension funds and may drive up the price for stocks. The existing principle is that the taxation of pension funds is deferred until converted to income. A better way to make Canadian stocks more attractive, they suggest, is through economic policies such as deficit reduction.

Other tax measures in the Budget of some importance to the elderly include: an increase in the Disability Tax Credit from $575 to $700 a year starting in 1991, a $35 million expenditure; an expanded definition of eligible medical expenses under the Medical Expenses Tax Credit; and a provision to allow recipients of CPP/QPP disability benefits to spread the tax over the years of disability rather than include the full amount in the year received.

The 1991 Budget further proposes to extend to 1995-96 the Expenditure Control Plan introduced in the 1990 Budget. Under the Plan, annual spending for programs is constrained, frozen or reduced. Income support programs for seniors, however, along with some other social programs are exempted from this Plan. Maximum benefit rates for these elderly benefits programs are estimated to increase by 5.9 per cent over 1991-92 as a result of indexation to the CPI.[54]

The Budget contains a total program spending increase of $7.5 billion in 1991-92, of which $1.6 billion or 21 per cent is for the elderly benefits programs. On the clawback of OAS benefits to higher-income seniors, the Budget states: "Although this measure does not directly affect program spending, it does reduce the deficit and ensures that the benefits are better targeted than in the past."[55] As noted earlier, the mature clawback system is effective in 1991. For increasing numbers of seniors this will mean that their old age pensions will only jingle in their pockets.

The Mulroney government also announced in the Budget that legislation will be introduced to limit annual spending increases in federal programs to an average of three per cent over the period 1992-93 to 1995-96. While total program expenditures in 1991-92 are estimated to increase by 6.9 per cent, for the elderly benefits it is 9.2 per cent. The Budget notes that: "The aging of the population and full indexation of benefits to inflation have made benefits to the elderly one of the fastest growing areas of government spending."[56] The exemption of elderly benefits from the Expenditure Control Plan combined with the aging population, full indexation of benefits and legislated spending limits, will gently accelerate the "greying" of federal program spending.

For 1991-92, spending on the elderly benefits transfers is estimated to be $18,904 million, an increase of 9.2 per cent. This breaks down into increases of 9.6 per cent for OAS ($14,065), 8.0 per cent for GIS ($4,335 million) and 8.8 per cent for SPA ($504 million). It is worth noting that the 1990-91 forecast is now $202 million or 1.1 per cent lower than the 1990-91 Main Estimates of $17,502 million. The decrease is due to lower than expected numbers of eligible beneficiaries and average rates paid.

CPP benefit payments are estimated to rise $1,449 million or 13.6 per cent in 1991-92 to $12,096 million. In January 1991, federal and provincial finance ministers agreed to increase contribution rates for the next 25 years. Under the proposed change, which must be approved by federal and provincial governments, the average wage-earner will pay $7 a year more to CPP in 1992 and $42 more by 1996. Each worker's contribution is matched by the employer. In the face of higher than expected early retirements since 1986 and lower than expected productivity increases in the Canadian economy, this change in CPP contributions was made to ensure that the plan has funds of two years' worth of benefits.

The finance ministers also agreed that federal legislation will be introduced to increase benefits for children of CPP contributors who are disabled or deceased. These survivor benefits will rise by $35 a month to $148 monthly, benefiting about 165,000 children.[57] Besides this reform, the Estimates reveal that there are no major new income security initiatives in National Health and Welfare's priorities for 1991-92. The department does plan to offer as a voluntary service the automated deposit of OAS and CPP payments directly into a client's account in a financial institution. Also during 1991-92, Health and Welfare will undertake a survey "to analyse the low take-up rate in the splitting of CPP contributions upon a divorce or a separation."[58]

The department is actively engaged in defending the elderly benefits programs against various challenges launched under the Canadian Charter of Rights and Freedoms. About a dozen such Charter challenges are currently before the courts and the department expects more in the future. At issue is whether differential elderly benefit structures based on age of spouse or survivor, marital status, sexual orientation and length of residency in Canada are justified in relation to the Charter. The Charter's impact on the retirement income system, especially the direct transfer payments and contributory CPP, may well be immediate, manifold and significantly expansionary. For example, the department estimates that if the court decided that the SPA program discriminates against single, divorced and separated persons aged 60 to 64, then the contingent liability is $1.1 billion a year.[59] The Charter might become more impor-

tant than the Government's fiscal plan in determining the scope
of spending on elderly programs.

Federalism and Pension Policy in the 1990s

Pondering the future for Canadian federalism and, in turn,
for pension policy, we are faced with many questions. What is
the real or potential impact of the death of the Meech Lake
Accord on the retirement income system? How do recent changes in elderly benefits outlined above affect federal-provincial
relations? Will the demise of Meech jeopardize the **entente**
between the governments of Canada and Quebec in co-ordinat-
ing the CPP and QPP? If we are entering a new era of federalism
in Canada, what are the implications for pension programs? In
a renewed federal system, will Quebec and perhaps other
provinces assert their constitutional authority and demand
more autonomy in the old age pensions field? Can further power
over pensions be granted only to Quebec? In short, what are the
possibilities or scenarios for the further decentralization of
federalism in the pension field?

In speculating on these prospects, it is worthwhile to recall
past events at least for reflections if not recommendations. "The
failure of the constitutional review of 1968-71 marked the
beginning of a period," David Ross reminds us, "when reduced
federal-provincial co-operation meant that respective jurisdictions tended to go separate ways on income security issues."[49]
The 1970s featured unilateral actions by the provinces and
Ottawa in creating their own social programs. With less
buoyant economies and larger deficits now, is this as likely in
the 1990s? Or, will the political pressures of competitive
federalism spur governments to take unilateral action? In contrast to the 1968-71 Victoria Charter process, the 1986-90 constitutional Meech Lake reform discussions did not founder on
the issue of control over social policy, although some questions
about the federal spending power were raised.

The legal distribution of powers in the Canadian constitution has continuing significance for the reform and management of the CPP, the regulation of occupational pension plans,
the provision of tax assistance for retirement savings and the
direct transfer programs to seniors. Federal powers to make
payments to seniors via the OAS, GIS, SPA, to regulate certain
private pensions, to use the income tax system and to enact the
CPP are already constitutionalized. Thus, the death of the

Meech Lake Accord, which gave constitutional recognition to the right of Ottawa to spend in areas of exclusive provincial jurisdiction, does not weaken the federal spending power on elderly benefits.

While the death of Meech does not officially hurt federal powers in the pensions field, the Accord's ghost may politically haunt Ottawa. Debate arises, though hardly for the first time, about how this may affect the centralist-decentralist balance. Will the federal government be able to secure intergovernmental agreement on additional reforms to the CPP? Will post-Meech Lake pension reforms be of a checkerboard variety that deviate from the process of convergence in the 1980s? The answers to these and other questions depend, of course, on the actual unfolding of events (including the Bélanger-Campeau Commission, and constitutional review initiatives in other provinces as well as in Ottawa).

Given both historical patterns and recent events in Canadian federalism, our post-Meech politics may well produce the next round in the pension debate and reform process. The stage will be federal-provincial relations with the main players being Quebec, Ottawa and Ontario. Pension policy, specifically old age pensions, promises to be caught up in the dynamics of our charged intergovernmental arena. The issues and battle lines are not yet clearly drawn, but they concern the appropriate division of powers between the federal and provincial governments. At stake is the legitimacy and role of Ottawa in the pensions field.

A case can be made that there will be renewed pressures within governmental circles for a public sector response to retirement income needs. With the election of an NDP government in Ontario in September 1990, the Ontario government, for the first time in the modern age of pension politics, is no longer the assured champion of the private pension industry. We may also see NDP governments elected in British Columbia and Saskatchewan in 1991. An expanded CPP with significantly improved benefit levels naturally fits with the NDP's philosophy, social policy preferences and political support from the women's movement and organized labour, among others. The Ontario NDP government also supports the mandatory protection of pension benefits from inflation, guaranteeing workers' rights to surplus funds in pension plans, promoting the co-management of plans and expanding the coverage of occupational pensions. Legislation may be introduced in 1991.[50]

Quebec governments since at least the early 1960s have advocated the introduction and expansion of public pension plans. Compared to the other provinces, Quebec's attitudes towards federal involvement in public pensions have been different. While other provinces accepted a federal role in public pensions, Quebec has been more defensive about its jurisdiction; traditionally objecting to federal action, insisting on the 1951 constitutional amendment that acknowledged the paramountcy of the provinces in the old age pensions field, and opting out of the CPP in 1966 and establishing the related but separate QPP. Quebec also manages the investment of QPP surplus funds differently from what the other provinces and Ottawa do with CPP funds, using the funds to acquire equity in key industries in Quebec.[51]

With the death of the Meech Lake Accord, the Quebec government may become less willing to endorse the existing federal-provincial division in income security. This would be a return to more historical stances taken by Quebec. In fact, most of the groups appearing before the Bélanger-Campeau commission studying Quebec's political future, called for more powers for Quebec in numerous sectors. And many groups, including the Quebec Chamber of Commerce, called for exclusive Quebec jurisdiction in old age pensions. The Bourassa government may well press for provincial supremacy over OAS and the GIS, as it did in 1971 during the then constitutional review process.

In the pension politics of the early 1990s, the federal government could conceivably side with Ontario (and perhaps Quebec) in expanding the CPP. Perhaps more likely is that Ottawa will take some further reforms of the GIS and SPA programs, possibly the tax credits, and the PBSA rules on occupational plans within federal jurisdiction. Such pension reforms would help emphasize the national and social dimensions of Canada. In the ongoing struggle over the divided loyalties of Quebeckers and other Canadians, pension reform might also help reinforce Ottawa's shaken legitimacy and challenged authority in the Canadian political community.

CONCLUSION

Overall, pension reform by the Mulroney government since 1984 is predominantly a neoconservative record as opposed to a centrist (liberal social reform) or a mixed record. The Government's main strategy is to rely on the private market through retirement savings plans and occupational schemes to extend pension rights and benefits. Federal policy makers have emphasized selectivity over universality, private plans over public programs and income subsistence over income adequacy for all. Tory pension reform has involved restraining public programs and promoting private arrangements. The shift is toward market-based equity over citizenship-based entitlements.

Four factors have largely influenced this pattern of policy instrument and value choices. First, when the Tories came to office in 1984, they inherited a federal-provincial pension reform process that was well advanced. The Canadian pension debate had begun in earnest in the late 1970s and by the early 1980s much of the reform agenda, although certainly not all, had taken shape, especially with respect to the CPP, occupational plans and tax assistance. Second, the neoconservative philosophy of the Mulroney Tories, which became increasingly evident and potent over the 1984-90 period, was an important factor. It was evident in the Tories' non-decision-making in the area of public pensions and their private sector orientation to reform. Third, the pension reform agenda was related to the Tories' wider fiscal plan of government restraint and deficit reduction. The greater selectivity of elderly benefits pursued by the Tories was frugal redistribution aimed at expenditure savings rather than purposeful redistribution motivated by social equity. Bureaucratic politics within the federal government was a fourth factor that influenced the pattern of pension policy choices. This involved bargaining between Finance and National Health and Welfare over the relative reform emphasis and direction. In the end, Finance largely prevailed in promoting tax-assisted savings and modest occupational pension changes instead of Health and Welfare's preference for substantially expanding the CPP and leaving the OAS intact.

Other less important factors included demographic trends and "grey power." As our analysis indicates, except for their notable success on the OAS de-indexation issue, seniors' groups have had little influence on the Mulroney government's pension and social policy record.

To further privatize the retirement income system has been the main thrust of Tory pension reforms. But the privatization is in large part an illusion and raises some serious issues as a policy trend. Increasing signficantly the contribution limits to RRSPs represents private retirement savings but with substantial and regressive public revenue subsidies. This measure contradicts the fairness objective of tax reform and accents income inequalities in Canada. Furthermore, the narrow scope of reform to the occupational pensions sector leaves untouched the critical flaws of that sector concerning insufficient coverage and inadequate inflation protection. For many elderly Canadians the outcome will be continued reliance on the under-developed public pension system.

Appendix 10.1

Conservative Reforms to the Retirement Income System, 1984-90

Levels and Programs	Initiatives and Reforms

1. Direct Transfer Payments

Old Age Security	Abandoned effort at partial de-indexation of benefits, 1985.
	Clawback of payments from recipients with annual incomes over $50,000, 1989.
Guaranteed Income Supplement	No action.
Spouse's Allowance	Extension to all widowed in need aged 60-64, 1985.
Unemployment Insurance	Retirement benefit for workers at age 65 eliminated and UI Act modified in 1989 to allow continued coverage by workers aged 65 and over.

2. Contributory Public Pensions

Canada Pension Plan	Modest improvement of some benefits and new 25-year schedule of contribution rate increases to make financing more secure, 1987.
	Changes to CPP Appeals System, 1990.
	CPP Survivor-benefits issue studied, consultation paper 1987, government response 1988, federal-provincial discussions in progress 1990-91.
	Homemakers' pension issue unresolved.

Levels and Programs	Initiatives and Reforms

3. Occupational Pension Plans

Pension Benefits Standards Act	New legislation implemented in 1987, with improved minimum standards for benefits in private pension plans.
Federal Public Service Plans	Statute Law (Superannuation) Amendment Act, 1989, improved survivor benefits.

4. Tax Assistance and Regulation

Age Exemption of $2,670	Converted to non-refundable flat rate age tax credits of $850 in 1988.
Pension Income Deduction up to $1,000	Converted to credit in 1988, 17 per cent of eligible pension income, maximum $170.
Canada Pension Plan Contributions Deductions	Converted to a credit of 17 per cent of contributions, 1988.
Investment Income Deduction up to $1,000	Eliminated, 1988.
Dividend Tax Credit	Reduced from 33 1/3 per cent to 25 per cent of cash dividends, 1988.
RRSP, RPP & DPSP contribution deductions	Reforms first promised in May 1985 Budget finally enacted in June 1990. Include higher dollar limits on contributions phased-in over 1991-95.
Deferred Income Trusts and other Registered Retirement Funds	Increased limits on foreign investment assets by Canadian pension funds from 10 to 20 per cent over 1990-95 period.

Notes

Special thanks to Ken Battle and Steve Kerstetter of the National Council of Welfare and to Frances Abele and Keith Banting for their comments on the first draft of this chapter. I would also like to thank those officials who provided documents on pension reforms.

1   This first part is drawn from Michael J. Prince, "Startling Facts, Sobering Truths and Sacred Trust: Pension Policy and the Tories," in Allan M. Maslove (ed.), *How Ottawa Spends, 1985* (Toronto: Methuen, 1985), pp. 150-53.

2   Reported in *The Globe and Mail* [Toronto], August 11, 1984, pp. 1-2.

3   "Statement on Social Policy of Progressive Conservative Government," *Perception*, vol. 8, no. 1, 1984, p. 8.

4   Speech from the Throne to open the first session, Thirty-Third Parliament of Canada, November 5, 1984.

5   For a discussion of the Liberals' pension proposals, see Michael J. Prince, "Whatever Happened to Compassion? Liberal Social Policy 1980-84," in Allan M. Maslove (ed.), *How Ottawa Spends, 1984* (Toronto: Methuen, 1984), chapter 3.

6   Department of Finance, *A New Direction for Canada: An Agenda for Economic Renewal* (Ottawa: November 1984), p. 71.

7   A fuller description of the retirement income system is given in Michael J. Prince, "Startling Facts, Sobering Truths and Sacred Trust: Pension Policy and the Tories," in Allan M. Maslove (ed.), *How Ottawa Spends, 1985* (Toronto: Methuen, 1985), pp. 115-21.

8   Department of Finance, *A New Direction for Canada: An Agenda for Economic Renewal* (Ottawa: November 1984), p. 74.

9   Department of Finance, *A New Direction for Canada: An Agenda for Economic Renewal* (Ottawa: November 1984), p. 77.

10 Ibid.

11 Department of National Health and Welfare, *Child and Elderly Benefits, Consultation Paper* (Ottawa: January 1985).

12 Department of National Health and Welfare, *Child and Elderly Benefits, Consultation Paper* (Ottawa: January 1985), p. 8.

13 Michael Wilson, *The Budget Speech*, February 16, 1986, p. 12.

14 Department of Finance, *Pension Reform: Improvements in Tax Assistance for Retirement Saving* (Ottawa: December 1989).

15 Department of Finance, *Pension Reform: Improvements in Tax Assistance for Retirement Saving* (Ottawa: December 1989), p. 5.

16 Government of Canada, *Better Pensions for Canadians* (Ottawa: December 1982), pp. 1 and 11.

17 Department of Finance, *Pension Reform: Improvements in Tax Assistance for Retirement Saving* (Ottawa: December 1989), pp. 5-6. A previous document, Department of Finance, *A Better Pension System: Savings for Retirement* (Ottawa: October 1986), p. 17, stated that the 18 per cent limit of earned income to a prescribed dollar amount for tax assistance for retirement saving, "was chosen because it is the percentage of earnings required to be set aside each year to build a pension of 60 to 70 per cent of income—a level appropriate for the tax system to support."

18 Mark Novak, *Aging in Society: A Canadian Perspective* (Toronto: Nelson, 1988), p. 330. See also, D. Bercuson, J.L. Granatstein and W.R. Young, *Sacred Trust? Brian Mulroney and the Conservative Party in Power* (Toronto: Doubleday, 1986), chapter 6.

19 Ann Finlayson, *Whose Money Is It Anyway? The Showdown on Pensions* (Markham: Penguin, 1988), p. 24. See

also, R. Verzuh, "Grey power comes out of the closet," *Perception*, vol. 9, no. 1, pp. 13-15.

20   Allan Moscovitch, "'Slowing the Steamroller:' The Federal Conservatives, the Social Sector and Child Benefits Reform," in Katherine A. Graham (ed.), *How Ottawa Spends, 1990-91* (Ottawa: Carleton University Press, 1990), p. 201.

21   Elizabeth Riddell-Dixon and Gretta Riddell-Dixon, "Seniors Advance, The Mulroney Government Retreats: Grey Power and the Reinstatement of Fully Indexed Pensions," in Robert J. Jackson, Doreen Jackson and Nicolas Baxter-Moore (eds.), *Contemporary Canadian Politics* (Scarborough: Prentice-Hall, 1987), p. 289.

22   Mark Novak, *Aging in Society: A Canadian Perspective* (Toronto: Nelson, 1988), p. 331.

23   Michael Wilson, *The Budget Speech*, April 27, 1989, p. 9.

24   Department of Finance, *The Budget Papers* (Ottawa: April 27, 1989), p. 9.

25   Department of National Health and Welfare, *Child and Elderly Benefits, Consultation Paper* (Ottawa: January 1985), p. 6. Moreover, increasing the universal OAS benefit would have progressive impacts on the distribution of lifetime disposable income. See Bruce Kennedy, "Some Distributional Impacts of Marginal Changes to Public Pension Parameters," *Canadian Public Policy*, vol. 16, No. 1, March 1990, pp. 73-85.

26   National Council of Welfare, *The 1989 Budget and Social Policy* (Ottawa: September 1989), pp. 2-3.

27   Department of Finance, *The Budget Papers* (Ottawa: April 27, 1989), p. 11.

28   Michael Wilson, *The Budget Speech*, April 27, 1989, p. 10.

29   National Council of Welfare, *The 1989 Budget and Social Policy* (Ottawa: September 1989), p. 15.

30 National Council of Welfare, *Pension Reform* (Ottawa: February 1990), p. 18. See also, Ken Battle, "Clawing back," *Perception*, vol. 14, no. 3, pp. 34-38.

31 For more details and comments, see Richard Lee Deaton, *The Political Economy of Pensions* (Vancouver: University of British Columbia Press, 1989), chapter 4, Department of Finance, *A Better Pension System: Saving for Retirement* (Ottawa: October 1986), pp. 9-10, and National Council of Welfare, *A Pension Primer* (Ottawa: September 1989).

32 National Council of Welfare, *A Pension Primer* (Ottawa: September 1989), p. 29.

33 Treasury Board of Canada, *News Release* (Ottawa: June 16, 1989). The Statute Law (Superannuation) Amendment Act, 1989, amends the following eight federal pension laws:

The Public Service Superannuation Act,
The Canadian Forces Superannuation Act,
The Royal Canadian Mounted Police Superannuation Act,
The Members of Parliament Retiring Allowances Act,
The Diplomatic Service (Special) Superannuation Act,
The Defence Services Pension Continuation Act,
The RCMP Pension Continuation Act, and
The Pension Act that applies to disabled veterans.

34 Department of Finance, *The Budget Papers* (Ottawa: May 28, 1985), pp. 45-49.

35 Department of Finance, *The Budget Papers* (Ottawa: February 15, 1984), p. 18.

36 Office of the Superintendent of Financial Institutions, *PBSA Update*, Issue No. 4, (Ottawa: March 1990).

37 Grattan Gray, "Social Policy By Stealth," *Policy Options*, Vol. 11, No. 2, p. 27.

38 *A Pension Primer*, p. 46.

39   Herbert Hanmer, "Seniors: Sales tax, health issues pro-
      vide new challenges," *Perception*, vol. 12, no. 2, p. 50.

40   House of Commons, Standing Committee on Finance and
      Economic Affairs, *Report on the White Paper on Tax
      Reform (Stage 1)* (Ottawa: November 1987).

41   Department of Finance, *Tax Reform 1987, Income Tax
      Reform* (Ottawa: June 18, 1987), p. 38.

42   House of Commons, Standing Committee on Finance and
      Economic Affairs, *Proceedings* (Ottawa: September 17,
      1987), p. 106:26.

43   Government of Canada, Task Force on Retirement In-
      come Policy, *Report* (Ottawa: 1980), p. 173. See also,
      Department of National Health and Welfare, *Survey of
      Old Age Security and Canada Pension Plan Retirement
      Benefit Recipients* (Ottawa: Income Security Programs
      Branch, Health and Welfare Canada, 1990). This 1987
      survey found that 39 per cent of respondents deemed their
      income as inadequate to cover basic needs.

44   Patrick Grady, "The Distributional Impact of the Federal
      Tax and Transfer Changes Introduced Since 1984," *The
      Canadian Tax Journal,* vol. 38, no. 2, pp. 286-97.

45   Ibid., pp. 294-97. See also C. Lindsay and S. Donald,
      "Income of Canada's Seniors," *Canadian Social Trends,*
      no. 10, Autumn 1988, (Ottawa: Statistics Canada), pp.
      20-25.

46   National Council of Welfare, *Social Spending and the
      Next Budget* (Ottawa: April 1989), p. 2.

47   Ibid., pp. 2-3. These are revised totals provided to the
      author by the NCW.

48   P.S. Heller, R. Hemming and P. Kohnert, *Aging and So-
      cial Expenditure in the Major Industrial Countries 1980-
      2025* (Washington, D.C.: International Monetary Fund,
      1986). These projections assume a steady rate of
      economic growth and that existing program levels are
      maintained. See also R. Holzman, *Social Policy Studies*

No. 5: Reforming Public Pensions (Paris: Organization for Economic Co-operation and Development, 1988).

49   David P. Ross, *The Working Poor* (Ottawa: Canadian Institute for Economic Policy, 1981), p. 77.

50   "Rae vows to protect pensions," *The Globe and Mail* [Toronto], November 27, 1990, p. A5, and "Grappling with pensions," *The Financial Post* [Toronto], January 21, 1991, p. 12.

51   Kenneth Bryden, *Old Age Pensions and Policy-Making in Canada* (Montreal: McGill-Queen's University Press, 1974), pp. 201-202, and Bruce Kennedy, "Refinancing the CPP: The Cost of Acquiescence," *Canadian Public Policy*, vol. 15, no. 1, March 1989, pp. 34-42.

52   Michael Wilson, *The Budget*, February 26, 1991, pp. 153-57.

53   Barrie McKenna and Dennis Slocum, "Pension money eyed for stocks," *The Globe and Mail* [Toronto], February 27, 1991, pp. B1 and B7; Bruce Cohen, "Tax may force fund switch," *The Financial Post* [Toronto], February 27, 1991, p. 27; Dennis Slocum, "Pension industry fears tax grab," *The Globe and Mail* [Toronto], February 28, 1991, p. B7; William Johnston, "Penalty wrong way to steer pension funds," *The Globe and Mail* [Toronto], March 2, 1991, p. B4; and "Pension proposal needs more study," *The Financial Post* [Toronto], March 11, 1991, p. 7.

54   Health and Welfare Canada, *1991-92 Estimates*, Part III (Ottawa: Supply and Services, 1991), pp. 3-25.

55   Michael Wilson, *The Budget*, February 26, 1991, p. 62.

56   Ibid., pp. 61-2.

57   See *The Globe and Mail* [Toronto], January 29, 1991, p. B2.

58   Health and Welfare Canada, *1991-92 Estimates*, Part III (Ottawa: Supply and Services, 1991), pp. 3-16.

59   Ibid., pp. 3-15.

FISCAL FACTS AND TRENDS

This appendix presents an overview of the federal government's fiscal position, includes certain major economic policy indicators for the 1981-90 period, and some international comparisons.

Facts and trends are presented for federal revenue sources, federal expenditures by policy sector, the government's share of the economy, interest and inflation rates, Canadian balance of payments in total and with the United States in particular, and other national economic indicators. In addition, international comparisons on real growth, unemployment, inflation and productivity are reported for Canada, the United States, Japan, Germany and the United Kingdom.

The figures and time series are updated each year, providing readers with an ongoing current record of major budgetary and economic variables.

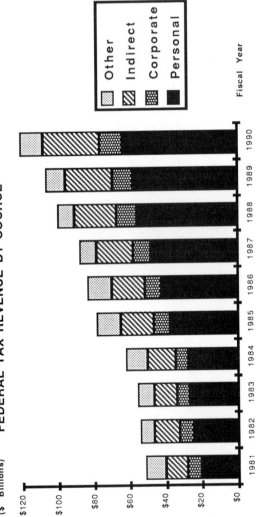

FEDERAL TAX REVENUE BY SOURCE

($ Billions)

Fiscal Year

Other
Indirect
Corporate
Personal

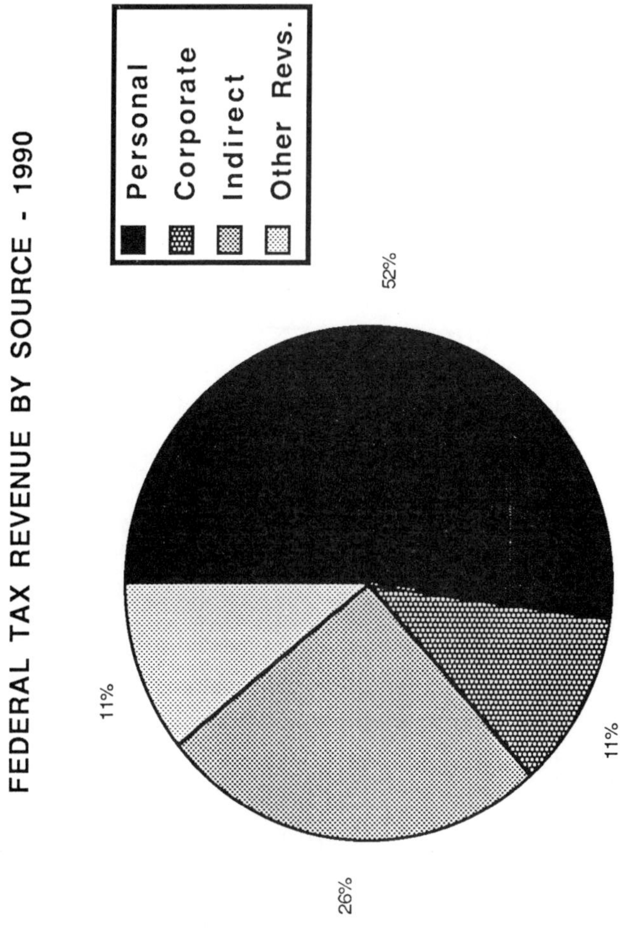

FEDERAL TAX REVENUE BY SOURCE - 1990

Personal
Corporate
Indirect
Other Revs.

52%

11%

11%

26%

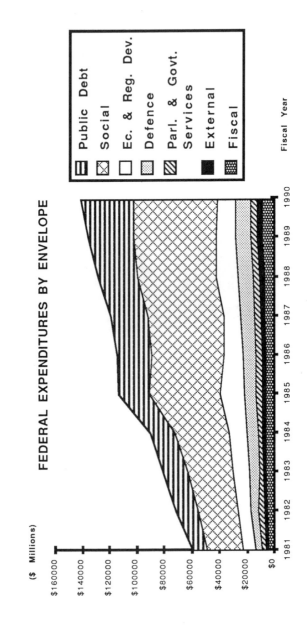

FEDERAL EXPENDITURES BY ENVELOPE

($ Millions)

Public Debt

Social

Ec. & Reg. Dev.

Defence

Parl. & Govt.
Services

External

Fiscal

Fiscal Year

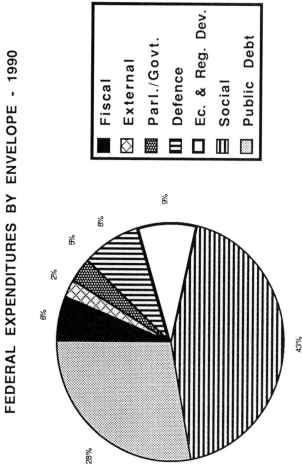

FEDERAL EXPENDITURES BY ENVELOPE - 1990

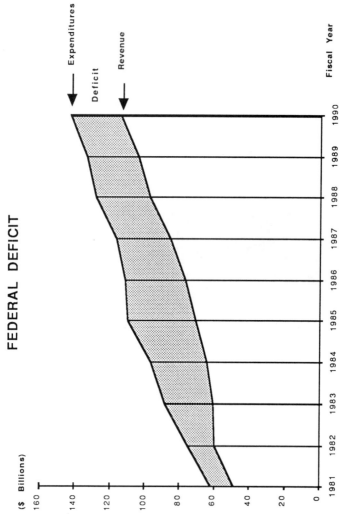

FEDERAL DEFICIT

($ Billions)

Expenditures

Deficit

Revenue

Fiscal Year

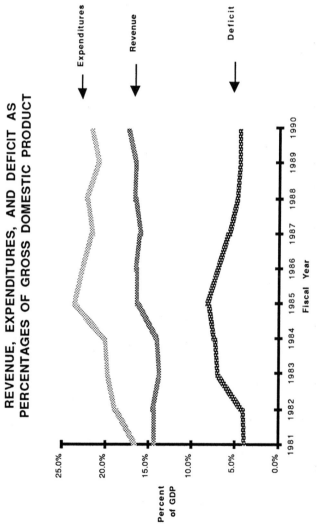

REVENUE, EXPENDITURES, AND DEFICIT AS
PERCENTAGES OF GROSS DOMESTIC PRODUCT

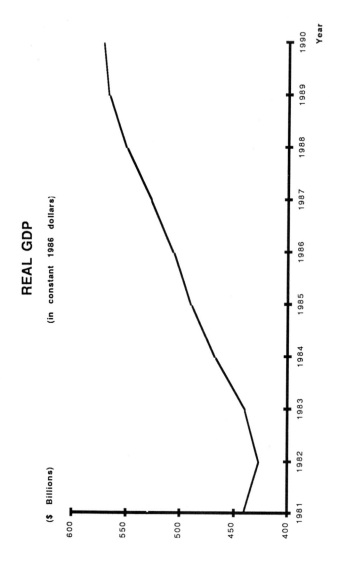

REAL GDP

(in constant 1986 dollars)

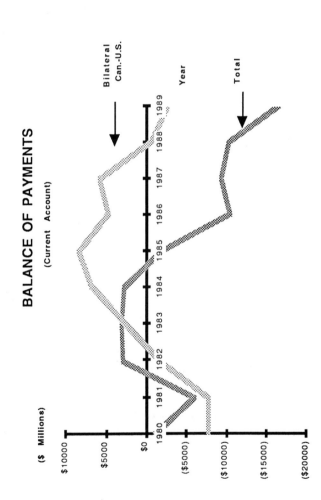

BALANCE OF PAYMENTS

(Current Account)

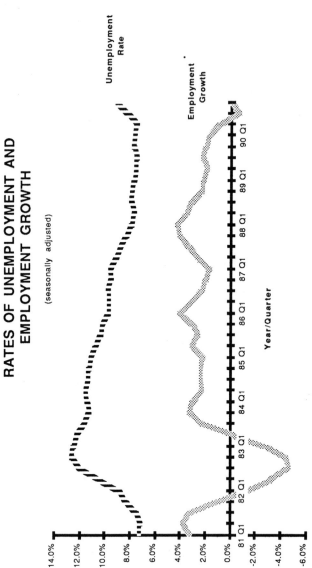

RATES OF UNEMPLOYMENT AND
EMPLOYMENT GROWTH

(seasonally adjusted)

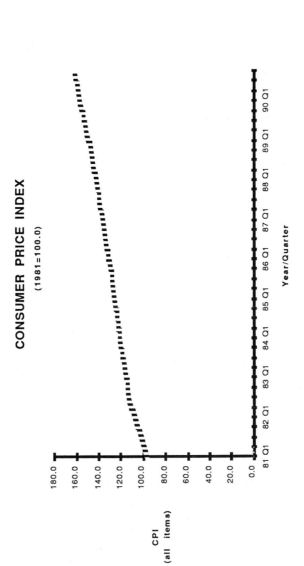

CONSUMER PRICE INDEX

(1981=100.0)

CPI
(all items)

Year/Quarter

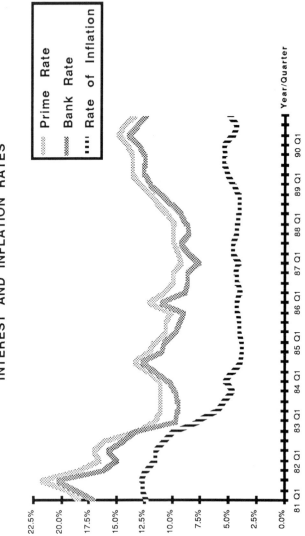

INTEREST AND INFLATION RATES

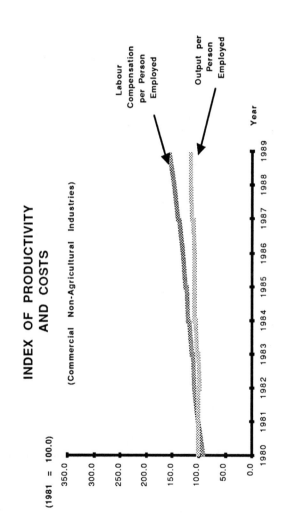

INDEX OF PRODUCTIVITY AND COSTS

(Commercial Non-Agricultural Industries)

(1981 = 100.0)

Labour Compensation per Person Employed

Output per Person Employed

Year

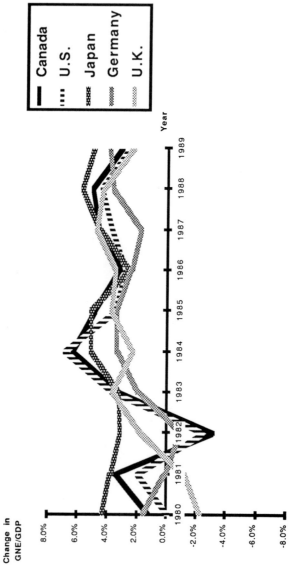

GROWTH IN REAL GNE/GDP

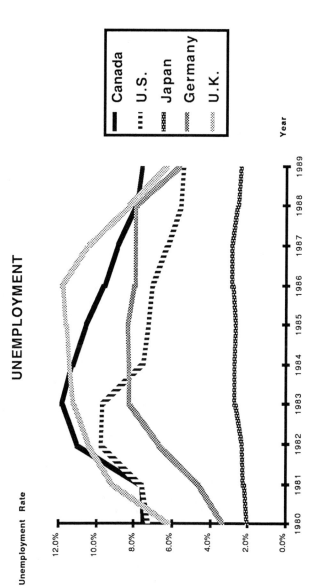

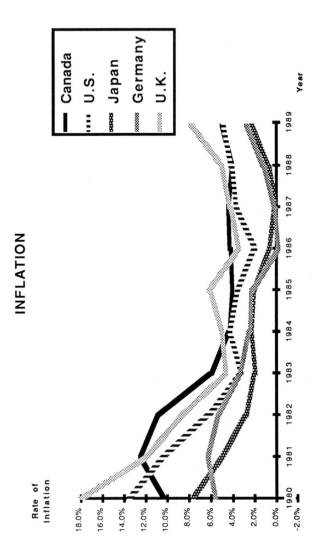

INFLATION

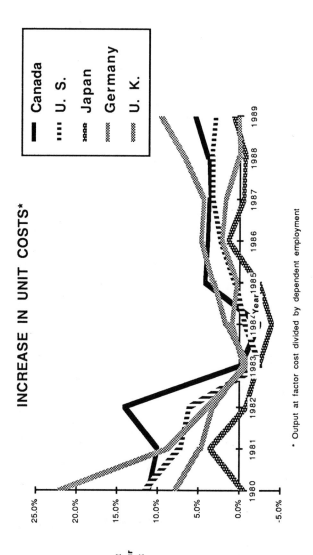

INCREASE IN UNIT COSTS*

Canada
U. S.
Japan
Germany
U. K.

Unit Labour Cost

25.0%
20.0%
15.0%
10.0%
5.0%
0.0%
-5.0%

1980 1981 1982 1983 1984 Year 1985 1986 1987 1988 1989

* Output at factor cost divided by dependent employment

FEDERAL REVENUE BY SOURCE*
($ million)

Fiscal Year	Personal Tax (1)	Corporate Tax	Indirect Taxes (2)	Other Revenue (3)	Total Revenue	Per cent Change	As a % of GDP
1981	19,837	8,106	11,714	11,164	50,821	23.0	14.3
1982	24,046	8,118	13,789	8,115	54,068	6.9	14.4
1983	26,330	7,139	12,748	8,906	55,123	2.0	13.6
1984	26,967	7,286	15,234	12,550	62,037	12.5	14.0
1985	36,807	9,379	18,186	13,702	78,074	25.9	16.3
1986	41,720	9,210	18,896	13,136	82,962	6.3	16.4
1987	47,436	9,885	20,897	9,359	87,577	5.6	15.9
1988	55,550	10,878	23,505	9,661	99,594	13.7	16.6
1989	57,294	11,730	26,167	10,994	106,185	6.6	16.4
1990	62,633	13,021	31,064	12,911	119,629	12.7	17.2

1 For the years 1985-88 unemployment insurance contributions are included in the total.

2 Consists of sales taxes, energy taxes (except for petroleum & gas revenue tax and incremental oil revenue tax), excise duties, custom imports, and other excise duties and taxes.

3 Consists of non-resident income tax, petroleum and gas revenue tax, incremental oil revenue tax, miscellaneous other taxes, and non-tax revenue.

SOURCE: Public Accounts, various years.

FEDERAL EXPENDITURES BY ENVELOPE*

($ million)

Fiscal Year	Fiscal Arrang.	External Affairs	Parl/Govt Services	Defence	Ec. & Reg. Develop.	Social	Public Debt	Total Outlays	Per cent Change	Total As % of GDP
1981	3,908	1,421	2,962	5,058	8,957	25,846	10,687	58,839	14.0	16.5
1982	4,734	1,702	4,483	6,031	9,457	28,963	15,168	70,538	19.9	18.8
1983	5,661	2,028	2,808	6,990	11,981	33,433	16,971	79,872	13.2	19.7
1984	5,862	2,261	3,493	7,973	13,101	38,704	18,146	89,540	12.1	20.1
1985**	5,985	2,659	4,227	9,021	17,641	50,977	22,455	112,965	26.2	23.6
1986	5,941	2,500	4,797	9,366	13,630	52,264	25,441	113,939	0.8	22.6
1987	6,302	2,912	4,355	10,270	12,625	55,059	26,658	118,182	3.7	21.5
1988	7,007	3,461	4,744	11,074	15,231	57,132	29,028	127,677	8.0	22.2
1989	8,127	3,584	4,714	11,291	14,401	59,619	33,183	134,919	5.7	20.8
1990	8,836	3,383	4,697	11,340	12,372	60,977	39,400	141,005	4.5	21.7

* PEMS basis; reflects 1984-85 envelope system; includes loans, investments and advances.
** Expenditure base in Public Accounts modified in 1985.

Source: Economic Review, reference table 51 for 1979-84 data.
Public Accounts, Table 1.7, various years.

INTERNATIONAL ECONOMIC COMPARISONS*

(PERCENTAGE CHANGES)

	1980	1981	1982	1983	1984	1985	1986	1987	1988	1989
Growth in Real GDP (1)										
Canada	1.1	3.4	-3.2	3.2	6.3	4.8	3.1	4.5	5.0	3
U.S.	-0.2	1.9	-2.5	3.6	6.8	3.4	2.7	3.7	4.4	2.5
Japan	4.3	3.7	3.1	3.2	5.1	5.1	2.5	4.5	5.7	4.9
Germany	1.5	0.0	-1.0	1.9	3.3	3.3	2.3	1.7	3.6	3.9
U.K.	-2.3	-1.2	1.7	3.6	2.2	3.7	3.4	4.7	4.2	2.2
Unemployment Rate (2)										
Canada	7.5	7.6	11.0	11.8	11.2	10.5	9.5	8.8	7.8	7.5
U.S.	7.2	7.6	9.7	9.6	7.5	7.2	7.0	6.2	5.5	5.3
Japan	2.0	2.2	2.3	2.7	2.7	2.6	2.8	2.8	2.5	2.3
Germany	3.3	4.6	6.7	8.2	8.2	8.3	7.9	7.9	7.9	5.6
U.K.	6.1	9.1	10.4	11.2	11.4	11.6	11.8	10.4	8.2	6.2
Inflation (3)										
Canada	10.2	12.5	10.8	5.9	4.3	4.0	4.2	4.4	4.0	5
U.S.	13.5	10.3	6.1	3.2	4.3	3.5	1.9	3.7	4.1	4.8
Japan	7.7	4.9	2.7	1.9	2.3	2.0	0.6	0.1	0.7	2.3
Germany	5.5	6.3	5.3	3.3	2.4	2.2	-0.2	0.2	1.2	2.8
U.K.	18.0	11.9	8.6	4.6	5.0	6.1	3.4	4.2	4.9	7.8
Unit Labour Costs in Manufact. (4)										
Canada	11.1	10.0	14.2	-0.1	-2.3	4.3	3.9	3.7	4.0	5.7
U.S.	11.6	7.3	6.1	-2.5	-0.6	0.6	2.4	3.3	3.4	2.9
Japan	-0.4	3.7	-0.8	-2.3	-3.9	-2.2	1.4	-0.5	-0.7	0.9
Germany	7.8	4.8	3.3	-0.5	1.0	0.3	2.2	1.7	0.1	0.3
U.K.	22.1	8.8	3.9	-1.0	1.8	3.3	4.8	3.1	6.0	9.8

* According to figures compiled by the OECD.
1. GNE data are reported for the U.S., Japan, Germany, and Canada, while GDP data are reported for the U.K.
2. Unemployment rates are on the basis of national definitions.
3. As measured by the year-to-year variation in the Consumer Price Index.
4. Defined as output at factor cost divided by dependent employment.

FEDERAL DEFICIT*
($ million)

Fiscal Year (end Mar. 31)	Total Revenues	Total Expenditures	Budgetary Deficit	Per cent Change	As a % of GDP
1981	48,775	62,297	13,522	17.6	3.8
1982	60,001	74,873	14,872	10.0	4.0
1983	60,705	88,521	27,816	87.0	6.9
1984	64,216	96,615	32,399	16.5	7.3
1985	70,891	109,222	38,324	18.3	8.0
1986	76,833	111,237	34,404	-10.2	6.8
1987	85,784	116,389	30,605	-11.0	5.6
1988	97,452	125,535	28,083	-8.2	4.7
1989	103,981	132,715	28,734	2.3	4.4
1990	113,707	142,703	28,966	0.0	4.4

* Revenues are calculated on a net basis.

Source: Public Accounts 1989-90, Table 1.2.

Subscribers

We thank the following organizations for assisting in meeting the financial costs of producing *How Ottawa Spends* by subscribing to the 1991-92 edition.

Department of Secretary of State
Government of Canada

Ministry of Intergovernmental Affairs
Government of Ontario

Petro-Canada Inc.
Calgary

The Southam Newspaper Group
Toronto

Xerox Canada Inc.
North York

The Authors

Frances Abele is an Associate Professor in the School of Public Administration, Carleton University.

James Bickerton is an Assistant Professor in the Department of Political Science, St. Francis Xavier University.

Marina Devine is a graduate student in the School of Public Administration, Carleton University.

G. Bruce Doern is a Professor in the School of Public Administration, Carleton University.

Alain-G. Gagnon is an Associate Professor in the Department of Political Science, McGill University.

Roger Gibbins is a Professor in the Department of Political Science, University of Calgary.

David C. Hawkes is an Adjunct Professor with the School of Public Administration, Carleton University

Leslie A. Pal is a Professor in the Department of Political Science, University of Calgary.

Susan D. Phillips is an Assistant Professor in the School of Public Administration, Carleton University.

Michael J. Prince holds the Lansdowne Chair in Social Policy, University of Victoria.

Daiva Stasiulis is an Associate Professor in Department of Sociology/Anthropology, Carleton University.

Brian W. Tomlin is a Professor of Political Science and International Affairs, Carleton University.

THE SCHOOL OF PUBLIC ADMINISTRATION
at Carleton University is a national centre for the
study of public policy and public management
in Canada.

The School's Centre for Policy and Program Assessment
provides research services and courses to interest groups, businesses, unions and governments in the evaluation of public
policies, programs and activities.